2000
Year B

AN ALMANAC OF PARISH LITURGY
SOURCEBOOK
FOR SUNDAYS AND SEASONS

Peter J. Scagnelli

LTP
LITURGY
TRAINING
PUBLICATIONS

ACKNOWLEDGMENTS

Excerpts from the English translation of *Documents on the Liturgy: 1963–1979: Conciliar, Papal, and Curial Texts* © 1982, International Committee on English in the Liturgy, Inc. All rights reserved.

Excerpts from *Gather Faithfully Together,* copyright © 1997, Archdiocese of Los Angeles, are used with permission.

Sourcebook for Sundays and Seasons, 1999, copyright © 1998, Archdiocese of Chicago: Liturgy Training Publications, 1800 North Hermitage Avenue, Chicago IL 60622-1101; 1-800-933-1800; fax 1-800-933-7094; e-mail: orders@ltp.org. See our website at www.ltp.org. All rights reserved.

Printed in the United States of America

ISBN 1-56854-293-3

The turn of the millennium and the Gospel of Mark converge in this year of the Lord 2000. What better time to reflect on "Mark's Apocalypse": "If anyone says to you at that time, 'Look! Here is the Messiah!' or 'Look! There he is!'—do not believe it. False Messiahs and false prophets will appear and produce false signs and omens, to lead astray, if possible, the elect. But be alert; I have told you everything." (Mark 13:21-23)

CONTENTS

OVERVIEWS
vii

ADVENT
1

CHRISTMAS
25

WINTER ORDINARY TIME
53

LENT
81

TRIDUUM
113

EASTER
143

SUMMER AND FALL ORDINARY TIME
169

Foreword

WELCOME to *Sourcebook for Sundays and Seasons, 2000!* For more than a decade, people all over the United States and Canada, and wherever there are English-speaking Catholics, have looked to *Sourcebook* to help prepare their communities' liturgies. If *Sourcebook* is new to you, you are about to discover a treasure chest of information, instructions, ideas and good common sense. If you are one of *Sourcebook*'s longtime friends in the work of liturgical renewal, thanks for your confidence in us.

■ WHAT'S NEW? The Jubilee of the Year 2000 will soon be upon us! Liturgy planners will focus as always on the primary feasts and seasons of the year, but many of these celebrations will take on a millennial flavor. In Rome, different groups will gather with the Holy Father for special celebrations and blessings. Where appropriate, these have been noted throughout *Sourcebook* so that parishes might celebrate in harmony with Rome.

Here also is the latest scholarship on this year's evangelist, Mark. In addition, the Winter Ordinary Time section suggests a worthy undertaking for any liturgy committee: studying the Holy Father's recent Apostolic Letter on the liturgy, *Dies Domini,* in conjunction with the late Cardinal Joseph Bernardin's *Guide for the Assembly: Our Communion, Our Peace, Our Promise* (1984) and Cardinal Roger Mahony's *Guide for Sunday Mass: Gather Faithfully Together* (1997). Our author notes that these documents "together constitute a rich and challenging resource for recovering a sense of Sunday and translating that sense into life-giving celebration."

■ WHAT'S THE SAME? Peter J. Scagnelli is this year's author again. Peter is a diocesan priest and a native of Boston, where he is currently working on a doctorate in liturgical theology. He has served as parish priest and diocesan worship office director, and he still serves as a member of various committees of the International Commission on English in the Liturgy (ICEL). In addition to being a priest and liturgist, Peter is a linguist and translator — you may have sung some of his hymn texts, translated from Latin. Peter is also a very funny guy, and his humor comes through in his writing.

This year's *Sourcebook* is similar in many ways to previous years' books. The basic design of the sections and pages has been kept. Rita Corbin's artwork again graces the cover and inside of this year's book. Rita has worked in religious and liturgical art for many years. You may be most familiar with her work from *The Catholic Worker.*

Because *Sourcebook for Sundays and Seasons* evolves much as an almanac does, the work of many previous authors and compilers remains a part of this book. The hands of Larry Mick, Jerry Galipeau, G. Thomas Ryan, Peter Mazar, Mary Beth Kunde-Anderson, David Anderson, Barry Moorehead, Neil Kraft and Anthony DiCello may still be detected herein. *Sourcebook* is all the richer for their contributions over the years, and so, we hope, is your parish's liturgical life.

■ WHO BRINGS IT ALL TOGETHER? Many people work hard and long to move this book from being a few electronic impulses (all of this book was sent to LTP via e-mail) to being the book you are holding in your hands. Copyediting and general editorial assistance were provided by Audrey Novak Riley. LTP's graphics department takes all these words and makes them into a thing of beauty. Jane Kremsreiter designed the 1991 book. Mary Bowers made some modifications to the original design, and Ana Aguilar-Islas designed the cover. These last three have all moved on from LTP, but it's nice that their work is here to remind us of them. M. Urgo did the layout for this year's book, and Mark Hollopeter did the typesetting.

Work on the year 2001 book has already begun, but we are interested in hearing your comments and suggestions at any time.

Victoria M. Tufano

Welcome to 2000!

WELCOME to *Sourcebook for Sundays and Seasons 2000,* the thirteenth edition of Liturgy Training Publications' annual almanac of parish liturgy, and the first of the new millennium!

The years leading up to the year 2000 have provided a fresh opportunity for many people around the world, in varied walks of life and of differing cultures and religions, to reflect on the mystery of time. If the changing of the centuries reminds the world that *time marches on,* then surely the dawning of a new millennium proclaims with particular urgency *tempus fugit* — time flies! Indeed, the records and writings that survive from the last time one millennium ended and a new one began testify to the strange and sometimes frightening ways in which human beings try to cope with such a momentous milestone.

Many in the waning years of the 900s were certain that Christ's Second Coming and the final judgment were at hand. All over Europe there were "prophets" who claimed to know from secret revelations the exact identity and specific activities of the Antichrist, as preachers by the score warned that natural catastrophes and divine chastisements were imminent, accompanied by fearful plagues and fiery punishments.

By contrast, the advent of the present millennium has been significantly less hysterical. Chalk it up, perhaps, to technology, or maybe blame it on the ever-expanding World Wide Web. Whatever the cause, this time around, the direst millennarian predictions have forecast not cosmic cataclysms but computer glitches! When the world holds its breath at midnight on January 1, 2000, the only earth-shaking phenomena dreaded among us will be caused by Y2K, the millennium bug.

No sincere believer laments the absence of that strange blend of panic and pietism that marked the turning of centuries a millennium ago. On the other hand, none of us who turn to a publication like *Sourcebook* would want to dismiss the mystery of time's unfolding or the wonder of the seasons' ever-recurring changes. Even our secular society treasures some aspects of mystery: almost any bookstore stocks at least as many books on angels as on computers. How much more sensitive to the mystery of time should we believers be — we who have been sealed with the Holy Spirit, whose sevenfold gift includes *timor Domini.* The International Commission on the Liturgy (ICEL) translated this Latin expression a generation ago not by the literal but misleading phrase "fear of the Lord," but by the more accurate expression "awe and wonder in the Lord's presence."

The Second Vatican Council's primary aim in the reform of the liturgy, "to be considered before all else," was that all the People of God be enabled to celebrate the liturgy of Sundays and seasons with "full, conscious and active participation," their "right and obligation by reason of their baptism" (*Constitution on the Sacred Liturgy,* 14). The Council reasoned that this would open the whole community of the church to a more vivid experience of awe and wonder in God's presence, which will, in the mind of the Council, lead all people to a greater sensitivity to the presence of God in the world and in our sisters and brothers (see CSL, 8 – 9).

Worship and witness: these two elements are meant to be constitutive in every believer's life in both the Jewish and Christian covenants. To serve the community's worship and witness has been the goal of *Sourcebook* since its inception. In the new millennium, many things will undoubtedly change and much more than we now imagine will stay the same. For all who celebrate the sacredness of time through the liturgy, for all who go forth to serve the sacred place we call Earth, its habitat and its inhabitants, in "the liturgy beyond the liturgy," *Sourcebook* seeks to serve as a guide during the year 2000.

Here you will find notes concerning what will change this year and what will stay the same as last year in the principal sources that anchor the liturgy as reformed by Vatican II: the calendar, the lectionary and the sacramentary.

Again this year, I thank Gabe Huck both for his inspiration to begin *Sourcebook* and for his invitation to return to work on it this year. Editor Vicky Tufano has once again eliminated any need for extra penance during the official season of Lent by making her desert journey in summer and fall, helping me meet deadlines. At times she almost succeeded! Her patience and perseverance, tempered understanding and unfailing good temper, are any author's dream and have been this grateful author's blessing for years.

During the first draft of *Sourcebook 2000*, in the autumn of 1998, an event occurred that brought my work to a standstill, an event that has changed my life forever. On September 8, the feast of Our Lady's Nativity, my mother, Valeria Scagnelli, suffered a cerebral hemorrhage and fell into a coma. She made her Passover to the Lord on October 2, the memorial of the Guardian Angels. The thoughtful words and supportive presence of our family and friends, neighbors and colleagues during this month-long vigil remain in the hearts of my father, sister and myself as an incarnation of the communion of saints. But there is another group of people I would like to acknowledge: the doctors, nurses and other medical staff members who assisted my mother and us during her final pilgrimage home to God. I dedicate *Sourcebook 2000* to them: our dear friend Bruce McNulty, MD, of Ravenswood, Chicago; Robert E. Johnson, MD, and Vincent Yuan, MD, of Framingham; Sin Choo, MD, Salvatore Primo, RN, and everyone attached to the Surgical Intensive Care Unit at Boston University Medical Center. At your hands we felt the gentle touch of the Divine Physician. Accept the dedication of this book as a sincere token of my family's gratitude and esteem.

From all of us at LTP, to all our friends, old and new, both within and beyond the Roman Catholic community, on behalf of *Sourcebook* and its related publications, thank you for letting us serve you. Feel free to suggest ways we can serve you more effectively. Let us remember and rejoice as we gather at the table of the word and the table of the eucharist, and as we go forth to live the word and to set the table of kindness and compassion in the new millennium. Welcome! Come, let us worship! Come, let us witness!

Sourcebook 2000: Organization

COMMUNITIES using beautiful ritual books are aware that it is enough to *look* at that book to know that it contains a message of supreme importance. Official liturgical books should be handsomely crafted, bearing a look of importance and conveying a sense of permanence.

Sourcebook is not an imposing book like the lectionary or sacramentary, but rather a humble servant to them and the revered texts they contain. Remember *Sourcebook*'s subtitle, *An Almanac of Parish Liturgy,* and consider *The Old Farmer's Almanac,* which to this day hangs on a hook by the kitchen window in many New England homes. No almanac tries to replace the calendar or pretends to control the tides or rule the sun. But every almanac alerts its users to the movements of these phenomena, points out what is different this year from last year, where adjustments must be made and where those things that are constant will recur again. And a good almanac sprinkles in tips on yearly planting and daily housework. Each year's issue is only a few weeks old when it starts to show signs of daily consultation. Well-thumbed and battered a bit, any almanac worth its salt presents essential information and important insights in an unselfconscious and user-friendly format. The basic structure of an almanac and much of the information in it remain the same from year to year, organized and adjusted according to the year at hand.

Sourcebook strives to be such an almanac, and those who have used it in the past will see that its structure is essentially unchanged.

OVERVIEWS

Sourcebook begins with a series of Overviews designed to provide planners and presiders with a broad perspective of the liturgical year and a clear blueprint with which to plan specific liturgical celebrations. These Overviews offer basic tools of the liturgical craft for those whose ministry includes preparing the assembly's words of prayer or songs of celebration, planning and rehearsing its ritual movement and gesture, and arranging or adorning the place of worship.

The focus is on the basics: the calendar for 2000, the lectionary of Year B, the sacramentary, and liturgical celebrations other than the eucharist.

The conviction underlying the Overviews is that no matter how often we may have celebrated — or even planned — the liturgical year, we need to take time annually for a thorough and thoughtful review of the basics. The Overviews are meant to provide the essential background that should precede any planning for specific seasons or liturgies.

Let this portion of *Sourcebook* serve first as homework for planners and presiders, and then as an outline for the agenda of autumn's first meeting. Resist the temptation to head right for Advent! Although the celebration of the liturgical year begins with Advent, planning for the liturgical year ideally should not. Take time for a thoughtful examination of the Calendar, Lectionary, Sacramentary and Celebration Overviews. Confront the questions the exercise will raise; for instance, see Calendar Overview, page x. This kind of preliminary effort will repay planners and presiders with a firm foundation on which to build the year's liturgy planning.

RESOURCES

Each Overview section concludes with a list of helpful and accessible publications for those who wish to do further reading or add to their parish or personal libraries. For video resources, readers are urged to obtain the catalogs of LTP and other liturgical publishers. For Internet websites an indispensable reference work is Thomas C. Fox's *Catholicism on the Web* (New York: MIS Press, 1997).

SEASON

The seasonal sections of *Sourcebook* are arranged according to the following pattern in order to present the liturgical aspects of the season in a comprehensive and concise way:

- *Setting of the Season:* the feel of each season in the context of nature and of society
- *Sense of the Season:* the historical evolution and orientation of the season according to Vatican II reforms
- *Look of the Season:* in and around the worship space and at home
- *Sounds of the Season:* appropriate music, new and old
- *Rhythm of the Season:* preparing the parish to embrace each season
- *Word of God:* structure and themes of Year B's lectionary for each season
- *Eucharist:* seasonal suggestions for the elements of the Mass
- *Celebrations:* forms of worship and pastoral rites appropriate to the season
- *At Home:* prayer and ritual in the domestic church

CALENDAR

The calendar sections of *Sourcebook* present a day-by-day outline of the liturgical year. Every calendar entry for a Sunday or solemnity features these components:

- *Orientation:* historical origins and Vatican II's sense of what each solemnity and special observance is about
- *Lectionary:* comments on each Lord's Day scripture in the context of the entire season or, during Ordinary Time, of each block of Sundays
- *Sacramentary:* ideas for appropriate prefaces, eucharistic prayers and other liturgical texts
- *The Week Ahead:* advance notice, when needed, of upcoming feasts and of weekday readings whose displacement may suggest the permitted rearrangement of the weekday lectionary

TEXTS

The first *Sourcebook for Sundays and Seasons* in 1988 contained a selection of scriptural opening prayers translated from the Italian sacramentary that matched the lectionary readings. Suggestions for the general intercessions and other liturgical elements for which there was no other English source were also provided: for example, the Proclamation of Christmas, the Epiphany Proclamation of the Date of Easter, and the Reception of the Holy Oils at the Holy Thursday evening Mass of the Lord's Supper. We who have compiled *Sourcebook* over the years note with satisfaction that the *Sacramentary Supplement* (Catholic Book, 1994) and the forthcoming revision of the sacramentary for the United States incorporate these elements of *Sourcebook* as part of the official liturgical use of the church in this country.

This year's *Sourcebook* continues to provide some of those elements, as well as seasonal dismissals for the catechumens and ministers of the eucharist to the sick and homebound. These texts can be found in the body of the appropriate season and calendar sections, rather than in their own section, as in the past. For scriptural collects and general intercessions, as well as introductions to the Lord's Prayer, invitations to communion and dismissal formulae, please see this *Sourcebook*'s companion volume, *Prayers for Sundays and Seasons, Year B* (LTP, 1996).

RESOURCES

The Liturgy Documents: A Parish Resource. Third Edition (LTP, 1991; on disk, 1997). Most of the major Roman liturgical documents, along with documents of the Bishops' Committee on the Liturgy.

Documents on the Liturgy, 1963–1979: Conciliar, Papal and Curial Texts (Collegeville: The Liturgical Press, 1982). Translation and compilation of everything official. Extensive indices and cross-references make this a gold mine of information.

Documents of Christian Worship: Descriptive and Interpretive Sources, James F. White, editor (Louisville: Westminster/John Knox, 1992). From the beginning (scripture, Fathers, councils), across traditions (Jewish, Catholic, Orthodox, Anglican, Reformed), grouped by topic (space, time, sacraments, word, etc.). Where we all come from, what we have in common, how we differ.

Newsletter of the Bishops' Committee on the Liturgy. Washington: United States Catholic Conference. Pertinent information regarding liturgical developments, documents and regulations for the United States. Contact the Liturgy Secretariat at 3211 Fourth Street NE, Washington DC 20017-1194; 1-202-541-3060.

National Bulletin on the Liturgy. Canadian Catholic Conference. Published four times per year. Offers helpful background on many topics on the liturgy. Contact Novalis, P.O. Box 990, Outremont, Quebec, H2V 4S7; 1-800-668-2547.

Liturgy 90 (The name will change to *Rite* in January 2000). LTP. Published eight times a year. Accessibly written and pastorally relevant articles on parish liturgy. Each issue also includes a ready-to-copy bulletin insert focusing on a particular element of liturgical practice.

Calendar Overview: November 28, 1999 – December 2, 2000

A popular approach depicts the liturgical year as consisting of two major seasons, one centered on Christmas and the other on Easter, with a few ordinary (meaning "nothing special") Sundays between Christmas and Lent, and a longer ordinary block stretching from Pentecost until the next Advent.

But a careful reading of the foundational principles set forth above suggests a different approach. Those two paragraphs make Sunday, the Lord's Day, "the first holy day of all." In fact, according to the Vatican norms, even Easter's preeminence derives from Sunday: "The solemnity of Easter has the same kind of preeminence in the liturgical year that Sunday has in the week" (GNLYC, 18).

THE LORD'S DAY

"The day which reveals the meaning of time": thus does John Paul II in his recent pastoral letter, *Dies Domini: An Apostolic Letter on Keeping the Lord's Day Holy,* describe Sunday — not only a day that brings the past into the present, Christ's resurrection and our eucharist, but a day that propels the community toward the future.

> [Sunday] has nothing in common with the cosmic cycles according to which natural religion and human culture tend to impose a structure on time, succumbing perhaps to the myth of eternal return. The Christian Sunday is wholly other! Springing from the Resurrection, it cuts through human time, the months, the years, the centuries like a directional arrow which points them toward their target: Christ's Second Coming. Sunday foreshadows the last day, the day of the Parousia, which in a way is already anticipated by Christ's glory in the event of the Resurrection. (75)

Thus from the perspectives of history and theology Sunday is the real kernel of the liturgical year. Centuries before there was a First Sunday of Advent or even a Third Sunday of Lent, there was just Sunday. The earliest disciples, after their encounters with the risen Lord and their empowerment by the Holy Spirit, all of which occurred on "the first day of the week," continued to assemble on this day "for the breaking of the bread," as the Acts of the Apostles describes it.

Indeed, Luke's story of the journey to Emmaus, also "on the first day of the week," has long been considered by many commentators to be a eucharistic paradigm. The risen Lord, unrecognized, meets the disciples on the road of life's journey; opens their minds to the scriptures; then, at their invitation, comes to table with them. With gestures that have not changed to this day, Jesus *takes, blesses, breaks* and *gives* the bread. In that moment, in those gestures, "their eyes were opened and they recognized him." The consequence of such recognition has also remained the same. The Pope describes it as "from Mass to mission": The two disciples (and how many since!) rose from the table and hurried forth, although it was night, to tell their story and to proclaim their faith. Indeed, as we shall see in a moment, the Pope's letter is at its most eloquent when it restates the inseparable link between the liturgy and social justice.

The Emmaus story presents the Sunday worship of the early Christian community in skeletal form, and it did not take long to flesh out that outline. By the next century both the preeminence of Sunday and the order of Sunday worship were well established enough to look like what we do every week. Catholics and all Christians who make word and table the center of Sunday worship will find familiar a Lord's Day celebration whose description comes to us from the first generation after the apostles. Sometime before 160 CE, the Roman convert Justin described for his pagan audience the Sunday liturgy that he knew:

> On Sunday we have a common assembly of all our members, whether they live in the city or in the outlying districts. The recollections of the apostles or the writings of the prophets are read, as long as there is time. When the reader has finished, the president of the assembly speaks to us; he urges everyone to imitate the examples of virtue we have heard in the readings. Then we all stand up together and pray.
>
> On the conclusion of our prayer, bread and wine and water are brought forward. The president offers prayers and gives thanks [literally, *makes eucharist*] to the best of his ability, and the people give their assent by saying, "Amen." The eucharist is distributed, everyone present communicates, and the deacons take it to those who are absent.
>
> The wealthy, if they wish, may make a contribution, and they themselves decide the amount. The collection is placed in the custody of the president, who uses it to help orphans and widows and all who for any reason are in distress, whether because they are sick, in prison, or away from home. In a word, he takes care of all who are in need.
>
> We hold our common assembly on Sunday because it is the first day of the week, the day on which God put darkness and chaos to flight and created the world, and because on that same day our savior Jesus Christ rose from the dead. For he was crucified on Friday and on Sunday he appeared to his apostles and disciples and taught them the things that we have passed on for your consideration. (Justin, *First Apology in Defense of the Christians*, 66 – 67; Third Sunday of Easter, Office of Readings)

John Paul expands on Justin's characterization of Sunday with a veritable litany of titles:

- *Day of the Lord:* day of the Creator God at work in the first creation
- *Day of Christ:* day of the Risen Lord and of the Gift of the Holy Spirit, the day therefore of the new creation, thus the first day and, as some early Christian writings liked to call it, the "eighth" day
- *Day of the Church:* day of the heart of Sunday, the celebration of word and eucharist; day when the Mass becomes mission in the sending forth of the community
- *Day of the Human Race:* day of joy, of rest and relaxation, of solidarity, that is, "mercy, charity and apostolate" (*Dies Domini*, 69).

■ SUNDAYS IN ORDINARY TIME: In his discussion of the Lord's Day, the Pope is not speaking of a Sunday within the two main liturgical seasons. The Pope is speaking about Sunday *in and of itself,* an ordinary Sunday, we might say.

A fresh understanding of the word "ordinary" in a liturgical context reinvests the thirty-four or so Sundays in Ordinary Time with their original dignity and sets them up as the model for the Sundays of the liturgical seasons. Far from meaning "nothing special," *ordinary* in contemporary liturgical usage means *ordinal:* Sundays counted in order as we make our way through the lectionary.

While the lack of a specifically festive title renders a Sunday blank for some, from the perspective of the lectionary, the Sundays in Ordinary Time are blank only if the pages of the synoptic gospels are blank! The content of these Sundays is nothing less than and no one else but Jesus himself. Jesus is, of course, the content of the festal seasons as well, but one might note this difference. During the festal seasons, the gospel passages proclaim and celebrate specific saving deeds accomplished by God in Christ. A certain fragmentation is inevitable, as gospel excerpts are lifted out of their narrative context and arranged episodically, thematically, even chronologically. The Sundays in Ordinary Time, however, allow the theological purpose of each evangelist to appear in sharper relief. Protestant liturgist Fritz West observes:

> Matthew emphasizes the teacher Jesus and the Church; Luke stresses the universality of the gospel brought by the prophet of the kingdom. The [arrangement in Year B] employing both Mark and John as a whole addresses the question, "How do we know Jesus Christ?" Taken alone, the selections from Mark find the answer in the Cross; those from John find it in the Eucharist. (Fritz West, *Scripture and Memory: The Ecumenical Hermeneutic of the Three-Year Lectionaries.* Collegeville: The Liturgical Press; A Pueblo Book, 1997, 117)

THE PASCHAL CYCLE

In addition to the weekly observance of the Lord's Day, history attests to the early observance of an annual Christian Pasch or Passover. Originally a unified observation of the Lord's passion, death and resurrection celebrated in one all-night Vigil, this observance came to be spread out over three days, the Three Days of the Lord's Pasch, or the Sacred Paschal Triduum. Preceded by the Forty Days of Lent and flowering into the Great Fifty Days of Easter, culminating in the celebration of Ascension and Pentecost, this paschal cycle occupies over a quarter of the calendar year.

The elements of each Lord's Day are especially dramatic within the Triduum. There is a prolonged liturgy of the word as the greatest stories of salvation history and the most intense messages of the prophets are proclaimed. Christian initiation is celebrated and the assembly of the baptized renews the baptismal covenant. The eucharist is celebrated with special solemnity on the night when the neophytes partake of the Lord's table for the first time. All this is preceded by Thursday night's word, footwashing and supper, and by Friday's passion proclamation, prolonged intercession for the needs of all, and veneration of the cross. For these three days, the disciplinary fast of Lent yields to the anticipatory paschal fast, a period of holy rest and recreation for those about to be baptized and for those renewing their baptismal covenant.

The Lent preceding the Triduum is marked by a devout reading of the word in the weekday lectionary, which presents the principal disciplines of Christian commitment, and an enhanced Sunday lectionary that presents the principal scriptures from the Hebrew Bible and New Testament alluding to baptism. Lent also invites a more intense commitment to justice and charity in the traditional disciplines of prayer, fasting and almsgiving.

The "week of weeks," as ancient writers described Eastertime, is a period of "holy rest" for the neophytes as they reflect peacefully and prayerfully on the initiation they have just experienced. The first reading in the liturgy of the word on the Sundays and weekdays of this season is from the Acts of the Apostles. These passages challenge the contemporary community to the baptismal conversion, eucharistic sharing and dynamic evangelism that marked the worship and witness of our forebears.

THE INCARNATION CYCLE

The incarnation cycle takes many of its emphases from the Lord's Day celebration. It also points more clearly than might first be imagined to the Triduum. The Word becomes flesh not only to dwell among us but to die on our behalf: "What child is this who, laid to rest on Mary's lap, is sleeping . . . Nails, spear shall pierce him through, the cross be borne for me, for you." The proclamation of the word throughout Advent resounds with the calls of the prophets, especially Isaiah and John the Baptist, for the justice that is the hallmark of the Messiah's reign. The Twelve Days of Christmas are filled with the *comites Christi,* the companions of Christ, saints who manifest in their lives, most of them also in their martyrdom, the cost of discipleship. Epiphany and the Baptism of the Lord likewise celebrate the revelation of the Word made flesh and challenge the community to embrace the cost of discipleship and the work of evangelization.

ADDITIONAL RESOURCES

General Norms for the Liturgical Year and Calendar, Overview by Kevin W. Irwin, in *The Liturgy Documents: A Parish Resource,* Third Edition. Chicago: Liturgy Training Publications, 1991 (on disk, 1997).

H. Boone Porter, *The Day of Light: The Biblical and Liturgical Meaning of Sunday.* Washington: The Pastoral Press, 1987 (now available from Oregon Catholic Press)

Laurence Hull Stookey, *Calendar: Christ's Time for the Church.* Nashville: Abingdon Press, 1996.

Thomas J. Talley, *Origins of the Liturgical Year.* Collegeville: The Liturgical Press; A Pueblo Book, Second Emended Edition, 1986, 1991.

James F. White, "The Language of Time," in *Introduction to Christian Worship: Revised Edition.* Nashville: Abingdon Press, 1990.

Lectionary Overview 2000: Year B

RAYMOND Brown summarizes the enduring contribution of the Gospel of Mark this way:

> By the time Mark wrote, Jesus had been preached as the Christ for several decades. To appreciate what this earliest preserved written portrayal contributed to our Christian heritage, one might reflect on what we would know about Jesus if we had just the letters of Paul. We would have a magnificent theology about what God has done in Christ, but Jesus would be left almost without a face. Mark gets the honor of having painted that face and made it part of the enduring gospel. (*Introduction to the New Testament,* 157–158)

Brown describes the tone of this earliest and briefest of the gospels:

> The motifs of disobedience, failure, misunderstanding, and darkness are prominent in Mark; but the death of Jesus on the cross, which is the darkest moment in the Gospel, is not the end. God's power breaks through, and an outsider like the Roman centurion is not excluded but understands. No matter how puzzled the women at the tomb are, the readers are not left uncertain: Christ is risen and he can be seen. (154)

BASIC INFORMATION ABOUT MARK

Scholars date the Gospel of Mark between 60 and 75 CE and locate its origin in Rome, although Syria, northern Transjordan, the Decapolis and Galilee are alternate possibilities. The early church attributed the gospel to Mark, reputedly a follower and interpreter of Peter, usually considered to be the same person as John Mark of Acts, whose mother had a house in Jerusalem and who accompanied Barnabas and Paul on the first missionary journey.

But Brown proposes another authorship "detectable from the contents":

> A Greek-speaker, who was not an eyewitness of Jesus' ministry and made inexact statements about Palestinian geography. He drew on preshaped traditions about Jesus (oral and probably written) and addressed himself to a community that seemingly had undergone persecution and failure. (127)

He describes that community in greater detail, and this background sets the stage for what we find in Mark:

> The Gospel's envisioned audience consisted of Greek-speakers who did not know Aramaic. Either the author or the audience or both lived in an area where Latin was used and had influenced Greek vocabulary. For the most part the recipients were not Jews since the author had to explain Jewish purification customs to them . . . they were probably Christians who had been converted by evangelizers familiar directly or indirectly with Jewish Christian tradition. Most likely they had heard a good deal about Jesus before Mark's Gospel was read to them. Theologically the recipients had an overheated expectation of an imminent parousia

(wherefore Mark 13), probably activated by persecution which they had undergone and during which a considerable number had failed. (163)

But Donald H. Juel challenges the theory that Mark directs his gospel to a persecuted people:

> Contrary to much current opinion, that audience does not appear to be simply a beleaguered minority barely holding on. Mark writes for people who have tasted success. The portrait of the first generations of Christians as persecuted members of Greco-Roman society drawn principally from the lower classes does not square with the information Mark provides. Their "problems" may well include self-satisfaction, competition for positions of leadership, and taking the gospel for granted, rather than the often advanced concern about the delay of the *parousia* or discouragement in the face of persecution. (*Augsburg Commentary on the New Testament: Mark,* 20)

To illustrate his point, Juel examines Mark 10:35–45, the gospel for the Twenty-ninth Sunday in Ordinary Time:

> The question is not willingness to die but rather willingness to lead without flaunting authority. The whole passage has to do with status and leadership — hardly of interest or concern to a community of desperate, persecuted believers. Such comments would be of interest to a community that has tasted power and likes it, a community that is already experiencing the pressures of institutionalization. Most of chapter 10 has to do with social relations and organization. The disciples serve once again as examples of inadequate discipleship, and here their problem is self-seeking ambition . . . In the shadow of the cross we get a brief glimpse of a new community in which relations are not governed by power and status but by service and hospitality for those without status — a community in which those who have been ransomed live for others. (149)

CHARACTERISTICS OF MARK

In his *Fortress Introduction to the Gospels* (Fortress, 1998), Mark Allan Powell identifies ten characteristics of this gospel:

- *An unusual urgency pervades the telling of the story.* The ministry begins with the news that "The time is fulfilled" (1:14) and unfolds almost breathlessly, appearing to take place within a few weeks, in contrast to three years in John. The word *immediately* (*euthys* in Greek) occurs 42 times, 11 in the first chapter alone (only *once* in the much longer gospel of Luke). There is urgency about the future as well: Jesus will come soon (13:30); therefore, leaders especially, be vigilant! (13:32–37).

- *Mark appears to emphasize Jesus' deeds over Jesus' words.* Less space is given to formal teaching in Mark, while the mighty works of Jesus take up more space in Mark than in the other gospels.

- *Mark's Gospel is dominated by the passion narrative.* The last three chapters move day by day, even hour by hour, through the final events.

- *The linguistic style is less refined.* All the gospels are written in *koine* (common) Greek, but Mark's Greek is the most *koine* of all.

- *Three literary devices* characterize the effective rhetoric of this deceptively simple gospel:

    Narrative anticipations: references that prepare readers for what will come later. *Example:* in Mark 3:9 a boat is readied that is not needed until 4:1.

    Two-step progressions: repeating a statement to add precision or clarity. *Example:* in 1:15 the announcement is made: "The time is fulfilled; the kingdom of God has come near." Repetitions like this get the reader used to taking a second look.

    Intercalation: the "Markan sandwich." One story is inserted within another. *Example:* in Mark 5, Jesus is summoned to Jairus' house to cure his daughter; on the way a woman with a hemorrhage is healed; then Jesus arrives at Jairus' house. This technique prompts readers to consider two otherwise unrelated stories in light of each other.

- *The geographical focus is Galilee.* The story makes an abrupt switch to Jerusalem in Chapter 10, but the disciples are told to go back to Galilee after Jesus' death: "There you will see him" (16:7).

- *Mark appears to be written for a Gentile audience.* Although Mark's Gospel assumes some familiarity with elements of Judaism, it was probably written for Gentile Christians who respected Jewish scriptures but were ignorant of basic Jewish rituals.

- *Mark offers the most human portrait of Jesus in the gospels.* Mark paints a refreshingly human and comforting portrait of Jesus, who becomes tired (6:31) and hungry (11:12) as any human being would, and he feels a wide range of human emotions: pity (1:41), anger (3:5), wonder (6:6), compassion (6:34), indignation (10:14), and love (10:21). Surprisingly, Jesus does not know everything (13:32), and his power is sometimes limited (6:5). But he is identified from the beginning as the Son of God (1:1), teaches with divine authority (1:22), and works awe-inspiring miracles by God's power (1:44).

- *There is a secrecy motif.* Jesus refers to the secret of the kingdom (4:11), and sometimes extends this secrecy theme to his deeds and person. But not consistently; he tells a demoniac whom he has healed to go and preach to his family and friends (5:19), and sends out his disciples as missionaries (6:7; 13:30) to proclaim the gospel to all nations (13:10).

- *Mark highlights the failures of Jesus' disciples from beginning to end.* They are unperceptive (8:14 – 21) and sometimes even opposed to him in their thinking (8:33, 9:33 – 34, 10:37 – 38). They often fail to live up to Jesus' expectations. For instance, Jesus gives them authority over demons (6:7), but they are unable to cast one out (9:17 – 19). After bold statements about their willingness to die with him (10:38 – 39; 14:29 – 31), Judas betrays Jesus (14:43 – 45), the rest desert him (14:50), and Peter denies three times that he even knows him (14:66 – 72). (Powell, 40 – 45)

Discipleship and the cross are major themes in Mark's Gospel. Paradoxically, the failure of the disciples becomes an opportunity for the gospel's clearest note of hope. The announcement of the resurrection contains the good news that Jesus has not abandoned those who had once abandoned him. Indeed, Jesus wants them back (16:7):

> At the end of this story, readers may recognize that, like the disciples, they have failed to understand the gospel of the cross and so have failed to meet the expectations of the one they call Messiah and Son of God. Even so, they may realize that they can still continue with Jesus, knowing that this relationship is (and always has been) sustained by his faithfulness, not theirs. Such a message would have specific pastoral relevance for a community in which many had suffered persecution and some had no doubt lapsed on account of it (see 4:16 – 17). (58)

THE YEAR OF MARK?

It is not exactly precise to designate Year B as the Year of Mark. Although 60 percent of the Gospel of Mark will be read in the course of this year, generous portions of the other gospels, particularly the Gospel of John, will also be proclaimed.

The lectionary departs from the year's principal synoptic gospel at several points in each year of the cycle. The Matthew and Luke infancy stories, for example, are too powerful and too beloved not to be proclaimed each year during Advent and Christmas. The baptismal passages from the Gospel of John prescribed for Year A may be used each Lent, especially in communities with catechumens: the Samaritan Woman (Third Sunday of Lent), the Man Born Blind (Fourth Sunday) and the Raising of Lazarus (Fifth Sunday). During Eastertime each year, the Gospel of John is used, since it is particularly well suited to this period of mystagogical reflection on the new life of baptism.

But Year B turns to the Gospel of John even more than do Years A and C. Sometimes the reason is practical. Mark does not feature an extensive account of the preaching of John the Baptist for Advent. During Lent, when the baptismal gospels are not used, Year B relies on the Gospel of John to provide reflections on the glorification of Christ through cross and resurrection. Also, at the beginning and end of Ordinary Time, the gospel readings are from John: the call of Andrew and Peter (Sunday 2), and a discussion between Pilate and Jesus on the nature of kingship (Christ the King).

But the most important digression from the Gospel of Mark takes place in the center of Ordinary Time. From Sundays 17 through 21 Year B presents five sections of John 6 on the Bread of Life.

CHARACTERISTICS OF YEAR B

Despite the admixture of readings from the other three gospels, Year B does derive its predominant character from the Gospel of Mark. Many commentators consider the principal motif of Mark to be the question Jesus poses to his disciples in Mark 8:29, the gospel for the Twenty-fourth Sunday in Ordinary Time: "Who do people say that I am?"

Others point out that Mark lets us know who Jesus is right from the start: "The beginning of the good news of Jesus Christ, *the Son of God*" (1:1). The question for these scholars is not "Who is Jesus?" but "How do we know?" and "What are the practical consequences of believing that Jesus is the Son of God?" Still others phrase the challenge of Mark somewhat differently and find their answer in Mark and John:

[The Year B arrangement] employing both Mark and John as a whole addresses the question, "How do we know Jesus Christ?" Taken alone, the selections from Mark find the answer in the Cross; those from John find it in the Eucharist. (Fritz West, *Scripture and Memory*, 117)

Raymond Brown looks for the principal characteristics of each gospel in its passion account. Mark's account of the passion is replete with themes that recur throughout Year B: misunderstanding, rejection, betrayal, denial, desertion and failure.

Juel looks at the end of the Gospel of Mark for the key to understanding it. Most scholars accept Mark 16:1–8 as the original ending. The lectionary places this passage at the heart of this liturgical year as the Easter Vigil gospel: "So [the women] went out and fled from the tomb, for terror and amazement had seized them; and they said nothing to anyone, for they were afraid" (Mark 16:8).

Juel provides an intriguing thought about this unsatisfying ending to take with us on our journey through Year B:

> Endings are important for what they do. Understanding the meaning of these verses must involve a sense of their function in Mark. Do they, like some endings, tie up loose ends? Do they resolve some tension the story has generated? Do they finally reveal a mystery concealed from the reader throughout? Or are the verses intended to disappoint a reader who has been lured into believing that something good will come of Jesus' death? Readers of stories by Kafka or plays by Beckett will be aware of how endings can be used to devastate the naïve.
>
> If 16:8 is the last verse of Mark's Gospel — and that, to the best of our knowledge, is the case — it establishes *a vantage point from which the whole story must be read.* How can the "good news about Jesus Christ" have led to this — frightened women who say nothing to anyone? (231. Emphasis added)

Juel notes that most likely the Gospel of Mark was written to people who already knew the story that Jesus had been raised:

> Yet the world is not the same. The tomb is empty. Jesus is out, beyond death's reach, on the loose. Readers know this cannot be the end of the story. There has been too much preparation for the next chapter. Someone must have spoken, since the Gospel has been written. (233)

He concludes with a thought planners and presiders might keep in mind as Year B unfolds: "Interpretation must respect the two impressions with which the story concludes: disappointment and anticipation." (233)

Disappointment and anticipation: welcome to the lectionary of Year B!

THE INCARNATION CYCLE

Mark begins the liturgical year, but the liturgical year does not begin at the beginning of Mark! Advent opens with Mark 13's warning about the need to be vigilant and stay awake for the Lord's second coming. The chapters of Mark that follow today's gospel selection chronicle the Lord's passion; thus the First Sunday of Advent points us toward the paschal mystery with a passage that, in the gospel narrative, leads directly to the passion. The Second Sunday of Advent continues this paschal orientation by presenting John the Baptist, God's messenger sent before the Messiah. John's fate and Jesus' fate are martyrdom in witness to the truth. The baptism with the Holy Spirit, which John promises that the Messiah will administer, will be a baptism of blood.

Matthew, Luke and John provide the readings throughout the Christmas season. Mark reappears on the Sunday after Epiphany, the Baptism of the Lord, with a brief summary of that event. The lectionary goes back to the story that began on the Second Sunday of Advent with the promise of the Messiah's baptism with the Holy Spirit. A voice from heaven proclaims what Mark has already told us: Jesus is the Son of God. With Jesus anointed by the Spirit and proclaimed by the voice to be the Beloved, we are ready for Ordinary Time, when we will see the mighty deeds of Jesus and reflect on the cost of discipleship.

THE PASCHAL CYCLE

The Gospel of Mark provided the readings for the first two Sundays of Advent, thus opening the incarnation cycle. Now Mark opens the paschal cycle with his versions of the stories we hear at the beginning of every Lent: the Lord's Temptation (First Sunday of Lent) and the Transfiguration (Second Sunday).

On the First Sunday of Lent, Mark's account of Jesus' temptation is spare compared to the detailed drama of Matthew and Luke. But look closer to see how Mark tells it. The shadow of the cross settles over the scene. Jesus survives the testing, but there is a hint that the real test lies ahead. As in Advent, John's fate comes to mind: He has been arrested, and what will happen to Jesus? Then comes the proclamation, "The time is fulfilled; the kingdom of God has come near," and the call to of discipleship: "Repent, and believe in the good news."

On the Second Sunday of Lent, Mark's version of the Transfiguration is proclaimed. There are some unique elements in Mark's story. The disciples' lack of perception, so characteristic in Mark, is hinted at. Whereas in Matthew, Peter calls Jesus "Lord" and in Luke "Master," here Peter calls Jesus simply "Rabbi," though he has made his profession of faith in Jesus' messiahship barely a chapter before. The heavenly voice corrects him: Jesus is the Son, the Beloved, to whom they must listen. The secrecy motif is here: They are to tell no one what they have seen "until the Son of Man has risen from the dead." The disciples still lack perception, "questioning what this rising from the dead could mean."

The Gospel of John takes over for the rest of Lent, with Mark reappearing on Passion (Palm) Sunday. The passion narrative is replete with the Markan themes. Jesus' abandonment is profound: All the disciples desert him, there is no family or beloved disciple at the foot of the cross on which Jesus hangs for six hours, not three. Even God seems to have abandoned Jesus, whose only word from the cross is "a loud cry." Some would translate the Greek word as *scream:* "My God, my God, why have you forsaken me?" At that point a Roman centurion identifies Jesus in almost the same words Mark used in the first verse of his gospel. The word is out; this truly was God's Son! The message must be proclaimed! But the disciples fail again; in the Easter Vigil gospel the women are afraid to convey the message they have been given.

The Gospel of John provides the readings throughout the Fifty Days of Easter. The final Mark passage of the paschal cycle is proclaimed on the Ascension; an additional ending to Mark (16:15 – 20). There are echoes of John's Gospel in the text: Signs accompany those who believe. So the disciples are sent to evangelize, never abandoned by the one they abandoned, but intensely united to the risen Christ whose ministry now becomes their own.

ORDINARY TIME

In Year A, Ordinary Time is constructed around Matthew's five blocks of alternating narrative and teaching, the five "Great Sermons" of Jesus. Year C uses Luke's "Travel Narrative" to order that long period of time and vast amount of scripture. The Gospel of Mark, however, is not so neatly structured. There is a *division by geography:* the ministry in Galilee (chapters 1 – 9) and the journey to Jerusalem (chapter 10) for the passion and death (chapters 11 – 15). There is also a *division by audience:* Jesus preaches and heals among the crowds (chapters 1 – 8:26), then Jesus interacts with his disciples, though not exclusively (from 8:27 until the passion). Bonneau notes:

> Because of the lack of consensus among biblical scholars in discerning the organizing structure of Mark's gospel, the compilers of the Lectionary do not appear to have followed either pattern but rather were content to select passages that portrayed Jesus in all facets of his ministry. (*The Sunday Lectionary,* 149)

Any chart of Year B's Ordinary Time, therefore, can be misleading and is bound to be somewhat arbitrary. It is always artificial to divide Ordinary Time into a series of miniseasons, but what the intent here is to clarify the shadings of the season of Sundays that is Ordinary Time. It will be helpful to see what the lectionary's supranarrative has omitted from Mark's gospel or moved to another place in the liturgical year. The chart combines the insights of John Fitzsimmons, a Scottish pastor and scripture scholar who has graciously permitted us to adapt his outline, and the research of Normand Bonneau, whose book on the Sunday lectionary has already been recommended. The material used in preparing the chart appeared in his article, "The Synoptic Gospels in the Sunday Lectionary: Ordinary Time" (*Questions Liturgiques* 75 [1994]: 154 – 169).

Before charting Year B's Ordinary Time, it may be helpful to summarize Fritz West's view of the lectionary's supranarrative, which he sees organized around three principal themes (*Scripture and Memory,* 116 – 117). The first theme is the *cross* as the Messiah's and the disciple's way to glory. Then *miracles* are crucial in the Markan Messiah's ministry, indeed, as the way the Messiah teaches. Finally, the *disciples* provide the interaction with Jesus that ties these themes together:

- *Cross.* Episodes from the journey to Jerusalem (Mark 8–10) convey the centrality of the cross. The lectionary includes the first two predictions of the passion on Sundays 24 and 25; on Sunday 29 the dialogue of Jesus with Zebedee's sons that follows the third passion prediction; and the concluding episode of the journey, the healing of Bartimaeus on Sunday 30.

- *Miracles.* The lectionary's supranarrative includes eleven of Jesus' miracles: Sundays 4, 5, 6, 7, 9, 12, 13, 17 (John's account of the miraculous feeding), 23 and 30. Related to the miracles is the injunction to silence on Sundays 5, 6, 13 and 23.

- *Disciples.* Jesus' interaction with them ties the themes of the cross and miracles together. Like Mark's gospel, the lectionary uses the disciples to raise the question of comprehension. The supranarrative includes 15 of Mark's 25 accounts of Jesus' encounters with his disciples and followers: Sundays 3, 4, 5, 12, 15, 16, 17 (John's gospel), two each on Sundays 24 and 25, 26, 27, 28 and 29.

WINTER ORDINARY TIME

■ Transitional Sundays

[moved to Advent 2	Beginning of the gospel and John the Baptist	Mark 1:1–6]
Sunday 1	The Baptist's messianic preaching; baptism of Jesus	Mark 1: 6–11
Sunday 2	Call of Andrew and Peter	John 1:35–42

■ The mystery progressively revealed, stage I: Jesus with the Jewish crowds

[moved to Lent 1	Temptation of Jesus	Mark 1:12–13]
Sunday 3	First preaching in Galilee; call of first disciples	Mark 1:14–20
Sunday 4	Teaching and healing in the synagogue	Mark 1:21–28
Sunday 5	Healing Peter's mother-in-law; healing many sick in the evening; withdrawing to pray; searched out; moving on	Mark 1:29–39
Sunday 6	Healing a man with leprosy	Mark 1:40–45
Sunday 7	Healing a paralyzed man and forgiving sin	Mark 2:1–12
[omitted:	Call of Levi	Mark 2:13–17]
Sunday 8	Question about fasting: old vs. new	Mark 2:18–22
Sunday 9	Violations of the Sabbath: eating, healing	Mark 2:23 — 3:6

In a block of nine Sundays, the most that can occur before Lent, the lectionary presents the initial stage of the Gospel of Mark. The principal themes of Mark are in clear evidence, especially on Sunday 5, "a day in the life of proclaiming the kingdom" (Brown). Healing, controversy and misunderstanding recur, especially as Jesus becomes "the transgressor of the boundaries" (Juel). Two episodes are omitted from Ordinary Time and used as seasonal readings: the preaching of John the Baptist (to Advent 2), the temptation story (to Lent 2). The call of Levi is omitted in Year B and presented in Year A.

SUMMER ORDINARY TIME

■ The mystery progressively revealed, stage II: Jesus with the crowds and with his disciples

[omitted:	Healing multitudes	Mark 3:7–12
	Call of the Twelve	Mark 3:13–19]
Sunday 10	Accusations; house divided; Jesus' true relatives	Mark 3:20–35
[omitted:	Parable of the sower and explanation	Mark 4:1–25]
Sunday 11	Seed parables	Mark 4:26–34
Sunday 12	Calming the storm	Mark 4:35–41
[omitted:	The Gerasene demoniac	Mark 5:1–20]
Sunday 13	Jairus' daughter, a woman's faith	Mark 5:21–43
Sunday 14	Jesus rejected at Nazareth: misunderstanding	Mark 6:1–6

This year, Ordinary Sundays 10, 11 and 12 are omitted, and the cycle resumes with Sunday 13 the week after the Solemnity of the

Body and Blood of Christ. Important passages dealing with the nature of the reign of God, a major theme in Mark, are therefore omitted. A deeper problem in this block of Sundays involves the construction of the Year B lectionary. The parable of the sower and Jesus' interpretation of it are omitted from the Year B lectionary, since the same story appears on Sunday 15 of Year A. At least one scholar sees that parable as the key to the entire Gospel of Mark. In her *Sowing the Gospel: Mark's World in Literary-Historical Perspective* (Fortress 1989, 1996), Mary Ann Tolbert asserts that, as in the Greek secular literature of the period, the parable functions as a plot synopsis (*prooemium*) for the whole work:

> The material that precedes the parable introduces the audience to the habits and responses of several major groups in the Gospel: the disciples, those healed, and the scribes, Pharisees, and other Jewish opponents. That initial perspective then assists the audience in identifying the Gospel groups that illustrate each of the four basic types of responses to the word outlined by the parable. The stories immediately succeeding the parables distinguish sharply between those representing the rocky ground and the good earth, the two responses most easily confused because of the positive beginning of the rocky ground type. (175)

Omitted also is the healing of the Gerasene demoniac, one of the few instances when Jesus both refuses a vocation (he will not let the man come with him and his disciples) and contravenes his usual preference for silence, "Go home to your friends and tell them." What remains in this year's lectionary is the healing of Jairus' daughter and of the woman with the hemorrhage. The section ends with misunderstanding in Jesus' hometown.

■ THE MYSTERY PROGRESSIVELY REVEALED, STAGE III: JESUS BEGINS TO MANIFEST HIMSELF

Sunday 15	Jesus sends out the Twelve	Mark 6:7–13
[omitted:	Herod, the death of John the Baptist	Mark 6:14–29]
Sunday 16	The Twelve return; Jesus' compassion for the crowd	Mark 6:30–34
[omitted:	Feeding 5000; walking on water; healing	Mark 6:35–56]
Sunday 17 through 21	Feeding 5000; bread of life; incredulity and faith	John 6:1–70
[omitted:		John 6:16–23; 36–40; 59–60]
Sunday 22	What defiles a person	Mark 7:1–8, 14–15, 21–23
[omitted:	Syro-Phoenecian woman	Mark 7:24–30]
Sunday 23	Healing a deaf-mute person	Mark 7:31–37
[omitted:	Feeding of 4000; demand for a sign; discourse on leaven; healing blindness	Mark 8:1–26]

As summer's harvest ripens, Year B's lectionary turns to the Bread of Life section of John. *Sourcebook* provides reflections on these Sundays in the calendar section of Summer/Fall Ordinary Time. Note the architecture of this block of Sundays. Evangelization begins in Christ and leads to Christ: In liturgical terms, the liturgy is the source and summit of Christian life and witness. We go out from Jesus, we return to Jesus. Worship gives strength for witness, witness compels us to return to worship.

Two omissions in the lectionary supra-narrative should be noted. Year B replaces Mark's two feeding stories (5,000 and 4,000 people) with the single feeding story from John. The Gospel of Mark uses these two stories to reinforce the motif of the disciples' misunderstanding. The reflections of one commentator might be kept in mind when preaching on the feeding story from John:

> Students of the Gospel have often taken the parallels as a sign that Mark is reproducing a doublet of one tradition . . . . The inadequacy of such exegesis should be obvious. The repetition is intentional; the details of the two stories are recalled with precision, and in the summary of the two accounts . . . the small differences in wording are reproduced exactly. . . . The effect of the repetition on readers is perhaps more to the point. Those who have listened to the whole Gospel read at one sitting generally laugh at this point. It is almost comical. It has all happened before — and the disciples do not yet understand about the loaves. They still do not expect a miracle. (Juel, 111–112)

Some also question the omission from the Sunday lectionary of Jesus' healing of the blind man in stages and with saliva. Some scholars think this is an allusion to early initiatory rites; all note the way the story reinforces the motif of the disciples' misunderstanding and prepares the way for Peter's confession of faith.

FALL ORDINARY TIME

■ THE MYSTERY OF THE SON OF MAN, STAGE I: TEACHING THE WAY TO THE DISCIPLES

Sunday 24	Peter's confession; first prediction of the passion; instruction to disciples	Mark 8:27–35
[omitted:	Conditions of discipleship	Mark 8:34—9:1
moved to Lent 2	Transfiguration	Mark 9:2–8
omitted:	Coming of Elijah and healing	Mark 9:9–29]
Sunday 25	Second prediction of the passion; dispute about greatness	Mark 9:29–37
Sunday 26	Strange exorcist; on temptations	Mark 9:38–47
[omitted:	Teaching on salt	Mark 9:49–50]
Sunday 27	Marriage and divorce; Jesus blesses the children	Mark 10:1–16
Sunday 28	Rich man	Mark 10:17–31
[omitted:	Third prediction of the passion	Mark 10:32–34]
Sunday 29	Ambition of the sons of Zebedee	Mark 10:35–46
Sunday 30	Healing of the blind Bartimaeus	Mark 10:46–52

Fall Ordinary Time begins with a pivotal scene in Mark's gospel: Peter's confession of Jesus as Messiah. True to form, misunderstanding is immediate, and Jesus calls Peter "Satan" for opposing the way of suffering Jesus points out. With the second prediction of the passion, also misunderstood by the disciples, a journey through Galilee begins. Several lessons on the nature of life in the reign of God follow. The fitness of children for the reign of God contrasts with the inability of the rich man to give up his wealth for that reign. For those who do make the commitment, the rewards are great, but, significantly, Mark adds to the litany of blessings—persecutions! Misunderstanding on the part of Zebedee's sons becomes, through the anger of the rest, a tribute to the disciples' continuing lack of perception into the nature of Jesus and his teaching. The healing of Bartimaeus sets the stage in the Gospel of Mark for the final revelation of Jesus as Son of God through the passion. In the lectionary, it prepares us to see Jesus as universal Lord and King in the final weeks of the liturgical year.

NOVEMBER ORDINARY TIME

■ THE MYSTERY OF THE SON OF MAN, STAGE II: FINAL REVELATION IN JERUSALEM

[moved to Passion/ Palm Sunday	Entry into Jerusalem	Mark 11:1–10
omitted:	The Jerusalem ministry and teaching	Mark 11:11—12:27]
Sunday 31	The greatest commandment	Mark 12:28–34
[omitted:	Question of David's son	Mark 12:35–37]
Sunday 32	Hypocrisy of the Pharisees' religious observance; authenticity of the widow's religious observance	Mark 12:37–44
[omitted:	Predictions about the end	Mark 13:1–23]
Sunday 33	Parousia of the Son of Man; parable of the fig tree; time of the parousia	Mark 13:24–32
[moved to Advent 1	Watch! Stay awake!	Mark 13:33–37]

■ THE MYSTERY OF THE SON OF MAN, STAGE III: FULFILLMENT OF THE MYSTERY

Sunday 34	(Christ the King) Jesus before Pilate: what kind of king?	John 18:33–37

The gospel ends with the passion. The lectionary and the liturgical year end, as they began, with the parousia. Christians prepare for judgment by learning again the greatest commandment. Combining Deuteronomy and Leviticus, Jesus presents this Jewish teaching as the hallmark of his own community of disciples. He describes the perceptive scribe of the Torah as being "not far from the reign of God." Phony and sincere religious observance is next on Jesus' teaching agenda. He who is about to give all that he has sees a perfect model for discipleship in the poor widow. The Year of Mark ends as it began: with a call for vigilance and a reminder that, for a disciple awaiting the coming of the Son of Man, the best way to *get* ready is to *be* ready! The last Sunday in Ordinary Time goes to the Gospel of John to place the paschal mystery before our eyes one last time in the liturgical year 2000: Jesus before Pilate, confounding his and our notions of kingship.

MARK AND ANTI-SEMITISM

In Year B, as in every year, it is difficult to listen to parts of the gospel and not hear an anti-Jewish polemic. Raymond Brown reminds us that when the Gospel of Mark was taking shape, this was not a problem, since those on both sides of "the Jesus issue" were, in fact, Jewish. When the first Christians thought of those who had conspired against Jesus, they did not think in terms of "them" and "us." The leaders were Jewish and the believers were Jewish, too. The situation then was not unlike the persecution of the prophet Jeremiah centuries before: he was a Jewish prophet opposed by Jewish leaders. But soon enough, as large-scale conversions of Gentiles changed the Christian community, the situation changed. It was no longer an intra-Jewish setting, but one in which Jews were on one side and Gentile Christians were on the other.

The passion narrative in particular during Year B needs to be handled with a sensitivity that does not permit an "our," "your" or "their" attitude to develop between Christians and the holy people of the covenant from whose midst came Jesus, our Messiah.

Additional Resources

GENERAL INTRODUCTIONS (SCHOLARLY BUT ACCESSIBLE)

Normand Bonneau, *The Sunday Lectionary: Ritual Word, Paschal Shape.* Collegeville: The Liturgical Press, 1998.

Raymond E. Brown, *An Introduction to the New Testament,* especially chapter 7. New York: Doubleday, 1997.

Mark Allan Powell, *Fortress Introduction to the Gospels,* especially chapter 2. Minneapolis: Fortress, 1998.

"Reading Guide to the Gospel of Mark," in *The Catholic Study Bible.* New York: Oxford University Press, 1992.

ONE-VOLUME COMMENTARIES

Donald H. Juel, *Mark.* Augsburg Commentary on the New Testament. Minneapolis: Augsburg, 1990.

Forthcoming volume on Mark in the *Sacra Pagina* series from The Liturgical Press.

NARRATIVE APPROACH

Janice Capel Anderson and Stephen D. Moore, editors, *Mark and Method: New Approaches in Biblical Studies.* Minneapolis: Fortress, 1992.

David Rhoads and Donald Michie, *Mark as Story: An Introduction to the Narrative of a Gospel.* Philadelphia: Fortress, 1982.

Mary Ann Tolbert, *Sowing the Gospel: Mark's World in Literary-Historical Perspective.* Minneapolis: Fortress, 1989, 1996.

ECUMENICAL RESOURCES

Susan A. Blain, editor, *Imaging the Word: An Arts and Lectionary Resource* (several volumes). Cleveland: United Church Press, 1995. Rich illustrations in all styles and from all periods. Suitable for placement at the entrance of the worship space as a contemporary icon.

Fritz West, *Scripture and Memory: The Ecumenical Hermeneutic of the Three-Year Lectionaries.* Collegeville: The Liturgical Press, 1997.

Wayne L. Wold, *Tune My Heart to Sing: Devotions for Choirs Based on the Revised Common Lectionary.* Minneapolis: Augsburg Fortress, 1997. Brief reflections for all three cycles in one volume. Each entry is coordinated with the gospel of the Sunday and refers to a hymn text appropriate to that gospel.

Sacramentary Overview: Preparing for Liturgy

The label "liturgy planning" is problematic if it leads us to believe that our task is to invent, devise or create the liturgy. All these paths are dead ends. Worship is not something we invent; it is the given, it is our duty, it is what we do. Prayer is not something we devise; it is a relationship. Christian ritual is not something we create; it is concerned with what we do naturally: we bathe, we eat and drink, we forgive and we marry. (Austin Fleming, *Preparing for Liturgy,* 30)

FLEMING suggests substituting the word *preparing* for *planning* to better orient ourselves to the real task:

Although we are unable to plan our encounter with the Lord, we are called, always and everywhere, to be ready, open to, and prepared to encounter the Lord who comes to meet us — and this is our duty and our salvation. Although we are unable to plan the graced moment of encounter with the Lord, we are obliged to prepare for it. Each person, and the whole community is called to "prepare the way of the Lord" and to make straight the paths along which we encounter the divine Traveler. (32)

Such reflections remind us of two basic truths to fix in our minds and hearts before we dare to prepare or preside at any liturgy.

First, the liturgy is not our personal possession to do with as we please without reference to the history and heritage that transcend our own limited space and time and insight. Nor is it a hobby with which to experiment, heedless of the community's wisdom that is enshrined in its official suggestions, directives, and legislation.

Second, the basic unit of all liturgical preparation, the primary focus of creative energy and prayerful devotion, is neither the liturgical year nor a season within it, but the Sunday eucharist itself. No amount of planning for a season or feast, no matter how well-intentioned or sophisticated, can succeed without attention to the worthy celebration of this basic liturgical element. The week-by-week proclamation of the scriptures and blessing of the community's table in the great prayer of thanksgiving form the fundamental setting, the "basic outline," to use Fleming's term, within and around which any seasonal or festal variation takes place.

BASIC PRINCIPLES

From these truths come two principles that good liturgical planning strives to hold in creative tension, two principles that have marked the Roman rite from time immemorial:

- *Ritual requires repetition:* Whatever made us think that the liturgy should constantly change?
- *Liturgical seasons create variation:* Whatever made us think the liturgy should never change?

On the one hand, no human community can function effectively if it has to fashion anew, at the dawn of each new day or at the beginning of each new year, the ritual patterns by which it lives and moves. Knowing not only *who* does *what,* but *how* and *when* is part of that "noble simplicity" long considered the hallmark of the Roman liturgy.

On the other hand, common sense dictates that an early morning Sunday Mass in the heat of midsummer need not be identical to the principal Mass of Christmas day. The concept of *progressive solemnity* suggests that there should be an easily perceived difference between the Sundays of Easter and Sundays in Ordinary Time, between Ash Wednesday and the Easter Vigil. Even within the Order of Mass, the basic components vary in importance. For instance, there ought to be, visually and audibly, a noticeable difference between the quiet, even silent preparation of the gifts and the proclamation or chanting of the eucharistic prayer, between the inaudible prayer at the washing of the hands and the invitation to communion.

BASIC QUESTIONS

With the calendar as a framework and the lectionary as the primary text, those preparing the liturgy can outline the community's Sunday eucharist by asking two questions:

- What elements in this community's celebration of the eucharist rarely change from Sunday to Sunday?
- What variations might help the assembly enter more prayerfully into the spirit of Advent and Christmastime, Lent and Eastertime, or the solemnities and feasts within them (such as

Epiphany and Ascension) or related to them (such as Presentation and Holy Cross)?

Thoughtful study of the outline that emerges from such questions will reveal two dimensions of the community's worship:

- *The unchanging backdrop:* "by heart" patterns that lend steadiness and stability to the community's celebration of the Lord's Day.
- *The variable highlights and shadings:* contrasting and complementary seasonal variations of decor and music, ritual gesture and special texts that permit the nuances of the liturgical seasons to enhance the community's celebration of the liturgical year.

In order to translate these truths, principles and questions into action:

- Look at the shape of the Sunday eucharist as it has been given to us by the church.
- Examine the elements of it, what each is meant to accomplish and how each fits into the whole (see the sacramentary's General Instruction).
- Reflect on how the community celebrates each component through the successive seasons of the liturgical year.

Following are suggestions for varying the introductory rites and for linking the two principal components of the Mass, the liturgy of the word and the liturgy of the eucharist. They can serve as examples of the celebration can be customized according to the season. It may be that the situation of the community suggests looking first at other elements in the Order of Mass, or those preparing the liturgy may wish to review each component in the Order of Mass over a period of years.

INTRODUCTORY RITES

Beginnings are crucial. Liturgical beginnings are both crucial and tricky. Reflect on the embarrassment of riches in the introductory rites of the present Order of Mass:

- Gathering song and procession
- Sign of the cross, formal liturgical greeting, less formal introductory remarks
- Penitential rite with invitation, silence, spoken words and sometimes sung acclamations
- Gloria, on most Sundays
- Opening prayer or collect.

One author called this "our cluttered vestibule." When ICEL began its research in preparation for the revised sacramentary, it found that the English-speaking bishops were aware of the problem, too:

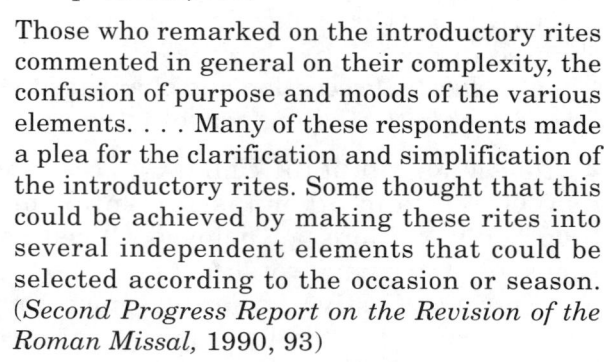

> Those who remarked on the introductory rites commented in general on their complexity, the confusion of purpose and moods of the various elements. . . . Many of these respondents made a plea for the clarification and simplification of the introductory rites. Some thought that this could be achieved by making these rites into several independent elements that could be selected according to the occasion or season. (*Second Progress Report on the Revision of the Roman Missal,* 1990, 93)

Accordingly, ICEL has proposed that the revised sacramentary give communities freedom to choose among the various elements, rather than celebrating all of them sequentially. The present Order of Mass already provides such a solution in certain instances. For example, when the blessing and sprinkling with holy water begin the Sunday liturgy, the penitential rite is omitted. When the blessing of candles or palms or any similar rite precedes the Mass, that becomes the introduction and, unless the Gloria is prescribed, the opening prayer follows immediately. On Ash Wednesday, when the blessing and imposition of ashes becomes the day's dramatic penitential rite, the liturgy begins simply, with the greeting and opening prayer.

Consider applying this principle seasonally according to the current rubrics, mapping out distinctive introductory rites for the entire liturgical year. Throughout each season, a distinctive introductory rite could set the tone for the entire liturgy within the first few moments. Each introductory rite would consist of these elements:

- Preparation
- Entrance
- Greeting
- Conclusion.

One possible pattern follows:

■ ADVENT: *Preparation:* The church in semi-darkness as people arrive; Advent hymn tunes or chants are playing softly; the appropriate number of Advent wreath candles is already burning (or perhaps are lighted after the greeting).

Entrance: Procession of ministers enters to instrumental or chanted version of the Advent hymn used throughout the season and pauses under the hanging Advent wreath or near a standing one.

Greeting: Greeting, introduction and chanted litany.

Conclusion: Procession and chant resume. Presider chants opening prayer at chair.

■ CHRISTMAS THROUGH EPIPHANY: *Preparation:* Organ (and other instrumental) preludes or variations on beloved Christmas tunes greet arriving worshipers.

Entrance: Festive gathering song accompanies procession led by fragrant incense. Song continues throughout incensation of altar, congregation and perhaps even the nativity scene. On the Feast of the Lord's Baptism, this incensation might be omitted, and the simple greeting ("The Lord be with you") followed by blessing and sprinkling with water.

Greeting: Greeting and litany follow.

Conclusion: Joyous singing of the Gloria. Opening prayer follows.

■ LENT: *Preparation:* Congregation enters silent church. Entrance procession may also be silent or accompanied by distinctive chant-style entrance song.

Entrance: The principal liturgy of the First Sunday of Lent should begin with a penitential procession. This procession begins ideally at the place where the Passion Sunday blessing of palms and the Easter Vigil's new fire will be. The assembly moves to the place of the eucharistic celebration accompanied by the litany of the saints.

Greeting: On other Sundays of Lent the congregation may kneel for the "I confess" and absolution.

Conclusion: Introductory rite closes with chanted Greek *Kyrie* from among the chants of the old Vatican "Kyriale" (especially Masses XV, XVI, XVII, XVIII although some prefer the more dramatic Mass XI, "Orbis Factor"). Opening prayer is offered.

■ EASTERTIME: *Preparation:* The Roman heritage of chant and the wide variety of Reformation chorales and hymns provide innumerable possibilities for festive preludes to greet the worshipers as they gather in the light of the Easter candle. It should appear that this candle has been burning since the Vigil! The Easter candle is always lighted before anyone arrives and extinguished after everyone leaves.

Entrance: Incense and alleluias! Incensation of the altar, font and the assembly in whom the risen Christ dwells.

Greeting: The greeting is chanted.

Conclusion: Throughout Eastertime, blessing and sprinkling with water replaces the penitential rite. Sprinkling is accompanied by proper Eastertime chant, leading into sung Gloria. Opening prayer is sung.

■ OTHER SPECIAL DAYS:

Presentation of the Lord (with its candle blessing) and the *Annunciation:* incorporate more visual or aural elements from the Christmastime introductory rites.

Transfiguration, Exaltation of the Holy Cross and *Mary's Assumption:* echo elements from Eastertime's beginnings.

All Saints: sung litany but not in the penitential style of Lent. Some parishes continue this practice at the principal liturgy throughout November, culminating in Easter-style triumph on the Solemnity of Christ the King.

■ SEASON OF SUNDAYS: There can be variety here, too, whether it is Winter Ordinary Time, Summer or Autumn, or November.

A *procession* of ministers may not always be appropriate or desirable. A diminished assembly during summertime or an increased assembly in vacation communities might suggest different approaches. The ministers could simply enter and take their places during the quiet time before the celebration. Sometimes the gathering song begins quietly with everyone seated, growing until the presider stands to greet the assembly. Or when the moment to begin has come, the presider stands and then the community's song begins. Or there may be no song — only the simple greeting.

The *litany of the saints* as the November entrance has already been mentioned. In some communities the images of the saints or the Book of the Names of the Dead are incensed during the introductory rite to signal the bonds that unite the community here with the community gone before through death to glory.

GOSPEL AND EUCHARISTIC PRAYER

Just as the *proclamation of the gospel* is the culmination of the liturgy of the word, the *eucharistic prayer* is the high point of the liturgy of the eucharist. Three sung acclamations should punctuate this prayer at even the simplest celebration: the Holy, the memorial acclamation, the Great Amen. The *Ceremonial of Bishops* makes provision for the incensation of bread and cup as these are shown to the people for adoration after the words of institution.

Consider linking these major elements by song and ceremonial. These traditions could be adapted creatively and selectively by season. Some possibilities:

■ ACCLAMATIONS: In Latin Mass days, those who used the Vatican *Kyriale* could tell what season and even what rank a day was by the opening notes of the Kyrie. One was reserved for Eastertime, two for feasts of Our Lady, one for Sundays of Advent and Lent, another for the weekdays of those seasons.

Choose distinctive chants that sound like Advent, that are sung only during Eastertime, or that signal a Marian feast, a festive occasion, a penitential season.

Choose Mass settings with gospel acclamations and eucharistic prayer acclamations that incorporate the same musical theme and tone.

Foster this by-heart and by-season approach by a judicious limiting of the community's repertoire of acclamations: one set for Advent, another for Christmastime, a third for Lent, one for Easter's Fifty Days, perhaps one each for summer, autumn and November Ordinary Time. November's chants might even anticipate Advent.

■ CEREMONIAL: Candles, incense and ritual movement traditionally mark the high points in the liturgy of the word and liturgy of the eucharist. With some adaptations a link may be established:

Gospel Proclamation. Determine *when* there will be a procession with candles, incense, gospel book. (See LTP's videos *The Word of the Lord* and *New Life: A Parish Celebrates Infant Baptism* for a joyous carry-around of the book and an energetic acclamation.)

Proclamation of the Eucharistic Prayer. Let the same incense, candles and ministers who led the assembly in honoring the gospel do the same for the eucharistic prayer.

The danger of an overly intense focus on the words of institution and adoration of the consecrated elements suggests that the use of torches and incensation during the institution narrative *not* be revived. But consider the thoughtful updating of this tradition that took place at the ordination of Paul Pluth, OSB, at Padre Serra Parish in Camarillo, California. Liturgical dancers led the entrance procession with bowls of incense. They accompanied the deacon for the gospel procession, and stood with smoking, fragrant bowls uplifted throughout the gospel proclamation. Later, during the proclamation of the eucharistic prayer, they knelt with their bowls of incense on the lowest step of the altar. The assembly, which had sung enthusiastic alleluias before and after the gospel proclamation, sang reverently joyous acclamations throughout the eucharistic prayer.

Thus the ministers and assembly proclaimed, by sight, sound and even smell, the parallel importance of the gospel and the eucharistic prayer. The assembly was drawn equally into the prayerful experience of both.

ADDITIONAL RESOURCES

General Instruction of the Roman Missal and Appendix to the General Instruction for the Dioceses of the United States. Overview (includes Overview of the Appendix) by Mark R. Francis, CSV. In *The Liturgy Documents: A Parish Resource.* Third Edition. Chicago: Liturgy Training Publications, 1991 (on disk, 1997).

Austin Fleming, *Preparing for Liturgy: A Theology and Spirituality.* Revised Edition. Chicago: LTP, 1997.

Kevin W. Irwin, *Advent and Christmas: A Guide to the Eucharist and Hours.* Collegeville: The Liturgical Press, 1986.
Lent, 1985.
Easter, 1991.

Richard McCarron, *The Eucharistic Prayer at Sunday Mass.* Chicago: LTP, 1997.

Celebrations Overview

THE major portion of any liturgy team's energy and efforts is rightly directed toward preparation of the community's Sunday and seasonal eucharist. Well prepared, prayerfully offered and enthusiastically celebrated, the principal Sunday eucharist should be a work of art. Gathering varied gifts and talents together, blending diverse voices of praise and petition into a balanced chorus, coordinating word and gesture, song and silence, sight and even smell — this is nothing less than the weaving of a complex and beautiful tapestry.

Compared to the preparation of Sunday eucharist, the fabric of communal and individual life beyond the Sunday assembly is more like a quilt than a tapestry, a multitude of varied patches. Some patterns are repeated over and over again, as regular as the daily sunrise and sunset. Other designs recur less frequently, but with enough regularity to be recognizable when one looks at the whole. There are bright patches of joy that add beauty to the quilt. There are subdued patches of sorrow, often unforeseen and difficult to fit into any orderly pattern. The liturgical ministry of every parish needs to care for this fabric of human existence on several levels, the communal and the personal, the expected and the impromptu, the recurring and the rare.

THE LITURGY OF THE HOURS

Not just another devotion but the formal daily liturgy of praise and intercession to be offered everywhere by everyone, the Liturgy of the Hours belongs to the whole people of God, as Vatican II made clear.

True though this is, even the most enthusiastic devotees have been daunted by the complexities of translating theory into practice. The Anglican and Lutheran liturgical reforms of the sixteenth century found considerable success in restoring the Hours to the whole community, both by the use of the vernacular and by a vast simplification of the complex monastic version of this prayer. Most would agree that Vatican II's revised Liturgy of the Hours is not simplified enough for user-friendly, popular celebration, but there is wide latitude for pastoral adaptation. In recent years, many simplified resources have appeared to help parish communities embrace this cherished heritage.

One of the most accessible, available from LTP, is Joyce Ann Zimmerman's *Morning and Evening,* which has three components:

Morning and Evening: A Parish Celebration. A concise overview of the background and components of the Liturgy of the Hours. A practical step-by-step manual by an author with experience in restoring the Hours in real communities.

Morning and Evening. This booklet provides everything necessary for popular participation in the Hours.

Morning and Evening: Order of Service. Everything needed by presider, cantor and accompanist in a loose-leaf format.

INITIATION

Adult and infant baptism, confirmation and first eucharist are defining moments not only in the lives of individuals but in the life of the whole community.

- *Adult initiation.* Always reserved to the Easter Vigil. The *Rite of Christian Initiation of Adults* spells out in great detail the elements involved in its celebration.
- *Infant baptism.* How often and in what context is this sacrament celebrated? At Sunday eucharist? Communally, outside the eucharist?
- *Confirmation and first eucharist.* Their essential connection to baptism should be highlighted. Good ways to do this are scheduling them as close to Easter as possible, emphasizing the renewal of baptismal vows (with participants gathered around the font) and making the Easter candle prominent.

HEALING

The sacramental rites that touch body and soul with the healing presence of Christ also need to be part of the liturgy team's reflections.

- *Reconciliation.* When and how is this sacrament celebrated? The official rite suggests communal celebrations during Advent and Lent. Planners need to prepare these to balance the twofold call to personal and communal conversion, the individual commitment to public witness and the community's obligation to justice.
- *Pastoral Care of the Sick.* How often and when does the community celebrate communal anointing? Who brings the eucharist to the sick and when? Is there a clear connection between the Lord's Day eucharist of the community and the reception of communion by those separated from us by sickness, disability or advanced age?

LIFE PASSAGES

Liturgy teams should help in the preparation of attractive and informative brochures that explain necessary policies and procedures.

- *Marriage.* Liturgy planners should be involved in helping couples prepare a celebration that respects the church's expectations. Music, decor, ritual movement and scriptural selections are all to be included in such planning.
- *Funerals.* Families often need and appreciate help in planning vigil services and in making their way through the choices of texts and music for the funeral Mass.

ONCE-A-YEAR CELEBRATIONS

Besides the eucharist and Liturgy of the Hours, other services can serve as prayerful signposts as the community journeys through the liturgical year.

- Patronal feast and anniversary of dedication (local parish and diocesan cathedral)
- Advent service of lessons and Advent carols
- Christmas and New Year's Eve vigils
- Penitential procession for the First Sunday of Lent
- Extended vigil for Pentecost Eve

DEVOTIONAL LIFE

The long and ongoing work of liturgical renewal rightly demands the full attention and first commitment of energy and resources of planners and presiders. But no community's prayer can be complete without some devotional dimensions as well. In reflecting on the devotional life of the parish, it may be helpful to consider several categories.

CHRIST-CENTERED DEVOTIONS

- *Solemnity of the Body and Blood of Christ (Corpus Christi).* Some parishes celebrate the Lord's abiding presence with a procession, a prolonged time of quiet and prayerful adoration, Evening Prayer and Benediction.
- *First Friday* is an important day in many communities, and *Catholic Household Blessings and Prayers* contains the beautiful scriptural litany associated with this devotion.

In one cathedral parish, the group that organizes the community's yearly and monthly eucharistic adoration also works as the justice outreach committee, serving Christ alive and present in the needy of the neighborhood.

- *Stations of the Cross.* This continues to be an important part of lenten prayer in some communities.

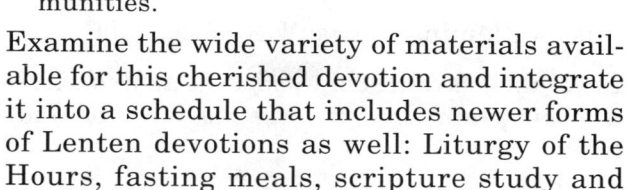

Examine the wide variety of materials available for this cherished devotion and integrate it into a schedule that includes newer forms of Lenten devotions as well: Liturgy of the Hours, fasting meals, scripture study and social justice outreach.

MARIAN PRAYER

The intimate association of Mary with the redeeming work of her Son and the life of her Son's disciples is celebrated in feasts throughout the year.

- *Saturday commemoration during Ordinary Time.* See the *Collection of Masses of the Blessed Virgin Mary* (published by The Liturgical Press), which relates Marian titles to the seasons of the liturgical year and roots most of these in the scriptures.
- *Evening Prayer* on Marian feastdays
- *August 15.* Fragrant herbs and first fruits of the forthcoming harvest are blessed in some places, reflecting Mary's special sharing in Christ's resurrection through her Assumption.
- *December 12.* The Guadalupe feast and the Las Posadas customs can be a way of joining diverse ethnic groups together around the woman whose Son is Lord of all nations and Liberator of all the oppressed.
- *The Rosary* is a time-honored prayer. Modern arrangements of it, modeled on public celebrations conducted by Pope John Paul II, combine scripture, song and silent prayer along with the customary Hail Marys.

COMMEMORATIONS OF THE SAINTS

To which saints does the community have long-standing devotion? Patronal dedication titles and varied — sometimes changing — ethnic backgrounds will suggest at least a short litany of names. Some local or national saints may also provide that human link with God's kingdom which the cloud of witnesses in every age always offers those of us still running the race. Certainly no living community can be fully alive in faith without a sense of its participation in the communion of saints across time and space.

ADDITIONAL RESOURCES

Mary Beth Kunde-Anderson and David Anderson, *Handbook for Church Music for Weddings.* LTP.

Austin Fleming, *Parish Weddings.* LTP.

Graziano Marcheschi, *Scripture at Weddings: Choosing and Proclaiming the Word of God.* LTP.

Order of Christian Funerals (ritual and study editions) and *Cremation Appendix.* LTP. Assembly participation cards for the vigil and committal, and prayer cards for the funeral home are also available.

Margaret Smith, *Facing Death Together: Parish Funerals.* LTP, 1998.

LTP's Sourcebooks: *Baptism, Marriage, Reconciliation, Death.*

ADVENT

The Season
The Setting of Advent / 3
A Sense of Advent / 4
The Look of Advent / 6
The Sounds of Advent / 7
The Rhythm of Advent / 8
The Word of God / 8
The Eucharist / 10
Other Celebrations / 13
At Home / 14
The Calendar
November 30 – December 24 / 16

The Setting of Advent

WHAT is the context in which your community will celebrate its first Advent of the new millennium? Responsible liturgical planning strives to be sensitive to the several dimensions in which most members of the Sunday assembly live. Approaching each season from a variety of perspectives will give those who prepare and preside at the community's worship a feel for the richness of the real-life setting of that worship. Vast and beautiful indeed is the treasury of the church's liturgical heritage. But as Pope John XXIII (1958 – 1963) reminded us, "the church was not put on earth to guard a dusty museum but to cultivate a flourishing garden of life." The prime objective of the art of liturgical planning must be to transform that timeless treasury into a living legacy, made tangible and given voice in the "full, conscious, and active participation" of the whole People of God (*Constitution on the Sacred Liturgy,* 14).

So as Advent 2000 draws near, planners and presiders should confront a variety of questions long before designing the Advent wreath or choosing the first Advent hymn. Think of this reflection as the first steps in building a bridge between our life-giving heritage and our daily life.

■ THE GLOBAL CULTURE is showing contrasting emotions as the year 2000 comes closer. Anticipation and apprehension seem to be everywhere! These emotions are not exactly twins, but they are at least relatives. They usually show up together deep in the heart of anyone awaiting something momentous or someone very important.

These emotions have been abroad in the world these last few years. Inflamed by some doomsday groups and manipulated more subtly by others, they have surfaced as well in more reasoned mainline discourse. As the population of planet Earth prepared for the event that is now at hand, anticipation and apprehension echoed in every kind of writing, from papal and political to popular, and showed up in every field of endeavor, from the sacred and scientific to retail sales.

True, some concerns are specific to this particular millennium's beginning, for instance, the famous Y2K computer bug. But much of the political upheaval, societal turmoil and spiritual energy that seem to be unique to the coming of the year 2000 have in fact been part of every year in modern history. Nevertheless, such matters did seem to assume a more prominent presence in these last few years. It is as if the human race wants to start the new millennium with a clean slate. This, then, could be called the global or cultural dimension of the context of Advent 2000. Nor is it unrelated to the mood of the liturgical season of Advent. Anticipation and apprehension recur in the scriptures of the Advent lectionary, in the Advent prayers of the sacramentary and liturgy of the hours; they echo and reecho through the season's formal chants and popular hymns. The comforting promise of coming fulfillment only intensifies the urgency of the disturbing challenge to change, to convert, to prepare a straight path!

■ NATURE is a world of contrasts during Advent, at least in much of the Northern Hemisphere, a strange blend of bleakness and brightness. On some days a crisp, clear (and late!) dawn provides us with a spectacular sky awash in all the shades of the Advent palette — purple, blue and rose. But on other mornings the sky stays the color of the squirrels that turn out in force to defy all the laws of gravity as they raid every feeder in sight. Here, too, the liturgy of the season of Advent is a mirror image of the world around us. The texts and tunes of Advent, translating the message Israel's prophets and sages, can sing cheerfully of God's bright promise of salvation or poignantly of the nation's — and the individual's — bleak experience of exile.

■ CONFLICT RATHER THAN CONTRAST might best describe most evenings during Advent. If Advent mornings provide a setting for nature's contrasting moods, then Advent evenings set the stage for a battle waged in many a worshiper's heart. Advertise this wrestling match as Hearth vs. Mall, the modern day version of the struggle between the contemplative and the active, between the tranquil peace of the Advent season and the commercial compulsion of the Christmas countdown.

Oddly, both sides of the conflict have enlisted one of the season's basic symbols: light. Every culture in the Northern Hemisphere has a winter custom involving light, every religious group a ritual employing it. So while the gentle glow of candles in the Advent wreath might bid our hearts stay close to home on these long and increasingly colder nights, the malls are ablaze with holiday lights — and have been since Halloween! Perhaps we cast a wistful eye toward the Advent wreath as we pull on hat and gloves.

As much as our spiritual commitment may draw us to the Advent candles, the reality of the world we live in hardly permits us to ignore the mall lights. But could our Roman forebears ignore their world's celebration of the Birth of the Invincible Sun at the time of the winter solstice? Not likely, one imagines. In fact, liturgical history shows that, while Roman Christians may have had other, more traditional reasons for commemorating the birth of Christ on December 25, they did not hesitate also to redeem the imagery of their pagan neighbors. Who else could the *true* Invincible Sun be but Jesus "the true light, which enlightens everyone coming into the world" (John 1:9) and "the Sun of Justice risen with healing in its wings" (Malachi 4:2)?

Thus Advent planning and preaching might find ways to suggest that the lights of the mall, too, can be signals of the season pointing to Jesus. Is there not something deeply spiritual about going out into a cold winter night to find just the right present to surprise and delight someone we love?

In all of this, of course, a balance is needed. But a liturgical planning that is at once respectful of the tradition and sensitive to the contemporary world needs to appreciate the Advent place of both quiet evenings by candlelight and bustling evenings at the mall. Each can turn us toward the Incarnation by revealing the splendor of the Holy One already in our midst and the mystery of the holy hidden in the ordinary.

A Sense of Advent

O come, O come Emmanuel ... It is difficult to imagine celebrating Advent without these words and without the plaintive chant to which they are invariably sung. Though not the most ancient of Advent hymns, it is, arguably, the most familiar Advent song. And it begins with the word, the plea, the command most representative of the season: Come! Come, Lord Jesus!

■ THE THREE "ADVENTS" OF CHRIST: The hymn and the word give voice to what the official liturgical documents consider the defining mood of the season: devout and holy expectation (*General Norms for the Liturgical Year and*

Calendar, 39). But for a full sense of Advent's richness, this central verb of the season needs some conjugation! The first set of alternative invocations for Penitential Rite C accomplishes this task in an admirable way:

> Lord Jesus, you *came* to gather the nations into the peace of God's kingdom:
>
> You *come* in word and sacrament to strengthen us in holiness:
>
> You *will come* in glory with salvation for your people:

Monastic authors and preachers of the middle ages loved to explore the concept of Christ's advent from the three perspectives of history, mystery and glory. Christ's first advent, at a certain time and place in history, was mostly hidden, marked by humility; it set him on the path of service, suffering and death. Christ's second advent would be in great glory, fully manifest to all, even to those who had rejected him, for this time Christ would come as Lord of the ages and Judge of the world, with judgment for some and salvation for others.

In the meantime there was Christ's coming in mystery: in the proclamation of the word, in the celebration of the eucharist, in the mystery of every person. Our response to Christ in this, his intermediate advent, signaled to these authors how well we understood his first advent and how prepared we would be for his second one.

■ MYSTERY, NOT HISTORY: Such an approach orients us toward the liturgy's multi-faceted way of engaging the human person. Liturgical celebration embraces at once past, present and future. It is simultaneously remembrance, revelation and anticipation. This broad perspective safeguards us against the recurring temptation to historicize the liturgical year and turn it into a kind of salvation-history pageant, a sacred play in two parts, coming and birth, death and resurrection, with the intermission of Ordinary Time in between. The liturgical year and, indeed, all of Christian worship, is neither a "let's pretend" attempt to recapture someone or something past, nor a simple "going in circles" through a recurring cycle of ritual and nostalgia. A more accurate image is a lively and progressive spiral motion by which, year after liturgical year, as "the church unfolds the entire mystery of Christ," (GNLYC, 1), we who celebrate are drawn deeper and deeper, or higher and higher, into the mystery and toward the mystery's fulfillment. The liturgy then is neither child's game nor adult drama, but a for-real shaping of our mortal lives according the pattern of Christ's sacrificial love, a lifelong preparation for immortal life at the wedding feast of the Lamb.

■ CONTEXT AND CENTER: Because the liturgical year celebrates the whole mystery of Christ and centers on Christ's paschal mystery, Advent cannot be planned or celebrated apart from Christmas. Nor can Christmas, with its stories of acceptance and rejection, danger and deliverance, its marvels and its martyrs, be separated from the paschal mystery. Planners and preachers need to let the scriptural texts, the songs of the season, and even the worship environment, proclaim and reflect the destiny of the Child: the passion, death and resurrection to glory. Note that the first memorial acclamation, focusing on the paschal mystery, echoes the penitential rite quoted above in its use of three verb tenses and incorporates Christ's second advent:

> Christ *has* died;
> Christ *is* risen;
> Christ *will* come again.

Perhaps the memorial acclamation most commonly used during Advent also keeps the center of the liturgical year in focus:

> Dying you destroyed our death.
> Rising, you restored our life.
> Lord Jesus, come in glory.

■ ADVENT'S TWO PHASES: Having looked at Advent in terms of verb tenses, however, we should note that the celebration of Advent actually reverses the order given in those texts. Advent begins with the *will come* phase, placing the end of all things before us. Occurring at the end of the civil year and, in many places, at the end of nature's yearly cycle, the beginning of the new Advent dovetails with the ending of the old liturgical year. The eschatological themes that marked the lectionary readings of the final weeks in Ordinary Time recur in the scriptures of the first weeks of Advent, particularly the First and Second Sundays in Advent. On these Sundays the prescribed preface, Advent I, speaks of us "watching for the day, hoping that the salvation promised us will be ours, when Christ our Lord will come again in his glory." This end signals not only the end of time and the culmination of history, but the inevitability of our own death and the certainty of judgment.

But in this first phase of Advent there are also elements of a new beginning. A new gospel book is opened on the First Sunday of Advent, and week by week another candle is lighted in the wreath. The challenging "Keep awake" is balanced by the comforting "Rejoice always." The community moves into a new year's uncertainty with trust in that "sure and certain hope" of resurrection, reunion with the community of saints gone before us, the "blessed hope" of the coming of the Christ whose reign is one of service, forgiveness, and true peace.

From December 17 on, the lectionary signals a change. Prophetic promises become very specific, matched by gospels that portray their fulfillment. Mary's expectation, the Baptist's mission as herald, and the joy that should be ours are all keynotes of this phase's preface, Advent II, which bids us greet the Lord, "our hearts filled with wonder and praise."

The Look of Advent

THE scriptural themes proclaimed inside the church and the seasonal characteristics of nature outside should be allowed to work together in guiding the creativity and informing the decisions of those planning the Advent environment. In this and in every season, the single most valuable resource and reference work any community can own is Peter Mazar's *To Crown the Year* (LTP, 1995).

Mazar seconds the concern for context and focus, challenging planners whose ministry is decorating to attend both to broad perspective and finer detail:

> There is both continuity and discontinuity between the seasons. Many of the scriptures, psalms and hymns of one period seem to prepare for the next; as the weeks pass, there is a gradual shifting of imagery.
>
> But there is also discontinuity between seasons. Some images do not carry over. These abrupt changes can bring an unsettling discomfort (not always a bad thing) but also delightful surprise. One of your tasks is to strike a balance between connections and breaks. (205–206)

PRELIMINARIES PLAIN AND SIMPLE

Taking his own advice, Mazar discusses the particular details of decorating for Advent within the broad perspective of decorating throughout the winter season:

> The span of time from the First Sunday of Advent to the day before Ash Wednesday is not very long, 15 weeks at most. Use common elements of decoration throughout these winter weeks, things that draw the season into our common prayer and bring light and cheer to what can be a depressing time of year. (205)

He characterizes the worship environment for Advent as being "plain and simple" and suggests five preliminary and practical steps toward achieving this:

1. Clean and simplify the whole place: worship space and vestibules.

2. Consider retaining some of the autumn (harvest) decor, but mute the colors.

3. Hang a large Advent wreath and light it for every gathering (although this was originally a home custom and not essential to the community's liturgy).

4. Decorate Mary's shrine and attend to images of John the Baptist, Elizabeth, the archangel Gabriel, and the prophet Isaiah.

5. Decorate the parish's outdoor area, the parking lot with its landscaping and even the building's doorways in a way that speaks of Advent, not of Christmas. (With the exception of the Advent wreath, an abundance of evergreens, says Mazar, is for Christmas, not for Advent.)

Complete details on Advent decorating appear on pages 200–221 of Mazar's book.

COLOR

Every parish should own at least two sets of violet vestments. The Advent vesture should not parallel Lent's penitence but speak of Advent's unfulfilled expectancy and provide a quiet prelude to the dramatic effect of Christmas brightness. Consider various ways of establishing the contrast:

- *Advent violet:* Choose the dark blue-violet of a winter sky. In fact, there seems to be historical precedent for the use of dark blue, especially in northern Europe.

- *Lenten violet:* Select royal or "Roman" purple, the *vexilla regis*, the "royal banners" of the king. A traditional, ancient lenten hymn has this title in the original Latin (see *Worship III*, #435).

Or:

- *Advent vesture:* Employ more elaborate adornment, orphreys, banding and so forth.
- *Lenten vesture:* Let this be utterly simple. In fact, traditional English usage called for a "lenten apparel" that was simply unbleached linen or even sackcloth.

And:

- *Advent paraments:* Let various shades of blue be dominant and let them complement the violet vestments.
- *Lenten paraments:* If used at all, these should reflect the austerity proper to Lent.

ADVENT WREATH

Proportion and *placement* are two principal matters to attend to in preparing the assembly's Advent wreath. Now a basic part of parish Advent décor, the Advent wreath was originally a visual aid to domestic prayer. When making the transition to the home of the whole people of God, the church, make sure it is proportionate to the size of the room it adorns and place it so that it engages the assembly's attention without distracting from ambo (the word) and altar (the eucharist). A possible solution:

Make it as big as a wagon wheel, with fine fat pillar candles.

Hang it over the center aisle and place a table with a bowl of fragrant incense under it (pick a special "Advent only" scent). Let the incense waft up through the wreath toward heaven.

The entrance procession could pause under it for the greeting and perhaps a chanted litany. Then, as the liturgy continues, attention turns toward ambo and altar, while the wreath continues shining in the midst of the assembly.

Let the same wreath, with renewed greenery, and holly or cranberries added, become a central Christmas decoration as well to maintain both the continuity and distinctiveness that Mazar speaks of in his reflections.

For other creative possibilities, see Mazar, 222–228. For practical thoughts on candlelighting, see G. Thomas Ryan's *The Sacristy Manual* (LTP, 1993), 147–149.

Remember, in Advent, less is more. Increasing clutter prepares for nothing. Keep in mind the small but significant change of lighting one more candle on the Advent wreath each week. Any attempt to make visible the growing anticipation of Advent should be as subtle as that candle-lighting.

The Sounds of Advent

LONGING and *fulfillment:* As these two movements alternate in Advent's scriptures and prayers, so Advent hymnody can generally be divided into two styles "tones" that reflect this alternation of moods:

Minor key melodies create a sense of haunting beauty and profound longing.

Carol-like tunes with gentle rhythms express a joy-filled faith that expects fulfillment.

The music chosen for Advent will ideally reflect the liturgical multivalence of the season, eliciting various moods and reflections from our hearts. There is an exceptional aesthetic beauty and theological depth to many traditional Advent texts. Since the season is too brief for learning many hymns, and since the restrained quality of the Advent liturgy cautions against musical excess, choose few pieces, but let them be deep enough to be worthy of the season. One or two carefully chosen hymns used each Sunday can unify the season, or choose two styles in succession:

■ EARLY ADVENT: Select something in a minor key with a haunting melody, unaccompanied or with single wind instrument sustaining melody. "O come, O come Emmanuel" represents this genre, as does the contemporary "Each winter as the year grows older."

Remember that chant works best with minimal or no accompaniment. Reed instruments or flute and oboe stops carry the chant melody lines well. Recent arrangements incorporate handbells for chord clusters at the end of each phrase. Handbells with chant create an effect of prayerful dignity and peaceful contemplation perfect for Advent's tenor and tone. Bells also keep the assembly on pitch.

■ LATE ADVENT: Switch to carol-style hymn and richer accompaniment, anticipating the coming feast in an aurally pleasing way. "O come, divine Messiah" and "People, look east" are fine representatives of this genre.

■ PLANNING THE SOUND OF ADVENT: A good way to begin planning is to read prayerfully, preferably aloud and in a group setting, all the verses of these traditional hymns:

O come, O come, Emmanuel

Savior of the nations, come

The King shall come when morning dawns
O Holy City seen of (by) John
Creator of the stars of night
Rorate Coeli (You clouds of heaven)
Wake, awake (Wake, O wake), and sleep no longer
On Jordan's bank
The Word of God proceeding forth

At this beginning of the liturgical year, make sure to obtain copies of the fine new ecumenical resources that have become available:

- *New Century Hymnal* (United Church of Christ). Contains new, inclusive translations of older hymns and impressive new texts.
- *With One Voice* (Lutheran Church). Look at "Light one candle," a text that combines the weekly Advent candle-lighting with Isaiah's prophecies.
- *A Year of Grace: Hymns for the Church Year.* (Hope Publishing Co., 1990) These are the collected hymns (original texts and translations) of the noted American hymn-writer, Carl P. Daw, Jr.
- *Redeeming the Time: A Cycle of Song for the Christian Year* by Herman G. Steumpfle, Jr. (GIA, 1997).

While official Roman directives ban the organ as a solo instrument in Advent, except on the Third (*Gaudete:* Rejoice) Sunday, contemporary usage suggests only that music in Advent be somewhat more restrained. This is done not out of a sense of penitence, but to achieve an effect similar to that of joyful white vestments appearing on Christmas after the violet of Advent. After the reflective quiet of Advent chants, the Gloria of the angels and carols of joy will resound with greater freshness on Christmas. Traditionally, the sound of Advent steers a middle course between Lent's austerity and Christmastime's exuberance. The mood is "devout and joyful expectation" for Advent: somewhat subdued befitting the expectant nature of the season, but gradually increasing in joy as Christmas approaches.

The Rhythm of Advent

Think of all the time we have wasted through recent decades listening to preachers lambast the evils of commercialism, the materialism of gift-giving, and all of the pagan atrocities of our cultural holidays, when what we hungered for were words of promise, of gospel, of the Coming One. (J. Neil Alexander, *Waiting for the Coming,* Washington: The Pastoral Press, 1993, 26–27).

AT this time of the year, more than at any other, we need to see society not as a world that is lost but as the world God refused to allow to be lost. "God so loved the world that he gave his only Son . . . not to condemn the world but that the world might be saved through him" (John 3:16–17).

In the parish setting, let any challenge to the culture be delivered gently, as a mutual reminder spoken by one who is part of the assembly and not above or apart from it. We all live in the same world and face together a pervasive consumerism that teaches us to measure love by purchases and to compensate for neglect by spending. Most people sense the need to recover the deeper meaning of Christmas and will appreciate practical and positive suggestions on how to do that:

- *Saturday or Sunday Evening Prayer, or a weeknight vigil by candlelight* with the soothing sound of Advent chants and carols. Schedule these services later in the evening, when meetings and the mall race are done; feature scripture, time for silent prayer, a simple sung litany, maybe a brief meditation but perhaps no preaching.
- *Communal reconciliation* can foster a sense of watchfulness and prayer, offer an opportunity for conversion and renewal, and lead to a deeper involvement in the spirit of Advent.
- *Christmas music rehearsals,* for liturgy or for carol singing in the community. Follow these with a warm sharing of hot chocolate and homemade cookies (good practice for Christmas baking!) to give people a chance to pause and catch their breath.
- *Offer "an alternative Christmas"* by introducing the parish to groups who work with Third World countries and the poor in our own country.

The Word of God

THE SUNDAY SCRIPTURES

Each gospel reading [of the Sundays of Advent] has a distinctive theme: the Lord's coming at the end of time (First Sunday of Advent), John the Baptist (Second and Third Sunday), and the events that prepared immediately for the

Lord's birth (Fourth Sunday). (*Lectionary for Mass,* Introduction, 93)

- **GOSPEL**: Year B, the Year of Mark (and John), features these selections in fulfillment of that thematic format:
  - First Sunday: The return of the Lord *(Mark 13:33–37):* This gospel sounds very much like the Matthean gospels that brought the liturgical year just past to its conclusion. The moral of the story about the bridesmaids (Thirty-second Sunday in Ordinary Time, Year A) echoes here: "Keep awake, for you know neither the day nor the hour." The story of the talents (Thirty-third Sunday in Ordinary Time, Year A) comes to mind as well: "About the day and the hour . . . no one knows." Mark repeats the "no one knows" motif, twice in the Canadian lectionary which prefixes verses 31 and 32 to the Roman lectionary reading. Then he ups the ante by intensifying and repeating the commands: "Beware, keep alert . . . keep awake . . . keep awake." But our vigilance is to be an active and productive. Working and watching go hand in hand when it is Jesus whom we are awaiting: "He put his slaves in charge, each with a particular task."
  - Second Sunday: John the Baptist's call to conversion *(Mark 1:1–8):* With no infancy narrative or childhood stories, Mark begins his gospel with the essential information and the immediate setting for Jesus' ministry. From the beginning we know who John is and is not. His dress, diet and desert ministry mark him as one of the "sons of the prophets." Indeed, he looks and sounds like the prophet Elijah whose return, it was said, would herald the coming of the Messiah. John himself tells us that "one who is more powerful" is coming. Mark has begun his gospel and this Sunday's selection from it by telling us who Jesus is, "the Son of God." Since we already know this, how much more urgent for us, than for John's audience, is the call to confess our sins, repent, and prepare the way of the Lord.
  - Third Sunday: the relationship of John to Jesus *(John 1:6–8, 19–28):* Advent's urgency sounds most clearly in this passage, for in the unique time-perspective of the Fourth Gospel, the "one who is coming after," warns John the Baptist, "already stands among you — one whom you do not know." But we know him, don't we?
  - Fourth Sunday: Events immediately preceding Christ's birth *(Luke 1:26–38):* The annunciation story is made poignant by a tremulous question, "How can this be?" and a trustful commitment, "Let it be done to me according to your word." Binding question and commitment together is the promise that binds Christ's first coming and glorious return together, the promise that guides us on our pilgrimage in this meantime: "Nothing is impossible with God!"

- **FIRST AND SECOND READINGS**: Year B presents selections from Isaiah on the first three Advent Sundays, turning on the last Sunday to Nathan's promise that God will build David a house, and not vice-versa, the prophecy to which Gabriel alludes in the annunciation to Mary. While the prophetic readings set the stage for God's saving intervention in Israel, the second readings for each Sunday link the saving work of God in Christ to Christian life in today's world.
  - First Sunday: *Isaiah 63:16b–17, 19b:* Isaiah's prayer that God rend the heavens and come down is balanced by his understanding that God is here already, intimately at work in and through his people. His awareness of the shortcomings and sins of the people is balanced by his perception that we are still a work in progress. "We are the clay, and you are the potter, we are all the work of your hand." *1 Corinthians 1:3–9:* Paul reminds his faction-prone church at Corinth that "in every way you have been enriched in him . . . so that you are not lacking in any spiritual gift." They (we!) are to act on those gifts, so that we "may be blameless on the day" we are praying will come, the day of the Lord. God will accomplish his great work in us because he is faithful and can be trusted to fulfill his promises.
  - Second Sunday: *Isaiah 40:1–5, 9–11:* What a construction project to prepare the way of the Lord! Yet the keynotes of the passage are comfort and tenderness, for over all these rebuilt roads God's people will be carried by the shepherd who gathers them in his arms. *2 Peter 3:8–14:* Peter specifies what the building program envisioned by Isaiah and John entails: leading holy and godly lives, working while we wait, making the most of God's patience by making up for lost time.
  - Third Sunday: *Isaiah 61:1–2a, 10–11:* The joy of good news for the oppressed, a wedding between heaven and earth, a garden that brings forth the nourishment earth desperately needs: righteousness and praise. Such is Isaiah's vision of life with the Servant of the Lord. *1 Thessalonians 5:16–24:* How much more should be the joy of the disciple of Jesus, the disciple who is always at prayer, and always grateful, trusting in the fidelity of the God who calls us.
  - Fourth Sunday: *2 Samuel 7:1–5, 8b–12, 14a, 16:* Perhaps Nathan's prophetic eyes saw one of David's soon-to-be-born sons, but his words carried beyond his age into the message of Gabriel,

"the Lord God will give him the throne of his ancestor David." *Romans 16:25–27:* The mystery kept secret for ages is now open and accessible to all with its life-transforming power. The surprising part of the secret is that not only is the throne of David established forever in Jesus, but its saving power is extended beyond every human boundary "to all the Gentiles, according to the command of the eternal God."

PROPHECY AND FULFILLMENT

Discussing the coordination of the Hebrew scriptures with the Sunday gospels, the *Revised Common Lectionary* (1992) notes a positive advantage: "the desire . . . that the eucharistic liturgy and its readings be unified around the paschal mystery as it is proclaimed in the gospel reading" (18). However, in consequence of this coordination, our lectionary can seem to present the first reading solely as a prelude to the gospel.

This raises what is, in a way, the enduring theological issue with which Paul struggled throughout his ministry and epistles, that of the relationship of the Christian community to its Jewish heritage. Related questions have to do with Jesus as Messiah, the church as the New Israel, and the authority of the Old Testament in the Christian church today (16–17).

The Jewish scriptures need to be understood not only as preparation, but as a living challenge to us today. Specifically with regard to Advent, the United States' bishops write:

> The lectionary readings from the prophets are selected to bring out the ancient Christian theme that Jesus is the "fulfillment" of the biblical message of hope and promise, the inauguration of the "days to come" described, for example, by the daily Advent Masses. . . . This truth needs to be framed very carefully. Christians believe that Jesus is the promised Messiah who has come (see Luke 4:22), but also know that his messianic kingdom is not yet fully realized. . . . While the biblical prophecies of an age of universal "shalom" are "fulfilled" (i.e., irreversibly inaugurated) in Christ's coming, that fulfillment is not yet completely worked out in each person's life or perfected in the world at large (*Guidelines and Suggestions for Implementing the Conciliar Declaration "Nostra Aetate,"* no. 4, II, 1974 no. 2). It is the mission of the church, as also that of the Jewish people, to proclaim and to work to prepare the world for the full flowering of God's reign, which is, but is "not yet" (cf. 1974 *Guidelines* ii). Both the Christian "Our Father" and the Jewish "Kaddish" exemplify this message. Thus, both Christianity and Judaism seal their worship with a common hope: "Thy kingdom come!" (Bishops' Committee on the Liturgy, *God's Mercy Endures Forever,* 11)

The Eucharist

INTRODUCTORY RITES

■ BEGINNINGS BEFORE BEGINNINGS: Everything should be ready well before the assembly arrives. Nothing would kill the Advent spirit of quiet, contemplative longing more surely than distracted ministers busily putting things in place and scrambling to establish order just before the liturgy begins. Ideally, the ministers should be in sight only to serve the needs of hospitality as the church gathers.

■ THE ADVENT WREATH: Take seriously two concerns about the use of the Advent wreath during the liturgy: *visually* the wreath should not compete with the setting for the eucharist; *ritually* it should not compete with the rest of the liturgy (*Book of Blessings,* #1510, 1512).

In the dioceses of the United States, the Advent wreath is blessed on the First Sunday of Advent in a prayer that concludes the general intercessions (See *Book of Blessings,* chapter 47). There is no provision for a special introductory rite. On subsequent Sundays the appropriate number of candles are lighted before Mass begins or between the pentitential rite and opening prayer, but no additional rites or prayers are used. Alternatively, the Advent wreath blessing may take place during a celebration of the word of God or at Evening Prayer (see p. 13).

In the dioceses of Canada, the blessing of the Advent wreath takes place as part of a special introductory rite on the First Sunday of Advent (see p. 17). As the proposed Canadian sacramentary notes, "Since the lighted candle is a sign of Christ, the first candle of the wreath should always be lighted before the celebration begins."

In ethnic parishes in the United States that use ritual books in languages other than English (e.g., Hispanic parishes: *Bendicional*), the blessing of the wreath also takes place in the introductory rites.

LITURGY OF THE WORD

■ RESPONSORIAL PSALM: The principal consideration in choosing how to render the responsorial psalm is that the psalm should be sung. Three options are always available to make this possible:

- the *proper psalm* assigned in the lectionary
- a *seasonal psalm* chosen from among those at #174 in the revised lectionary
- a *common responsorial refrain* at #173 in the lectionary with verses of the proper psalm

The seasonal responsorial psalms and common refrains capture the central tone of a season. Advent's refrain sounds the timeless cry of longing, "Come, O Lord, and set us free." Sung with each Sunday's proper psalm, this refrain expresses our longing for salvation.

Psalms 25 and 85, beloved psalms of poignant longing and confident trust, are the seasonal psalms provided for Advent: "To you, O Lord, I lift my soul," and "Lord, let us see your kindness." Choose a memorable and melodic setting to become a text and melody known "by heart," shaping the community's sung prayer for the whole season. Some recommended musical settings for Psalm 25:

- "To you, O Lord": Marty Haugen, *Psalms for the Church Year* (GIA, G-2664); David Isele, *Psalms for the Church Year* (GIA, G-2662); Scott Soper, (OCP, 8979-CC); Christopher Willcock, *Psalms for Feasts and Seasons* (Liturgical Press); Ruth Artman, *Sing Out: A Children's Psalter* (WLP, 7190)
- Rawn Harbor, "Psalm for Advent," *Lead Me, Guide Me,* #500 (GIA)
- Howard Hughes, "To you I lift up my soul," *Psalms for Advent* (GIA, G-1905) or *Lead Me, Guide Me,* #499 (GIA)
- Robert E. Kreutz, "Come, O Lord," *Psalms and Selected Canticles* (OCP)
- Paul Lisicky, "You are my guide," *Psalms for the Church* (World Library Publications, 6204)

Some settings for Psalm 85:

- "Lord, let us see your kindness": J. Robert Carroll/J. Gelineau, *Worship,* #770 (GIA); Christopher Willcock, *Psalms for Feasts and Seasons* (Liturgical Press)
- Michael Connolly, "I will hear what God proclaims," (GIA, G-2401)
- Marty Haugen, "Let us see your kindness," *Psalms for the Church Year* (GIA, G-2664)
- Jack Miffleton, "Come, O Lord, and set us free," *Sing Out: A Children's Psalter* (WLP, 7190)

■ GOSPEL ACCLAMATION: Twenty-one verses from scripture and ancient liturgical sources provide gospel acclamations for Advent weekdays, a treasury of seasonal themes for daily prayer. See the lectionary for verses that go with each Sunday's readings. Proper to late Advent are the "O Antiphons," borrowed and abridged from Evening Prayer of the week before Christmas. The ecumenical importance of these powerful expressions of Israel's and the church's longing for salvation cannot be overstated. They incorporate the principal titles and themes of the prophetic messianic tradition and were universally preserved by the churches of the Reformation. If the complete version is being sung at parish Evening Prayer, there is no reason why it could not also serve as the gospel acclamation at Mass, provided that the people are able to join in an alleluia refrain before and after the antiphon. Besides the well-known metrical version, "O come, O come, Emmanuel," there are several vernacular adaptations of the ancient, well-loved chant from the *Antiphonale Monasticum* (see GIA's *Worship: Liturgy of the Hours,* Leader's Edition). Three suggested settings of gospel acclamations for Advent are:

- John Schiavone, *Gospel Acclamation Verses for Advent* (GIA, G-2110)
- *ICEL Lectionary Music* (GIA, G-2626)
- David Haas, *Advent Gospel Acclamation* (OCP, 8732)

■ DISMISSAL OF THE CATECHUMENS: The words of dismissal which send the catechumens forth from the assembly should allude to the Advent hopes and longings of the community, which they increasingly share. Here is a sample text:

> My dear friends: With the assurance of our loving support, this community sends you forth to reflect more deeply on the word we have shared. Our Advent prayer is that God bless you with every spiritual gift and strengthen you with the comfort of glad tidings, so that in due time you may share fully at the Lord's table and be found blameless on the day when Christ comes in glory.

■ GENERAL INTERCESSIONS: LTP's *Prayers for Sundays and Seasons, Year B,* presents suggested intentions that draw their inspiration and vocabulary directly from the day's scriptures. This resource also provides a presider's introductory bidding and two scripturally inspired collects from which one can be chosen to conclude the general intercessions (be sure to use the shorter prayer conclusion, "We ask this through Christ our Lord"). The calendar entry for each Sunday also provides a text from the prayer tradition of other Christian churches, written in the style of the Roman collect and related to the scriptural motif of the Sunday. Since the Roman rite does not prescribe a particular prayer to conclude each Sunday's general intercessions, planners or presiders may choose these texts freely.

LITURGY OF THE EUCHARIST

■ EUCHARISTIC PRAYER: Two Advent prefaces signal a twofold emphasis for the season.

- Advent I (used through December 16) speaks to the first, eschatological emphasis.
- Advent II (December 14 – 24) addresses the incarnational aspects. The eucharistic prayer could be one less frequently heard during the rest of the year:
- *Reconciliation II* neatly ties together both the incarnational and eschatological dimensions of the feast. Christ is proclaimed as "the word that brings salvation, the hand you stretch out to sinners, the way that leads to your peace." Later the prayer envisions the banquet of the kingdom at which are gathered "people of every race, language and way of life."

■ ACCLAMATIONS: Here are two possibilities:

- Unify and differentiate the Advent-Christmas seasons by singing the same acclamations during both seasons. In Advent do them in unison with no added instrumental or choral parts, except perhaps a single wind instrument as at the gathering song. For the Christmas season, add instrumental embellishments.
- Use one setting, simple and unadorned, for Advent and a completely different, very festive acclamation set for Christmas.

Richard Proulx's *Missa Emmanuel* (GIA, G-3489), based on "O come, O come, Emmanuel," for cantor, choir and congregation is an excellent choice. Its familiarity invites participation, important for parishes with holiday visitors. Christopher Walker's *Glastonbury Eucharistic Acclamations* (OCP, 7165) are similarly suitable for Advent-Christmas, as the assembly repeats each line after the cantor.

■ COMMUNION RITE: See LTP's *Prayers for Sundays and Seasons* for alternative texts to the invitations to the Lord's Prayer and to communion. Remember Advent's two phases: Use one set at every Mass until December 16; another from December 17. Heard on Sundays and weekdays, the repetition will permit the assembly to come to know the words by heart. For chanting the Lord's Prayer as an assembly, the unadorned simplicity of the chant adaptation by Robert Snow (found in every missalette) is most appropriate to Advent. Its chant-style doxology likewise connotes Advent and, when sung, serves to emphasize the particularly Advent-style prayer that precedes it: "as we wait in joyful hope for the coming of our Savior, Jesus Christ."

Vatican II's official chant manual, *The Simple Gradual,* prescribes Psalm 85 for the communion procession during Advent. If not used as a common responsorial psalm during the liturgy of the word, it would be most appropriate here. Marty Haugen's setting, "Lord, make us turn to you" (*Gather,* #37) effectively captures the spirit of the season. Other refrain-style choices are Haugen's "My soul in stillness waits" (GIA, G-3331), based on the "O Antiphons," or Jacques Berthier's "Wait for the Lord" (Taizé; GIA, G-2778). Also fitting in Advent is any responsorial-style setting of the Magnificat. James Chepponis' version (GIA, G-2302) has an easy refrain for the assembly, with verses for one or two cantors. Practically, learning Psalms 25 and 85 provides two convenient choices for Advent Evening Prayer. The *General Instruction of the Liturgy of the Hours* permits divergence from the official psalmody to facilitate community participation. Incorporating the Magnificat into the assembly's repertoire during Advent provides several benefits: the late Advent scriptures celebrate Mary's role in salvation history; the Magnificat is appropriate for Marian feasts throughout the year; and the assembly has learned a Magnificat for celebrations of Evening Prayer.

CONCLUDING RITES

■ DISMISSAL OF EUCHARISTIC MINISTERS: A seasonal dismissal of those bearing the eucharist to the homebound may be used. Here is an example:

Go forth in peace to the sick and homebound of our community, bearing the word of life and the Body of Christ together with the assurance of our love and concern. Be to our brothers and sisters heralds of glad tidings and ministers of Christ's abiding presence.

- BLESSING AND DISMISSAL OF ASSEMBLY: The blessing and dismissal of the entire assembly should likewise be seasonal and stable throughout Advent. The best way to cue the congregation's "Amen" to the threefold solemn blessing is to chant each paragraph of it. *Prayers for Sundays and Seasons* offers a seasonal dismissal for both phases of Advent.

Other Celebrations

LITURGY OF THE HOURS

Saturday or Sunday Evening Prayer is especially appropriate during Advent, since the hour itself celebrates God's gifts of light and darkness and so is a perfect way to incorporate one of the principal themes of Advent into a non-eucharistic time of prayer. Begin with everyone gathered under, or at least turned toward, the Advent wreath for the introductory verse, response and opening hymn. Follow with a ceremonial lighting of the candles of the wreath or other candles in the church from the wreath. If Morning Prayer is celebrated during Advent, check the daily Office of Readings for appropriate patristic readings to serve as a meditation after the psalmody.

LESSONS AND CAROLS

This traditional service, especially popular in the Episcopal tradition, combines elements from Vespers and Vigils. The most useful formats, for both Advent and Christmas, may be found in the Episcopal Church's *Book of Occasional Services* (Church Hymnal Corporation, various editions).

BLESSING THE ADVENT WREATH

This is another good way to celebrate a service of light with Evening Prayer. As noted, chapter 47 of the *Book of Blessings* (BB) suggests Evening Prayer I of the First Sunday of Advent as an appropriate time to bless the Advent wreath and light its first candle. Modified to include these elements, Evening Prayer could look like this:

- Introduction (not a lucernarium) and hymn
- Psalmody
- Reading (perhaps Isaiah as in BB, #1526)
- Homily, followed by silence (response)
- Gospel canticle (Magnificat)
- Intercessions (BB, #1530) and Lord's Prayer with proper introduction (BB, #1531)
- Prayer of blessing (BB, #1532 or #1533)
- Lighting of first candle
- Concluding rite (BB, #1534)

If the parish usually begins Evening Prayer with a lucernarium, use the prayer of blessing from the *Book of Blessings* and light the first candle at the start of the celebration. Then the first Advent candle symbolizes the light praised in hymn and thanksgiving. In subsequent weeks, use the Advent candles for the lucernarium.

COMMUNAL PENANCE

Though not officially a penitential season, Advent is an appropriate time to seek peace within and around oneself. The preaching of the prophets and John the Baptist resounds in Advent's scriptures and summons us to a conversion that prepares the world and ourselves for the Lord's unexpected yet certain coming. Communal celebrations can include elements from a complete Advent service in appendix II of the *Rite of Penance*. As with all the liturgies of Advent, careful use of darkness and light will provide the mood of the season.

COMMUNAL ANOINTING OF THE SICK

Sundays in Ordinary Time, especially those with scriptural healing stories, seem best for communal anointing. If celebrated during Mass on an Advent Sunday, the ritual Mass is not permitted. One of the scripture passages from the *Pastoral Care of the Sick* may be used, perhaps as a second reading, though the readings of the day may be just as suitable.

FUNERALS

Funeral Masses are not celebrated on Advent Sundays or on the Immaculate Conception.

Maintain the spirit of Advent by lighting the Advent wreath and choosing the Isaiah and Revelation readings from among those provided for funerals. These offer a consolation of eschatological hope and promise to the bereaved that have an Advent tone. Psalms 25 and 85, two of the common psalms for Advent, are most suitable as responsorial psalms. Acclamations at the gospel and in the eucharistic prayer should be those used on Advent Sundays. Much traditional Advent music and many of Advent's eschatological texts express well the longing for redemption proper to Advent and to funerals. They are also generally well known to diverse congregations and visitors from other churches.

MARRIAGE

The *Rite of Marriage* (#11) directs those preparing couples for marriage to advise them about the "special nature" of Advent and Lent, a polite way of suggesting that we help people see how contrary to the spirit of both seasons the celebration of marriage is! The presumption is that the whole community is caught up in Advent's "devout and joyful expectation," just as during Lent the catechumenal journey toward initiation and conversion will absorb everyone's time and energy. Nevertheless, legitimate circumstances may require the celebration of marriage during these seasons, and those minimally involved in community worship or completely removed from it may wish to be married during these times. How the community deals with such delicate and personal issues may vary from place to place. But the church's liturgical sense presumes that these marriages are the exception. On Advent Sundays and on the Immaculate Conception, all Mass texts must be of the Advent day. It is not desirable and may not even be possible to alter the parish's Advent decor to accommodate wedding decorations, and at all liturgical gatherings, including weddings and funerals, the appropriate number of candles should be lit in the Advent wreath.

CHRISTIAN INITIATION

Neither the Rite of Acceptance into the Order of Catechumens nor the Rite of Welcoming Candidates is appropriate for the First Sunday of Advent. Such scheduling usually indicates a desire to compress the catechumenate into a nine-month school year, a largely ineffective approach to formation. Advent's liturgy is somewhat quiet and focused to sustain a mood of expectancy and watchful prayer. Powerful rites of acceptance and welcoming are better on Sundays in Ordinary Time, where they can become the community's focus. Liturgies of the word and other celebrations with catechumens and candidates should be prepared with Advent in mind. These people should be joyfully welcomed into the prayer experiences of this important season.

At Home

THE JESSE TREE, A GIVING TREE

A recent adaptation of the Jesse Tree custom is an Advent "Giving Tree" on which are hung cards listing gifts for people in need. Parishioners take the cards home at the beginning of Advent and return the gifts near the end of the season for distribution at Christmas. This custom helps us realize the deeper purpose of gift-giving. It links Christmas shopping to the Christian love that should mark all who follow the One whose birth at Bethlehem is God's enduring gift to us. The Giving Tree is best placed in the entryway or some location other than the sanctuary, lest the simplicity of Advent decor be compromised.

HOME ADVENT WREATH

Although increasingly associated with parish decor and worship, the Advent wreath began as a home custom. It offers an excellent way to link Sunday worship visually and verbally with daily prayer and Christmas preparation at home. To make it easy to observe the custom, many parishes stock Advent candles and wreath forms, which a youth group, religious education program or parish prayer group can sell on the last weekends of Ordinary Time.

14 ADVENT: OTHER CELEBRATIONS

FAMILY ADVENT DAY

A day for families with activities for various age groups and an educational program about Advent's history, scriptures, themes and customs might be welcome, especially by parents who want to hand on Catholic traditions but aren't sure how. This also can be a helpful way to set the parish clock to the new season. Brief midday prayer could open an afternoon gathering featuring an Advent hymn sing, making household Advent wreaths, ideas for Advent prayers and mealtime rituals. The day could conclude with all joining in the parish celebration of Evening Prayer.

Advent-Christmas meal prayer cards.

Keeping Advent and Christmastime, a pocket booklet for prayer and scripture reading throughout the day.

Take Me Home, pages for families and children for the beginning of Advent, St. Nicholas, Our Lady of Guadalupe, St. Lucy and the "O Antiphons" of Advent's final week. *Take Me Home, Too* is more along the same line.

Additional Resources

Book of Blessings, 1989, published by Catholic Book Publishing Company and The Liturgical Press.

J. Neil Alexander, *Waiting for the Coming: The Liturgical Meaning of Advent, Christmas, Epiphany.* Washington: The Pastoral Press, 1993.

For the Millennium Jubilee:

Vatican Internet site for the Jubilee: *http://www.Jubil2000.org*

Pope John Paul II, *The Mystery of the Incarnation (Incarnationis Mysterium)* The papal bull on the Jubilee, proclaiming the Holy Year and outlining some events of the year. Washington: United States Catholic Conference (800-235-8722; Publication No. 5-313).

From LTP:

An Advent Sourcebook.

Fling Wide the Doors, adaptation of traditional Advent calendar with booklet of prayers for each day.

Mary Ellen Hynes, *Companion to the Calendar* (see especially O Antiphons, 4–6).

Peter Mazar, *Winter: Celebrating the Season in a Christian Home.*

Welcome, Yule! Sunday handouts that unify the observance of Advent and Christmas and link prayer at church to prayer in the household.

CALENDAR

November

Lectionary #2
(Lectionary for Masses with Children, #2)   violet

28 First Sunday of Advent

■ ORIENTATION: From the parking lot, through the doorway and into the vestibule, let silent signals of the new season greet worshipers as they arrive, heralding the opening weekend of Advent and the beginning of a new liturgical year. Plaintive reeds in a minor key set the mood as the assembly gathers. The introductory rites will be different and distinctive today, the "Advent only" format.

The unconquerable Light shining in darkness is one of Advent's principal motifs, and the spirit of Advent is one of watchfulness and joyful expectation. On this first weekend of Advent, think about celebrating Evening Prayer on both Saturday and Sunday evenings. These gatherings will illumine the dark of this first Advent weekend with the presence of the One who comes among us as Light of the world. On the remaining Advent weekends, celebrate Evening Prayer on either Saturday or Sunday.

■ LECTIONARY: Each lectionary cycle opens with history's close. The ending of one millennium and the beginning of a new one has seen speculation on the "end times" become obsessive in some quarters. But for those who live by the spirit of the liturgy, Advent in any year always directs our thoughts toward the setting of history and the dawn of the eternal "day of the Lord."

It has been a commonplace in biblical studies to think of Mark as the gospel of "imminent eschatology": that is, Mark's community lived as if the end was just around the corner. People expected the Lord's return at any moment. But at least one scholar, tipped off by Jesus' repetition of the command to "Stay awake," offers a different theory:

> The danger of falling asleep exists for those who read the story. The warning seems more appropriate for the indifferent than for the desperate. Mark seems directed to believers, perhaps especially those in authority, who have experienced some success and are tempted not so much to lose heart as to drift off into indifference, unaware of the tests that lie ahead. . . . It may well be that these words were addressed to a sleeping church — one in which believers had tasted success and liked it, a church in which there were already positions of authority to which people aspired, perhaps even competing for power. (Donald H. Juel, *Augsburg Commentary on the New Testament: Mark.* Minneapolis: Augsburg, 1990)

For Isaiah, waiting for God to act and working as partners with God go hand in hand. We are clay in the hands of the potter (First Reading), but this potter is also going to come again in glory. So Isaiah begs the Lord to "rend the heavens and come down," and reminds us pointedly that God brings redemption to only those who "gladly do what is right." Paul's challenge to the Corinthians (Second Reading), and to us, is similar to Isaiah's message. The Christian community is to prepare for the end by working in the present. Paul's ideal Christian makes industrious use of the "spiritual gifts given," "in speech and knowledge of every kind."

■ SACRAMENTARY: For the penitential rite, use Form C, invocation set *i* throughout the season, or chant these invocations drawn from the scriptures of the day:

- You came to deliver us from the guilt of our sins and to show us the face of God: Lord, have mercy.
- You come to enrich us with every spiritual gift and to keep us watchful in our work as your servants: Christ, have mercy.
- You will come on a day we cannot know to gather us home and to give us new life: Lord, have mercy.

Advent I, with its eschatological emphasis, is the preface prescribed from now through December 16. The *Liturgical Calendar for Canada* notes that "Sensitivity to inclusive language suggests changing 'as a man' to 'in our human flesh.' The same consideration applies to the solemn blessing for Advent: 'as man' in the third paragraph could become 'in the flesh.'" Eucharistic Prayer for Reconciliation II is especially appropriate during Advent and may be used with the Advent prefaces (see *Notitiae* 19 [1983], 270). It speaks of "your Son who comes in your name" and pictures the great eschatological banquet "in that new world" at which are gathered "people of every race and language and way of life." Use LTP's *Prayers for Sundays and Seasons, Year B,* for an appropriate introduction to the Lord's Prayer, invitation to communion and dismissal sentence. This same book contains collects based on the lectionary readings that could be used to conclude the general intercessions. Also appropriate would be text composed for this Sunday in 1549, here adapted from the Episcopal *Book of Common Prayer:*

> Almighty God, give us grace to cast away the works of darkness and put on the armor of light now, in the time of this mortal life in which Christ came among us in great humility; that in the last

16 ADVENT: NOVEMBER

NOVEMBER

day, when he shall come again in glorious majesty to judge the living and the dead, we may rise to life immortal with him, who lives and reigns for ever and ever.

- BLESSING THE WREATH: The Advent wreath may be blessed during Mass, during a celebration of the word or at Evening Prayer. (See p. 10.)

In the dioceses of the United States, see *Book of Blessings,* chapter 47, for a blessing of the wreath at the conclusion of the general intercessions.

In the dioceses of Canada, this special introductory rite may be celebrated: "Since the lighted candle is the sign of Christ, the first candle of the wreath should always be lighted before the celebration begins."

- Sign of the Cross and Greeting
- Presider's Invitation:
  My brothers and sisters,
  as we wait in joyful hope for
     the coming of our Lord Jesus
     Christ in glory,
  let us pray that God will make
     us witnesses of Christ, the
     Light of love,
  who has taken on our humanity
     to bring salvation to all
     people.
- Silent Prayer
- Blessing (with hands joined):
  Lord God,
  our Source of hope and
     Fountain of love,
  you gather all peoples and
     nations
  to be one in your kingdom
     of light and peace.
  On this day that we celebrate
     Jesus' victory over sin
     and death,
  we look forward to his return
  when we will share the vision of
     your glory.
  Bless your people + who use
     this wreath
  as the evergreen sign of your
     faithful love.

Dispel the darkness of sin,
that the light and joy of Jesus
   may shine in this waiting
   world.
We ask this through Christ our
   Lord. R. Amen.
- Litany of Praise: invocations from the penitential rite.
- Opening Prayer
  Copyright Concacan Inc., 1999. All rights reserved.

- THE WEEK AHEAD: *Tuesday:* On Saint Andrew's feast, preachers will find it easy to connect the readings prescribed for the feast to the motifs of Advent.

In preparing the general intercessions and bulletin notes, remember a number of events that claim our prayerful attention this week:

Wednesday: World AIDS Awareness Day, sponsored by the World Health Organization, and the anniversary of Rosa Parks' refusal to move to the back of the bus (Montgomery, Alabama, 1955).

Thursday: martyrdom of Maura Clarke, Ita Ford, Dorothy Kazel and Jean Donovan (El Salvador, 1980). The Advent prophets' call for justice in preparing the way of the Lord makes it especially appropriate to pray for those deprived of human rights, those who work for justice, those who suffer from AIDS and those who care for them. Many HIV/AIDS ministries host ecumenical or interfaith prayer services to lift up the role of pastoral and spiritual care. Since 1990, AIDS Interfaith New York has sponsored "An Interfaith Service of Hope and Remembrance." Contact them: 175 Ninth Avenue, New York NY 10011 (212-627-7759) or American Association for World Health, 1129 20th Street NW, Suite 400, Washington DC 20036 (202-466-5883).

MON 29 Advent Weekday
#175 (LMC, #172–175) violet

"Swords into plowshares and spears into pruning hooks": What a vision Isaiah saw, what a dream for every generation since that has not yet seen the prophet's vision come true! For Isaiah, the fruit of that peace was to be the gathering of all nations in unity. Jesus in the gospel sees the nations gathering in faith and feasting on healing. Eucharistic Prayer for Reconciliation II, already suggested for Advent Sundays, echoes these readings. Its vivid eschatological vision and portrayal of Christ's universal redemptive mission make it appropriate throughout the season.

TUE 30 Andrew, apostle
#684 (LMC, #423) red
FEAST

- ORIENTATION: Although liturgists may regret that the Advent just begun is so soon displaced by a saint's feast, Andrew experienced his own Advent. In today's Office of Readings Saint John Chrysostom notes: "Andrew's words reveal a soul waiting with the utmost longing for the coming of the Messiah, looking forward to his appearing from heaven, rejoicing when he does appear, and hastening to announce so great an event to others." A good description of how Advent should be for today's believers!

- LECTIONARY: The selection from the Letter to the Romans and the account of Andrew's call from the gospel of Matthew both emphasize the responsibility of disciples to share the good news with others. How beautiful are our feet upon the mountains of our neighborhoods? In John's

NOVEMBER

account, Andrew brings his brother Peter to Jesus. In Matthew, Peter and Andrew are sent fishing for people. Here is a perfect Advent motif and challenge: We ourselves are waiting, but how many others wait to hear the good news that we already know? To whom could we be apostles this Advent?

■ SACRAMENTARY: Light the Advent wreath and use the Advent introductory rites, along with the Advent acclamations before the gospel and during the eucharistic prayer. The preface entitled Apostles II emphasizes the call of the church to be "the living gospel for all to hear." Most hymnals have a generic saints' hymn, "By all your saints still striving," which has verses specific to particular saints, including Andrew.

December

WED 1 #177 (LMC, #172–175) violet
Advent Weekday

All peoples, *all* nations, *all* faces, *all* the earth: The promise of God's gift of universal salvation shines today in Isaiah's vision and in the compassion of Jesus who heals the crowds and feeds the multitudes. As we wait for all to be gathered into the great feast, we can catch a glimpse of what that great feast will be like, whenever disciples are willing to place their little bit in the hands of Jesus.

Today is World AIDS Awareness Day and the anniversary of Rosa Parks' refusal to move to the back of the bus. The homily should note that both observances speak to "the shroud that is cast over all peoples." And while Isaiah bids us wait in patient faith for the day of rejoicing, Jesus, in his ministry, acts on Isaiah's vision.

THU 2 #178 (LMC, #172–175) violet
Advent Weekday

Advent, and particularly today's scriptures, says: Deeds, not words! Or better, Turn your words into deeds. Talk is cheap. Real love pays a price. On this day, American Catholics must remember four missionary women who paid for their love of the poor with their lives. Maura Clarke, Ita Ford, Dorothy Kazel and Jean Donovan were martyred in El Salvador on this date in 1980.

FRI 3 #179 (LMC, #172–175) white
Francis Xavier, presbyter, religious, missionary (+1552)
MEMORIAL

Deaf people who hear, blind people who see, barren fields that bear fruit: In Isaiah's vision God's bounty springs forth. And God's justice reigns: "The neediest people shall exult . . . the tyrant shall be no more!" The healing touch of Jesus made this vision come true in his day. Fifteen hundred years later, today's saint went to the ends of the earth to make the prophet's vision true and Jesus' touch a reality for countless people.

The opening prayer asks that zeal like that of Francis Xavier mark each of us. In today's intercessions remember Christians in India and throughout the Far East, the apostolates of local Jesuit or Xaverian communities and the labor of missionaries throughout the world. The saint's opening prayer replaces the Advent weekday one. Conclude the intercessions with the Advent collect of the day or one from the Masses "For the Spread of the Gospel," using the shorter ending "We ask this through Christ our Lord."

■ HANUKKAH: Tonight is the beginning of an eight-day festival of lights for our Jewish neighbors. Hanukkah celebrates fidelity to the covenant in the face of tyranny and forced assimilation (see 1 and 2 Maccabees). Remember the sensitivity necessary in relating Christianity to Judaism in preaching and teaching, especially at this time of the year and during the Triduum. Consult LTP's helpful publication, *Teaching Christian Children about Judaism*.

SAT 4 #180 (LMC, #172–175) violet
Advent Weekday

John of Damascus, presbyter, religious, doctor of the church (+ eighth century), optional memorial/white. ■ An important part of the community's Advent and Christmas ministry is outreach to the hospitalized and homebound, for whom this time of year can bring loneliness more painful than physical ailments. Isaiah envisions the compassionate God binding up the people's injuries. Matthew shows the compassionate Jesus healing and sending his disciples out to be ministers of healing as well. Those engaged in such work — eucharistic ministers, hospital visitors, hospice workers and hospitality groups — might gather on this first Saturday in Advent to be refreshed together in prayer and to coordinate their ministries for the weeks ahead. This might also be a good occasion to invite others to turn Advent resolutions into reality by joining them.

Today's saint was a Christian official in a Moslem government, a biblical commentator and a gifted poet. Here is a patron for all who seek to forge unity of purpose and witness out of ethnic and religious pluralism.

D E C E M B E R

■ OPTIONAL MEMORIALS: This first optional memorial of the liturgical year provides an occasion for reviewing the policy on observing these days. The *General Calendar,* supplemented by calendars of nation, diocese or religious community, establishes memorials that must be observed. When an optional memorial occurs, especially during Advent or another season, the decision is local. For detailed norms see the *General Instruction of the Roman Missal* (chapter VII); for selecting readings, see *Introduction to the Lectionary* (chapter IV). Unless the community has special devotion to a saint whose optional memorial it is, these principles apply:

1. Respect the primacy of the season. Keep the seasonal color. Use the acclamations chosen for the season.

2. Respect the integrity of the lectionary. During major seasons, optional memorials should not displace the appointed texts. Even in Ordinary Time, there should be no interruption of continuous readings.

3. Integrate the saint's commemoration. While the saint's opening prayer may replace that of the season, it could also be transferred (with the shorter ending) to conclude the general intercessions.

5 Second Sunday of Advent
#5 (LMC, #5) violet

■ ORIENTATION: Review the community's sacred art: statuary, stained glass, icon or tapestry. Are any of Advent's principal personages depicted there: Mary, Joseph, John the Baptist, Elizabeth, Isaiah or other prophets, the archangel Gabriel? If so, these images should be honored during Advent by simple and tasteful adornment (Mazar, 215–218).

■ LECTIONARY: This week and next, the community hears the challenging preaching of John the Baptist in light of the Isaiah's comforting prophecies. Both Sunday gospels invoke the imagery of major road construction, but the call to conversion is at its heart a call of comfort and hope. The Lord whose advent demands the renovation of our heart's highway speaks tenderly, casts out fear and gathers us into his arms for the journey home (First Reading). The author of 2 Peter reminds us that the Day of the Lord will be sudden and severe. But the same author brackets that warning with praise for the patience of the Lord "who wants none to perish," and whose promise is "a new heavens and a new earth, where righteousness shall be at home" (Second Reading).

■ SACRAMENTARY: No additional ceremonies or prayers mark the lighting of the Advent wreath on this Sunday. Use a seasonal penitential rite or these invocations from the day's scriptures:

> You came to comfort God's people and to banish our fear: Lord, have mercy.
> You come to feed your flock like a shepherd and to carry us gently in your arms: Christ, have mercy.
> You will come to establish new heavens and a new earth where righteousness and peace shall dwell: Lord, have mercy.

Neither the prayers nor preface prescribed for today refer to John the Baptist. Yet this prophetic figure dominates the gospel this Sunday and next. For prayers that do mention John and that could conclude the general intercessions see LTP's *Prayers for Sundays and Seasons, Year B,* the alternative prayer for June 24, or use this text adapted from the *Book of Common Prayer:*

> Merciful God, you sent your messengers the prophets to preach repentance and to herald the dawn of our salvation. Give us grace to heed their warnings and to listen to the voice of John the Baptist, that we may forsake our sins and prepare the way for the mighty One, who comes to baptize us in the Holy Spirit and to establish your kingdom of righteousness and peace: your Son, Jesus Christ, who is Lord for ever and ever.

■ ADVENT PENANCE SERVICE: This Sunday and next, John the Baptist calls us to conversion of heart and reform of life to facilitate the Lord's advent. This weekend, therefore, is a perfect time to announce pre-Christmas penance services. Bulletin inserts should offer times and dates for communal and individual celebrations of reconciliation, and some of the texts that are part of the rite: for instance, an Advent examination of conscience and the new forms of the act of contrition.

■ THE WEEK AHEAD: *Monday* is Saint Nicholas' Day and no community should forget to honor the legendary bishop renowned for his compassion and generosity. *Wednesday* is the holy day of the Immaculate Conception and, in the United States, next *Sunday*'s observance of the Third Sunday of Advent displaces the feast of Our Lady of Guadalupe. Announcements, spoken or printed, could point to the appropriateness of honoring Mary during Advent.

ADVENT: DECEMBER 19

DECEMBER

MON 6 — Advent Weekday
#181 (LMC, #172–175) violet

Nicholas, bishop (+ fourth century), optional memorial / white. ■ Weak hands, feeble knees, fearful hearts: can we relate to these? Isaiah wants us to see life's road as a highway to heaven, and the proper mode of travel along it is leaping and dancing for joy. As the roof is torn open above him and a paralyzed man lowered through the opening, Jesus sees a faith that heals, and speaks a word of forgiveness that raises the man up. The whole event foreshadows our own resurrection from the paralysis of sin.

Today's observance of Nicholas' legendary compassion coincides with Isaiah's vision of God's compassion, and with Luke's portrait of the compassionate Jesus. The parish may want to give small gifts to children after Mass today to remind children of the true origin of Santa Claus. A Saint Nicholas children's party might also provide an opportunity to gather gifts for needy children.

TUE 7 — Ambrose, bishop, doctor of the church (+ 397)
#182 (LMC, #172–175) white
MEMORIAL

Sunday's Isaiah reading is repeated today with a gospel in which Jesus pictures God as a very inefficient shepherd. What kind of shepherd would leave the 99 sheep he was sure of to search for the one lost sheep, which he could be sure was not the brightest in the flock? With the Father whom Jesus reveals to us, compassion triumphs over efficiency, mercy over justice, and a small victory — one little sheep — is the goal of God's saving plan.

The entrance of today's saint into the church was dramatic, to say the least. He was still a catechumen when he was elected bishop of Milan by popular acclamation and ordained on this day in 374.

WED 8 — Immaculate Conception
#689 (LMC, #429) white
SOLEMNITY

■ ORIENTATION: This solemnity began in the East and spread to the West in the Middle Ages. It became common to the whole Roman church in the eighteenth century. Pius IX proclaimed the dogma in 1854. We celebrate Mary as firstfruits of Christ's redeeming harvest, preserved from sin from the moment of her conception.

Even before it became dogma, the bishops of the United States declared Mary the nation's patroness under this title.

■ LECTIONARY: A longstanding confusion labels the virgin birth of Jesus an "immaculate conception," a confusion reinforced by the prescribed annunciation gospel. But today's scriptures can be preached as a suite to focus our attention on what Catholic theology recognizes as a true and saving partnership. It is Christ who reverses Adam's disobedience (first reading), and Christ in whom we receive adoption as God's children (second reading). The gospel makes it clear that God's gracious will is to desire, not demand, our cooperation in the great plan of universal salvation. Mary is the model of such cooperation.

■ SACRAMENTARY: Since the angel's annunciation and Mary's faith-filled response match Advent's joyful expectation, it is certainly possible to celebrate today's liturgy in a way that keeps the Advent spirit:

- Advent elements:
    - introductory rites
    - alternative opening prayer links feast to season
    - gospel and eucharistic prayer acclamations
    - the customary Advent Sunday choice of eucharistic prayer
- Solemnity elements:
    - brief introduction after the greeting to focus on the subject of the feast
    - sung Gloria in a setting that offers a foretaste of Christmas
    - floral and candle arrangements near the image of Mary
    - the solemn blessing in the sacramentary has been updated for inclusive language in the *Book of Blessings* #20, appendix II.

■ MUSIC: Some Marian music appropriate to Advent includes "She will show us the Promised One," "Behold a virgin bearing him," "The Angel Gabriel from heaven came" and "O Holy Mary" (Owen Alstott, OCP, 8724). The *New Century Hymnal* has an outstanding Marian hymn, "Mary, woman of the promise." Compline's Advent Marian antiphon is the simple and beautiful "Alma redemptoris mater."

THU 9 — Advent Weekday
#184 (LMC, #172–175) violet

Blessed Juan Diego (Cuatitlatoatzin), hermit, optional memorial / white. ■ The gospel passage today begins a series of daily readings on the message of John the Baptist and his role in salvation history. To Matthew, John is the last and greatest of the prophets, standing at the threshold of the kingdom. Commentators puzzle over Jesus' comment on the taking of that kingdom by force. Whatever it means, one thing is clear: We should humbly rejoice to be counted among the "worms and maggots" lifted up by the Lord. Do we gladly, graciously, humbly extend to the poor in our midst the same compassion the Lord has extended to us?

Today's optional memorial honors one who fits Isaiah's image of God's "poor and needy," the native Mexican who saw Our Lady of Guadalupe on the hill where the basilica now stands. Juan Diego's proper texts are in the *Sacramentary Supplement* (Catholic Book Publishing Company and Liturgical Press, 1994.)

FRI 10 #185 (LMC, #172–175) violet
Advent Weekday

Today's readings present Advent's challenge and comfort clearly. The challenge is God's call for us to attend to "the way you should go." The comfort is God's promise to grant his people "prosperity . . . success . . . offspring." Jesus sheds light on the problem: We are often obstinate children, refusing any message that challenges our complacency. Seeing that more clearly may be a first step toward embracing the challenge and attaining the comfort.

Today is the anniversary of the death of the Cistercian monk and spiritual writer Thomas Merton (+ 1968). See his *Seasons of Celebration* for fine pre–Vatican II liturgical writing on the liturgy.

SAT 11 #186 (LMC, #172–175) violet
Advent Weekday

Damasus I, pope (+ 384), optional memorial/white. • Elijah, John the Baptist and Jesus are linked by a common experience, which Jesus articulates in the gospel passage. For each, the way to glory led through rejection and suffering.

Today's saint recognized the shifting language of the local church. As Latin replaced Greek among the people, he commissioned Saint Jerome (September 30) to prepare a new translation of the scriptures in Latin so that all could understand the word of God.

12 #8 (LMC, #8) violet or rose
Third Sunday of Advent

■ ORIENTATION: *Gaudete in Domino!* Rejoice in the Lord! In an age when assemblies knew the sung prayers of the liturgy by heart, Sundays were identified by the first words of the entrance antiphon. Some of that heritage echoes in the traditional name for Advent's Third Sunday: *Gaudete!* Rejoice! Continue that legacy through:

- festive preludes and postludes at all liturgies today
- hymns sung by the assembly that incorporate the word and theme of joy
- flowers that bear joyful witness to growing anticipation

■ LECTIONARY: "Who are you?" and "Why are you doing that?" Better questions would have been, "What does this mean for us? What do you know that we don't know?"

"Among you stands one whom you do not know." That's the important information. Not who this baptizer is and not why he is doing that, but what it all means: The one who is to come is already here.

We are called to show by the way we live, by the way we love and by our joy (first and second readings) that this is the year of God's favor (first reading). The fulfillment of all God's promises is already in our midst if we have eyes to see, ears to hear and hearts daring enough to love one another as he has loved us! The promise of both testaments is linked by the canticle of Mary, which replaces the responsorial psalm. The Magnificat sets the stage for the second phase of Advent.

■ SACRAMENTARY: Suggested scriptural texts for the penitential invocations:

> You came to bring glad tidings to the poor and to heal the brokenhearted: Lord, have mercy.
> You come to announce a year of favor and to clothe us with rejoicing and salvation: Christ, have mercy.
> You will come to bring to completion the work of holiness you have begun in us: Lord, have mercy.

The original Latin text of the sacramentary's opening prayer for today speaks of "the coming festival of our Savior's birth." Unfortunately, the current English translation renders this "the birthday of Christ," an expression full of exegetical and pastoral difficulties. Today's gospel reading is our second encounter with John the Baptist, whose witness is celebrated in the preface Advent II, which is not called for by the rubrics until Friday (December 17). This prayer, which could conclude the general intercessions, is from the *Lutheran Book of Worship*:

DECEMBER

Eternal God, you sent John the Baptist to prepare the way for the coming of your Son and Grant us wisdom to see your purpose and openness to hear your will, that we, too, may prepare the way for the Christ who even now is among us, the Lamb of God and true Light of the world: your Son, Jesus Christ, who is Lord for ever and ever.

■ OUR LADY OF GUADALUPE: December 12 is usually the Feast of Our Lady of Guadalupe, the patronal feast of Mexico and an observance dear to many in the U.S. The Third Sunday of Advent must replace the feast, but parishes with a Hispanic presence may wish to honor the Virgin of Guadalupe on Saturday or even on Sunday with a judicious use of appropriate liturgical elements (general intercessions and hymns, for instance). Properly observed, the Guadalupe feast and the memorial of Blessed Juan Diego fit in well with the Second and Third Sundays of Advent. After all, these are the Sundays when we meet John the Baptist, the herald of righteous living. Parish plans for Christmas outreach to the needy can be seen as a response to his challenge. Together with the preaching of John the Baptist, the story of the Virgin of Guadalupe has something to say about righteousness toward the lowly and care for those in need.

■ THE WEEK AHEAD: On Friday, Advent's second phase begins. It runs from December 17 through 24 and features two important liturgical elements:

- *daily gospel passages* from the infancy narratives of Matthew and Luke present the most important events leading up to the Lord's birth and are matched to the appropriate precedent stories of the Hebrew Bible

- *the "O Antiphons"* present the Messianic images of the Hebrew scriptures in beautiful phrases: a prose version appears in the *Liturgy of the Hours;* a metrical version is the ever-popular "O come, O come, Emmanuel." Liturgy planners may wish to prepare a handout with scripture references, antiphon texts and proper dates for each.

#187 (LMC, #172–175)   red

MON 13 Lucy, virgin and martyr (+ fourth century)
MEMORIAL

"I see him but not now. I behold him but not near." Summoned from the east to use his occult arts against Moses and Israel, Balaam saw a star rising out of Jacob and prosperity for Israel. The late scripture scholar Raymond Brown says that Balaam was one of those who in Jesus' day were called *magi*. The magi from the East who followed a star saw the one whose kingship would be visible only after he hung beneath the sign saying "King of the Jews." Now as then, Jesus leaves acceptance of his kingship a matter for those with eyes, like Balaam's, sharp enough to see.

Fitting that today should be the memorial of Lucy, whose name means "light" and whose healing specialty, by tradition, is eyesight.

#188 (LMC, #172–175)   white

TUE 14 John of the Cross, presbyter, religious, doctor of the church (+ 1591)
MEMORIAL

Zephaniah's prophecy sings of "a people humble and lowly . . . the remnant who shall do no wrong and utter no lies . . . and no one shall make them afraid." Dare we see ourselves among them, or do we feel unworthy of the call? We know that we are sinners, so Jesus' gospel word is a comfort: The tax collectors and prostitutes can enter the kingdom.

Today's saint is perfect for Advent. John of the Cross was a mystical poet who suffered at the hands of his own brothers in religious life, yet saw clearly through that "dark night" to the vision of his Beloved.

#189 (LMC, #172–175)   violet

WED 15 Advent Weekday

Today's selection from Isaiah is the text from which the Advent chant *Rorate coeli* is adapted: "Shower, O heavens, from above, and let the skies rain down righteousness; let the earth open, that salvation may spring up." This beautiful text and chant should be part of the community's repertoire so it can be sung at the eucharist and Hours today and often during Advent. "Are you the one?" John's disciples asked, and we might imagine John adding, "because you don't look anything like the one I expected!" This Messiah has in his hand not the winnowing fork of final judgment, but the healing touch of mercy. To those who would prefer that God act decisively to inaugurate the kingdom and vindicate his disciples, Jesus offers a new beatitude: Blest are those who find no stumbling block in the compassionate way of this Messiah.

#190 (LMC, #172–175)   violet

THU 16 Advent Weekday

The first phase of Advent closes with Isaiah's exultant hymn celebrating the marriage between God and the human race. These commands are a joy: "Do not hold back . . . do not fear . . . do not be discouraged." The word *compassion* resounds through the reading. God's love for his people is everlasting and steadfast. Jesus asks us what we went

DECEMBER

out into the wilderness of Advent hoping to see. When we think immediately of John the Baptist, we hear the good news that we are in an even deeper relationship with God than John, who heralded the kingdom from afar.

■ LAS POSADAS: The Advent novena, *Las Posadas* ("the inns"), begins tonight. This devotion, popular in much of Latin America and the Philippines, commemorates the journey of Mary and Joseph from Nazareth to Bethlehem.

FRI 17 — #193 (LMC, #172–175) violet
Advent Weekday

O SAPIENTIA

". . . and teach us in her ways to go." Today the O Antiphons begin with praise of Lady Wisdom as image of God's messiah. Advent's second phase looks more directly toward the birth of Christ, without forgetting the Lord's glorious return and creation's transformation.

The "O Antiphons" appear in an abbreviated form as verses for the gospel acclamation (lectionary, #202). "O come, O come, Emmanuel" is a version known to all, and can be paired with an appropriate alleluia refrain for the gospel acclamation. Begin today with verse 2 ("O Come, thou Wisdom") and use the appropriate verse each day. Three other settings: Marty Haugen, "My soul in stillness waits" (GIA, 2652); Michael Joncas, "Let the King of Glory come"; and the chant adaptation in *Worship: Liturgy of the Hours,* Leader's Edition.

■ LECTIONARY: The countdown to Christmas begins at salvation's dawn, setting our feet on the path that stretches from Jacob's promise to Jesus' birth. The dying patriarch gathers his sons around him; the prediction to Judah is proclaimed in full. The long genealogy with which Matthew begins his gospel is read today. Its theology is profound. The cast of characters — especially the women — is comforting: There is room for all of us in the family of this Messiah who smashes down walls between Jew and Gentile, man and woman, saint and sinner.

SAT 18 — #194 (LMC, #172–175) violet
Advent Weekday

O ADONAI

"O Adonai and leader of the house of Israel . . . come and with an outstretched arm, redeem us!" To a nation whose spirit had been drained by apostasy and political collapse, Jeremiah spoke words of unlikely hope and daring promise. To a man whose betrothed was inexplicably with child, the angel of the Lord gave an explanation just as unlikely and a command just as daring. Yet "when Joseph awoke . . . he did as the angel had commanded." Look in the United Church of Christ's *New Century Hymnal* for a lovely carol that sings the story to a familiar tune: "Gentle Joseph, Joseph dear" (#105).

✸ 19 — #11 (LMC, #11) violet
Fourth Sunday of Advent

O RADIX JESSE

■ ORIENTATION: "O root of Jesse, raised up as a sign for all peoples; kings stand silent in your presence; the nations bow down in worship before you. Come! Let nothing keep you from coming to our aid." Even though on this Sunday the proper prayers and readings of the Fourth Sunday of Advent must be used, do work in this antiphon that celebrates the Advent Christ as the one who saves us through the paschal mystery.

■ LECTIONARY: The gospel passage was already proclaimed on the Solemnity of the Immaculate Conception. This is not a problem if we look at this gospel in light of the other two readings. The context of today's readings highlights the establishment of the Davidic dynasty beyond human imagination. "I will make your name great . . . The Lord himself will make you a house" (first reading). Paul expands our vision even further by telling us how unexpectedly inclusive that house will be: "all the Gentiles" (second reading). These thoughts suggest an emphasis for this weekend: Mary's faith-filled response is the dawn of salvation — for all people!

■ SACRAMENTARY: These invocations for the penitential rite are based on the scripture readings for this Sunday:

> You came as the child of the Virgin Mary to deliver your people and to build for them a house of peace: Lord, have mercy.
> You come as the revelation of God to proclaim good news and to bring us to the obedience of faith: Christ, have mercy.
> You will come as Son of the Most High God to rule over your people for ever and your kingdom will have no end: Lord, have mercy.

The first opening prayer is the old Angelus collect, freely translated, a clear link between the incarnation and the paschal mystery of Christ. If not used as the opening prayer, it could fittingly end the general intercessions. The alternative prayer has a clear Marian reference. There is an official annunciation preface (P-2) in the *Collection of Masses of the Blessed Virgin Mary.*

DECEMBER

■ THE WEEK AHEAD: Christmas eve is almost a week away! Send out an attractive outline to help everyone remember the richer-than-usual schedule.

MON 20 — #196 (LMC, #172–175) violet — Advent Weekday

O CLAVIS DAVID

> Answer quickly, O Virgin. Reply in haste to the angel . . . Answer with a word, receive the word of God. Speak your own word, conceive the divine Word. Breathe a passing word, embrace the eternal Word. (Bernard, Office of Readings, December 20)

Before Vatican II, Advent had only three proper Masses (the winter "ember days"). Today's Mass was one of those. It was the *Missa Aurea,* the Golden Mass. Beginning with the beautiful introit chant, *Rorate coeli* ("Shower your rains upon us, O heavens, from above"), it proclaimed the Isaiah prophecy and the annunciation to Mary. In the post–Vatican II liturgy, today's Mass is but one movement in a symphony of Masses that feature messianic prophecies and annunciation narratives. Today and tomorrow, with the visitation story, form an appropriate setting for honoring Mary's role in salvation history in preaching, prayer and song. There are proper texts for December 20 in the sacramentary; the preface is Advent II. But the prayers over the gifts and after communion are two that recur during Advent. See the *Collection of Masses of the Blessed Virgin Mary* for more annunciation-oriented prayer texts (Mass 2) and a special preface (P-2).

TUE 21 — #197 (LMC, #172–175) violet — Advent Weekday

O ORIENS

Peter Canisius, presbyter, religious, doctor of the Church, (+ 1597), *optional memorial.* ▪ "O Dayspring, splendor of eternal light, and sun of justice!" The perfect antiphon for the winter solstice! The Song of Songs pictures the bridegroom hastening across the hills to his beloved. Into the hill country hastens Mary to be of service to Elizabeth and to magnify the Lord. The prescribed preface is Advent II (P-2), but note that the *Collection of Masses of the Blessed Virgin Mary* has a beautiful Preface of the Visitation (P-3) that articulates several important aspects of this gospel passage and Advent mystery.

Liturgical norms for these final days of Advent provide for only passing commemoration of the two saints whose days are this week. They may be mentioned in the introduction to the Mass, and the opening prayer may be that of the saint or of the season, with the unused collect transferred to the end of the general intercessions.

Peter Canisius was a Jesuit who matched a university teaching career with popular preaching and catechisms for the laity. Peter is remembered for his courtesy in debate in those heated years after the Reformation and his use of the recently invented printing press to aid the Catholic revival of that time.

WED 22 — #198 (LMC, #172–175) violet — Advent Weekday

O REX GENTIUM

Hannah's prayer is fulfilled, and her heart bursts forth in a song that provided Luke with the model for Mary's Magnificat. Sing Hannah's canticle after the first reading, and Mary's canticle after communion. Today's O Antiphon sings of the unity brought about by the long-desired of nations. "O come, Desire of Nations, bind/all peoples in one heart and mind;/Make all our sad divisions cease/and be yourself our Prince of peace."

THU 23 — #199 (LMC, #172–175) violet — Advent Weekday

O EMMANUEL

John Kanty, presbyter (+ 1473), *optional memorial.* ▪ The scriptures of the next two days tell the story of the birth of John the Baptist and the return of Zechariah's speech in a canticle of praise. Zechariah's canticle should be sung today and tomorrow.

Like Tuesday's saint, Peter Canisius, John Kanty was a professor. He is remembered for urging his students to moderation in controversy and for the generous almsgiving that was the fruit of his austere personal life. In today's general intercessions remember college students who are traveling home for the holidays.

FRI 24 — [morning] #200 (LMC, #172–175) violet — Advent Weekday

Even the official texts are caught up in the joy about to "dawn upon us from on high": The collect breaks with Roman usage and addresses Jesus himself in a burst of urgency: *Come quickly, Lord, and no longer delay!*

Some Eastern churches commemorate our first parents on this day before Christmas, an expression of our deep longing to gather all our human family into the marriage of heaven and earth. So, Happy Feast Day! to all who bear Adam's name or Eve's name, and to all of us who have inherited their strengths and weaknesses, and who bring them all to the One who comes to make all things new.

CHRISTMAS

The Season
The Setting of Christmastime / 27
A Sense of Christmastime / 28
The Look of Christmastime / 30
The Sounds of Christmastime / 31
The Rhythm of Christmastime / 32
The Eucharist / 33
Other Celebrations / 37
At Home / 38
The Calendar
December 25 — January 9, 2000 / 39

The Setting of Christmastime

'Tis the Season!" bellowed the early November editorial of a major metropolitan newspaper, bemoaning the untimely beginning of the commercial holiday season:

> As Christmas trees and Santa villages go up in the malls, a person wants to shout: "Take them down! We haven't finished the Halloween candy yet." Not long ago — was it 1970? — a kid would have been down to a couple of lollipops and a box of hard raisins before retailers dared push the candy canes. No electric star twinkled before its time, which, as everyone knew, was the day after Thanksgiving, not the middle of August. (*The Boston Globe,* November 12, 1998, page A24)

This is only half the story and part of the problem for those trying to live by the liturgical calendar. Not only does Christmas arrive weeks if not months before Advent; the commercial Christmas season ends on the day after Christmas! Here an equal and opposite reaction occurs. Mental health workers, pastoral care ministers, even police officers attest to a dramatic increase in domestic violence and family conflict, relationship issues and personal crises during the Christmas holidays. Who can doubt that society's extended and exaggerated anticipation of Christmas contributes to the sensation of tremendous letdown and, in some cases, to devastating depression, once Christmas day is past?

Each year, on the day after Christmas, frantic traffic and frenetic crowds concelebrate a yearly ritual: the return of unwanted presents and the exchange of wrong sizes. There is always a post-Christmas sale, but it isn't a particularly festive event. It seems designed more to comfort those who were disappointed with what their loved ones gave them! So just as the liturgical calendar swings open a shining door on "the Twelve Days of Christmas," the commercial world that surrounds us slams its doors shut on all festivity.

But this Christmas a symbolic door, the holy door, swings open not only on the Twelve Days of Christmas, but on the Great Jubilee 2000. Recalling that Jesus has told us, "I am the door" (John 10:7), Pope John Paul II notes that the symbolic door of the Holy Year reminds us that the Christian life is pilgrimage of faith:

> To focus upon the door is to recall the responsibility of every believer to cross its threshold. To pass through that door means to confess that Jesus Christ is Lord; it is to strengthen faith in him in order to life the new life which he has given us. It is a decision which presumes freedom to choose and also the courage to leave something behind, in the knowledge that what is gained is divine life (cf. Matthew 13:44–46). It is in this spirit that the Pope will be the first to pass through the holy door on the night between 24 and 25 December 1999. Crossing its

threshold, he will show to the Church and to the world the Holy Gospel, the wellspring of life and hope for the coming Third Millennium. Through the holy door, symbolically more spacious at the end of a millennium, Christ will lead us more deeply into the Church, his Body and his Bride. (John Paul II, *Incarnationis Mysterium*, 8)

Long before we moderns labeled the phenomenon Seasonal Affective Disorder (SAD), our pagan ancestors, in the Northern Hemisphere at least, were coping with nature's enveloping darkness and its attendant emotional gloom by celebrating the increase of light that begins after the winter solstice. Halls lit with bright candles and fragrant oil lamps, rooms warmed by roaring fires, doors hung with wreaths and garlands of evergreen and blood-red berries, tables laden with rich foods and fine wines — all these were ways of chasing the winter's dark and cold away. Hand in hand with all of this, of course, went the gracious hospitality that brought people in and made them feel at home.

When upon that world "there dawned the Sun of Justice with its healing rays" (Malachi 3:20), Christ, "the Light of the world that no darkness can overcome" (John 1:5), our Christian forebears simply took many elements of the world's solstice celebration and made them their own, *our* own! We need to find ways to do that today.

There is no place here, then, for grim sermonizing about the world's lack of values, or a nostalgic idealization of "the good old days." More challenging and more enduring will be a thoughtful exploration of creative ways to make Christmas and the days that flow from it both holy and wholesome. Look across the boundaries of time and culture to see what other Christians have done or are doing. Our Latin-speaking ancestors, for instance, had a deep sense of the "commercial" that saw the Incarnation as a very "good deal" for us mortals: *O admirable commercium,* they sang, "O marvelous exchange: the Creator of human nature took on a human body." While British Christians were singing of themselves as "merry gentlemen," a Native American carol was transforming the manger into a lodge of bark, swaddling clothes into rabbit skin, shepherds into hunter braves and the Magi into tribal chiefs. Eastern European Christians bless wine and share it as a pledge of reconciliation before the New Year dawns. Hispanic Christians find the birth and manifestation of Christ a perfect opportunity to transform the divine visitation into a setting for human hospitality. And who knows what insights and customs newly-arrived Christians from Southeast Asia and other distant lands and diverse cultures may have brought to renew and enrich our Christmastime?

Let the local faith community, then, open wide its doors in a Great Jubilee of celebration, evangelization and reconciliation. especially during the shining days of Christmastime, so that, as the Pope has said, "the Christmas season will be the pulsing heart of the Holy Year, bringing to the life of the church an infusion of the copious gifts of the Spirit for a new evangelization" (*Incarnationis Mysterium*, 6).

A Sense of Christmastime

THE PASCHAL CONNECTION

Next to the yearly celebration of the paschal mystery, the church considers nothing more important than the memorial of Christ's birth and early manifestations. (*General Norms for the Liturgical Year and Calendar,* 32)

ALTHOUGH the official document is speaking about rank, take that "next to" in the broader sense of perspective as well. Picture in the mind's eye the parish nativity set arranged with a glorious triptych behind it. The left panel of the triptych depicts the footwashing in front of a table set with bread and cup, the center panel portrays the crucifixion, and the right panel celebrates the resurrection. The manger thus appears against the backdrop of the gospels' portrayal of the paschal mystery and Easter Triduum.

But only *in the mind's eye!* No liturgical decorator would ever overburden the community's space or the worshipers' minds by depicting all the mysteries at once! Yet holding the paschal mystery in our consciousness is a crucial requirement as we attend to the nativity, epiphany and baptism. There is no other way to get a proper sense of the simultaneous challenge and comfort of this season or to guarantee that the Christmastime liturgy will touch our hearts with tenderness and transform them with power.

■ SCRIPTURAL LINK: "An adult Christ at Christmas" was the expression Raymond Brown coined to describe this paschal sense of Christmas, and it was the title he gave to a popular adaptation of his research (*An Adult Christ at Christmas,* The Liturgical Press, 1978). Brown saw the infancy narratives as the gospel in miniature. Under the guise of the loveliest stories in literature, Matthew and Luke are teaching that, from the first moments of this Child's human existence, the choice of acceptance or rejection is set before all who encounter him. The characters that people the infancy narratives prefigure the cast of the passion play: lowly shepherds, curious Gentiles, nervous authorities, and always the Virgin Mother, model of the perfect disciple, who "pondered all these things in her heart." Brown urges us not to be discouraged that the infancy stories are known by many "who know little else of the gospel." Brown understands that some believers may find this disheartening:

> But this is to neglect the fact that the infancy narrative contains both the cross and the God-given triumph. Herod stalks the trail of the magi, a menacing reminder that, while the star of the newborn King has shone forth in purity and simplicity, there are those who will seek to blot out that light. If the infancy story is an attractive drama that catches the imagination, it also is a substantial proclamation of the coming of the kingdom and its possible rejection. (*The Birth of the Messiah.* Doubleday, revised edition, 1993, 232)

■ HISTORICAL-THEOLOGICAL LINK: "Winter Pascha" was the expression the preeminent Orthodox liturgical theologian Alexander Schmemann used to describe the Christmas liturgies. Explaining the Orthodox use of *pascha* to describe both Easter and Christmas, Schmemann's interpreter Thomas Hopko observes:

> The liturgical verses and hymns for Christmas and Epiphany, the Pascha of Christ's incarnation and manifestation in the flesh, repeat those of Easter, the Pascha of Christ's death and resurrection. The Lord's birth and baptism are directly connected to His dying and rising. He was born in order to die. He was baptized in order to be raised. (*The Winter Pascha.* St. Vladimir's Seminary Press, 1984, 10)

Contemporary research into the origins of the liturgical year suggests a historical foundation for this theological link of the winter and spring paschas, Christmas and Easter. Thomas J. Talley, Episcopal priest and expert on the liturgical year, challenges a theory that has been accepted for two hundred years, namely, that Christmas is the Christian adoption and adaptation of the Roman pagan festival *Dies natalis solis invicti,* the birthday of the invincible sun. First of all, says Talley, this was not a festival of great antiquity at Rome, having been established by the Emperor Aurelian only in 274 CE. Is it likely, he asks, that a persecuted minority would so wholeheartedly adopt the feastday of a pagan god? His research suggests that early Christians wanted to determine precisely the actual date of Christ's death, 14 Nisan according to scripture. They computed the fourteenth day of the spring moon in the year of the crucifixion to coincide with the Roman date March 25. Semitic tradition had it that patriarchs were born and died on the same date. That tradition was adapted and enhanced for Christ. Texts from Augustine and others show that Christians believed Christ was *conceived* and died on the same date, March 25. Counting forward, then, from the conception date of March 25, they determined his date of birth to be December 25 (See *Reforming Tradition.* The Pastoral Press, 1990, 135).

■ MUSICAL LINK: In more subtle ways, ancient hymns, traditional carols and even contemporary compositions, in their original forms, manifest a similar sense of the unity between incarnation and paschal mystery. From the fourth century comes Prudentius' lovely *Corde natus ex parentis,* "Of the Father's love begotten." It appears in every major hymnal as a quintessential Christmas hymn. But no hymnal dares to include the verse that occurs in the Latin original between what is commonly given as verses 1 and 2 in English:

> He assumed this mortal body,
>   frail and feeble, doomed to die,
> That the race from dust created
>   might not perish utterly,
> Which the dreadful law had sentenced
>   in the depths of hell to lie.
>   (Translation R.F. Davis, 1905,
>   in Eric Routley, *A Panorama of Christian Hymnody.* Chicago: GIA Publications, 1979)

Conversely, when presenting the fifth-century passion hymn of Venantius Fortunatus, *Pange, lingua, gloriosi praelium certaminis,* "Sing, my tongue, the glorious battle," every major hymnal omits this verse from the original:

> Hear the helpless infant crying
>   where the narrow manger stands;
> See how she, his Virgin Mother,
>   ties his limbs with slender bands,
> Swaddling clothes she wraps about him
>   and confines God's feet and hands!
>   (Anonymous translation,
>   pre–Vatican II daily missal)

More ancient than the Reproaches, this hymn is still prescribed for use during the Good Friday Veneration of the Cross, though that verse does not appear in it. Both hymns, in their original versions, consider it quite natural to sing of the incarnation and passion. There is the deep, perhaps even instinctive sense that the two mysteries need to be held together in consciousness even though only one is the principal focus.

Could it be that the violence and injustice of our own age have caused modern hymn writers to recover something of this paschal sense? Consider these hymns, worthy of addition to the parish's repertoire of carols:

> Child of gladness, child of sorrow,
> Crib today and cross tomorrow;
> Holy child, who comes to borrow
> Peasant robe and stable bare.
>   ("Child of Gladness, Child of Sorrow,"
>   Michael Perry, © 1987,
>   Hope Publishing Co., Carol Stream IL
>   in *Catholic Book of Worship III*)

> O Child of ecstasy and sorrow,
> O Prince of peace and pain,
> Brighten today's world by tomorrow's,
> Renew our lives again;
> Lord Jesus, come and reign!
>   ("Each winter as the year grows older,"
>   William Gay, © 1971, United Church Press)

> And who could be the same for having held
> The infant in their arms, and later felt
> The wounded hands and side,
>   all doubts dispelled.
>   ("Peace came to earth," Jaroslav J. Vajda,
>   © 1984 *With One Voice*)

The power of the Christmas liturgy flows ultimately from the Lord's paschal mystery; and this insight, so deeply part of the tradition across the ages, must shine forth in our celebration. We are, after all, celebrating a mystery, not simply commemorating a historical event. Making Christmas a remembrance or a symbolic reliving may seem at first to make those past events more present to the imagination. But in reality, the opposite happens. The celebration is emptied of transformative power; the impact of the saving event is removed from the present. The mystery is relegated to the realm of the make-believe or "let's pretend."

An authentic celebration of Christmastime delights to see the People of God drawn to the wood of the manger, but then directs us to look beyond it to the wood of the cross. A community that has placed Christmas next to the paschal mystery kindles the lights of the Christmas tree with joy, but turns for that Christmas light to the light of the Easter candle.

The Look of Christmastime

CANDLELIGHT

A festival of light; the revelation of Christ, Light of the World (John 8:12); and the Sun of Justice rising with healing in his wings (Malachi 4:2): thus do the scriptures, hymns, collects and prefaces of the season celebrate Christmas.

Among his many insightful ideas on Christmas decor (pages 230–264), Peter Mazar offers this caution about the use of Christmas lights in church:

> There are ways to use them well but even more ways to use them poorly. The worship environment is almost always better served by candles. A constellation of flickering votive candles—perhaps lining a beam or clustered in a corner—is a lot more magical and unexpected than electric lights. (*To Crown the Year,* 248)

See also Mazar's excellent ideas on electric lights for the Christmas tree or outdoors.

EVERGREENS

As candles are a universal symbol of light's triumph over darkness, so evergreens are an ancient sign of life's eternal victory over death. Many elements associated with Christmas decor point to Easter's paschal glory. Consider the link between the lights of the Christmas tree and the paschal candle. The Christmas tree itself is a link, a reminder of the tree of life and of the life-giving cross. Its trunk may even be suitable for the limbs of the Good Friday cross. The holly's thorns and blood-red berries, along with the red poinsettia, remind us of Christ's passion. Wreaths are ancient symbols both of victory (Christ's paschal victory) and of the mystical union of marriage (the marriage of Christ and the church).

MANGER SCENE

The manger can rekindle a sense of wonder in the most sophisticated heart and summon cluttered lives back to the simplicity in which God took flesh. To us who glory in self-sufficiency and wealth, the manger offers a visual reminder that Christ was born into homelessness and poverty. It can be a wonderful gathering place for personal and family prayer: Children love to visit the manger! Evening Prayer on Christmas Eve or Christmas day could fittingly be celebrated at the manger.

Design and location are critical. Too grand a scope or too prominent a place could cause the manger to overshadow or even unbalance the liturgy. Altar, ambo and assembly hall remain the principal focal points for the eucharistic celebration during Christmastime. Mazar's excellent proposals will prevent missteps and encourage creativity (*To Crown the Year,* pages 241, 250–255).

The manger scene may be blessed at Evening Prayer on Christmas Eve or at a vigil before Night Mass. The United States' *Book of Blessings* suggests that the blessing take place after the general intercessions, but the manger's location at some distance from the altar may suggest a stational stop during the entrance or recessional.

OUTDOORS

Christmas is one of the few times when otherwise reticent citizens make public displays of holiday cheer. Light and evergreens are used by believers and nonbelievers alike to adorn their homes. How much more fitting are they for the *domus ecclesiae,* the house of the church. Big, beautiful wreaths, along with lights and walkway luminaries, are signs of festivity and hospitality. Outdoor banners and flags increasingly brighten people's homes. These can proclaim the good news of salvation at the church when they are made of durable material, in a tasteful design appropriate to the building's architecture and large enough to be viewed from a distance.

CIVIC RESPONSIBILITY

It may be necessary to consult the local fire marshal or other civil authority before planning Christmas observances. Some important questions are these: In light of safety regulations, how much space is required for the numbers we expect? Are cut trees and real greens permitted? Our norms encourage real plant material; we should not accede to the use of artificial greenery too easily. Candles and incense are not optional elements in Catholic worship; therefore, we have a right as well as an obligation to use them. It is possible to arrange lit candles safely in relationship to evergreens, flowers and straw. If necessary, representatives from the parish or diocesan liturgical commission may wish to see how other religious groups reconcile their worship needs with civil regulations or meet with the responsible civil officials to ensure an approach that respects both liturgy and public safety.

The Sounds of Christmastime

CAROLS

All nations and cultures, each language and ethnic group, and almost every generation have contributed to the vast repertoire of music we call Christmas carols. In current usage, the term embraces everything from folk carols to hymns with a more biblical or doctrinal orientation. But even these retain some of the folk-carol feel and are often set to folk tunes. Familiar and beloved carols are sacramental in the deepest sense of the word: They both signify and effect the presence of Christ in the world, for they are heard at this time of the year not only as church hymnody but even as mall music. Many are truly known "by heart": The mere snippet of a tune or text can conjure up deepest joy or poignant pain.

The new hymnals published by many denominations reflect the blossoming of interest in carols and have vastly increased the repertoire. Contemporary compilations include English carols, German *Weihnachtslieder* ("songs to celebrate the Nativity"), French *noëls,* Polish, Slovak, Ukrainian, Italian, Hispanic and African American Christmas songs, representing a unique form of inculturation. The carols of our own generation express a particularly moving consciousness of sin. While every generation has prayed for "peace on earth, good will to all," those who analyze twentieth-century Christmas poetry must be struck by the social nature of the redemption we pray for. War and poverty are among the many things that have convinced us of our powerlessness to redeem ourselves. Such anxieties are very much a part of our modern experience of Calvary, so how could they not echo in our contemporary song to the Christ of Bethlehem? If not yet a part of the community's Christmas repertoire, some of these newer texts need to become so. Together with our old favorites, they are part of the heritage we will hand on to our children's children. The paschal mystery and personal conversion are here, and so is a deep awareness of social sin.

Interspersed with favorite carols, such contemporary pieces can set a prayerful tone as communal or choral prelude while the assembly gathers. If the parish is ethnically diverse, planners should invite suggestions of beloved Christmas songs of various cultures. Less diverse congregations will want to enrich their imagery of the incarnation by learning the carols of other cultures and adopting those insights as their own. During the preparation of the gifts, carols that echo the scriptures may be used to form a musical link between word and eucharist. This usually brief rite may be prolonged by incensation of altar, gifts and assembly. Carols known by heart eliminate the need for carrying participation aids and make a good accompaniment to the communion procession.

GLORIA IN EXCELSIS

The Gloria is an important part of the Christmas liturgy especially on Christmas night, both because the assembly has abstained from its joy throughout Advent and because it is inspired by the angels' song at Christ's birth. Since joy and fervor are the keynotes of this song, look for musical settings conveying strength and beauty. The same setting used until the Feast of the Lord's Baptism underscores the unity of the season. The rendition could be enhanced by vocal harmonies, handbells, flute, trumpet or whatever embellishments are available at each celebration. Choose a setting that will invite the participation of the whole assembly, even visitors. Selections that encourage the assembly's participation and are particularly suitable for the tone of Christmas are listed on page 34.

The Rhythm of Christmastime

HOSPITALITY

CHRISTMASTIME is a brief but intense period, and it is as rich as it is brief. The season is worth our best efforts to keep the spirit of celebration throughout these special days. At this season, perhaps even more so than usual, the goals of parish liturgy preparation are these:

to offer God glory;
to invite God's people to worship that is
    prayerful, reverent and beautiful;
to provide hospitality that is warm, inclusive
    and genuine.

Who are the people we liturgical ministers serve at this most wonderful time of the year? Excited youngsters, of course, whose presence renews in us the wonder of early Christmas memories. Hassled young parents, perhaps many single parents, working two or more jobs to garner a moderate harvest of toys. Anxious mid-lifers, working hard at staying employed, home-making and parenting, concealing their own worries to make yet another Christmas merry for loved ones. Precious but sometimes neglected are aged parishioners who may find themselves alone for the holidays with memories of far-away children or of spouse or friends long departed. Some faces are only vaguely familiar, people rarely seen at worship; other faces are suddenly recognized: students and former parishioners back to visit for the holidays. One and all, these are God's holy people. For us who minister, their presence is God's blessing in the flesh; supporting their prayer is our privileged purpose.

If serving them is not always easy for us, liturgical celebration is not always easy for them! Bombarded since Halloween by Christmas advertising campaigns and taped carols at the mall, some are glad to put Christmas to rest on the night of December 25! To be of best service to others in a ministry that counters the surrounding culture, we ourselves need to embrace the liturgical treasures of the Christmas season. Then we need to share these gifts cheerfully, enthusiastically, positively and patiently.

COMMUNICATIONS

As Jesus once suggested, we "children of light" need to take a lesson from the resourcefulness of the "children of the world." The malls publicize their holiday specials well. But the treasures we have to share are so much richer! Therefore, let the Christmastime schedule be carefully planned, thoughtfully arranged and well publicized. Present it in an attractive and convenient manner, have it printed and send to the full mailing list. Perhaps a guest book at the door during Advent services has collected the names of new people who will appreciate knowing what's going on. Attractive posters at church entrances and notices in the bulletin will reinforce whatever is mailed to the homes. Local newspapers and other media sometimes provide churches with free space and time for sharing Christmas schedules with a wider public.

The Eucharist

INTRODUCTORY RITES

THE ritual actions with which the liturgy begins should provide a nonverbal greeting that welcomes the assembly and sets a Christmas tone even before the words of greeting are spoken. The ritual beginning of Advent Masses could suggest a contrasting opening for the Christmas liturgies.

On Christmas Eve itself (whether early or at midnight), Mass might begin with an opening rite that echoes, but does not compete with, the uniqueness of the Easter Vigil. A suggested order of service for Christmas Eve appears in the calendar (page 39–40). In the absence of a prescribed vigil in the Roman rite, this *Sourcebook* offers some of the Ambrosian rite's resources of texts and prayers. In structure and content, this order is reminiscent of the Easter Vigil.

■ PROCLAMATION OF THE BIRTH OF CHRIST: In some places, the chanting of this ancient text, by candlelight, without explanation or introduction, marks the transition between the pre-Mass vigil and the opening hymn. The traditional form of the text is on page 48. A new form appears in the *Sacramentary Supplement* for the United States (New York: Catholic Book, 1994), along with a suggestion that it follow the greeting of the Mass. The penitential rite is omitted and the Gloria forms the response to the proclamation.

At other Masses, sing a beloved Christmas carol during the solemn incensation of the altar to provide an experience of sight, sound and smell that establishes a perfect setting for words of welcome and the return of the joyful Gloria.

■ BLESSING AND SPRINKLING OF HOLY WATER: Celebrated on both Epiphany and the Lord's baptism, this option would link the two celebrations ritually, and acknowledge that both manifestations were formerly celebrated on Epiphany. Incensation and greeting remain, followed by the water blessing.

Some communities renew baptismal vows on the Feast of the Lord's Baptism, sprinkling with water after the homily, as on Easter Sunday. This may at first seem appropriate, but there are several reasons to hesitate. In the Roman rite, the usual place for the ritual sprinkling with water is during the introductory rite, immediately after the water blessing. These blessings refer to the water specifically as a reminder of baptism, our passageway to word and eucharist. On Easter, the only day on which the sprinkling takes place after the liturgy of the word, there is no water blessing because the water for sprinkling has been blessed at the Easter Vigil. Renewing baptismal vows after the homily on the Feast of the Baptism of the Lord requires an overburdened rite: water blessing, renewal of vows and sprinkling. Nor should anything be done on this day that might diminish the uniqueness of Easter as the primary festival of initiation and baptismal renewal.

■ GLORIA IN EXCELSIS: On Christmas, the choice of a setting for the Gloria involves two considerations:

- The music should be suitably festive, in keeping with the importance of the solemnity, and the Gloria's inspiration drawn from the Lucan nativity.
- The setting should permit, indeed encourage, the participation of the whole assembly.

The well-known "Gloria in excelsis Deo" refrain from "Angels we have heard on high" provides an easy assembly refrain in several settings. "A Christmas Gloria" by Paul Gibson (OCP, 9551), for assembly, cantor, SATB choir, organ and trumpet in C, features imaginative use of this carol's melodic material for unison verses. Daniel Laginya's "Christmas Gloria" (GIA, G-2971) is a nice setting for cantor and congregation, as are Glorias by Benedictine composers Columba Kelly in *The Collegeville Hymnal* (Liturgical Press) and Becket Senchur's "Mass of Hope" in *The People's Mass Book* (World Library Publications). These invite creativity when used with choir and/or instruments. Richard Proulx's "Gloria for Christmastime" (GIA, G-3085) employs two-part mixed voices, cantor and congregation (with a flute/oboe obbligato). Look also at the "Chant-style Gloria" with optional Christmas refrain by Howard Hughes (WLP, 8534) and Peter Jones' "Glory to God" (OCP), especially good if brass is available, and Steven Janco's "Glory to God" (WLP, 8559). Almost any setting of the Gloria can be made more festive by imaginative use of handbells and by dividing verses between the choir's men and women.

■ THE COLLECTS: The Christmas image of light's increase as night gives way to day shine through the opening prayers, or collects, provided for the Christmas Masses. There are subtle and bold echoes of paschal words and images. Each of these liturgical formularies should only be used at the actual time of day for which it is prescribed. The lectionary rubric that permits a pastoral selection from among the many readings of the several Christmas Masses does not apply to the sacramentary. With the sacramentary texts, a thoughtful reading of the prayers reveals their power and beauty, and their potential usefulness as homiletic, devotional and educational resources.

LITURGY OF THE WORD

■ RESPONSORIAL PSALM: Proper psalms for solemnities and feasts are in the lectionary with the proper readings; seasonal psalms and refrains are found at #174 and #175.

Christmastime: Psalm 98, with the refrain "All the ends of the earth have seen the saving power of God," may be used throughout Christmastime. A different psalm is provided for Epiphany and the Lord's baptism, but Psalm 98 with its message of universal salvation is still appropriate. Several suggested arrangements include:

- David Haas and Marty Haugen, "All the ends of the earth" (GIA, G-2703)
- Rawn Harbor, "Psalm for Christmas," *Lead Me, Guide Me* (GIA), #504
- David Isele, "All the ends of the earth," *Psalms for the Church Year* (GIA, G-2262)
- Richard Proulx and John Hirten, "Psalm for Christmas Day" (GIA, G-3631)
- Michael Joncas, "All the ends of the earth" (GIA, G-3431)
- James Marchionda, "Psalm 98," *Psalms for the Cantor,* volume II (WLP)
- Mary Kay Beall's arrangement for children (with Christmas descant) in *Sing Out! A Children's Psalter* (WLP, 7990)

Canada's official *Catholic Book of Worship III* proposes Psalm 147 with the refrain "The Word of God became flesh and dwelt among us" as an alternative seasonal psalm for Christmas.

Holy Family: Psalm 128 with the refrain "Happy are those who fear the Lord and walk in his ways," a classic wedding psalm, is appropriate on a feast that celebrates the family. There are a number of arrangements; the Gelineau setting and refrain found in *Worship III* and in *RitualSong* is perhaps the best known. *We Celebrate* (World Library) contains a setting by Ron Rendek.

Mary, Mother of God: Psalm 67 with the refrain "May God bless us in his mercy" is an invocation of God's blessing on the new year. Consider Robert Batastini's expanded form in *Worship* and the Canadian hymnal's variation, "O God, be gracious and bless us, and let your face shine upon us."

Epiphany: Psalm 72 with the refrain "Lord, every nation on earth will adore you" is prescribed. Many settings are available: GIA's *Worship* offers five; *Service Music for the Mass,* vol. 1, from World Library has a setting by Noel Goemanne.

Baptism of the Lord: Psalm 29 with the refrain "The Lord will bless his people with peace" is prescribed. Many settings are available. Consult the sources already noted.

■ GOSPEL ACCLAMATIONS: Verses that supplement those proper to the season's several solemnities and feasts are at #212 and #219 in the lectionary. These liturgical texts would also be perfect to include in parish handouts, participation aids and mailings. They communicate in a concise way the spirit of the season and can provide a good springboard for personal prayer.

■ DISMISSAL OF CATECHUMENS: While each community will form catechumens in its own manner, the *Rite of Christian Initiation of Adults* suggests appropriate content:

> The instruction that the catechumens receive during this period should be of a kind that while presenting Catholic teaching in its entirety also enlightens faith, directs the heart toward God, fosters participation in the liturgy, inspires apostolic activity and nurtures a life completely in accord with the spirit of Christ. (78)

Direct the attention of the catechumens especially to the collects and prefaces of Christmastime as rich sources of solid theology and spirituality. Remember, too, that many Christmas carols are well known far beyond the setting of church and worship. Those familiar to the catechumens could be helpful in orienting them to this season's prayerful beauty and gospel challenge. Those that aren't familiar could be shared as an important and endearing part of the faith and family the catechumens are preparing to embrace.

■ PROFESSION OF FAITH AT CHRISTMAS MASSES: Only twice a year is liturgical language reinforced by body language during the profession of faith. We give a special reverence to the words that express our faith in the incarnation on Christmas and the Annunciation (March 25) by genuflecting as we pronounce them. In the pastoral experience of many, this genuflection just doesn't work. For one thing, no liturgical gesture can be a meaningful experience of reverence if it sneaks up on the assembly twice a year! More basically, this dramatic twice-yearly genuflection makes no sense if the bow, prescribed for every week's profession of faith, never happens. This seems to be the case in many parishes.

What is at stake here is not simply an insignificant rubric but a traditional Catholic, incarnational instinct to involve the whole self, all our senses, in the act of prayer. Even where such an approach is familiarity, it will be necessary to alert the assembly to the genuflection. A brief invitation before the profession of faith should be sufficient. Because the invitation to a posture of prayer is similar to that used during the solemn prayers of Good Friday, these or similar words are appropriately spoken by the deacon:

> Today, as we profess our faith together, let us genuflect at those words that enshrine our belief that the Word of God has indeed become flesh to dwell among us.

In times past, the profession of faith was set to some of the most stately chants in the church's Gregorian repertoire. Perhaps on this solemnity and other major days, it might once again be sung, of course, in a form that invites the participation of the whole assembly.

■ PROCLAMATION OF THE DATE OF EASTER ON EPIPHANY: The proclamation from the *Sacramentary Supplement* (1994) is found on page 50 of this *Sourcebook*. The *Ceremonial of Bishops* (#240) encourages observance of the custom. Although its practical purpose predates the wide availability of printed calendars, the symbolic value of the proclamation endures. The clear message of the text is that Christ's Pascha is central to the church's life in this and in every year, the fountain from which all feasts flow, the reason we pay honor to Mary and the saints as believers in whom Christ's passover mystery has triumphed. The ritual message can likewise be powerful.

The proclamation is made from the ambo. The *Ceremonial of Bishops* notes that a deacon or other minister may vest in a cope for the proclamation, giving unspoken, visual honor to the action. Especially when chanted, it serves as solemn consecration of the new calendar year.

LITURGY OF THE EUCHARIST

■ PREFACES TO THE EUCHARISTIC PRAYER: Vatican II's liturgical reform increased the number of prefaces for the eucharistic prayer from the 16 found in the Tridentine Missal to more than 85. There are three prefaces for Christmas now, one for Epiphany, a new preface of the Lord's baptism, and several Christmastime Marian prefaces in the *Collection of Masses of the Blessed Virgin Mary*. Each in its own way capsulizes the theology and spirituality of the season. They are discussed here in a slightly revised, inclusive translation. Remember, in matters liturgical, richness of resources should never result in randomness of choice! Planners and presiders will want to choose thoughtfully from among the three Christmas prefaces for the solemnity and throughout the octave (even when saints' days occur).

Christmas Preface I, "Christ the Light," begins immediately with a reference to John's prologue: "In the mystery of the Word made flesh your glory fills the eyes of our mind." Then it sings of the twofold movement God initiates in the incarnation: "seeing God made visible in Christ, we are caught up in love of things we cannot see."

Preface Christmas II, a new composition drawing on the homilies of Leo the Great, subtly links incarnation with paschal mystery in the title "Universal Restoration in the Incarnation." The wedding of opposites is celebrated in these beautiful lines: " the God we cannot see has now appeared in human form. The one begotten before all ages begins to live in time."

Christmas Preface III, "Exchange in the Incarnation of the Word," is drawn from ancient sacramentaries and celebrates the *admirable commercium*. This "marvelous exchange" is a series of redemptive paradoxes: ". . . your eternal Word assumes human frailty, our mortal nature takes on immortal value. . . . This union between God and ourselves makes us sharers in eternal life."

In the Northern Hemisphere, the steadily growing light in nature mirrors the growing light of salvation. The Epiphany Preface combines echoes of Christmas liturgical texts, the Magi story (Matthew) and the presentation (Luke). Christ is "the light to enlighten all nations," and "Now that he has appeared in our mortal flesh, you have refashioned us in the image of his immortal glory." Although the Epiphany preface may be used on weekdays following that solemnity, so may the Christmas prefaces be used, right up to the Feast of the Baptism of the Lord. The second and third Christmas prefaces are strikingly appropriate even after Epiphany, since they celebrate restoration of unity to creation, universal salvation and the "divinization" of our human nature in Christ. These are the special scriptural themes of Epiphany week, with its selections from the First Letter of John and gospel passages about Christ's healing outreach to Israel and beyond it to the Gentiles.

Finally, the Preface of the Lord's Baptism recapitulates the principal conviction celebrated in the Christmas season: "A voice came down from heaven to waken our faith in your Word dwelling among us." It also returns the church to Ordinary Time, which is characterized by the lectionary's weekly proclamation of the life and teaching of the Lord: "Christ your servant was anointed with the oil of gladness and was sent to preach the good news to the poor."

Planners and presiders will also want to become familiar with the Christmastime prefaces found in the *Collection of Masses of the Blessed Virgin Mary*. While there is no specific preface for the Holy Family provided in the sacramentary, the Preface of Our Lady of Nazareth in the *Collection* celebrates the scriptural and pastoral themes of the feast. On the Solemnity of Mary, Mother of God

(January 1), the sacramentary specifies the Preface of the Blessed Virgin I (inserting the name of the feast, "Motherhood") or II (which incorporates phrases from the Magnificat). A third Marian preface, Mary, Model and Mother of the Church, has been added to the sacramentary (see Votive Mass of Mary, Mother of the Church, appendix X of the 1985 sacramentary), and the *Collection* contains another beautiful preface, entitled Mother of the Savior. See, too, the preface Our Lady of the Epiphany, which celebrates the shepherds as the firstfruits of Israel and the Magi as the firstfruits among the Gentiles now gathered into the church.

■ EUCHARISTIC PRAYER: Eucharistic Prayer I (the Roman Canon) has special inserts for Christmas Day, its octave and Epiphany. The use of variable seasonal prefaces with Eucharistic Prayers for Reconciliation is permitted (see *Notitiae* 19 [1983], page 270). Reconciliation II with one of the Christmas prefaces might be a good choice on weekdays after Epiphany. Although it is always supposed to be used with its own preface, Eucharistic Prayer IV seems appropriate on the Feast of the Lord's Baptism with its lyrical praise of Christ who "lived as one of us in all things but sin. To the poor he proclaimed the good news of salvation, to prisoners, freedom, and to those in sorrow, joy."

■ ACCLAMATIONS DURING THE EUCHARISTIC PRAYER: Some parishes use the same acclamations for both Advent and Christmastime, others a set for each season. In either case, Advent's simplicity will undoubtedly give way to a more festive Christmastime sound. To encourage participation as guests and strangers join year-round participants, choose festive settings that feature a cantor-assembly call and response. Howard Hughes' "Mass of the Divine Word" (GIA, G-2415), Christopher Walker's "Glastonbury Eucharistic Acclamations" (OCP, 7165) and William Ferris' "Music for the Banquet" (WLP, 7555) are such arrangements.

■ COMMUNION RITE: For sample texts for the introduction to the Lord's Prayer, and the invitation to communion see LTP's *Prayers for Sundays and Seasons, Year B*.

■ MUSIC DURING THE COMMUNION RITE: Christmas is a perfect time for congregations to start singing during the communion procession, if they are not already doing so. An abundance of seasonal selections known to all eliminates the inconvenience of carrying participation aids. The parish's favorite carols, particularly those with refrains, are especially appropriate at communion throughout the season.

CONCLUDING RITES

■ BLESSINGS: Three solemn blessings are provided for use during the Christmas season:

Christmas: This blessing emphasizes the darkness/light theme of Christmastime and introduces a sense of the assembly's mission as "heralds of the gospel," speaking beautifully of the peace and goodwill celebrated in the carols and customs of the season.

January 1: Obviously the solemn blessing "Beginning of the Year" is appropriate, but unfortunately it does not incorporate explicitly the scriptural and liturgical themes associated with the season. The solemn blessing for feasts of Mary mentions both Christ's birth and the redemption of the human race.

Epiphany: Epiphany's solemn blessing successfully incorporates and recapitulates the seasonal themes. It mentions enlightenment of the world in Christ and our call as Christ's disciples to be a source of that light to our brothers and sisters.

■ DISMISSAL: For appropriate seasonal dismissals, see *Prayers for Sundays and Seasons, Year B*.

Other Celebrations

LITURGY OF THE HOURS

Perhaps Advent witnessed the beginning or growth of a parish custom of celebrating Morning or Evening Prayer. If so, continue the momentum during the Christmas season. Depending on the size of the group, such gatherings could take place at the manger or near the Christmas tree. In fact, the blessing of these beloved symbols may take place during the celebration of one of these hours. The *Liturgy of the Hours* (volume I) contains fine nonscriptural texts for these holy days.

NEW YEAR'S EVE

According to an ancient Catholic custom, the end of one year and the beginning of a new one is marked by a vigil of prayer, concluding with the solemn chanting of the Te Deum. Besides the well-known metrical version, "Holy God, we praise thy name," consider the chant adaptations of the Te Deum in contemporary hymnals. See the Episcopal *Hymnal 1982* for an adapted Latin chant (S 282) and Byzantine version (S 288).

COMMUNAL ANOINTING OF THE SICK

Because of the unique focus of the major feasts of this season, the ritual Mass for anointing is not permitted on Christmas, January 1 or Epiphany. At weekday celebrations with the sick, whether in small groups or the parish assembly, choose readings from the rite's selection of texts. As in Advent, the three Isaiah passages work well, and the reading from 1 John and the Lucan gospel of Jesus and John the Baptist fit the spirit of the season. Or why not simply use the readings appointed for the day? These are generally rich in messianic and manifestation images and would draw the sick into the image world of Christmas.

FUNERALS

Consider using the readings appointed for the day even at funerals, supplementing them perhaps with Isaiah or 1 John. The lectionary selections for the Christmas octave and the weekdays before and after Epiphany often present passages that lead easily to thoughts of the paschal mystery. In a church filled with Christmas decorations, it will be impossible to pretend that it is not Christmastime. Nor is there any need to do so. A thoughtful homilist can join reflections on Christian death to seasonal images of light and new life, and point the assembly toward Christ's victory over death.

MARRIAGE

On Christmas, January 1 or Epiphany, marriage celebrations must use the texts proper to these days. On the feasts of the Holy Family and the Baptism of the Lord, nuptial Masses that are not parish Masses can use the full set of marriage texts, and, as noted in the *Rite of Marriage* (#11), a reading from the rite's own scripture selections can be integrated into the feast day's proper readings. The Song of Songs, 1 John and the wedding feast at Cana are traditional and beautiful both for weddings and for this time of year.

At Home

ANCIENT Christian writers, such as Saint John Chrysostom, used the expression "domestic church" in their delight in seeing parallels and links between the place where the community gathered officially and the homes where Christian families lived. For early believers, there was an obvious relationship between the assembly's altar table, prepared for the Lord's sacrifice and supper, and the family table where the sacrifice of mutual love and care provided a feast for the household united in Christ. Ideally, public Morning and Evening Prayer, celebrated daily in church, began with prayer together at home and echoed in a family life of mutual service within and beyond the home.

While such customs may strike us as quaint, the term "domestic church" appears in the new *Catechism of the Catholic Church*. The tradition of prayer at home together is the object of renewed interest and the focus of several recent publications. Almost all families have religious customs and symbols they associate with Christmas. So Christmas is a perfect time to give new impetus to household prayer and ritual. The most basic thing the parish liturgy team can do to assist this effort is make a variety of materials widely accessible to the community.

CALENDAR

December

SAT 25 #13–16 (LMC, #13) white
The Birth of the Lord (Christmas)
SOLEMNITY

ORIENTATION

■ THEOLOGICAL, HISTORICAL AND PASTORAL: Three perspectives can help liturgists serve the community's prayer well on this rich solemnity. Focusing on only one or another might impoverish the community's prayer. Embracing all three helps us to serve the community where it is and to suggest new directions to deepen its celebration of the incarnation.

Theologically, the Christmas liturgy celebrates the saving event in which Christ "the true light, which enlightens everyone, was coming into the world" (John 1:9).

Historically, this theology expresses itself in a sequence of celebrations from Christmas Eve to Christmas night that features a corresponding sequence of texts. We heirs of the Roman rite ought to know this rich heritage of Christmas liturgies well:

- Nocturnal Liturgy: For 1500 years Roman Christians have celebrated the liturgy "at night" (the old and new Latin missals do not specify midnight) near a replica of Bethlehem's manger at Saint Mary Major, the principal Roman basilica dedicated to Mary.

- Morning (Dawn) Liturgy: Historically, there has been a papal Mass at Saint Anastasia's Basilica in honor of the patron of the basilica, since her feast is also December 25. Thus the notation in the old Latin missal, "Station at Saint Anastasia."

- Day Liturgy: Originally, this papal Mass was at Saint Peter's, and later moved to Saint Mary Major where the manger was. As late as 1962 the missal noted: "Station at Saint Mary Major."

- Liturgy of the Hours: In addition to the three Masses, there were gatherings throughout the day to keep the canonical Hours.

Pastorally, the first question is: What has worked in this local church in the past? Openness and humility are essential. However, so is the responsibility to move beyond the familiar when necessary. Liturgical leaders should be bold enough to offer, with patience and sensitivity, some treasures of the universal church's heritage.

EVENING PRAYER

When? Ideally before the (first) evening Mass. *Where?* In the main worship space, around the manger, near the Christmas tree, in a chapel, depending on numbers. *Who?* Everyone, including planners, presiders, ministers, musicians, decorators and staff. Here is a prayerful conclusion to all the frantic preparation, a peaceful way to usher in the solemnity and dispose heart, soul and senses to liturgical service.

Anyone may preside: ordained, religious, lay. Here is an order of service:

- Before prayer: Once all have gathered and spent a few moments in silent recollection, the presider stands and begins.

- Call to worship: Sung dialogue on light: V. Light and peace in Jesus Christ our Lord (or Christ our Light). R. Thanks be to God.

- Lucernarium: Candle lighting could include the lighting of the Christmas tree, or the tree could be blessed and lighted after the gospel canticle.

- Hymn: Prescribed is the anonymous sixth-century "Christe, redemptor omnium" (*Hymnal 1982,* #85). Another good choice is the lovely chant and text "Of the Father's love begotten," found in an increasing number of Catholic hymnals.

- Psalmody: 113, 147B; New Testament canticle: Philippians 2:6–11.

EARLY EVENING MASS

■ ORIENTATION: Who participates in this Mass? Their ages and numbers are important for determining everything from scripture selection to procession logistics. The hour may make this a Mass of convenience for many people. There are simple ways to enhance prayer and invite active participation.

■ WORSHIP SPACE: Let prayerful wonder and quiet anticipation reign as people arrive. Subdued light sets a good tone. Incense left over from Evening Prayer (or even from an informal incensing before anyone arrives) is an aromatic invitation to enter the mystery of this eve.

■ SCRIPTURE: Official norms permit use of the *Lectionary for Masses with Children* only with children apart from the main assembly. But on Christmas Eve, the children in the midst of the assembly are a living liturgical symbol. Luke's nativity gospel seems the most appropriate choice. Its power and beauty resound in any translation.

■ BLESSING THE MANGER: This is a beautiful ritual, particularly if the members of the assembly or at least the children process there with joyous song.

MASS IN THE NIGHT

■ ORIENTATION: Even if Midnight Mass is not practical, a community can make Christmas Eve special by scheduling an evening Mass that is truly "in the night." Depending on parish needs, this might end up replacing the early evening Mass, thus establishing a subtle link with the Easter Vigil.

■ WORSHIP SPACE: Soft candlelight, subdued artificial light, the scents of evergreens and incense — let these form the welcome. All is ready well before anyone arrives: no ministers busily preparing books or vessels, no unnecessary sound or movement to distract from the prayerful silence. Parishioners may be quietly greeting each other, but that is part of the gathering, the sacramental presence of one another.

■ BEGINNING WITH A VIGIL: Schedule a vigil of psalmody and silence, reading and prayer beginning no more than an hour before Mass begins. If it is made known to the assembly for a few weeks beforehand, many will come for the whole vigil. But let people know that they are free to arrive whenever they can.

The full Office of Readings (*Liturgy of the Hours*, vol. I, 399 and appendix I) is a challenge to most communities. The Ambrosian rite of Milan follows Easter or Pentecost Vigil model, incorporating Roman material but alternating reading, silence, song and collect. This order borrows from both.

- *Entrance procession:* Begin with the church in semi-darkness. The candles for the Advent wreath may be carried at the head of the procession, followed by the ministers, all carrying candles. The procession pauses a few times so that light can be passed to the assembly.

Choose a chant-like processional song that invites participation, perhaps with a refrain. "A child is born in Bethlehem," with its haunting Gregorian melody and quietly joyful refrain, is perfect, especially a cappella or with handbells.

When the procession arrives at the altar, many candles are lit there and throughout the church (pew candles, consecration candles on the walls).

- *Sung greeting:* V. Light and peace in Jesus Christ our Lord (or Christ our Light). R. Thanks be to God.
- *Hymn:* "Of the Father's love begotten" as at Vespers or another reflective piece.
- *Thanksgiving for light:* Sung by cantor, deacon or priest. As the community sings Amen, a few artificial lights may be turned on, but ideally the vigil continues by candlelight.
- *Welcome.*
- *Readings:* Several may be chosen from this list of traditional readings. Each is followed by a psalm or a carol, and a collect.
    I. Genesis 15:1–12, 17–18 (lectionary, #373); psalm or carol ("It came upon the midnight clear"); collect.
    II. Isaiah 7:10–14 (lectionary, #10); psalm or carol ("What child is this?", "Lo how a rose e'er blooming"); collect.
    III. Isaiah 11:1–10 (lectionary, #4); psalm or carol ("From heaven above," "God rest ye"); collect.
    IV. Micah 5:1–4 (lectionary, #12); psalm or carol ("O little town of Bethlehem," "Once in royal David's city"); collect.
    V. Christmas homily of Leo the Great (*Liturgy of the Hours*, vol. I, 404).
    VI. Proclamation of the Birth of Christ (traditional, page 48; revised, *Sacramentary Supplement*, 19) or: gospel of the genealogy (lectionary, #13, optional ending at v. 17).
    VII. The Gloria is sung by all; Mass continues as usual.

■ BEGINNING WITHOUT A VIGIL: Two forms are possible:

- *First form:* After preludes and congregational and choral singing, the church remains in subdued light. Following a brief silence, the Proclamation of the Birth of Christ is sung. The lights are raised, followed by the entrance procession and incensation of altar, followed by greeting, Gloria and opening prayer.
- *Second form* (suggested by *Sacramentary Supplement*): Begin with entrance procession, greeting, introduction and singing of the Proclamation. The Gloria and opening prayer follow.

■ ADDITIONAL NOTES FOR MASS:

- *Gospel:* A gospel procession with incense and candles, culminating in a chanted gospel, is a particularly effective way to proclaim the "good news of great joy" on Christmas. See *Chants for the Readings* (Joseph T. Kush, GIA, G-2114) and *Liturgical Music for the Priest and Deacon* (Columba Kelly, St. Meinrad's Archabbey, St. Meinrad IN).
- *Profession of faith:* Remember to genuflect.
- *Announcements:* Carefully chosen words of thanks to all who carried out the preparations for liturgy are appropriate. Avoid any suggestion that the laity helped the clergy conduct the liturgy! Thanks should be in the name of the entire assembly, gratefully acknowledging the assembly's participation as well.

EARLY MORNING MASS

■ ORIENTATION: *In Aurora:* even the Latin title for this Mass sounds like grace, beauty, peace and a quiet increase of light. Let these be characteristic of this liturgy. In many communities the early Mass is sparsely attended. Remember that the demographics — who attends — inform the style, tone and content of the homily, which therefore may be very different from that preached last night.

■ SCRIPTURE: Since this probably is the only Christmas Mass for many, the gospel from the night Mass may be added to the verses assigned to the dawn Mass.

■ MUSIC: It may not be possible to have musicians accompany this early Mass, but do try. Most assemblies will gladly join in an a cappella carol or two and the acclamations.

MASS DURING THE DAY

■ ORIENTATION: Let the Christmas morning liturgy ("the day Mass") stand on its own. It is not wise to import the unique elements of the Easter Vigil into the Easter morning Masses, and the same principle applies here. Do not import into Christmas morning those elements that make Christmas night special: the Proclamation of the Birth of Christ, for instance. Instead, plan enhancements that would not work with the quiet of the Vigil. Some parishes station a brass ensemble in the gathering area just inside the door to welcome people with festive music, and feature congregational carols before the liturgy begins. Additional instrumentation for these carols can also help to make the setting festive.

■ SCRIPTURE: Lectionary rubrics permit the interchangeable use of the four sets of Christmas readings. Proclaiming the prologue to the Gospel of John is a venerable tradition at the Mass during the day. It links us again to the light/darkness theme of the season. A solemn chanting of this prologue would give it the prominence called for by the tradition. The genuflection during the profession of faith will reinforce the importance of the community's conviction and joy that "the Word was made flesh and lived among us."

PRAYER DURING THE DAY

■ CHRISTMAS MIDDAY PRAYER: At the parish hall or at home, Midday Prayer is a good way to begin a festive Christmas dinner. Start with a Christmas carol. Use the parish's version of the Christmas responsorial psalm, "All the ends of the earth." Follow this with a scripture passage and the table blessing. The meal at the hall and Christmas dinner at home ideally gather neighbors, friends and homeless people who might otherwise dine alone or not at all on Christmas day.

■ TABLE PRAYER: The prayer in the *Book of Blessings* (#1038ff, 1048) might seem too much for the average household, but at the parish's festive dinner, this table blessing could be celebrated and even expanded with carols and a Christmas reading or two. At home, the form in *Catholic Household Blessings and Prayers* is beautiful and easy to celebrate.

■ AN OPEN DOOR: Leave the church open throughout the day, if possible, and announce this at Mass as an invitation to return. People may enjoy stopping in with their guests to show off their parish home and to spend a few moments in prayer before the manger.

CHRISTMAS VESPERS

Evening Prayer is the liturgical way to crown the celebration of Sunday or a solemn feastday. Late on Christmas afternoon, after the day's grand dinner is finished and the dishes done, many people like to step out for a breath of fresh air, and to prolong the holiday a little. The parish can offer an opportunity for communal prayer with Evening Prayer.

Use the pattern established for Advent Vespers or Sunday Vespers through the year, with some Christmas adaptation:

- Sing a well-known Christmas carol during an extended lucernarium in which all the church's candles are lighted.

- Use psalms the assembly can sing (*General Introduction of the Liturgy of the Hours,* #247). The appointed psalm is not one we would ordinarily choose for a festive day, Psalm 130, "De profundis" ("Out of the depths"); perhaps it was chosen for the line, "with the Lord there is mercy and fullness of redemption."

  The prescribed New Testament canticle is Colossians 1, the hymn to Christ that closes Christmas Day by linking the celebration again to the paschal mystery: "He is the first born from the dead."

- Scripture: 1 John 1:1–3, "What we have seen with our eyes, what we have looked upon, what our hands have touched — the word of life."

- Canticle of Mary, intercessions, Lord's Prayer and collect, blessing and dismissal.

DECEMBER

26 The Holy Family — FEAST
#17 (LMC, #14) white

■ ORIENTATION: Established as part of the Christmas season in 1921, this feast was linked to the octave of Christmas when Vatican II's reform of the calendar was published in 1969. The gospel passages chosen portray the holy family of Jesus, Mary and Joseph, as a model of unity and persevering love, despite the dangers and difficulties of their time and situation.

■ LECTIONARY: The new Year B lectionary offers a first reading that is a composite from Genesis: Genesis 15:1–6 and 21:1–3. The Canadian edition inserts 17:3b–5, 15–16 after the selection from Genesis 15 and adds 21:4–7 at the end of the official text. The theme is God's promise and its fulfillment. The Canadian addition gives Sarah equal prominence.

Because of their great faith, God wrought such miracles in the marriage of Abraham and Sarah that the only fitting response was holy laughter! The Hebrews passage continues the themes of promise made, promise fulfilled; faith tested, faith triumphant. Notice also the themes of witness and service, as this family became an instrument of blessing for all peoples and every generation.

The gospel passage for every year portrays the holy family as a very human family, too. Year B's gospel takes place at the temple. The focus is Simeon's prophecy about this child who will be "a sign of contradiction," and the mother, whose soul will be pierced. The longer form recapitulates the themes of the first two readings, trust in God's promises and faith proved through testing.

■ SACRAMENTARY: There is no specific Holy Family preface, but for an alternative text to the three Christmas prefaces provided, consult the *Collection of Masses of the Blessed Virgin Mary*, P-8, Our Lady of Nazareth. *Prayers for Sundays and Seasons, Year B* provides general intercessions and collects based on the readings.

■ BLESSING OF FAMILIES: For many families, life together or apart holds sorrow. This feast calls for sensitivity, since such wounds can be particularly painful in the holiday season. A blessing of families or renewal of marriage vows may not be appropriate today; it could unwittingly hurt more than help. On this feast in some parishes people bring devotional objects received as Christmas gifts to be blessed. Those who bring such gifts may gather at the manger where a priest or deacon can use the *Book of Blessings* (chapter 44, shorter form for use after Mass).

MON 27 John, apostle and evangelist — FEAST
#697 (LMC, #438 and 452–454) white

The first reading presents the incarnation as a tangible fact, a God we can get our hands on: The Word has been heard, seen, touched! The gospel connects Christmas and the Pasch through the story of the empty tomb. Exegetes rightly caution us about making connections too easily, but tradition identifies today's saint with "the beloved disciple" who "reposed upon Jesus' breast" at the Last Supper. John's feast, therefore, invites us to focus close to home and heart; to reflect on our love for those nearest to us.

In some Eastern European churches, this feast is also when enemies are reconciled, often over a glass of newly-blessed wine, this day also being the day for blessing wine in some ethnic groups. Keeping this custom, John Paul II went on this day to meet his would-be assassin face to face, hoping, the Pope said, "to know him as a man and as a brother."

TUE 28 The Holy Innocents, martyrs — FEAST
#698 (LMC, #439 and 456–459) red

The liturgy and the First Letter of John keep before our eyes the light-from-darkness motif of Christmastime. Nowhere does the struggle between light and darkness seem more intense than in the suffering of children, who for world-weary adults can be icons of holiness and innocence. This feast reminds us again that Christmas is not all "Silent night" and "Joy to the world." The Child is a sign of contradiction still, the one who reveals "the thoughts of many hearts."

WED 29 Fifth Day in the Octave of Christmas
#202 white

Thomas Becket, bishop, martyr, optional memorial/red. ■ The first reading reminds us that there can be no compromise

42 CHRISTMAS: DECEMBER

DECEMBER

with darkness, for where hatred reigns there is no love for our brothers and sisters and no light from the God who is love. In a movement from the gentle warmth of Bethlehem to the ominous atmosphere of Jerusalem, Luke has Simeon promise that Jesus will be "a sign of contradiction," revealing the inner thoughts of many hearts.

Today's saint, in the face of martyrdom (+ 1170), discerned that "the last temptation is the greatest treason: to do the right deed for the wrong reason" (T.S. Eliot, *Murder in the Cathedral*). Becket, who began as a worldly and ambitious politician, defied his old friend King Henry II in defense of the church's freedom to protect its own. As conflicts from Central America to Africa remind us, Becket was not the last bishop to lay down his life for his sheep.

THU 30 — #203 white — Sixth Day in the Christmas Octave

The First Letter of John challenges each age group in the community to embrace new life in Christ. Homilists may remind the assembly that "the world" in 1 John means a way of life unenlightened by the gospel, anchored in self-centeredness and sin. Contrast this to "the world" in the Gospel of John: "God so loved the world that he gave his only Son" (John 3:16). Luke likes to work in couplets and to present women who complement the men in his stories: Today's gospel completes yesterday's presentation story with the prophet Anna.

FRI 31 — #204 white — Seventh Day in the Octave of Christmas

Sylvester I, pope, optional memorial/white. ▪ The prologue of the Gospel of John reappears from the Christmas Mass during the day to mark this last day of the year. This text proclaims the life that will not die, that no darkness can extinguish God's light, that the baptized have been given a new life as God's own sons and daughters, and that in the Word made flesh we have been given the gift of God's enduring love.

Keep in mind that today is primarily a "day within the octave." If Pope Sylvester (+ 335) is commemorated, this takes place in the opening prayer and intercessions, and by linking today's gospel to the remembrance of Sylvester's defense of Christ's divinity against the Arian heresy.

NEW YEAR'S EVE

■ PARTIES AND PRAYER: "First night" inspires people in both directions! Parishes might consider welcoming the new year with a vigil that may culminate in the eucharist. The vigil may be scheduled to culminate at midnight, but some communities might prefer an earlier hour. Some parishes have found it popular to schedule their own "safe and sober" New Year's Eve party in conjunction with the vigil.

The *Liturgy of the Hours* has material for a vigil office of readings (vol. I, 479ff and appendix I). *Sourcebook*'s observations for Christmas Eve are pertinent here as well (see page 40); the focus is primarily on Mary's maternity. The Episcopal Church's *Book of Occasional Services* provides readings more oriented toward other themes of January 1: the sanctification of time and seeking the blessings of peace. The order of worship could be similar to the Christmas Eve vigil and may be adapted to conclude with the eucharist:

- *Entrance procession:* Church in semidarkness. Candle lighting during the continuation of the hymn that has accompanied the procession to the altar, or lucernarium after the greeting.
- *Sung dialogue:* V. Light and peace in Jesus Christ our Lord, Christ our Light (or Jesus Christ, the same yesterday, today and forever). R. Thanks be to God.
- *Hymn:* perhaps with references to Christ as Prince of Peace; the Te Deum for the Jubilee (or any musical version) might also be appropriate (see "Music" under the January 1 entry)
- *Thanksgiving for light.*
- *Readings:* Several may be chosen from this list:
    I. Exodus 23:9 – 16, 20 – 21; Psalm 111 or 119:1 – 8 or carol; collect.
    II. Deuteronomy 11:8 – 12, 26 – 28; Psalm 36:5 – 10 or 89, part I, or carol; collect.
    III. Ecclesiastes 3:1 – 15 or 12:1 – 8; Psalm 90 or 130 or carol; collect.
    IV. Ecclesiasticus (Sirach) 43:1 – 22; Psalm 19 or 148 or 74:11 – 22 or carol; collect.
- *If the eucharist is to follow,* Gloria, opening prayer and liturgy of the word from the lectionary as usual. The Te Deum might be sung after communion.
- *If the eucharist is not celebrated,* the vigil continues:
    V. 2 Corinthians 5:17 – 6:2; Psalm 63:1 – 8 or Canticle of Simeon; collect.
    VI. Hebrews 3:1 – 15 (or 3:1 — 4:13); Psalm 95; collect.
    VII. Revelation 21:1 – 14, 22 – 24; optional homily; Te Deum or Gloria; concluding prayer (Mass for Special Needs, #24).
- *Solemn blessing* #3.
- *Dismissal.*

January

S A T #18 (LMC, #15) white
Mary, Mother of God
Octave of Christmas
SOLEMNITY

ORIENTATION

On the first day of the new year, the Roman liturgy celebrates the octave day of Christmas by honoring the motherhood of Mary. Eastern Christians emphasize the Child's circumcision, and the churches of the Reformation celebrate the bestowal of the name of Jesus. In the 1960s Paul VI designated today as Day of Prayer for World Peace. For all of us, it is the beginning of the civil year and, this year it is also the first day of the first year of the new millennium!

It will take a judicious use of sacramentary and lectionary, thoughtful writing of intercessions, and careful choices of music to weave these several strands into the tapestry of today's celebration. In the U.S., January 1 is not a holy day of obligation this year, but many will want to consecrate the first hours of a new year and a new millennium with worship, prayer and praise. Perhaps only one Mass should be scheduled, late in the morning. Or if there was no Mass on New Year's Eve, or no eucharist with the vigil, some who stayed out late might appreciate Mass later on New Year's Day in the afternoon or early evening.

LECTIONARY

A symphony of scriptures is provided. Reading I: Words of peace and blessing. Reading II: Mary's motherhood, God's fatherhood, our adoption as free children of God in Christ. Gospel: A gentle link to the historical nativity, in which the continuity of the Jewish and Christian covenant is emphasized with the faithful obedience of Mary, Joseph and Jesus to the Law.

SACRAMENTARY

The collect for the votive Mass "Beginning of the Civil Year" (Various Needs and Occasions, #24) would be a good ending to intercessions that seek peace in the church, the world, our town, our homes, our hearts. The preface of Mary, Mother of the Savior (*Collection of Masses of the Blessed Virgin Mary*, P-5) keeps the focus on Christ through the scriptural imagery of the season. There is a solemn blessing for the New Year (#3).

MUSIC

Countless hymns and carols highlight the themes of the day: "What child is this?" "Of the Father's love begotten," "Hark! The herald angels sing," "At the name of Jesus," and "Sing of Mary." Consider also Dietrich Bonhoeffer's "By gracious powers." He wrote this New Year's poem for his mother when he was in prison, and it appears now in numerous hymnals (see GIA's *Worship*, #577). "For the healing of the nations" is another widely published hymn. The *New Century Hymnal* has "In the bulb there is a flower" (#433) and "I was there to hear your borning cry" (#351), both of which are appropriate for New Year's.

The Subcommittee on the Third Millennium of the U.S. conference of bishops recommends that parishes sing the Te Deum to bring in the new millennium. There are many versions, the best known being "Holy God, we praise thy name."

2 #20 (LMC, #16) white
The Epiphany of the Lord
SOLEMNITY

■ ORIENTATION: The Lord's incarnation as an "epiphany" or "theophany," the manifestation of God's presence, has been celebrated since the third century in the East and since the fourth century in the West. The Western church focuses on Christ's manifestation to the Magi, representatives of all the nations of the world. The Eastern church centers its commemoration on the Lord's baptism, the manifestation of Jesus as God's well-beloved Son. The official texts of both churches, mention both the Magi and the baptism, adding the wedding feast at Cana as well, when "his disciples believed in him."

MASS

- LECTIONARY: The second reading from Ephesians contains what was once the radical heart of the gospel: We Gentiles are now joined to the Jews as people of the covenant. The Western church reads the gospel of the Magi. To the gifts Isaiah foretold, gold and frankincense, Matthew adds the myrrh of burial. Hymns frequently use myrrh to link the glory of this feast to the suffering of the passion, and many include a reference to Herod's rage and fear at the Child he perceives as a threat to his throne. There is comfort in this gospel as well. The gospel portrays reason and revelation working together to lead to Christ, a journey that can be completed only by the gift of faith. Using their science, the Magi arrive in Jerusalem. There these Gentiles consult the Jewish revelation to determine the route to their goal, for reason alone cannot bring us finally to Christ. But the revealed word of itself seems insufficient as well, since the scribes who instruct the Magi do not make the journey. Could Matthew be telling his mixed community, and ours, that none of us has it all together, but that together we have it all?

- SACRAMENTARY: The *Ceremonial of Bishops* tells the bishop to "see to it that this solemnity is celebrated in a proper manner" (240), then provides an unusually detailed checklist. That list forms the basis for these suggestions, along with the reminder that "the invitations, comments and homily will explain the full meaning of this day with its 'three mysteries,' that is, the adoration of the child by the Magi, the baptism of Christ and the wedding at Cana."

- INTRODUCTORY RITES: "There will be a suitable and increased display of lights." Worshipers should arrive to a church building and worship space illuminated gloriously, proclaiming the splendor of Christ's manifestation. Whatever candlelight adorned Christmastime should also be present today: gathering area, altar, consecration candles, pew candles. The entrance procession could be a blaze of glory as well.

- LITURGY OF THE WORD: The gospel, accompanied by lights and incense, may be chanted to the old simple tone. "After the singing of the gospel reading, depending on local custom, one of the deacons . . . or someone else, vested in cope, will go to the lectern (ambo) and there announce to the people the movable feasts of the current year." See page 50.

- PRESENTATION OF GIFTS: "The custom of having a special presentation of gifts will be observed or renewed in accordance with local usage and tradition." The *Ceremonial*'s renewal of this custom raises many questions and suggests several possibilities. Who will come forward and with what? Children as well as adults should be involved. Gifts to assist those in need could stand for gold. Frankincense is used later to honor gifts, altar and assembly, and may be distributed afterward for Epiphany home blessings. What would pass for myrrh in this age? A gift for the homebound or the bereaved? Something associated with catechumens or penitents? Other gifts are possible: For instance, chalk that will later be used in home blessings, or parish calendars to be blessed before distribution.

But herein lies the ambiguity! Just after our presentation rite comes this prayer over the gifts: "Accept, O Lord, the gifts of your church, as we offer you today not gold, frankincense and myrrh but the very One who in these gifts is proclaimed, offered and received, Jesus Christ our Lord."

- EUCHARISTIC PRAYER: The Epiphany preface in the sacramentary is simple and direct. A text with more developed Epiphany themes is the preface entitled "Mary and the Epiphany of the Lord" (*Collection of Masses of the Blessed Virgin Mary*, P-6). There is a proper insert for Eucharistic Prayer I in the sacramentary, though Reconciliation II sounds custom-made for this solemnity: "Gather people of every race, language and way of life to share in the one eternal banquet with Jesus Christ our Lord."

- THE FAMILY HOME: *Catholic Household Blessings and Prayers* (page 126) provides a home blessing for Epiphany. The parish can provide simple materials to enhance the custom and make it a joy to celebrate. One custom is to trace crosses, the initials of the "kings" and the numerals of the year over the doorway with chalk: 20 + C + M + B + 00. Legend names the kings Caspar, Melchior and Balthazar. The initials were long ago reinterpreted by northern European Protestants who loved the custom but not the legend: CMB became *Christus mansionem benedicat*, "May Christ bless this house!"

JANUARY

EPIPHANY VESPERS

Epiphany Sunday night is a wonderful time to hold a parish Christmas choir concert. This could be preceded by Evening Prayer, featuring candlelight, incense and carols for everyone to sing (one last time!). The evening could conclude with a festive parish supper or open house. Some parishes take the opportunity at this gathering to show appreciation to all who worked to make Advent and Christmas a time of beautiful, glorious prayer.

MON 3 #212 white
Christmas Weekday

Throughout Christmastime, the First Letter of John forms the community in a faith life based on the incarnation. These are the sacred truths at the heart of Christian belief and identity: to believe in the name of Jesus Christ, who has come among us in flesh like ours, and to love one another. The gospels of the week present Christ, who heals, feeds, teaches and begins to gather around himself the community of the kingdom. Today's passage from the Gospel of Matthew shows the light of faith and the grace of healing coming to "Galilee of the Gentiles," and to all the world come the challenge to repentance and the proclamation of the kingdom's nearness.

TUE 4 #213 white
Elizabeth Ann Seton, married woman, religious founder, educator (+1821)
MEMORIAL

"Let us love one another" (first reading). ". . . and Jesus began to teach them many things" (gospel). In today's saint, the young United States saw God's love incarnated in the teaching ministry. This light shines among us still in Elizabeth Ann Seton's religious family and educational institutions. A glance at her titles in the calendar reminds us: She did it all! Our awe increases when we hear the litany of grief and suffering that formed the prayer of her life, suffering borne within her family and, sadly, in her dealings with some ecclesiastical authorities. Truly the saving ministry of Jesus described in today's gospel, was mirrored in Mother Seton's ministry.

■ SCHOOL LITURGY: Today's saint and tomorrow's were both educators, committed to quality education for all children. A Christmastime liturgy to welcome students back to school would be appropriate this week. Make sure the decorations are still up when the children return. A Christmastime celebration after vacation is far better than a Christmas Mass during Advent. Consult page 74 of LTP's *Preparing Liturgy for Children and Children for Liturgy* (originally published as the *Leader's Manual of the Hymnal for Catholic Students*) for helpful resources.

WED 5 #214 white
John Neumann, bishop, religious, missionary, educator (+1860)
MEMORIAL

The First Letter of John continues to call us to mutual love. Today it begins a line of reasoning that continues tomorrow: God, whom no one has ever seen, may be seen among us in our love. With New Year's resolutions still fresh in our minds, we know how long the path is between the real and the ideal! Today's gospel comforts us by showing that even the disciples who were Jesus' daily companions did not understand. To us, as to them, Jesus says, "Take heart, it is I; do not be afraid."

The Redemptorist John Neumann, bishop of Philadelphia from 1852 to 1860, was renowned for his love of the poor and his creation of a school system that would provide a first-class education for many who felt themselves to be second-class citizens. In the midst of the many practical tasks of building and organization that claimed his attention, Bishop Neumann appreciated the central role of the liturgy in the life of the local church. Among the personal effects on display at his shrine is the hand-written ordo he prepared annually for his diocese.

THU 6 #215 white
Christmas Weekday

Blessed André Bessette, religious, optional memorial/white. ▪ The Christian message is so clear: "Those who do not love a brother or sister whom they have seen cannot love the God they have not seen."

Holy Cross Brother André (+1937) was a humble servant of hospitality in Montreal. His compassionate prayer led to healing for many who came to him starving for physical or spiritual health.

FRI 7 #216 white
Christmas Weekday

Raymond of Penyafort, presbyter and religious, optional memorial/white. ▪ The Spirit, water and blood: Here is another subtle link to the Lord's passion. All three witnesses, says 1 John, agree: The eternal life God offers the human race comes to us through the flesh and blood person of Jesus Christ. And

JANUARY

this Jesus does not fear human touch — even the touch of those considered unclean or outside the Law. Jesus, who could have healed with a word alone, says "Be cleansed" to the leper only after he has touched the man.

Today's saint is easily seen in light of the readings. Raymond (+ 1275), a Dominican friar, learned Arabic and studied the Koran in order to communicate with Muslim leaders about Christian hostages.

SAT 8 #217 white
Christmas Weekday

This penultimate Mass of Christmastime summarizes the weeks just past and focuses our resolve on those just ahead. The scriptures affirm: "We know that we are God's children . . . and that the Son of God has come and has given us understanding" (1 John). Now let us join John the Baptist in proclaiming by the witness of our lives that "he must increase, but I must decrease" (gospel).

Some communities begin taking down the Christmas decorations today so that tomorrow's feast may signal a return to Ordinary Time. In preparation for tomorrow, do not set up a temporary font or special water display. Instead, make sure that the real font is suitably honored.

9 #21 (LMC, #17) white
The Baptism of the Lord
FEAST

■ ORIENTATION: The Feast of the Baptism of the Lord is also the First Sunday in Ordinary Time. The challenge is to blend a sense of Christmastime with images of the baptismal covenant, which we live out throughout Ordinary Time. Some parishes keep the Christmas decorations in place, and shift attention to the font by celebrating the rite of blessing and sprinkling there. Others begin modulating out of the Christmastime key by reducing the Christmas decorations and returning the church to its more usual appearance.

■ LECTIONARY: Part of today's gospel was proclaimed on the Second Sunday of Advent. It is as if having celebrated the mystery of the incarnation, we are ready to hear John the Baptist's challenge afresh in the light of our baptismal promises.

Thus the reading from Isaiah does not present an Old Testament foreshadowing of Jesus' baptism or ours, but relates the duties of one to whom God has said: "I will make with you an everlasting covenant . . . a witness to the peoples." We are commanded to eat what is good, incline our ear, come, listen, seek, call, return; and, in the second reading, to "love God and obey his commandments." Both readings remind us that the initiative is God's, as is the power to fulfill God's plan. The Isaiah reading ends by comparing God's word to rain: it will descend, accomplish its purpose, and then return to God and not be empty. The Johannine reading invokes the witness of "the Spirit, the water and the blood" as guarantee of God's victory in Jesus Christ. It is that victory in which we the baptized share.

■ SACRAMENTARY: Whether the setting of today's liturgy is simple or grand, some elements should make the transitional nature of this Sunday clear: The Christmastime Gloria and acclamation set should be sung one last time. Christmas carols may be wearing thin by now, but perhaps there could be one last hurrah for "Joy to the world" or another of the less Bethlehem-oriented carols. Musical options for this feast have increased as various Christian communities have taken it into their calendars. The Epiphany section of *Hymnal 1982* (Episcopal) and the *Lutheran Book of Worship* offer some fine selections. At least two hymns make explicit the traditional connection of Epiphany, baptism and Cana: "Songs of thankfulness and praise" and "All praise to you, O Lord."

The rite of the blessing and sprinkling of holy water should be used today, taking into account the cautions about making this feast echo Easter.

■ CONCLUDING CHRISTMASTIME: Celebrate Evening Prayer and follow it with one last round of carols. It might be a good idea to schedule an "undecorating party" as a festive conclusion to Christmastime.

PROCLAMATION OF THE BIRTH OF CHRIST

The twen-ty-fifth day of De-cem-ber. In the five thou-sand, one hun-dred and nine-ty-ninth year of the cre-a-tion of the world, from the time when God in the be-gin-ning cre-a-ted the heav-ens and the earth; the two thou-sand nine hun-dred and fif-ty-sev-enth year af-ter the flood; the two thou-sand and fif-teenth year from the birth of A-bra-ham; the one thou-sand five hun-dred and tenth year from Mo-ses and the go-ing forth of the peo-ple of Is-ra-el from E-gypt; the one thou-sand and thir-ty-sec-ond year from Da-vid's be-ing a-noint-ed king; in the six-ty-fifth week ac-cord-ing to the pro-phe-cy of Dan-iel; in the one hun-dred and nine-ty-fourth O-lym-pi-ad; the sev-en hun-dred and fif-ty-sec-ond year from the foun-da-tion of the cit-y of Rome; the for-ty-sec-ond year of the reign of Oc-tav-i-an

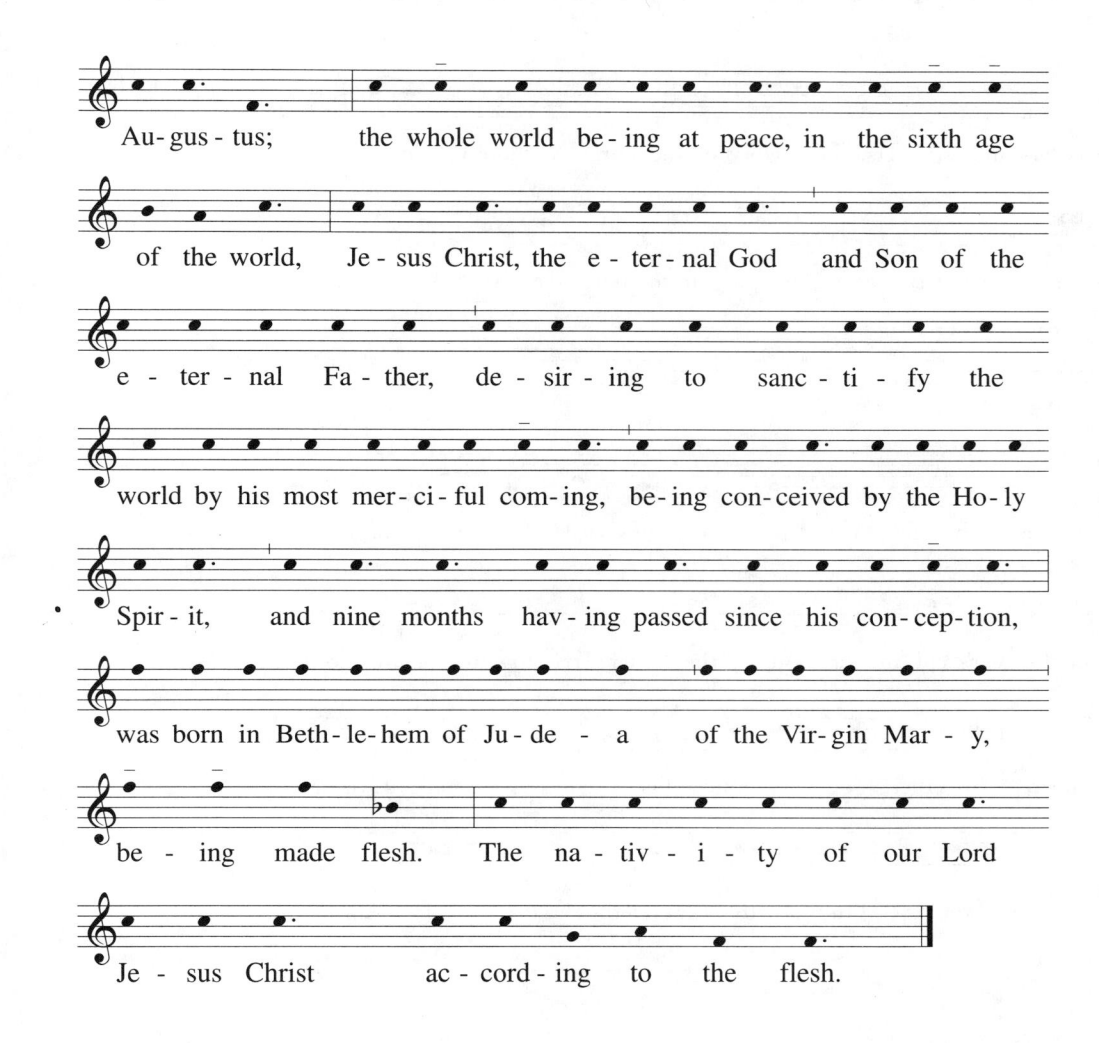

Au-gus-tus; the whole world be-ing at peace, in the sixth age of the world, Je-sus Christ, the e-ter-nal God and Son of the e-ter-nal Fa-ther, de-sir-ing to sanc-ti-fy the world by his most mer-ci-ful com-ing, be-ing con-ceived by the Ho-ly Spir-it, and nine months hav-ing passed since his con-cep-tion, was born in Beth-le-hem of Ju-de-a of the Vir-gin Mar-y, be-ing made flesh. The na-tiv-i-ty of our Lord Je-sus Christ ac-cord-ing to the flesh.

Suggestions for using the Christmas proclamation:

This is a traditional rendering of the Christmas proclamation, taken from the entry for December 25 in the ancient martyrology. It may be sung at the beginning of the Midnight Mass. It should be done without explanation, with great simplicity and reverence in the silence and darkness as the assembly keeps vigil.

Acolytes with lighted candles might accompany the cantor to the ambo or another appropriate place in front of the assembly. The cantor may indicate with a gesture that the assembly is to stand; when all are standing, the proclamation begins. The tradition calls for the assembly to kneel after the words "having passed since his conception . . ." and to rise before "The nativity of our Lord . . ." The cantor should stop at both times to allow this to take place. The acolytes and other ministers should know beforehand so that they can model for the assembly the kneeling and the rising.

When the proclamation is concluded, the entrance rites of Midnight Mass — which have truly begun with this chant — can continue with song.

Text was prepared by Rev. Richard Wojcik. Chant adapted from the original chant by Msgr. J. T. Kush. Music engraved by Marc Southard.

CHRISTMAS: PROCLAMATION OF THE BIRTH OF CHRIST

PROCLAMATION OF THE DATE OF EASTER

Dear brothers and sisters, the glory of the Lord has shone up-on us,

and shall ever be manifest among us, until the day of his return.

Through the rhythms of times and seasons

let us celebrate the mysteries of salvation.

Let us recall the year's culmination, the Easter Triduum of the Lord:

his last supper, his crucifixion, his burial, and his rising,

celebrated between the evening of the twentieth of April

and the evening of the twenty-second of April. Each Easter

as on each Sunday the Holy Church makes present the great and saving deed

by which Christ has for ever conquered sin and death.

From Easter are reckoned all the days we keep holy.

Ash Wednesday, the beginning of Lent, will occur on the eighth of March.

The As-cen-sion of the Lord will be commemorated on the first of June.

Pente - cost, the joyful conclusion of the sea - son of Easter,

will be celebrated on the eleventh of June.

And this year the First Sunday of Advent will be on the third of De-cem-ber.

Like - wise the pilgrim Church proclaims the passover of Christ

in the feasts of the holy Mother of God, in the feasts of the A-pos-tles and Saints,

and in the commemoration of the faith-ful de-part - ed. To Je-sus Christ,

who was, who is, and who is to come, Lord of time and history,

be endless praise, for ev - er and ev - er. A - men.

Alternate Amen

A - men.   A - men.   A - men.

This proclamation of the dates of Easter and other holy days is chanted by a cantor after the gospel reading or after the prayer after communion on the solemnity of the Epiphany. It may be sung from the ambo with lights and incense.

Proclamation of the Date of Easter on Epiphany copyright © 1994, United States Catholic Conference (USCC), 3211 Fourth Street NE, Washington DC 20017-1194. All rights reserved. Published with the approval of the Committee on the Liturgy, National Conference of Catholic Bishops. Music engraved by Emily McGary.

WINTER ORDINARY TIME

The Season
The Setting of Winter Ordinary Time / 55
A Sense of Winter Ordinary Time / 57
The Look of Winter Ordinary Time / 57
The Sounds of Winter Ordinary Time / 58
The Rhythm of Winter Ordinary Time / 58
The Word of God / 59
The Eucharist / 60
Other Celebrations / 61
At Home / 62
The Calendar
January 10 – March 7, 2000 / 64

The Setting of Winter Ordinary Time

"You know, this stretch of the year, at least in New England, reminds me of Pennsylvania!" The time was mid-January, and a colleague had just driven back to school in Boston after spending Christmas holidays and the semester break with his family in Kentucky. The remark brought silence to the coffee break and a puzzled response from the New Englanders present: "How in the world is January like Pennsylvania?" Our friend explained: "Not just January; but January, February, March. Winter around here is like driving the whole length of the Pennsylvania Turnpike. It doesn't seem to end! Like Pennsylvania, it just goes on and on and on — and it isn't even as pretty as Pennsylvania!"

That certainly clarified his meaning! Even those of us who had not navigated the entire breadth of the State of Pennsylvania could grasp exactly what our colleague meant.

After increasing cold from Thanksgiving on, and an advertising campaign that begins at least a month before that, Christmas arrives in a burst of colored lights and a round of festive gatherings. And there is snow. Not enough to shovel, mind you, but just enough to turn the green grass and gray asphalt into a romantic white landscape through which to travel to the magical beauty of midnight Mass.

But that is all over in the blink of an eye! The winter wonderland through which we traveled to the shining feasts of Christmastime melts into mounds of dirty snow and puddles of dirtier slush. And around the bend in that muddy road lurks Ash Wednesday followed by the Forty Days of Lent. Did anything ever seem as unending as this post-Christmas phase of winter?

Yet, wherever we may be and whatever the climate, we know that delightful changes are in store. Imperceptible to our eyes, the seeds from which the incomparable beauty of spring will burst into bloom are even now pulsing with life and preparing to germinate. A new semester begins with courses that offer students a fresh start. Some people are implementing New Year's resolutions, returning to diets after a holiday binge or starting exercise programs.

As with nature and society, so it is with the liturgy: Winter Ordinary Time is the setting for development that is secret but sure, growth that is unseen but steady. Thus, in Winter Ordinary Time, the lectionary begins a series of sequential readings from the evangelist of the year, in this Year B, from the Gospel of Mark and occasionally from John. Across the nine Sundays of Winter Ordinary Time, the most that can occur before Lent, the Year B lectionary presents a sampling of episodes and elements that characterize the Gospel according to Mark. With the crowds and those who come to him faith, Jesus responds by teaching, healing and forgiving. With the authorities, however, Jesus readily engages in confrontation and controversy.

Nature's hidden growth is mirrored in the quiet but important things that recur in many communities during Winter Ordinary Time.

- *Blessing of new liturgical ministers:* This could be celebrated on the Second and Third Sundays in Ordinary Time, when the lectionary pairs, on successive weeks, the vocation stories of Samuel and Jonah with the call of disciples in the Gospels of John and Mark.
- *Catholic Schools Week:* This celebrates the commitment of so many to the ministry of education, which in the communities of the inner city may also involve issues of justice.
- *The Week of Prayer for Christian Unity:* This ecumenical observance provides an opportunity for all who call upon Jesus as Lord to the visible unity of his church. This year an important opening event of the Great Jubilee will be the ecumenical prayer services taking place in Rome at both the beginning and end of this week of prayer.
- *Martin Luther King Jr.'s Birthday* and *Black History Month:* Christians join with all people of good will to reach beyond the sin of racism and the barriers of racial prejudice to celebrate a great man within the context of an inspiring history.
- *Roe vs. Wade.* The anniversary of the Supreme Court's decision legalizing abortion occurs during this time and offers an occasion for communal and individual bearing of witness on behalf of the sanctity of human life.

Further, Jubilee events in Rome during Winter Ordinary Time may inspire similar celebrations in the local community.

- *February 2: Feast of the Presentation:* A liturgy of light with the Candlemas procession will mark the jubilee of those consecrated to the service of God and the community in the religious life. Religious serving in the local community might be given the opportunity for public recommitment to their ministries and be honored with a parish celebration.
- *February 11: Memorial of Our Lady of Lourdes:* This day has been designated as a day on which the Anointing of the Sick will be celebrated at St. Peter's, with special recognition of the sick and of health-care workers. Parallel celebrations in parishes may be fitting.
- *February 18: Memorial of Blessed Fra Angelico:* A celebration of artists and of the arts is scheduled in Rome and may be an opportunity to honor the community's artists and to display their works.
- *February 20: Seventh Sunday in Ordinary Time:* As permanent deacons celebrate the Jubilee with the Pope in Rome, the local community may wish to celebrate the ministry and presence of its deacon(s).
- *February 27: Eighth Sunday in Ordinary Time:* On this day when Jesus proclaims in Mark's Gospel, "New wine — fresh wineskins!" a study convention will be held in Rome on the implementation of Vatican II. The long stretch of Winter Ordinary Time might be an excellent occasion to reflect on the documents and the spirit of Vatican II, the major formative event in the church's recent life.

Finally, an essential aspect of Winter Ordinary Time, especially in the final days of Winter Ordinary Time, is a shining sense of fun and feasting called *carnival*. Before we embrace the discipline of the Forty Days, before we embark with the catechumens on the path of discipleship to the waters of the font, we celebrate what our ancestors called *carnivale,* literally "farewell to the meat." Carnival celebrations have traditionally featured liberal amounts of the foods and beverages given up during Lent, and parades that evoke the great processions of salvation history, like the Exodus and Jesus' entrance into Jerusalem. Costumes in some places involved dressing up in a way that called to mind your most obvious sins and failings. Perhaps this bit of self-deprecating humor served as a preparation for the time of Lent when all masks must come off and the reality of our sinfulness confronted face to face. Winter Ordinary Time concludes, therefore, with *Mardi Gras,* literally "Fat" or "Greasy" Tuesday, also known as Shrove Tuesday, from the custom of confessing one's sins before Lent began.

Winter Ordinary Time, therefore, is neither bleak nor barren nor lacking in focus. It has its own special character and dynamism determined by the scriptures set forth in the ordered system called the lectionary; by the ministerial needs of parish life; and, this year, by the celebrations in Rome of the Great Jubilee.

A Sense of Winter Ordinary Time

WHAT is the shape of Sunday in our community? How do we prepare and gather for the eucharist? How often do we celebrate the eucharist, at what times, in what styles? How do we mark the sunsets of Saturday and Sunday, and greet the dawn of the Lord's Day? Getting a sense of Ordinary Time means recovering a sense of Sunday as the original kernel of liturgical time and of the liturgical year, Sunday simply as the Lord's Day.

In his Apostolic Letter, *Dies Domini* (The Day of the Lord), issued on Pentecost Sunday 1998, Pope John Paul II provides the whole church with an exploration of the multiple dimensions of this weekly celebration:

> The coming of the Third Millennium, which calls believers to reflect upon the course of history in the light of Christ, also invites them to rediscover with new intensity the meaning of Sunday: its "mystery," its celebration, its signficance for Christian and human life. (*Dies Domini*, 3)

The categories for reflection set forth by the Pope are indeed comprehensive. He examines the theological, historical, liturgical, pastoral and human dimensions of the Lord's Day observance. The perspectives from which he views these dimensions form a veritable litany of titles, each of them suggesting an important aspect for liturgists to reflect on, all of them together forming a rich resource for study and planning. Consider this outline of the Apostolic Letter:

- *Dies Domini: the Lord's Day.* The celebration of the Creator's work, "Shabbat": the Creator's joyful rest.
- *Dies Christi: the Day of Christ.* The day of the risen Lord and of the Gift of the Holy Spirit. The weekly Easter. The first day of the week. The day of the new creation. The eighth day: image of eternity.
- *Dies Ecclesiae: the Day of the Church.* The eucharistic assembly: the heart of Sunday. A pilgrim people. The day of hope. The table of the word. The table of Christ's body. Easter banquet and the gathering of sisters and brothers.
- *Dies Hominis: the Day of the Human Person.* Sunday: day of joy, rest and solidarity (by which the Pope means witnessing to social justice).
- *Dies Dierum: the Day of Days.* Sunday: the primordial feast, revealing the meaning of time.

This year's long stretch of Winter Ordinary Time provides a good opportunity for the community's liturgists to explore the multiple challenges of the Pope's Apostolic Letter, but not only his letter! Two other pastoral letters offer many practical suggestions for making Sunday the kernel of the liturgical year and the Sunday assembly the center of the community's week. Study Cardinal Joseph Bernardin's *Guide for the Assembly: Our Communion, Our Peace, Our Promise* (1984) and Cardinal Roger Mahony's *Guide for Sunday Mass: Gather Faithfully Together* (1997) in conjunction with the Pope's letter. All three are available from Liturgy Training Publications and together constitute a rich and challenging resource for recovering a sense of Sunday.

The Look of Winter Ordinary Time

IN the understandable exhaustion that follows the intensity of Christmastime, two extremes need to be avoided in the décor of Winter Ordinary Time. The first motif could be dubbed "Christmas leftovers," for its hallmarks are slowly dying poinsettias and rapidly shedding evergreens. The atmosphere points backward to the season just past, indicating non-verbally that not much is happening right now. The other motif could be called "lenten anticipation" and likewise misinterprets the "ordinary" of Ordinary Time. In this approach, the worship space is stripped of all decorations the moment Christmastime is over — just like the malls!

For an appropriate alternative, reflect on the winter plant life in your part of the world. Consult nature and the florist shops to see what kinds of things people are buying for their home decoration and celebration, and then incorporate these elements in simple, tasteful decorations for the setting of the eucharist. See Peter Mazar's many helpful suggestions in *To Crown the Year* (268 – 274).

The Sounds of Winter Ordinary Time

LITURGICAL *Music: Exploring the Genres* was the title recently suggested by a pastoral liturgist-musician for a workshop devoted to designing a core repertoire of music for parish liturgy. Categories and subcategories were organized according to a schema that, adapted for local circumstances, might recommend itself for reflection during Ordinary Time:

I. Service Music
  A. Eucharist
    1. Congregational Mass Settings: Advent (1); Christmastime (1); Lent (2: early Lent; Holy Week and Triduum, except Easter); Easter Vigil, Day and the Fifty Days (1); Ordinary Time (4: Winter, early Summer, late Summer, Autumn, November)
    2. Choral Mass Selections: enhancements for congregational settings; extra settings of the Gloria (4: Christmas, Easter, Solemnities, Latin)
    3. Antiphons, Refrains and Acclamations: alternatives to hymnody at the gathering rite and especially at the communion rite; proper or common texts for the responsorial psalm
  B. Sacramental Rites: antiphons and refrains
  C. Liturgy of the Hours: psalms and canticles; special antiphons; verses and responses; intercessory litanies

II. Hymnody
  A. Major Seasons, Solemnities and Feasts:
    1. Thematic: texts based on the varied motifs of season or day being celebrated
    2. Theological: texts based on the specific doctrine of the mystery being celebrated
  B. Ordinary Time: winter, summer, autumn, November:
    1. Lord's Day Hymnody: texts that celebrate various aspects of the rich symbolism and theology of Sunday; Easter hymns not overly specific to that solemnity but celebrating the paschal mystery (e.g. At the Lamb's High Feast; Alleluia! Sing to Jesus)
    2. Seasonal Hymnody
      a. Scripture-related: texts based on the themes of the lectionary readings assigned to the Sunday or block of Sundays being celebrated
      b. Nature-related: texts that celebrate aspects of the different seasons occurring world of nature
    3. Functional Hymnody: texts that refer to particular moments in the eucharistic celebration: gathering, presenting and preparing the gifts, communion or dismissal rites

Most newer hymnals and missalette guides feature multiple indices entitled topical, liturgical and scriptural. Many provide a church-year index that relates at least one hymn to the Sunday lectionary readings. In Winter Ordinary Time, such hymns might be drawn from selections listed under Christian Life, Ministry, Mission, Discipleship, Healing and Social Concern.

The Rhythm of Winter Ordinary Time

THE rhythm that pulsates through all the phases of Ordinary Time — winter, summer, autumn and November — measures the beat of several movements that play in harmony to form the great symphony of this major portion of every liturgical year.

Throughout the thirty or so weeks of Ordinary Time, several calendars govern our lives, the seasonal calendar of nature, the social calendar of the business, academic and civic worlds, and the scriptural calendar of the liturgy.

During Winter Ordinary Time, however, liturgy planners may wish to reflect on the several cycles that are in continual motion in our lives. Picture these cycles as circles, not concentric but intersecting. The reflective Christian life, whether of an individual or a community, is lived precisely at the point where these cycles intersect. Each cycle has what could be called a secular and a sacred dimension to it. Each cycle brings its own richness; a conscious, thoughtful participation in each cycle can be the key to a deeply experienced spiritual and human life.

■ THE ANNUAL CYCLE: In the major seasons of the liturgical year, the rhythm of the annual cycle is marked by a succession of celebrations rooted in the *life* of Christ, his incarnation and manifestation, his passion, death and resurrection. In Ordinary Time, the focus is on the *person* of Christ as presented by the predominant evangelist of that lectionary year; in Year B, Mark, with a supplementary selection from chapter 6 of the Gospel of John.

Each synoptic evangelist offers us a distinctive vision of Christ in a *narrative* whose inner dynamism is unique. From each narrative, the lectionary constructs a *supranarrative* by arranging passages semi-continuously during Ordinary Time and selectively for feast days. Lectionary Overview presents Year B's Markan supranarrative organized around Mark's three principal themes of cross, miracles and disciples. Consult the Sunday entries in the calendar sections for further reflections based on this overview.

The rhythm of Ordinary Time, determined by the lectionary, is thus uniquely Bible-based and offers the community a perfect opportunity to begin a systematic study of Mark. Refer to the Additional Resources at the end of Lectionary Overview for a bibliography of readily available commentaries on the Gospel of Mark.

Planners will want to be attentive to other elements of the annual cycle that recur during Ordinary Time, elements already mentioned in the Setting of Winter Ordinary Time: Martin Luther King Jr.'s Birthday, Roe vs. Wade anniversary, the Week of Prayer for Christian Unity, and the Jubilee Year events.

■ THE WEEKLY CYCLE: The secular weekend, especially in academic circles, now begins on Thursday evening, or certainly by early afternoon on Friday. Spiritually, our Hebrew ancestors had the rhythm of God's creation exactly right: "There was setting, there was dawning: one day" (Genesis 1:5, translated by Everett Fox, in *The Five Books of Moses*. New York: Schocken Books, 1995). The weekly observance of the Lord's Day begins with sundown on Saturday evening and concludes with sundown on Sunday evening. During Winter Ordinary Time examine how or if the community marks this beginning and ending, and consider instituting Evening Prayer on one or both of these evenings. The practice is specifically recommended by Pope John Paul in his Apostolic Letter on the Observance of Sunday (*Dies Domini*, 52). Friday, too, is part of the Christian weekly cycle, traditionally a day of special discipline in honor of Christ's death and of preparatory penitence for the Sunday eucharist, a kind "mini-Lent" before the weekly Easter. Is fasting or another discipline involving personal asceticism and community outreach part of life in our parish?

■ THE DAILY CYCLE: Secular society has its rituals for rising and beginning the day's work, ending it and returning home, taking nourishment and retiring for the evening. So, too, does the Christian community. Take advantage of this year's long stretch of Winter Ordinary Time to offer suggestions and resources to help the community and its members realize the spiritual potential of the daily cycle.

The Word of God

THIS year's late Easter makes Winter Ordinary Time as long as it can be and thus gives the community nine Sundays to become acquainted with the principal characteristics and motifs of the Year B lectionary.

THE SUNDAY SCRIPTURES

After the Feast of the Lord's Baptism, which is also the First Sunday in Ordinary Time, the Second Sunday in Ordinary Time leaves the synoptic gospel of the year to present a passage from the Gospel of John. The Second Sunday in Year B is a transitional Sunday, pointing both backward to the Lord's Baptism and forward to the rest of Ordinary Time. The selection from the Gospel of John is the testimony of John the Baptist concerning the identity of Christ. On the Feast of the Baptism, in Mark's account, the heavenly voice had identified Jesus as "my beloved Son." Now John the Baptist hails Jesus as the Lamb of God. This testimony is followed by the twofold response that should be the consequence of knowing who Jesus is: the disciples of John follow Jesus; then one of them, Andrew, hastens to share his discovery with someone else, his brother Simon, whom Jesus renames Cephas. Thus the Second Sunday leads us into the rest of Ordinary Time, for the gospel of the Third Sunday presents the Mark's very different account of the call of the disciples.

The sequential readings from the Gospel of Mark that begin on the Third Sunday of Ordinary Time continue for a full seven Sundays. Despite this considerable length of time, only the first two chapters of the Gospel of Mark are read, together with six verses of chapter 3. These first two chapters, brief as they are, suffice to demonstrate a number of the characteristics that make Mark's vision of Jesus, and that of the Year B lectionary, unique and challenging. For instance, on the Fourth Sunday in Ordinary Time we are told at the beginning and end of the gospel that the people are astounded for Jesus "teaches as one with authority." Yet Mark does not present that teaching in the form of extensive sermons, as Matthew does in Year A of the lectionary. Instead, Mark presents the *actions* of Jesus as living sermons in themselves. *Miracles of healing* attend the ministry of Jesus (Fourth, Fifth, Sixth, Seventh, Ninth Sundays). Jesus performs *exorcisms* (Fourth and Fifth Sundays) and engages in *controversy* with the religious leaders and their disciples (Seventh, Eighth and Ninth Sundays), for conflict with both these groups is characteristic of Mark's Jesus. Twice he commands *silence* (Fourth and Sixth Sundays). At the breathless pace characteristic of him, Mark leads us during the Sundays of Winter Ordinary Time through an experience of Jesus that is both filled with the comfort of healing and replete with the experience of conflict: conflict with evil, conflict with authority, conflict with tradition, conflict within ourselves!

THE WEEKDAY SCRIPTURES

The weekdays of Winter Ordinary Time are dedicated each year to a reading of the Gospel of Mark, chapters 1 through 12. Thus the weekday lectionary offers a reinforcement and enhancement of the Sunday experience of Mark. Not only do Weeks 1 and 2 provide an intensive review of the chapters of Mark covered in the first nine Sundays, but important passages omitted from the Sunday lectionary are proclaimed sequentially in the weekday gospels of Weeks 3 through 9.

In even-numbered years, the first readings on weekdays are from the Year II series. This year, the first readings of Weeks 1 through 5 present a broad sweep of Israel's history, with all of its beautiful and tragic stories. The series begins with Samuel's call in the Temple during his service to the old priest Eli, then God's choice and eventual rejection of Saul. David's anointing and victories are celebrated, and his sin and repentance are recalled. Solomon's wisdom is extolled, yet it cannot prevent the eventual disintegration of Israel and the apostasy of some of the people. Weeks 6 and 7 feature sequential readings from the practical and poetic advice of the Letter of James, while Weeks 8 and 9 set forth similar exhortations to holy living, rooted in reminders of the baptismal calling.

The Eucharist

WINTER Ordinary Time, especially in the lengthy period it spans in this Jubilee Year, offers planners and presiders an opportunity to reflect on and to refine the style of celebration that marks the community's Sunday eucharist. All who plan and preside might want to spend the first two weeks after Christmastime reading the trilogy of pastoral letters discussed in the Sense of Winter Ordinary Time section of this chapter.

After time alone with these documents, spend some time together, well before lenten preparations become too intense, to discuss how these letters confirm what the community is already doing and how they challenge the community to refine or even correct its practices. Many communities will discover that much or even most of what is being done is liturgically sound and pastorally effective, faithful to the vision enshrined in the church's documents and helpful in engaging the assembly in worship. Still, every community can do things better; though no community can or should try to fix everything all at once.

Winter Ordinary Time is an opportunity to focus on the transitional rites of the Sunday eucharist, the gathering moments, the presentation of the gifts and preparation of the altar, the concluding rites and sending forth of the assembly.

■ GATHERING TOGETHER. Rediscover—and use for nine Sundays in a row!—that most ancient and meaningful of Christian greetings: *Dominus vobiscum, the Lord be with you.* Let it be spoken from the heart and joined to the age-old gesture prescribed by the rubrics, the extending and joining of the hands that, when done thoughtfully and gracefully, expresses a reverent embrace of the entire assembly.

Consider the unofficial gathering rite that precedes that liturgy's formal entrance procession. In his letter, Cardinal Mahony notes that we usually think of liturgical preparation as involving the ministers. What about the assembly, the Cardinal asks. Have we communicated any sense of what needs to happen at home, before gathering, to bring our whole selves, body, mind and spirit, ready for the liturgy and hungry for word and eucharist?

How does the ministry of usher function in our community, with special attention to the very young, the seniors and those with special physical needs? Is greeting done in such a way that no one is host and no one is guest, but rather all are at home? The announcement of the opening hymn and any greeting by the cantor does not introduce the "cast" of the "show" ("Our lector this morning is . . . our eucharistic ministers are . . .). And there is a clear understanding that it is *Christ in one another* whom we stand to greet with song, *not,* "Let us stand now and greet our celebrant, Father . . . ."

No matter what the seating arrangements in the church, do all turn toward the aisle, as the procession passes? For that is to turn and face one another and greet the Christ in one another with festive song (see Cardinal Mahony, *Gather Faithfully Together,* 40 – 48; 63).

■ PREPARING THE TABLE. Rediscover the simple elegance of an altar on which we place the basic objects needed for worship with such careful reverence and such obvious purpose that no words need be said aloud. One plate with bread sufficient for this particular assembly's communion; one cup and a single flagon from which other cups will be filled at the breaking of the bread; the sacramentary with the presider's prayer texts. That is all, and that is enough.

Is the collection in our community truly almsgiving — gifts for the upkeep of the assembly's house of worship and gifts reflecting the community's sense that Mass opens into mission (John Paul II, *Dies Domini,* 45).

■ TAKING LEAVE. The ancient Latin words of dismissal, *Ite, missa est,* while defying easy translation, contain some sense of commissioning, of being sent forth to live what we have just celebrated. Resist the temptation to add a casual farewell. This is not a pitch for stuffiness but a reminder that we are about serious business here. Let the celebration end as it began: with simple, strong and ancient words of greeting, the gesture that embraces the assembly, a blessing that invokes the Name under which we have been reborn and that uses, in broad and graceful lines, the sign of the cross that shapes our lives. There may be an echo of the readings in the actual words of dismissal, but the formula must be concise and people's cue-line clear.

Our earlier question about the informal "gathering rite" before the entrance procession has a parallel in the procession out. The going forth from the eucharistic assembly is a wonderful time to exchange greetings, renew friendships and speak words of care, concern and encouragement. In referring to this "liturgy after the liturgy," Cardinal Mahony says, "I mean the true procession of this Church: one, two, and five at a time going back to the neighborhoods and homes, role and jobs, studies and waiting. But Sunday by Sunday the world is here being transformed in Christ!" (*Gather Faithfully Together,* 78)

Other Celebrations

LITURGY OF THE HOURS

THERE are different ways of introducing Morning and Evening Prayer, different opinions as to the best time of the liturgical year to do so, and a host of materials available to help make this ideal a reality.

Some find the limited commitment of four Sunday evenings in Advent a good way to begin. Add a Christmas or New Year's Eve vigil, especially to welcome in the new millennium and the Great Jubilee, and the custom is well on its way to becoming a tradition! If the Hours were celebrated for these special seasons and feasts, keep the momentum going in this period of Ordinary Time until Lent begins.

The simple form of weekday Morning or Evening Prayer during Ordinary Time may prove an easier way to introduce this form of prayer than coping with proper texts during the major seasons. One day a week or even daily, this is a good way to prepare an enthusiastic core group to lead a larger assembly in the celebration of the Hours during Lent. Morning Prayer might precede the usual starting time of morning Mass. Evening prayer could be scheduled in a similar way before parish meetings so that parishioners can celebrate prayer together before business. A solid resource is *Proclaim Praise;* a more complete sung version is *Morning and Evening: A Parish Celebration* (both from LTP).

When daily Mass is not celebrated on some weekdays, consider celebrating Morning or Evening Prayer rather than having a communion service. This could help the assembly learn a noneucharistic prayer form and deepen the community's sense of the eucharist's uniqueness.

PRAYER FOR CHRISTIAN UNITY

In his many homilies and addresses preparing for the Jubilee Year 2000, Pope John Paul II has often highlighted the responsibility of Catholics to join all Christians in working during the third millennium to overcome the divisions of the second. January 18 through 25 is the annual week of intercession for unity among Christians, as we pray "that all may be one . . . that the world may believe" (John 17:21). Resources in both English and Spanish are available from Week of Prayer, PO Box 300, Garrison NY 10524-0300 (914-424-3458) and the National Council of Churches, 475 Riverside Drive, Room 850, New York NY 10115 (212-870-2227). The "Order for Blessing of Ecumenical Groups" (*Book of Blessings,* #553) may be useful when joining other Christian communities for prayer during this week.

BLESSINGS

Two liturgical blessings related to particular feasts occur in Winter Ordinary Time: the blessing of candles on the Feast of the Presentation and of throats on the memorial of Saint Blase. The *Book of Blessings* provides an opportunity to revive customs that may have been neglected in recent years and offers an occasion to initiate new ways of blessing God and praying together. See the several forms for the blessing of families and of homes. Consider inviting people to stay after Mass to receive a special blessing if they will be celebrating a birthday during the week (#340) or going away for winter holidays or ski trips (#635). If the blessing of liturgical ministers occurs during this time of the year, when the gospels proclaim the inauguration of Christ's public ministry, be sure to look at the many resources provided in part VI of the *Book of Blessings.*

CIVIC OBSERVANCES

See the calendar entries of Monday, January 17, for the observance of Dr. Martin Luther King, Jr.'s birthday and of Saturday, January 22, for the anniversary of the Roe vs. Wade decision.

JUBILEE OBSERVANCES

Some dates of particular Jubilee celebrations have been noted above in the Setting of Ordinary Time. Parishes might wish to reflect these liturgies of the universal church being celebrated in Rome with their own celebrations on the local level.

At Home

SCRIPTURES AT HOME

Because the lectionary so shapes the church's prayer during Winter Ordinary Time, these nine weeks are a most opportune time to begin or revive parish Bible study and to encourage parishioners to read the scriptures for Sunday eucharist during the week before celebration. Some practical steps that can be taken:

- Print the biblical references of the weekday lectionary and of next Sunday's readings in the Sunday bulletin.
- Provide resources like LTP's *At Home with the Word* and its Spanish counterpart *Palabra de*

Dios, and similar resources such as *Share the Word* or *The Word Among Us.*
- Encourage the religious education ministry to sponsor a book table and assist them in providing affordable and accessible commentaries on the Gospel of Mark. Some titles listed in the Additional resources section of the Lectionary Overview may be suitable. Raymond E. Brown's *Christ in the Gospels of the Ordinary Sundays* (Liturgical Press, 1998), with essays on the entire three-year lectionary cycle, will prove serviceable year after year.

DOMESTIC PRAYER AND RITUAL

Consult *Catholic Household Blessings and Prayers* as a valuable resource for prayer that teaches us to sanctify all of life in a very natural way. Many formulas are modeled on Jewish blessing prayers and are easily learned by heart, to come easily from the heart. Awakening, opening the eyes, washing and dressing, prayer at table: Everything is here and all the seasons provided for, including the Week of Prayer for Christian Unity, Martin Luther King Day, Washington's Birthday, and Receiving Blessed Candles at Home (Candlemas Day).

A resource for teaching children to pray in this way is LTP's *Blessings and Prayers,* with wonderful illustrations by Judy Jarrett.

A beautiful introduction to prayer at the turnings of the day may be found in Melissa Musick Nussbaum's *I Will Lie Down This Night* and *I Will Arise This Day,* both from LTP.

CALENDAR

January

MON 10 — Weekday
#305 (LMC, #193–231) green

The first five weeks of Winter Ordinary Time feature an almost uninterrupted proclamation of God's power at work in Israel's history. For solid commentaries on 1 and 2 Samuel and 1 and 2 Kings, see the Reading Guide section of the *Catholic Study Bible* (New York: Oxford University Press, 1990). Today and tomorrow, the story of the childless Hannah and Elkanah provide a comforting witness to God's care for the lowly.

The gospel passages from now until Ash Wednesday are from Mark. These weeks are, in Jesus' words, "the time of fulfillment."

TUE 11 — Weekday
#306 (LMC, #193–231) green

Eli's harsh misinterpretation of Hannah's distress at the temple in Shiloh cautions us against judging quickly the troubled souls we sometimes encounter in the Lord's house.

Today's responsorial psalm, the canticle of Hannah, is the model for Luke's canticle of Mary (the Magnificat). Sing the responsorial psalm with the prescribed antiphon or another Magnificat antiphon the community may know from vespers, then sing Mary's canticle as a thanksgiving after communion.

Jesus reaches out in compassion to the afflicted man and in power against the ancient enemy of humankind. The healing stories in the gospels now through Friday and the call of Levi on Saturday suggest the use of the Eucharistic Prayer for Various Needs and Occasions IV, "Jesus, the Compassion of God."

WED 12 — Weekday
#307 (LMC, #193–231) green

"Speak, Lord, for your servant is listening!" Samuel's response to the God he does not yet know is a perennial model for believers. Unfortunately the lectionary omits God's answer, "See, I am about to do something in Israel that will make the both ears of anyone who hears of it tingle" (verse 11). In Mark's gospel God is indeed doing something new. Those who have been healed at Jesus' hand, like Simon's mother-in-law and like us, are "lifted up" so that we may "begin to serve" others.

THU 13 — Weekday
#308 (LMC, #193–231) green

Hilary, bishop and doctor of the church, optional memorial / white. • The First Book of Samuel moves swiftly from the end of Eli's house in today's reading, to the people's demand for a king in tomorrow's reading, to the anointing of Saul in Saturday's text.

In the healing of the leper, Jesus does not simply will and effect the cure — first he does the unthinkable and touches the man with leprosy. Is the charity of our community hands-on or arm's-length?

Hilary was noteworthy in his day (fourth century) for his firm and courteous defense of Christ's divinity. A married man, he was elected bishop of his native city.

FRI 14 — Weekday
#309 (LMC, #193–231) green

Samuel points out to the people exactly what a king is going to cost them. Like a wise parent dealing with demanding children, the Lord God gives the Israelites exactly what they ask for. If there is no worship on Saturday morning, lectionary norms permit the joining of tomorrow's first reading to today's so that the community hears the story of the anointing of Saul, which is important for understanding next week's narrative.

SAT 15 — Weekday
#310 (LMC, #193–231) green

Blessed Virgin Mary, optional memorial / white. • Both readings tell stories of vocation: Saul is anointed as Israel's ruler, and Levi instantly accepts Christ's invitation. The banquet with tax collectors and sinners foreshadows the guest list that Jesus will draw up for the feast of the kingdom and challenges our own restrictions on eating and drinking at the Lord's table.

In a tradition dating back to Charlemagne's time (ninth century), on the Saturdays of Ordinary Time the votive Mass of the Blessed Virgin Mary may be celebrated. The weekday lectionary is to be used. Every parish should have *Collection of Masses of the Blessed Virgin Mary,* Volume I: Sacramentary (Catholic Book and Liturgical Press). Mass #39, "Mary, Mother of Mercy" might be used today, for as Jesus' banquet with sinners reminds us, Jesus is dining with sinners still!

16 — Second Sunday in Ordinary Time
#65 (LMC, #60) green

LECTIONARY

Each year on the Second Sunday in Ordinary Time, the gospel reading is from the Gospel

64 WINTER ORDINARY TIME: JANUARY

JANUARY

of John. This selection alludes to the Lord's destiny and the hour of his passion, a subtle reminder that discipleship requires our own baptism into the death and resurrection of Jesus.

In this year's gospel, John the Baptist's announcement of Jesus' identity, "the Lamb of God," impels two of his disciples to leave the places and people familiar to them and follow Jesus. The question Jesus asks is the ancient question with which every baptismal rite has begun since long ago: "What do you seek?" In asking where Jesus is staying and in going to stay with him, the disciples are not just finding lodging! The Greek verb is more intense than our English "stay" and means "to abide with," "to remain with." Jesus will ask these same disciples at his final supper with them to "remain in me." One of the disciples hastens to the next task of those who discover Jesus: He seeks out someone else to share the good news with and brings that person to Jesus. The Isaiah passage presents another vocation story, that of Samuel in the service of the old priest Eli. The call is personal and insistent. Samuel's response is a perfect prayer with which to begin Ordinary Time: "Speak, Lord, for your servant is listening."

SACRAMENTARY

See LTP's *Prayers for Sundays and Seasons, Year B* for suggested intercessions, collects, introduction to the Lord's Prayer, invitation to communion, and words of dismissal.

Since the Johannine gospel complements the Markan passage of last week's feast, some texts from last Sunday's liturgy might be retained today. The Preface of the Baptism of the Lord (P-7) would go well with Eucharistic Prayer III, but so too would be the simplicity of Eucharistic Prayer II with its own preface's summary of Jesus' mission and gathering of disciples. The Preface of Christian Unity (P-76) is a beautiful text. Its use is appropriate in light of the Week of Prayer for Christian Unity and Martin Luther King, Jr.'s Birthday. Consider also Eucharistic Prayer for Reconciliation II.

THE WEEK AHEAD

Martin Luther King, Jr.

This weekend the United States observes the birthday of this prophetic preacher. Prepare by ordering materials for bulletin inserts and ecumenical prayer services (available in English, Spanish and Vietnamese) from the National Catholic Conference for Interracial Justice, 202-529-6480. The prayer in *Catholic Household Blessings and Prayers* (page 195) might conclude the general intercessions.

Liturgy Training Publications offers two resources for commemorating Dr. King: "Evening Prayer Commemorating the Birthday of Dr. Martin Luther King, Jr." and "Amazing Days: Martin Luther King's Birthday," a handout with prayers and commentaries that can be used as a bulletin insert.

The Week of Prayer for Christian Unity

From January 18 to 25, daily intercessions at Mass and the hours should include prayer for unity. Gatherings in Unity Week that include children from school or religious education can rely on LTP's *Preparing Liturgy for Children and Children for Liturgy* for prayer service ideas (page 77). The formularies for Christian Unity are in the Various Needs section of the sacramentary, #13. One thematic variation of the new Eucharistic Prayer for Various Needs and Occasions is titled "The Church on the Way to Unity" and would be appropriate this week.

Anniversary of Roe vs. Wade

See notes for Saturday, January 22.

MON 17 #311 (LMC, #193–231) green
Anthony, abbot
MEMORIAL

U.S.: Birthday of Martin Luther King, Jr., civil observance. • How appropriate to the day's commemorations are the weekday lectionary readings! In the first reading Samuel confronts Saul with his failure to obey God's command. Saul answers with rationalizations for his reinterpretation of God's clear instructions! Such convoluted "justifications" for racial discrimination abounded in the days when Martin Luther King Jr. began his ministry. Nor have they been completely silenced yet! Wherever there is a prophet in our midst, those who prefer to avoid harsh truths will find an excuse to dismiss the messenger.

Today is also the memorial of Anthony of the Desert, who took the gospel we hear at Sunday liturgy, "Sell what you have, give to the poor, and come, follow me!" as a personal invitation. His response was radical. The sacramentary texts for the memorial of Saint Anthony are to be used today.

WINTER ORDINARY TIME: JANUARY

JANUARY

TUE 18 #312 (LMC, #193–231) green
Weekday

Beginning of Week of Prayer for Unity. ▪ God sends Samuel off immediately to anoint one of Jesse's sons. There is, at first glance, an interesting contradiction in the reading. God tells Samuel, "Do not judge by his appearance or height." Then we hear of the young man's appearance in detail: "He was ruddy, and had beautiful eyes, and was handsome." But scholars say there is in fact no contradiction. A mere child, and a beautiful one at that, is exactly what you would not be looking for when choosing a leader to terrify the nation's enemies. Terror was certainly no part of Jesus' agenda. He depicted himself as a good shepherd, and in today's gospel, as Lord of the Sabbath he makes love of God and neighbor the heart of the law.

Remember to incorporate prayers for Christian unity into today's celebration.

WED 19 #313 (LMC, #193–231) green
Weekday

The battle between David and Goliath has been the subject of hundreds of paintings and sculptures, and in the poetry of Christian sermons it is a preview of Christ's victory over evil. One orator even saw in the five smooth stones a foreshadowing of Christ's victorious wounds! The point of the story is a truth Israel always had to rediscover, a message Christians have forgotten over and over: size and strength, strategy and wealth, as this world measures such things, mean nothing to God. Meanwhile, verse 5 of the gospel passage focuses on the heart as it records Jesus' emotions: "Jesus looked around at them with anger; he was grieved at their hardness of heart."

THU 20 #314 (LMC, #193–231) green
Weekday

Fabian, pope and martyr; Sebastian, martyr; optional memorials / red. ▪ Jealousy and friendship: painful contrasts then and now. Saul and Jonathan embody emotions with which we can all identify. Like many charismatic leaders, David inspires both reactions, and God uses all the contradictory stuff of human relationships to advance the course of salvation history.

Of one of today's saints, Sebastian, nothing is known for certain, though the legend endures that he was a Roman soldier who converted his allegiance to the Prince of Peace and suffered death because of it. Thanks to Eusebius, the historian of the early church, we know that Fabian was elected pope even though he was "a married man and a stranger."

FRI 21 #315 (LMC, #193–231) green
Agnes, virgin and martyr
MEMORIAL

David's righteousness and reverence move even the jealous Saul to tears. All of us, from time to time, find that we are not at peace with those around us. Our culture finds it difficult to honor people whose ideas we cannot understand. An example is today's saint, Agnes, whose pledge of virginity in commitment to Christ so infuriated the worldly powers of her time that they inflicted the cruelest of tortures upon a girl barely past childhood. Respect and kindness for a person with whose ideas we disagree would go a long way toward bringing peace not only to our own hearts but to our world. In the same way, the gospel account of the call of the apostles — people so different from one another yet formed by Christ into the core of his new people — can help us celebrate Augustine's formula for church unity: "In essentials, unity; in non-essentials, diversity; in all things charity."

SAT 22 #316 (LMC, #193–231) green
Weekday

Vincent, deacon and martyr, optional memorial / red; Blessed Virgin Mary, optional memorial / white. ▪ In the hearts of the great there is no room for hatred, not even of one's enemies. Nor does the child of God delight in the misfortunes of others. David is impressive: honest enough to sing of the good Saul did for Israel and unashamed to proclaim how dear Jonathan's friendship was to him. If we shared such attitudes, surely some would think us crazy. But we would be in good company! The brief gospel passage is always jarring, for our picture of Jesus' relatives is colored by the loving image of Mary, as she is portrayed in the gospels of Luke and John. But Mark is setting the stage for next Tuesday's gospel, when "his mother and brothers" appear. In the kingdom Jesus proclaims, "family" has a new meaning, and the good news is that Jesus' new definition can include us!

Parishes with a deacon may choose to keep the memorial of today's martyr, the fourth-century deacon Vincent, first martyr of the church in Spain. If the Saturday memorial of Mary is celebrated, consider choosing from the *Collection of Masses of the Blessed Virgin Mary* formulary #14 from the lenten section, "Mary, the Mother of Reconciliation."

JANUARY

Anniversary of Roe vs. Wade

The anniversary of the Supreme Court decision gathers crowds, pro and con, in Washington and around the nation. Such public witness by those who uphold the right to life at all its stages and in all related issues is a matter of Christian commitment. So, too, is reflection on this issue at the eucharist but, according to the mind of the church, in a way that does not take over the Mass. Let today's first reading and responsorial psalm challenge us to reflect on how our Israelite ancestors viewed victory and defeat, glory and shame. Let the unusual gospel selection provide food for thought on the cost of bearing witness to any truth in any age. Include in the intercessions those who are endangered by disregard for the holiness of life, and those who work to protect life. Let today's observance challenge all of us to adopt a respect for life that embraces all life issues and all life's victims.

23 Third Sunday in Ordinary Time
#68 (LMC, #63) green

LECTIONARY

Year B's sequential readings from Mark begin with Jesus' "proclamation of the gospel of God." What is this good news? God's time has come; God's kingdom is at hand. The phrase "at hand" is ambiguous: It can mean either *here* or *near* — or both. The gospel, remember, is proclaimed to a community that lives between the "already" of God's decisive inbreaking through Christ's historical coming and the "not yet" of history's fulfillment in Christ's glorious return. Jesus calls his listeners to action: "Repent, and believe in the gospel." We will hear them again; they are the primary formula for the imposition of ashes in the Vatican II sacramentary. Mark sets forth the call to continual conversion that should characterize the disciple's daily life. In contrast to Matthew's gospel, with its great blocks of verbal teaching, Mark's gospel teaches less in words and more in action. Thus, immediately after Jesus' proclamation, Mark translates Jesus' message into action: Simon and Andrew abandon their livelihood and follow Jesus; James and John abandon their livelihood and family and follow Jesus. Clearly, Jesus speaks with authority.

SACRAMENTARY

Because this week's scriptures continue the themes of call and response that were part of the Feast of the Lord's Baptism and of last Sunday's vocation story, the textual elements of the liturgy could remain the same this week. The invocations of the penitential rite, for instance, the preface and eucharistic prayer, introduction to the Lord's Prayer and invitation to communion might all be repeated. The observance of the Week of Prayer for Christian Unity and the possibility of blessing liturgical ministries might make the Preface for Christian Unity (P-76) a good choice.

THE WEEK AHEAD

On Tuesday and Wednesday the sequential readings from 2 Samuel are interrupted by proper readings from the sanctoral lectionary. See the calendar entries for a realignment as permitted by the *Introduction to the Lectionary for Mass*, 82. An important goal of the weekday lectionary is to present the biblical books in a way that respects their integrity and preserves their narrative continuity. The Saturday passage is also an important part of 2 Samuel, and the calendar entry for Friday suggests a way to make sure it is heard if there is no morning worship on Saturday. On Tuesday even the gospel passage is superseded, but this does not seriously fracture the continuity of the Markan narrative.

Catholic Schools Week

This week, which includes the memorials of Angela Merici and Thomas Aquinas, is usually designated as Catholic Schools Week. The National Catholic Education Association provides preaching and worship suggestions for use this Sunday, January 23, and a prayer service for next Sunday, January 31. Care should be taken to respect the integrity of the Sunday if either is chosen as the day to celebrate the school in the local community. Religious education programs should also be celebrated: These programs are the school of Christian living for many young people.

Liturgical Ministries

Call, service and ministry are themes that typically appear in the readings of this section of Ordinary Time as a new synoptic gospel is begun each year.

JANUARY

Thus, these weeks become for many parishes a time to reflect on the formation and ongoing education of liturgical ministers, and maybe to make plans for blessing them as well. The *Book of Blessings* (chapters 61 and 62) provides orders for blessing readers, servers, sacristans, musicians and ushers. The word *commissioning* is used only in chapter 63 (Order for Commissioning Extraordinary Ministers of Holy Communion). Planners who wish to bless all the liturgical ministers at one liturgy can add sections from chapters 61 and 63 of the *Book of Blessings* to the more inclusive chapter 62.

MON 24 — #317 (LMC, #193–231) white
Francis de Sales, bishop, religious founder, doctor of the church
MEMORIAL

The third week of the Ordinary Time lectionary opens with Israel's recognition of David as King and with King David's ascent to Mount Zion. The anointing in today's reading ritualizes the nation's acceptance of David as King. Tomorrow's first reading would recount the carrying of the ark to Zion and its reverent placement in the tent David had prepared there. This ritual act complemented King David's accession and signified God's abiding presence with him and the people. But tomorrow's first reading in the weekday lectionary is superseded by the readings proper for the Feast of the Conversion of Paul. Take advantage of the lectionary rubrics that foresee this possibility and join together the two days' readings to present the assembly with the complete episode (*Introduction to the Lectionary for Mass*, 82).

As bishop of Geneva, the city of Calvin's reform, Francis was renowned for serving his neighbors with gentle love (opening prayer) and for his courtesy in his dealings with the Protestant Christians of that city. His teaching, unlike the polemics of both sides in those days, was respectful and persuasive, anticipating the ecumenical approach of Vatican II.

TUE 25 — #519 (LMC, #247) white
The Conversion of Paul, apostle
FEAST

End of Week of Prayer for Unity. • During his historic visit to Cuba on this day in 1998, Pope John Paul II noted the irony of celebrating the liturgy in the Plaza of the Revolution. "From Saul to Saint Paul," the Pope remarked, "Ah, now *that* is a real revolution!"

Paul's conversion is the subject of both forms of the first reading, and the gospel proclaims the apostolic ministry that became his. Paul's conversion experience is a powerful reminder that we who are Christ's disciples are the Body of Christ. Paul learned this truth from Jesus: "Saul, Saul, why do you persecute me?" In the second form of the first reading, Ananias suggests that God might think twice about this fiery young Pharisee. But God explains and Ananias obeys. And what does Ananias call the murderous persecutor? "Brother!"

The general intercessions should include prayers for Christian unity and for all those on conversion journeys, not only the catechumens, but those who have been away from the community and may be making the journey home. Although one of the prefaces of the apostles is prescribed for today, neither one mentions Paul specifically. The Eucharistic Prayer for Masses of Reconciliation II, in the preface and the body of the text, speaks of change and mercy, of God's hand extended to sinners and of God's love, which not only brings us back to God but helps us "find our way to one another."

WED 26 — #319 (LMC, #193–231) white
Timothy and Titus, bishops
MEMORIAL

Timothy and Titus had Paul as mentor in the faith; with him they participated in the Council of Jerusalem, and from him, tradition says, they received the pastoral epistles that bear their names. Interrupting the sequential readings from 2 Samuel, the lectionary provides a choice of first readings from the letters addressed to the saints, each describing the ordering of the community through the laying on of hands and the appointment of elders. The gospel, taken from the weekday lectionary, is fitting for the memorial of two missionaries and founders of churches. Jesus tells the parable of the sower and gives his own homily explaining its meaning.

THU 27 — #320 (LMC, #193–231) green
Weekday

Angela Merici, virgin, educator, religious founder, optional memorial/white. • The prayer of King David needs to be proclaimed with the same reverence and awe as a eucharistic prayer. Indeed, there are similarities in its structure of praise, consecration, remembrance, intercession and eschatological hope. Yesterday's memorial superseded the part of the story just before David's prayer. It would make for a long first reading, but it might be advisable to combine yesterday's first reading with today's.

JANUARY

Alternatively, the presider might summarize yesterday's reading before the lector begins today's passage. Note that yesterday's reading in the United States' edition of the lectionary begins abruptly with the Lord's word to Nathan. The Canadian lectionary begins at verse 1 to put God's message in the context of David's proposition.

Angela Merici, whom we may commemorate today, is a patron of teachers. She was convinced that "disorder in society is a result of disorder in the family." How contemporary that sounds! Her solutions included a creative way for women to exercise a ministry in the church as a secular institute (today's Ursuline community) and education for girls, who were then usually excluded from that possibility.

FRI 28 — Thomas Aquinas, presbyter, religious, doctor of the church — MEMORIAL
#321 (LMC, #193–231) green

David's sin with Bathsheba and his treacherous set-up of Uriah form one of the more shocking stories in the Bible. The daily news testifies to the decadence the human heart is capable of, and the responsorial psalm reminds us that the problem begins in me! We wonder, with Wednesday's gospel, why can't we be good soil all the time? Why isn't there more good soil and more abundant fruit everywhere in the world — or even in my own life? Today's gospel is the comforting response. The seed grows and the harvest comes, we know not how, nor do we even perceive it. This is because the Farmer knows his business very well! Although it would make for a long first reading, tomorrow's first reading might be joined to today's in parishes where there is no Saturday morning worship. Alternatively, the homilist may wish to tell the rest of the story, Nathan's confrontation and David's response.

The work of today's saint is officially honored now, but in his own day, Thomas Aquinas was no stranger to opposition. His contribution was indeed original, as he harnessed the newest philosophical insights of his day to the service of the faith. Thomas was not only wrote formal theological expositions of enduring value but also set forth his faith in moving poetry. Any modern hymnal carries his name and contributions.

SAT 29 — Weekday
#322 (LMC, #193–231) green

Blessed Virgin Mary, optional memorial/white. • "You are the man!" Nathan confronts David with the truth of his sin and its consequences. The lesson is about accepting responsibility for our actions. It is also a lesson about trust in God's steadfast love and infinite mercy. As the gospel reminds us, whenever God draws near to us in Christ, his greeting is always "Peace" or "Do not be afraid." The one who stills the storm challenges us to have faith in the peace of his abiding presence.

If the Saturday memorial of the Virgin Mary is celebrated, today's readings are echoed in several formularies from the *Collection of Masses of the Blessed Virgin Mary*. Mass #35, Mary, Pillar of Faith celebrates Mary's faith that becomes our own by God's grace and through Mary's intercession. Mass #37, Mary, Mother of Divine Hope presents Mary as an example of hope, the virtue that accompanies faith.

30 — Fourth Sunday in Ordinary Time
#71 (LMC, #66) green

LECTIONARY

Moses, in the first reading, promises the people "a prophet like me." The Hebrew Bible shows us what a tall order that is! Moses' authority is bestowed directly by the God who calls him by name. Moses is God's chosen instrument, and through him God freed the people of Israel from slavery. He is the teacher through whom the Torah is given. He is the miracle worker who confirms Israel's strength and confounds Israel's enemies. Centuries later, in the person of Jesus, such a prophet comes into the synagogue at Capernaum. Although it is a Sabbath, Jesus begins the work of the kingdom, teaching, healing and redeeming. Note the response of the people in the synagogue at Capernaum. Mark records Jesus' command to the demon, upon which the crowd exclaims: "A new teaching with authority." But they also question: "What is this?" In the first verse of his gospel, Mark had identified Jesus as "the Son of God." But on this first Sunday of Jesus' ministry, the challenge for each of us is to determine, "Who is this — *for me?*"

SACRAMENTARY

From now until Lent, with the exception of the Eighth Sunday in Ordinary Time, the gospel selections from Mark present Jesus as the teacher who confronts and heals every kind of physical and spiritual illness.

JANUARY

Although this can be seen in Mark's portrait of Jesus all through the liturgical year, it is especially prominent in this block of Sundays. Texts for the penitential rite and general intercessions, and for introductions and invitations might reinforce Mark's portrayal. Prepare texts that reflect the titles Mark gives Jesus and the deeds Mark shows Jesus doing. Stay with these choices so that the words become a steady part of the assembly's weekly prayer. For example:

> Lord Jesus, you are the Prophet raised up by God, and you teach with power and authority: Lord, have mercy.
>
> Christ Jesus, you are the Holy One of God, and your touch brings healing and forgiveness: Christ, have mercy.
>
> Lord Jesus, you are the Lord of the Sabbath, and you feed us with bread of finest wheat: Lord, have mercy.

Or:

> Lord Jesus, you teach with authority and rescue us from the grip of evil: Lord, have mercy.
>
> Christ Jesus, you touch us with healing and lift us up for the service of others: Christ, have mercy.
>
> Lord Jesus, you forgive our sins and feed us with the bread of life and the new wine of your kingdom: Lord, have mercy.

Choose one eucharistic prayer and stay with it for this whole block of Sundays. Eucharistic Prayer IV, in the long section of praise that follows the Holy, holy, celebrates the redemptive mission of Jesus. The Eucharistic Prayer for Masses of Reconciliation II likewise speaks of the forgiveness of sins and the healing of division. Each should be used with its respective preface.

THE WEEK AHEAD

The readings for Wednesday's feast supersede the weekday lectionary's choices, but this does not seriously damage its continuity. The *Introduction to the Lectionary for Mass,* 82, permits the rearrangement of the weekday readings. See LTP's *Prayers for Sundays and Seasons, Year B* for further suggestions. Conclude the eucharist on these Sundays with Solemn Blessings for Ordinary Time III or V.

Preparing for Candlemas

The Sunday assembly should be reminded of Wednesday's feast and invited to bring candles for blessing, candles to be carried in procession and candles to be used with prayer in the home. The feastday liturgy, with its candlelight procession, requires darkness. This, as well as the convenience of the majority of parishioners who are at work or school during the day, suggests that this Mass be celebrated in the evening. If Mass must be celebrated in the morning, vespers could be celebrated in the evening with the candle blessing and procession attached to the beginning of the service as an extended lucernarium. See LTP's *Preparing Children for Liturgy and Liturgy for Children* (page 78) for practical ideas for preparing students at school or religious education to take part in the blessing of candles. In many communities, the blessing of throats takes place on the memorial of Saint Blase, February 3.

Black History Month

Communities that wish to mark Black History Month in the liturgy may do so with homilies, intercessions and the rich heritage of spiritual music (see especially GIA's hymnal *Lead Me, Guide Me*). Like many observances, this one expresses genuine human dreams and sentiments, but the timing is difficult to mesh with the liturgy. Days of saints especially revered in black Catholic communities, Peter Claver (September 9) or Martin de Porres (November 3), for example, might be alternative days for parishes to reflect on the histories of black Americans.

#323 (LMC, #193–231) white

MON 31 John Bosco, presbyter, educator, religious founder
MEMORIAL

Perhaps after being confronted by Nathan's accusations (Saturday, Third Week in Ordinary Time), David was ready to try to discern God's purpose in the criticism — or as in this case, the cursing — of others. Today's long and slightly strange healing story is of a piece with the two healings in tomorrow's gospel. The homilist may note that all three would have jolted the sensibilities of Mark's first audience because of the common thread: ritual impurity. The possessed man living among tombs and near a herd of swine, the woman with the flow of blood, and the dead child were all "untouchables." Yet Jesus places compassion above ritual observance and, in some way, touches all three with his healing power. Both texts thus challenge believers to consider those who seem outside the faith not as outsiders but as brothers and sisters called to eventual inclusion with us in God's plan.

"Give me souls!" was the motto of today's saint, but "Don Bosco" did not stop at serving the spiritual needs of his flock. To Turin's street children, the

FEBRUARY

founder of the Salesian community brought a parent's love and concern for their future. Asked by Pius IX to write out in detail the secret of his success, John Bosco sent the pope a single sheet of paper bearing the Lord's Prayer.

February

TUE 1 #324 (LMC, #193–231) green
Weekday

The treachery of Absalom is matched by the grief of his father David. Certainly among the daily worshipers there are parents who know the heartache of broken relationships with their children. A sensitive word about parental love, unconditional though sometimes painful, may be appreciated, as well as a petition in the general intercessions for the healing of such situations.

WED 2 #524 (LMC, #252) white
Presentation of the Lord
FEAST

ORIENTATION

Today's feast was celebrated as early as 386 in Jerusalem. It soon evolved into a torchlight procession, a vigil of expectation for the Lord who comes to meet his people with the light of salvation. The feast is still known throughout the Eastern church as "The Encounter," the cosmic encounter symbolized by the meeting of Jesus with Simeon and Anna in the Temple. By the seventh century, the feast had come to Rome, where its observance also involved a candlelight procession, although this seems to have been penitential, possibly a reflection of its replacing a pagan ceremony of expiation. The feast is set 40 days after Christmas, observing Luke's computation of the Jewish rite of the infant's presentation and the parents' purification.

LECTIONARY

The theme of "the encounter" runs through all three readings, but there is a wonderful contrast between the first and second. Malachi's question is eschatological, even apocalyptic: "Who can endure the day of his coming? Who can stand when he appears?" The Letter to the Hebrews suggests the response, "We can," for it says that Jesus is "not ashamed to call [us] brothers and sisters."

SACRAMENTARY

The order of service appears in the sacramentary and more fully in the *Ceremonial of Bishops* (CB):

- Gathering: Begin in a place other than where the eucharist will be celebrated, perhaps where the penitential procession on the first Sunday of Lent begins or the Palm Sunday procession. Ministers, vested for Mass (presider may wear cope), go there to begin. Ushers or greeters offer candles to all who gather.

If it is not possible to gather in a separate place, use the "solemn entrance" option and fill the worship place with candlelight. The procession should be an action of the whole assembly, not just a few people moving from a table holding candles to the altar.

- Candles are lit while the assembly sings the proper antiphon or a hymn.
- sign of the cross, greeting, invitation by presider
- blessing prayer over the candles
- candles are sprinkled with water in silence
- incense placed in the censer
- deacon (or presider) announces the procession as in sacramentary
- Procession moves to the site of the eucharist. As on Palm Sunday and at the Easter Vigil, the assembly follows the presider, who follows the censer, the cross borne between two candles, and the Book of Gospels (CB, 246). All bear lit candles and sing the antiphon and Canticle of Simeon (or a metrical version of the canticle).

The processional antiphon, *Lumen ad revelationem,* is easy to sing. It is sung with the Canticle of Simeon during the candlelight procession. At least one hymnal (*Worship,* #1023) has an English adaptation that works well.

- Entrance into church: The rite calls for the entrance chant and then the Gloria. But two different pieces of music followed by a sung Gloria makes the rite unwieldy. Perhaps an opening hymn or the Gloria might be sung to mark the transition from procession to eucharist. The setting for the Gloria should be that used during the Christmas or Easter seasons to link this feast to those solemnities (wear the Christmas or Easter vestments too). During this song, the altar is venerated and incensed by the presider. When the singing and movement cease, the opening prayer is chanted at once.

WINTER ORDINARY TIME: FEBRUARY

FEBRUARY

- Candles may be extinguished as everyone sits for the liturgy of the word. Alternatively, the liturgy of the word or even the entire Mass might be celebrated by candlelight. The candles should be lit again as the assembly stands for the gospel and later, according to ancient tradition, for the eucharistic prayer.

MUSIC

The best hymns for the feast are in the Latin *Liturgy of the Hours.* The English text of the hours has "When Mary brought her treasure." See *Hymnal 1982* and *Worship* for "O Zion, open wide thy gates" and "Hail to the Lord who comes." The *Lutheran Book of Worship* offers "In his temple now behold him." A new hymn that celebrates the humanity we share with Jesus is the striking "O God, we bear the imprint of your face," #585 in the *New Century Hymnal.* See the hymnals for metrical versions of the Canticle of Simeon (the Nunc Dimittis).

THU 3 Weekday
#326 (LMC, #193–231) green/white

Blase, bishop and martyr; Ansgar, bishop, religious, missionary; optional memorials/red. ■ Solomon succeeds his father David as king. David's final advice to his son is to fulfill the responsibility God has given him by walking in the Lord's ways and holding fast to the Lord's commands. Jesus sends the disciples out with "authority over unclean spirits," and specific mention is made of a ministry that continues to this day: "They anointed with oil many who were sick and cured them." The gospel story leads perfectly into the blessing of throats, if that custom is observed in your community today.

■ BLESSING THROATS: This rite, which may be presided over by a priest, deacon or lay minister, is clearly part of the memorial of Blase. There is no provision for transferring it to the nearest Sunday. The blessing may be celebrated during Mass, at its own liturgy of the word or as part of Morning or Evening Prayer before the gospel canticle. The order for the blessing is in the *Book of Blessings,* chapter 51.

FRI 4 Weekday
#327 (LMC, #193–231) green

The lectionary often celebrates a figure whose story has just concluded with a final canticle from the beautiful book of Sirach. In today's praise of David, his liturgical work receives special mention. In contrast to the peaceful death of King David, the gospel relates the violent death of John the Baptist. The miracles Jesus has performed and, perhaps, the sending forth of missionaries in Jesus' name, have come to Herod's attention. This gives Mark the opportunity to recall the preaching and witness of John the Baptist. Surely the fate of the Baptist does not portend peace for Jesus. There is a foreshadowing of Jesus' death in the story of John, and there is a poignant difference as well: The last line of the passage notes that John's disciples came to bury his body. When Jesus' final hour comes, all his disciples, the ones now working miracles in his name, desert him and flee.

SAT 5 Agatha, virgin and martyr
#328 (LMC, #193–231) red
MEMORIAL

To Solomon, as to his father David before him, the Lord God offers a wish and is pleased that Solomon does not seek what many of the world's rulers would covet. Solomon asks neither for long life, riches, or his enemies' destruction, but the one gift still in short supply, an understanding heart (or, another possible translation, a discerning mind). The gospel tells the story of the day off that never happened: The longing for time to rest for the mission yields to the compassion of the shepherd's heart and the fulfillment of the teacher's responsibilities.

Because of the nature of her martyrdom, Agatha might be an appropriate patron of women with breast cancer; indeed her memory should inspire prayer and action on behalf of all women who suffer in any way. Include these women and their families in the general intercessions, as well as nurses, who claim Agatha as the patron of their profession.

6 Fifth Sunday in Ordinary Time
#74 (LMC, #69) green

LECTIONARY

An image of resurrection is incorporated in the healing of Simon's mother-in-law, since the same Greek word is used both for Jesus' action in raising her up and Jesus' being raised up in Mark 16:6. Unfortunately neither of the two English-language lectionaries captures the sense of this. The NRSV of the Canadian lectionary is closer ("lifted her up") than the RNAB of United States' edition ("helped her up"). The point is

FEBRUARY

important: Simon's mother-in-law, being raised up, gives herself over to "serving" (NRSV; "waiting on them" in the RNAB). In any case, the Greek verb is *diakonei,* to minister. Simon's mother-in-law becomes the first woman of whom this ministerial verb is used in the gospel, but not the last.

SACRAMENTARY

Leave the choices for this block of Sundays in place, remembering that planners and presiders sometimes want to change texts that have become familiar to them, but are still fresh in the ears of their assemblies. The Eucharistic Prayer for Masses for Various Needs and Occasions is restricted by an introductory rubric to special Masses with those themes. Nevertheless, this prayer in its Form IV, Jesus, the Compassion of God, was the Pope's choice for the Sunday Mass he celebrated in Havana, Cuba, during Winter Ordinary Time 1998. Its preface and intercessory section make it fitting for this block of "healing" Sundays. "(Jesus) was moved with compassion for the poor and powerless, for the sick and sinner . . . Open our eyes to the needs of all; inspire us with words and deeds to comfort those who labor and are burdened." If the parish has not commissioned eucharistic ministers to the homebound or other parish ministers to the sick, these would be good Sundays for such celebrations.

MON 7 — #329 (LMC, #193–231) green
Weekday

This week and next, the weekday lectionary cycle is uninterrupted. This gives the assembly the opportunity to hear, in full, the sad conclusion of 1 Kings' presentation of Israel's history, and to start with the Letter of James next Monday. The gospel begins this week where we left off last week: Jesus continues his healing ministry.

TUE 8 — #330 (LMC, #193–231) green
Weekday

Jerome Emiliani, presbyter; optional memorial/white. • Solomon's prayer of dedication is a model of solid liturgical prayer. Phrases from it have found their way into the dedicatory prayers of the church throughout the centuries. The importance of the Temple as the focus of the people's prayer and a place of God's presence shows the great comfort God gives us by choosing to be accessible to us on earth. Yet this assurance is balanced by the understanding that even the heavens cannot contain the Infinite One. We look for God here, but expect to find God everywhere as well, even in unlikely places and people! Jesus challenges the Pharisees — and us — to keep tradition pure, a living expression of devotion.

Jerome Emiliani, a former army officer and prisoner of war, died on this date in 1587 while ministering to victims of the plague. The memorial might remind us of men and women far from home in military service, or of those who work with people with AIDS.

WED 9 — #331 (LMC, #193–231) green
Weekday

The Queen of Sheba comes to Jerusalem to verify the reports she has heard of Solomon's surpassing wisdom. This becomes the occasion and the motivation for her to bless the Lord, the God of Israel, as the source of Solomon's wisdom. Jesus explains to the crowd and then to his disciples the meaning of his teaching on defilement within the heart. Recall that Jesus offered a similar private instruction after the parable of the sower. This could signal a link: Jesus seems to be speaking of the human heart as the field in which God's word is sown.

THU 10 — #332 (LMC, #193–231) white
Scholastica, virgin, religious founder
MEMORIAL

In one turn of the lectionary page, Solomon falls from the pinnacle of wisdom to the depths of idolatry. From now until the end of the week, we read of the demise that followed upon Solomon's folly. The gospel offers a challenge: What are we to make of Jesus' treatment of the Gentile Syro-Phoenician woman who seeks healing for her daughter? Commentators offer various explanations for the harshness of Jesus' initial response and try to soften it by pointing out the diminutive form of the original Greek. Brown suggests that we simply accept that Mark is quoting Jesus as a first-century Jew who assigns first place to the "children" of the household (Jews), as does Paul and 1 Peter. Brown thinks it better to see this encounter in continuity with the previous discussion of food, since the admission of Gentiles and the suppression of Jewish dietary laws were subjects of intense debate in the early church for which Mark's gospel was written (Introduction, 137).

Today's memorial honors another woman of great faith, Benedict's twin sister Scholastica. See the Office of Readings for Gregory the Great's delightful story of how Scholastica got Benedict to stay at her guesthouse when he was determined to go back to the monastery.

WINTER ORDINARY TIME: FEBRUARY

FEBRUARY

FRI 11 #323 (LMC, #193–231) green
Weekday

Our Lady of Lourdes, optional memorial/white. ■ Rebellion and division among God's chosen people, and Jeroboam's idolatry, are the theme of today's reading and tomorrow's concluding episode from 1 Kings. If there is no Saturday morning worship, consider combining episodes for the sake of continuity.

For more than a century the shrine at Lourdes has been a place of deep faith and abundant healings both physical and spiritual. Unshakable confidence in God's power always goes hand-in-hand with the wholehearted embrace of God's will: the lesson not only of Lourdes but of Mary's own life. In Rome today the jubilee of the sick and of health-care workers will be marked with a celebration of communal anointing presided over by the pope. Local communities may wish to arrange a similar celebration to which the homebound and their caregivers are invited and for whom transportation and care at the church will be provided.

SAT 12 #334 (LMC, #193–231) green
Weekday

Blessed Virgin Mary, optional memorial/white. ■ Jeroboam's apostasy leads to hardened hearts and deadly sin. Today's gospel story, along with with Jesus' reluctance to heal (Thursday) and difficulty in doing so (Friday), suggests that hardened hearts diminish Jesus' power. Jesus feeds fewer people this time with more food, and afterward, only seven baskets are left over, not twelve.

The week's memorial of Mary may have been celebrated yesterday, but if the Saturday is also celebrated in her honor, consider using #20 from the *Collection*, "Holy Mary, the New Eve" with its emphasis on Mary's steadfast faith and obedient discipleship.

13 #77 (LMC, #72) green
Sixth Sunday in Ordinary Time

LECTIONARY

From now until Lent (that is, through Mark 3:6), Jesus is shown to be "the transgressor of the boundaries" (Donald H. Juel, *Mark*. Augsburg, 1990, 43). It seems that Jesus does this deliberately and pointedly. He did not touch the possessed man (Fourth Sunday), nor will he touch the paralyzed man (Seventh Sunday). Moreover, the leper does not ask for healing by saying, "If you are able," as does the father of the possessed boy in Mark 9:22–23. The leper says, "If you wish." What actually moves Jesus to act is a matter of dispute. "Moved with pity," the final translation has it. A variation in manuscripts has "and having become angry" — angry at the Law's restrictions on people with the disease? Jesus touches the man and makes the choice, "I do will it," and heals the man. In that moment, Jesus effects a change far beyond the man's skin: The boundaries established by Leviticus have fallen. In and through the person of Jesus, the man has been put in touch again with the community of God's people. The healing touch of Jesus transforms not just the individual but the whole community.

SACRAMENTARY

Much is made in contemporary literature of the healing power of human touch. There is a ritualized form of interpersonal contact in the liturgy: the sign of peace. Among the liturgical refinements of Winter Ordinary Time might be the community's approach to the sign of peace. From the stylized gesture among clergy at Solemn High Mass in the days before Vatican II, the sign of peace has diminished in some places to a perfunctory exchange of social greetings. That's better than nothing, but the sign of peace could be so much more. In some Eastern liturgies the verbal exchange that goes with the gesture is prescribed: V. Christ is among us. R. He is and ever shall be. And during the Eastertime's Fifty Days: V. Christ is risen! R. Christ is truly risen! What does the gesture look like among us? What do we say to one another while exchanging it?

MON 14 #335 (LMC, #193–231) white
Cyril, monk, and Methodius, bishop
MEMORIAL

The opening sections of James, read now through Wednesday, invite us to reflect on two ways of looking at and living life. In the gospel Jesus refuses a sign to those who demand one. To us who so often look for special signs ourselves, the wisdom of James should be self-evident in light of the sign we have been given: the cross of Christ.

Pope John Paul II declared today's saints co-patrons with Saint Benedict of a reunited Europe. These "Apostles to the Slavs" knew the importance of reinforcing their teachings with a liturgy that spoke to the people they were evangelizing. The

74 WINTER ORDINARY TIME: FEBRUARY

FEBRUARY

brothers, translators of the scriptures and prayers of the church, developed the alphabet that still bears Cyril's name. They can be seen as prophets and pioneers of what we now call inculturation. Cyril and Methodius remind us that while the gospel is timeless, it must be presented in images and idioms the people can recognize and embrace.

TUE 15 #336 (LMC, #193–231) green
Weekday

As James reminds us, we often blame our testing on God, when in reality we lead ourselves astray by our own self-centeredness and greed. Only by practicing a generosity modeled on that of the Father can we save ourselves from such self-absorption. Jesus warns against inner corruption (the "yeast" of the Pharisees and Herod) as he refers his uncomprehending disciples to the feeding of the vast multitude.

WED 16 #337 (LMC, #193–231) green
Weekday

Today's themes will recur in later readings from James. Gracious speech will be discussed Saturday, and would be on Tuesday, if it were not superseded this year by a feast day. Doing and not just hearing the word is counseled on Thursday, Friday and next Monday. Practical care for those in need as the measure of true religion is proclaimed on Thursday and Friday. In the gospel, the progressive cure of the blind man seems odd: Jesus has to lay hands on the man twice. Some commentators see this as a reference to gestures in the initiation rites Mark's community used.

THU 17 #338 (LMC, #193–231) green
Weekday

Seven Founders of the Order of Servites, religious; optional memorial/white. ▪ What are the implications of the maxim James calls the royal law, "You shall love your neighbor as yourself" (verse 8)? Peter gets the title right — Jesus *is* the Messiah — but misses the definition.

Today's seven saints were prominent Florentine businessmen who abandoned their fortunes shortly after the death of Francis of Assisi to become mendicant friars, in a commitment to evangelical poverty. In our own competitive, profit-driven world, what difference might we be called to make?

FRI 18 #339 (LMC, #193–237) green
Weekday

James makes an important point: You can't feed hungry people with words. So what's a Christian to do? "This teaching is not based on what is specifically Christian, but on faith in the one God" (*The Catholic Study Bible,* Reading Guide, 550). James points us toward continuity with our Jewish forebears by showing how the teachings of Jesus do not oppose but refine Torah.

Today the Dominican Order observes the memorial of Blessed John, known to art lovers everywhere as Fra Angelico. He preached through his painting. When John Paul II beatified the friar-artist, he proclaimed that he did so with confidence for "no one whose art so reflected the divine could have failed to be holy himself." In Rome today there is a Jubilee celebration for the artists of the world. Are there creative and talented people in the local community who can be honored with celebration today?

SAT 19 #340 (LMC, #193–231) green
Weekday

Blessed Virgin Mary, optional memorial/white. ▪ "From the same mouth come blessing and cursing. My brothers and sisters, this ought not to be so." Thus does James conclude his essay on the immense power of speech. And there is James' recurring theological point: "Religious language and practical human care must go together" (Johnson, 551). Mark's account of the transfiguration concludes the week's gospel readings. The glimpse of glory is meant to strengthen us to see the passion with eyes of faith.

To keep the Saturday memorial of Mary, consider Mass #27, "Mary, Image and Mother of the Church III," from the *Collection of Masses of the Blessed Virgin Mary.* This formulary incorporates some of the themes of the transfiguration.

☀ 20 #80 (LMC, #75) green
Seventh Sunday in Ordinary Time

LECTIONARY

A new and important element links the gospels of this Sunday to next Sunday and to the last Sunday before Lent. The scribes and the Pharisees begin to ask questions as Jesus' transgression of the boundaries comes to the attention of those whose office is to keep the boundaries intact. Homilist and hearers need to approach the situation of the man who is the object of Jesus' ministry with caution. Because Jesus says first, "Your

FEBRUARY

sins are forgiven," we might think that Jesus is confirming that illness is the result of sin. Jesus does not link the two: Notice that after the man's sins are forgiven, he does not immediately get up and walk away. The crowd is more amazed at the physical healing than at the forgiveness of sin, but Mark's principal emphasis is that Jesus has authority over sin as well as sickness. Jesus' mission is the healing of the whole person; and that radical healing eventually leads to "receiving a hundredfold now in this age — with persecutions — and in the age to come eternal life" (Mark 10:30, Twenty-eighth Sunday).

The Isaiah reading ties into this cosmic context. This is the message of Deutero (Second) Isaiah to the Jewish exiles in Babylon just before King Cyrus of Persia conquered the city (539 BCE). Through the events of history, says the prophet, God is going to "do something new." Whatever the political dimensions are, the spiritual side of God's promise is, "your sins I remember no more."

SACRAMENTARY

Reconciliation II would be a fine choice for a eucharistic prayer today, "the hand you stretch out to sinners." It is not too early to pick up on the theme of forgiveness in Isaiah and Mark. Perhaps this would be a good way to begin catechesis on the sacrament of reconciliation, especially if this will be offered communally during Lent. Provide attractive brochures with reflection and prayer material to help in the examination of conscience and in celebrating the rite.

THE WEEK AHEAD

Tuesday's feast has proper readings that interrupt the weekday lectionary series from James. Since James is read so infrequently, consider the solution in Monday's calendar entry. The gospel interruption is less troublesome, since the same theme will recur in the passage for Wednesday of next week.

Lenten Countdown

This was Septuagesima Sunday in the pre–Vatican II calendar, literally, 70 days before Easter. This weekend's bulletin and the parish notice-board should carry the first signs of the approaching season. Lenten participation materials, scripture calendars and prayerbooks should be available in the vestibule or gathering area beginning this weekend. LTP has several useful resources. See, for instance, *Keeping Lent, Triduum and Eastertime,* as well as the beautiful "Noah's Ark" calendar for helping children through the 40 days. *Bible Stories for the Forty Days* by Melissa Musick Nussbaum makes great lenten family reading.

MON 21 #341 (LMC, #193–231) green
Weekday

Peter Damian, bishop and doctor of the church, optional memorial / white. • Today's passage from James, together with tomorrow's (superseded by the feast day readings), is considered by one commentator to be a self-contained essay. He has nicknamed it, "Friendship with God or with the World?" Although it would be a somewhat long reading, consider joining tomorrow's passage to today's. We do not often read James in the assembly, and this wisdom is too good to miss. With Lent coming up, the words of Jesus are a reminder: Some unclean spirits can be cast out "only by prayer and fasting."

Peter Damian was an important figure of his time (eleventh century). His influence reached beyond the cloister to the wider world, which knew him as a theologian, an ascetic and champion of church reform.

TUE 22 #535 (LMC, #263) white
Chair of Peter, apostle
FEAST

First observed in fourth-century Rome, today's feast primarily celebrates Peter's role as leader of the church in Rome. In the academic world, as in the church and civil society, the "chair" (Latin: *cathedra*) is a symbol of teaching or governing authority. Today's feast celebrates also the role of the successor of the bishop of Rome, the pope, and his teaching authority. By celebrating this feast of unity with the bishop of Rome, local churches throughout the world proclaim our unity in one universal communion of faith and love.

WED 23 #343 (LMC, #193–231) red
Polycarp, bishop and martyr
MEMORIAL

Many United States Catholics were taken aback last year when the Pope directed a challenging homily against capitalism. Knowing of his experience in communist Poland, we expect John Paul II to zero in on communism. But the Pope is a frequent and forceful critic of capitalism. So is James today and tomorrow. James upbraids Christians whose lives are consumed with "doing business and making money." It is easy to make plans with no thought

76 WINTER ORDINARY TIME: FEBRUARY

of God's commands and, as tomorrow's reading makes clear, with no thought for those in need. Jesus adds: In matters of religion, there is no need to control everyone and everything. Whether people belong to our community or not, "whoever is not against us is for us."

Polycarp is said to have been a disciple of the apostle John. An authentic account of Polycarp's martyrdom and final prayer are in today's office of readings in the *Liturgy of the Hours*. The prayer echoes early texts that link sharing in the eucharist to participating in Christ's passion. Polycarp gives thanks for being permitted to "share in the cup of Christ." Do we offer the cup to all communicants at every Mass? It makes little sense to observe the practice once a year on Holy Thursday, if the daily eucharist does not take seriously the commands, "Take and eat; take and drink."

THU 24 Weekday
#344 (LMC, #193–231) green

Amos is called the voice of social justice in the Hebrew Bible. James is its most forceful advocate in the New Testament. Two weeks from now we will be in Lent, committed to its threefold discipline of prayer, fasting and almsgiving. Today might be an opportunity to reflect on our lenten almsgiving. The gospel offers a blessing on hospitality and a warning against scandalizing others. Both challenge us to recognize the sacred dignity of every human person.

FRI 25 Weekday
#345 (LMC, #193–231) green

The Letter of James closes with more reflection on the tongue and the damage it can do. In the community, says James, "Do not grumble against one another" for this is lack of charity. Nor is one to speak beyond plain meanings, "Do not swear an oath." Divorce is always a delicate subject, especially in a church that tries to obey the literal teaching of Jesus. Today Jesus appeals to Genesis over Deuteronomy, to God's plan "at the beginning" over Moses' interpretation "because of your hardness of heart." Jewish law permitted only men to initiate divorce. Jesus is addressing more here than the indissolubility of marriage:

> In the debate with the Pharisees, Jesus takes an even more radical stance — on behalf of women. Women whose vocation is the raising of children require the protection of the law. It has always been thus. Jesus' attack on a tradition of law that granted divorce easily — however "realistic" that tradition may have seemed to those engaged in the practice of the law — represented an attack on the social position of men. Jesus' position therefore seems to be that society has fundamental investments in the family that the law is intended to protect. (Juel, 140)

SAT 26 Weekday
#346 (LMC, #193–231) green

Blessed Virgin Mary, optional memorial/white. • In times of suffering, pray. In times of joy, sing songs of praise. In times of illness, let the elders anoint the sick. James knows that the community's daily life will be marked by a variety of needs. He knows, too, that within the community there are resources for every occasion if, we are "doers of the word and not hearers only." Yesterday's teaching from Mark on marriage leads naturally to today's passage about children. The disciples were products of a society where children were viewed as property with no legal rights or protection. Jesus' kingdom is radically different: Children are models of how to receive the kingdom. Not only are their requests for attention heard by Jesus, he honors them with a loving embrace and blessing.

For the Saturday memorial of Mary, look at Mass #8 in the Christmas section, Our Lady of Nazareth, which emphasizes Mary's role as wife, mother and first disciple of the kingdom (gospel), or #44, Mary, Health of the Sick (first reading).

27 Eighth Sunday in Ordinary Time
#83 (LMC, #78) green

LECTIONARY

"I will lead her into the desert and speak to her heart." Hosea provides an invitation to the lenten journey that homilists will want to mention. In the prophet's view, the covenant renewal is a wedding celebration involving the whole assembly of God's people. The communal aspect of this covenant is important to remember in this age of individualized spirituality. God relates intimately to the individual believer, and this intimacy is intensified by the marriage metaphor. But we are called to be part of a community, and that challenges us to discover and love in one another what the divine Bridegroom has discovered and loved in each person.

This image of a renewed covenant of marriage is the context of this Sunday's gospel proclamation and homily. When read

FEBRUARY

in the context of the Hosea passage, the gospel is not primarily a defense of the disciples' failure to fast. The point is that the great wedding of God and humanity is at hand in Jesus; this needs to be recognized and rejoiced over, even if others do not understand. "When the bridegroom is taken away from them," in his passion and death, "then they will fast on that day." But even then the fasting of the disciples will be nothing like the fasting of John's disciples. John's disciples fast in anticipation of the inbreaking of God's kingdom. The fasting of Jesus' disciples, from now until his glorious return, is a fast of preparation for a joyful reunion with the beloved. Like new clothing and new wine, new life in Christ should fill the disciple with confidence, freedom and exaltation!

SACRAMENTARY

All that was said last week about Reconciliation II as a eucharistic prayer holds true today as well, especially if the gospel proclamation or homily includes the call of Levi and the banquet with sinners. The choice for Lent (and possibly for next week, see below) should be different from this week's. It might be good to begin practicing the lenten gospel and eucharistic prayer acclamations today. The ideal is a good setting, perhaps in a minor key, that will become the community's "Lent only" chants.

COUNTDOWN TO LENT

Everything that will call the community to the lenten observance needs to be in place today. Special posters and notices, prayerbooks and spiritual reading, boxes and handouts and other materials to assist in almsgiving all should be ready. Besides being a thoughtful convenience to parishioners, these preparations are a signal that those who lead the community's worship take Lent seriously and, indeed, are even looking forward to it with excitement.

■ OLD PALMS FOR ASH WEDNESDAY: Invite people to bring their old palms from home to next week's liturgy so that the ashes for Ash Wednesday may be prepared next weekend.

MON 28 Weekday
#347 (LMC, #193–231) green

Between now and Ash Wednesday, the weekday lectionary (Year II) presents a much edited series of readings from 1 Peter, Jude (its only appearance in the lectionary) and 2 Peter.

Today's reading and Friday's puts Christian suffering in the context of our new birth in baptism and, therefore, makes it part of our intimate union with Christ. The selections from Mark's gospel on Monday, Wednesday and Thursday begin with reminders that Jesus is on a journey. By Friday we will be at the journey's destination, Jerusalem. Next week we begin the lenten journey, and today's gospel sets the prerequisite for journeying with Jesus: renunciation; giving to the poor; setting our hearts on heavenly treasure; following behind Jesus. Note two details in the story of the would-be disciple. "Jesus looked at him and loved him." "He went away sad [NRSV: "The man was shocked and went away grieving"] for he had many possessions." For that man, tangible possessions came first, as they so often do for us.

TUE 29 Weekday
#348 (LMC, #193–231) green

The good news is the surpassing treasure bestowed by God on the Christian community. What should be our response? Holy living, obedience, and readiness for action. Jerome commented on Peter's words in today's gospel, "Left everything? What did they leave? Some broken nets and leaky boats!" To Peter and his friends, that was everything. Note Mark's addition to the disciples' reward — and persecution besides.

March

WED 1 Weekday
#349 (LMC, #193–231) green

Note the details in Mark's gospel. The destination is Jerusalem. The disciples are walking behind Jesus until James and John come forward to make their request. In his response, Jesus uses the images of "baptism" and "drinking of his cup" to signify a share in his suffering. This should lead the faithful, penitent and elect, to reflection on the meanings of baptism and eucharist.

THU 2 Weekday
#350 (LMC, #193–231) green

With the lenten journey about to begin, we should all take to heart 1 Peter's wise advice to counter false accusations with the witness of good deeds. Close to Jerusalem now, in Jericho, Jesus heals the blind Bartimaeus. Jesus calls Bartimaeus, reminding us that the call to discipleship and community is a personal one. Jesus asks Bartimaeus the same question he asked James and John, and

MARCH

Bartimaeus, unlike them, asks not for personal glory but simply for the ability to see. Finally, unlike the rich man, Bartimaeus leaves his possessions — a beggar's cloak — and follows Jesus on the way of discipleship.

FRI 3 #351 (LMC, #193–231) green
Weekday

Blessed Katherine Drexel, virgin, religious founder, optional memorial/white. • The end is near! What are Christians to do? There is nothing here of panic or self-centered preoccupation. "Maintain constant love; be hospitable without complaining; serve as good stewards of whatever gift you have received; and rejoice to the extent that you share Christ's sufferings." There's a positive lenten program! In Jerusalem at last, and in Mark's "sandwich" construction, the gospel recounts Jesus' cursing of the fig tree, his cleansing of the temple, and further observation on figs and faith. The literary technique, and the note that "it was not the season for figs," alerts us to the symbolic nature of the story. This passage is not meant to make us critical of the Jewish religious authorities but attentive to our own faith response. The final line is a warning: We need not expect God to exercise his power if we do not join our faith to forgiveness.

An example of both passages in action was Mother Katherine Drexel, who died in 1955, as the civil rights struggle in the United States was just about to emerge in confrontation and legislation. Her ministry to Native and African Americans did much to pave the way for mutual enrichment.

SAT 4 #352 (LMC, #193–231) green
Weekday

Casimir; Blessed Virgin Mary, optional memorials/white. • Fortified by prayer and persevering in God's love, the strong are to extend to the wavering or confused the mercy they have received. The appropriateness of this short passage from Jude for the community's lenten preparation is obvious. The gospel ends on an ominous note: A stand-off between Jesus and the religious officials over the legitimacy of his own authority.

What did a late medieval court think of a peace-loving prince and his celibate lifestyle? The account of Casimir's life in the Office of Readings for his memorial makes it clear that he was busy being "father, son and brother" to all in need. Isn't that the point of celibacy for the sake of the kingdom?

If there is to be a final Saturday memorial in honor the Virgin Mary before Lent begins, consider using texts that speak of pilgrimage and discipleship. See #25, Mary, Image and Mother of the Church I or even one of the Masses in the lenten section, #13, The Commending of the Blessed Virgin Mary.

☼ 5 #86 (LMC, #81) green
Ninth Sunday in Ordinary Time

LECTIONARY

Winter Ordinary Time ends with foreboding in the religious-political alliance of enemies who are already plotting Jesus' death. Lent will begin with a reminder that whatever obligations we undertake as disciples, we do so in the freedom of love. Ours is a covenant with the God whose nature is love, and whose command to love him above all things is bound up with an equal command to love our neighbor.

SACRAMENTARY

■ ALLELUIA FAREWELL:

Alleluia though we cherish
and would chant for evermore.
alleluia in our singing,
let us for a while give o'er,
as our Savior in his fasting
pleasures of the world forbore.
  (*Hymnal 1982,* #122;
  slightly modernized
  in *Worship III,* #413)

Our eleventh-century, Latin-singing ancestors knew how to say goodbye to their alleluia, even singing it to its forty-day rest with this hymn. On this last Sunday that the assembly will sing alleluia until the Easter Vigil, alleluia banners, tapestries or scrolls, if they will be used again as decorations during the Easter season, can be carried out in procession at the end of the day's liturgy.

■ LENTEN ANNOUNCEMENTS, HANDOUTS AND COVENANTS: Masses on this last Sunday before Lent traditionally include many announcements and handouts. Some parishes provide a printed "lenten covenant" in a trifold pamphlet that outlines the schedule and suggestions for keeping the threefold discipline of prayer, fasting and almsgiving.

■ PREPARING ASHES: Consider burning last year's palms outdoors after the recessional or in the evening after vespers. Especially if the twofold alleluia in the Easter melody has

MARCH

been added to the dismissal, the transition to this activity will be striking.

MON 6 #353 (LMC, #193–231) green
Weekday

The first readings of the last two days before Lent are a unit, the only selections from 2 Peter in the weekday lectionary. The passages make good reading as a preparation for the season at hand and as a call to witness at the beginning of a new millennium. There is scholarly speculation that this may have been the last-written letter of the New Testament, addressed to a community that had begun to lose hope in the Lord's Second Coming. Today's passage is a call to appreciate the promises made to us, to be different from those who do not know of these promises, and to grow in a life of holiness. The elements of Christian holiness are set forth as interdependent qualities, crowned by mutual love. The parable of the unworthy tenants continues Jesus' confrontation with the authorities.

TUE 7 #354 (LMC, #193–231) red
Perpetua and Felicity, martyrs
MEMORIAL

■ LAST MASS BEFORE LENT. "To read the scriptures," Cardinal Newman said, "you would think Christ ever coming. To read the world, you would think Christ never coming again. Now, better a thousand times to think him coming and have him not come; than once to think him not coming, and have him appear!" Last year and this, religious people have heard the many predictions of chaos and the world's end. These expectations always seem to attend the turning of the centuries. Today's first reading, however, warns us: The Lord is coming again! In fact, by the our lives and our prayer we are to hasten the day when "justice will be at home." The last gospel before Lent relates one more confrontation and one of Jesus' more famous teachings. An early Father of the church said that the best way to render unto Caesar what is Caesar's was to make sure we had nothing that belonged to him. Now we render unto God what is God's, the Forty Days, our tithe of the Jubilee Year!

Today's saints, two African women, remind us of the catechumens and the elect who will be prominent in the assembly in the season about to begin. Perpetua, a young woman with a newborn son, and Felicity, a pregnant slave, were arrested with their catechist and several catechumens. Thrown to the wild beasts and then put to death by the sword, they died in each other's arms at Carthage about the year 203. How beautiful that they died embracing each other in the sign of peace, which, as neophytes, it was their privilege to share.

LENT

The Season
The Setting of Lent / 83
A Sense of Lent / 85
The Look of Lent / 86
The Sounds of Lent / 87
The Rhythm of Lent / 88
The Word of God / 89
The Eucharist / 90
Other Celebrations / 94
At Home / 95
The Calendar
March 8 – April 20, 2000 / 97

The Setting of Lent

RARELY does Lent begin as late as this first Lent of the new millennium does. In fact, it's been well over a decade since we've even come close to starting Lent this late, and it will be more than another decade before Lent is this late again. To find a year when Lent began later than this year's Lent does, you'd have to go all the way back to 1943!

So, March will be a week old already when this year's Lent begins. Depending on your geographical location, Lent may come in like a lion this year, but it will almost certainly go out like a lamb. This year's late Lent can be quite a different experience from an early, and therefore wintry, Lent!

The difference can be experienced positively or negatively. Some people prefer a Lent that is mostly winter. It's easier, say these folks, to enter into Lent's penitential mood and to keep focused on the spiritual life when you'd just as soon stay indoors anyway, curled up with a good book and warmed up with a cup of tea.

Others point to the origin of our English word for Lent and see in springtime's progress toward summer a perfect image of the journey toward the rebirth of nature and of the spirit that happens at Easter. The romance languages derive their word for the forty days of Lent from the Latin word for forty, *quadragesima*. Thus, in Italian Lent is *quaresima;* in Spanish, *cuaresma;* and in French, *carême*. But our English ancestors chose *lente,* the Middle English modification of an Old English word for spring, *lencten,* to name these forty days. The word even sounds like *lengthen,* which is exactly what the daylight hours do as March journeys toward April and spring toward summer.

Speaking of journeys, the increasing warmth of spring's lengthening days is custom-made for those first outdoor ventures in months. Hikes and bike trips, and eventually camping and canoeing, are all welcome springtime antidotes to a long winter's cabin fever. On the First Sunday of Lent this year, we celebrate the end of some real cabin fever in the story of God's covenant with Noah. After forty days and nights locked up together on that ark, imagine how welcome to human and beast alike was the sight of that dove, bearing in its beak the sprig of olive that told everyone it was safe to disembark!

We are more familiar, perhaps, with the "wintry" texts of Lent that remind us realistically of our mortality, "ashes to ashes and dust to dust." But there are also texts both ancient and modern, from lenten liturgies of the East and West, that strike a decidedly more spring-like tone. Consider these texts from the Eastern church that provide a formal, chanted announcement of the season:

The lenten spring shines forth,
the flower of repentance!

Let us enter the fast with joy, O faithful.
Let us not be sad.

Receive Lent with gladness, O people!
Prove yourselves to be children of God!

The poem, *Iam Christe, sol justitiae,* is perhaps as ancient as the sixth century, yet it is still the hymn prescribed for Morning Prayer in the Latin edition of the *Liturgy of the Hours.*

As spring awakes the frozen earth,
So Easter blooms from Lent's restraints.
Rejoice! For Christ will conquer death
And bring his grace to make us saints.
(Tr. Frank C. Quinn, © 1989)

Inspired by that ancient text, a modern poet has employed the same motif, spring, to create a lenten morning hymn:

As the sun with longer journey melts
   the winter's snow and ice,
with its slowly growing radiance warms
   the seed beneath the earth,
may the sun of Christ's uprising gently bring
   our hearts to life.

Through the days of waiting, watching,
   in the desert of our sin,
Searching on the far horizon for a sign of
   cloud or wind,
We await the healing waters of
   our Savior's victory.
(John Patrick Earls, OSB, © 1990
Order of St. Benedict, Inc., admin.
The Liturgical Press)

Despite the springtime feeling, all this talk of seeds and new life, movement and growth should remind us that even the warmer and lengthening days of spring are not meant to be a time of all play and no work! There is no harvest without the hard work of planting, and even the most elementary journey involves, if not the work of packing and the pain of farewells, at least a minimal preparation and some prudential planning.

So, too, there can be no Lent without authentic conversion, and no preparation for Easter without a sincere commitment to prayer, fasting and almsgiving. But the springtime we celebrate now at the beginning of the new millennium is a Lent enriched by the renewal decreed by the Second Vatican Council. For instance, the text of the imposition of ashes from the former liturgy remains as an option with its salutary reminder, "Remember that you are dust." But the newer formula for that ritual action quotes the Jesus who speaks in the gospel of this year, Year B, the Gospel of Mark. The sobriety of "Turn away from sin" is balanced with the call to embark on the journey and adventure of discipleship, "Be faithful to the gospel." Also, from 1570 to 1970, there was one Preface prescribed throughout Lent for use with the eucharistic prayer. It set forth a sober program, indeed: "Through our bodily fasting, you curb our vices and uplift our minds." But in the liturgy of Vatican II, that text is designated Lent IV, and the new text, Lent I, is remarkably exultant and adds an element of social consciousness to the discipline. It praises God because, "Each year you give us this joyful season when we prepare to celebrate the paschal mystery with mind and heart renewed. You give us a spirit of loving reverence for you, our God, and of willing service to our neighbor."

This joyful season! Not the way most people would instinctively describe Lent, yet perhaps it is a singularly appropriate description for this late-starting Lent. For those who prefer a winter Lent, the next couple of years will come soon enough. But for this first Lent of the new millennium, let the keynote come from two monastic texts written fourteen centuries apart. From early in the sixth century, the *Rule of Benedict* exhorts the community:

> During these days [of Lent] we will add to the usual measure of our service something by way of private prayer and abstinence from food or drink, so that each of us will have something above the assigned measure to offer God of his own will *with the joy of the Holy Spirit* (1 Thessalonians 1:6) . . . let each one deny himself some food, drink, sleep, needless talking and idle jesting, and look forward to holy Easter *with joy and spiritual longing.* (chapter 49)

Midway through the last century, one of Benedict's spiritual sons, the Trappist monk Thomas Merton, expressed the same thought this way:

> Ash Wednesday, the beginning of the Lenten fast, is a day of happiness . . . Lent is not so much a season of punishment as one of healing. There is joy in the salutary fasting and abstinence of Christians who eat and drink less in order that their minds may be more clear and receptive to receive the sacred nourishment of God's word, which the whole church announces and meditates upon in each day's liturgy throughout Lent. . . . In laying upon us the

light cross of ashes, the church desires to take off our shoulders all other heavy burdens — the crushing load of worry and obsessive guilt, the dead weight of our own self-love. We should not take upon ourselves a "burden" of penance and stagger into Lent as if we were Atlas, carrying the whole world on his shoulders. . . . Penance is conceived of by the church less as a burden than as a liberation. It is only a burden to those who take it up unwillingly. Love makes it light and happy. And that is another reason why Ash Wednesday is filled with the lightness of love. (Thomas Merton, *Seasons of Celebration,* 1958)

A Sense of Lent

LENT begins on Ash Wednesday and concludes quietly and without ceremony on Holy Thursday, before the Evening Mass of the Lord's Supper. At that point, the lenten fast, primarily a spiritual discipline, ceases so that after the Mass of the Lord's Supper, the more anticipatory paschal fast may begin, continuing until the Easter Vigil.

In giving the church a renewed sense of Lent, the Second Vatican Council set forth the liturgical agenda that we take into the new millennium:

> Lent is marked by two themes, the baptismal and the penitential . . . . More use is to be made of the baptismal features proper to the Lenten liturgy; some of those from an earlier era are to be restored as may seem advisable . . . During Lent penance should be not only inward and individual, but also outward and social. (*Constitution on the Sacred Liturgy,* 109, 110)

BAPTISMAL

The First Sunday of Lent is marked by two celebrations:

At the cathedral: the *Rite of Election.* The "elect," that is, those preparing for initiation at the Easter Vigil, enter into a period of final preparation, a time of purification and enlightenment. This rite gives public acknowledgement to the fact that God has "elected" or chosen these people. The inscription of names stands as a pledge of fidelity on the part of the elect to complete the process they have begun.

In the parish: a *Rite of Sending.* This can help the local community mark the day and enter into this important event in the lives of the elect, although as many parishioners as possible should accompany the parish's catechumens to the diocesan celebration.

■ ELECT: Present at the liturgy of the word as living icons of the season's baptismal character, the sisters and brothers who are the elect, together with their godparents or sponsors, are the principal symbols of Lent. It makes little sense to come up with lenten decorations when these living decorations are missing! Nothing can challenge the community to embrace that conversion proper to Lent more dramatically than the call to put our best foot forward in supporting, inspiring and assisting toward the font those who are about to join us. In two ways especially, do the elect act upon the community:

- *Scrutinies.* Celebrated during the principal Sunday eucharist on the Third, Fourth and Fifth Sundays of Lent, the scrutinies draw from and build upon the Year A gospel readings. These rites confer strength on the elect and confront all the faithful present with the need for conversion.

- *Dismissal.* The *Rite of Christian Initiation of Adults* restores the ancient dismissal rite by which those not fully initiated depart from the assembly after the liturgy of the word and before the creed and general intercessions. Their departure is neither an expulsion nor, worse, a statement of their unworthiness. Rather, it recognizes that from time immemorial initiation has been sealed admitting the neophytes to the community's "holy kiss" and "holy meal." A side effect of this dramatic rite is the impression made upon the faithful to treasure the great gifts which, having shared in so often, we too easily take for granted.

■ INFANT BAPTISM: Another way to emphasize the nature of Lent as a season of preparation for baptism is to refrain from baptizing infants during Lent (except as emergency or pastoral need may require). Instead, full participation in the liturgies of Lent, particularly presence at the scrutinies, provides a way for the parents and godparents of infants to receive appropriate formation. The infants might be baptized on Easter Sunday, either at the Vigil or one of the Masses during the day, or on one of the Sundays of Easter.

PENITENTIAL

A wonderful fifth-century homily sets before us the ideal of a full lenten observance, a journey that leads us back to God while leading us also to one another:

> Prayer, mercy and fasting: these three are one, and they give life to each other. Fasting is the soul of prayer, mercy is the lifeblood of fasting. Let no one try to separate them; they cannot be separated. If you have only one of them or not all together, you have nothing. So if you pray, fast; if you fast, show mercy; if you want your petition to be heard, hear the petition of others. When you fast, see the fasting of others. If you hope for mercy, show mercy. If you look for kindness, show kindness. If you want to receive, give. (Peter Chrysologus, Office of Readings, Tuesday, Third Week of Lent)

Prayer, fasting and almsgiving are the traditional disciplines that mark the observance of Lent. These practices are not meant to be an indulgence in masochism or an exercise self-improvement. Rather, as Benedict's *Rule* reminded us, they should be part of every Christian life in every season of the year. At this time of the year, they are meant to lead those already initiated back to the fervor that should flow continually from the grace of baptism. As their path leads the elect to the sacraments of initiation, the path of the faithful should take them to the sacrament of penance, which releases us from sin, restores us to baptismal innocence and reconciles us to God and the community.

The Look of Lent

FOR generations used to an environment whose audio-visual signals are all-pervasive and often subliminal, the liturgy begins even before we enter the space where the liturgy's beginning will be. The Orthodox priest and liturgical scholar Alexander Schmemann once described what the lenten atmosphere of the worship space should be: a climate that anyone walking into church should sense immediately. As with choosing texts, music and ritual patterns, so with decorations: it is best to plan the full season: the Forty Days (Lent); the Three Days (Triduum); the Fifty Days (Eastertime).

OUTSIDE

Liturgy begins before the beginning, and the very space that leads into the place of worship must be thought of as "the beginning before the beginning." This means that even when we have attended to the worship space and all the details of the liturgy to be celebrated there, the work is still not done!

People driving into the parking lot and walking onto the grounds should know immediately from what they see that Lent has begun. Think of the journey through the parking lot, up the walkway and into the church as a kind of entrance procession. Malls and marketplaces, businesses and homes do this sort of outdoor announcement with flags, colors, wreaths. Why not the house of God, the home of God's family, the community's gathering place? Consult Peter Mazar's important and practical guide, *To Crown the Year:* Parking lots, church grounds, paths and walkways, doorways and vestibule all can announce that business as usual has been suspended and that keeping Lent is the business of the day.

INSIDE

The lenten climate should greet the eye and signal the senses as we enter the building, proclaiming that Lent has begun, a time of serious and sustained reflection, a time of focus and attention to the things that really matter. This was the goal of the church's liturgical legislation in the past. The purpose of banning floral arrangements except on Laetare Sunday (Lent's midpoint) and solemnities like Saint Joseph and Annunciation was visual austerity. The suspension of instrumental music, festive preludes, postludes, interludes, and any instrumentation except that needed to sustain the assembly's singing ensured aural sobriety.

■ ASSEMBLY: The first focal point of decorating is often the last one we would think of: the place of the assembly. Decorating this area is neither to teach nor entertain but to create "an atmosphere and a mood" (*Environment and Art in Catholic Worship,* #100). Mazar develops the concept:

> The area high over the heads of the congregation or along the walls is usually a good area for strong decoration that signals the season. For example, a cluster of large branches . . .

an array of purple or gray fabric hangings grabs people's attention when they first enter the worship space, but it does not necessarily demand attention during the liturgy. (48)

"Winter-turning-into-spring" should be the approach, especially in this year of a late Lent. This motif reinforces the continuity of the whole paschal season, Ash Wednesday through Pentecost.

- **FONT**: A visual signal that Lent is a time of preparation for baptism is an empty font (and empty holy water stoups?). But mere emptiness, Mazar notes, can be misread as neglect. On the other hand, some recent attempts at creativity have misfired badly: Sand in the holy water fonts turns them into hotel lobby ashtrays! Mazar suggests that the baptismal font be "drained, cleaned and sealed in a noble manner" before Ash Wednesday. A bold and simple cross of purple cloth placed over the font says a lot without saying a word, as does putting the paschal candle away except for funerals and leaving the ambry open and empty of the chrism vessel. Place the Book of the Elect near the font, inviting prayer for those about to be initiated.

- **CROSS**: A primary symbol of Christianity, the cross is a supremely important item in Catholic worship. Except during the Easter Vigil when the paschal candle leads the way, the cross is the community's standard, shield and coat-of-arms, borne before us whenever we move in pilgrimage formation. The cross is at the head of the community for the penitential procession at the beginning of Lent. For the Palm Sunday procession it is to be "suitably adorned" (sacramentary). On Good Friday it is venerated with a solemnity usually reserved to the eucharist. Perhaps it leads the way into every Sunday eucharist during Lent and the rest of the year. Lent is the time to ask some questions:
  - What does the community's processional cross look like?
  - Is it the cross that is set in the sanctuary during the liturgy? Venerated on Good Friday? Should it be? Could it be?

- **VESTURE**: The prescribed liturgical color for Lent is purple or violet, and Lent's shade should be different from the purple of Advent. Avoid catalog offerings of gaudy purple with appliqué symbols that are busy, distracting, and often not very good art. Visual austerity, simplicity and plainness are the goals, whatever shade of purple is decided upon. On Laetare Sunday a dusky old-rose (not hot pink) may be used, and on Saint Joseph's day the Christmas whites could reappear, a visual signal of that lovely season with which he is so associated. For Palm Sunday, use the same red vesture reserved for the Triumph of the Cross, for Good Friday, and maybe for martyrs' days. Do not use the Pentecost set, and avoid, of course, anything with appliqué doves or flames!

The Sounds of Lent

As aural austerity and an aid to focus on essentials, traditional lenten liturgical usage restricts the use of instrumental music to "only as needed to accompany the voices." If there are no preludes during Lent, except perhaps on the Fourth Sunday, then the first piece the community hears and sings at Mass or the Hours must set exactly the right tone. Remember, however, that simplicity and sobriety need not mean gloominess! Remember, too, that the repertoire of refrains and hymnody for Lent is among the richest of the church.

- **CHANTS**: The recent public and commercial rediscovery of Gregorian chant confirms the power of this venerable music to move hardened hearts in every age. Unaccompanied chant, especially in the form of congregational refrain and cantor's verses, is powerful and prayerful. Because of the sense of solemnity and simplicity it communicates, and because the most ancient Roman tradition favors the approach, a chanted antiphon or refrain rather than the usual metrical hymn might be the best way to begin the eucharist. A perfect chant for this purpose is the traditional refrain to the Latin piece, "Attende, Domine." Appearing in several translations in all the major hymnals ("Draw near, O Lord our God"; "Hear us, almighty Lord"; "Hear our entreaties, Lord," etc.), the chant is a brisk and bright Mode 5 melody, quickly learned and easily memorized. There is nothing gloomy about this unadorned and straightforward piece, whose words and melody are perfectly matched. And, like so many of these chants, it has staying power; it will bear the weight of five weeks' use.

The restoration of responsorial psalmody in the Roman rite gives us perhaps the principal repertoire of refrain/verse chant. Learning a few of these settings will give the community material to use at worship during the communion procession as well as at celebrations of the hours. The normative lenten psalms (51, 33, 95, 23 and 130) contain a wide variety of themes: repentance, trust, openness to God, protection, supplication and hope. Refrain-style settings can be found in many hymnals, Catholic and Protestant, as well as in LTP's *Morning and Evening*.

Another option for refrain-style music at the eucharist comes from Taizé: "Adoramus Te Domine" (*Music from Taizé,* Volume I, GIA G-2433). Poetically gifted planners might write verses for each Sunday. For instance, for the First Sunday: "In the desert of repentance, *adoramus te Domine*"; "In a land parched dry and lifeless, *adoramus te Domine.*" On the Second Sunday: "On the mountain of your glory, *adoramus te Domine.*" Especially with the elect present, creative verses for the Third, Fourth and Fifth Sundays should draw on the rich scriptural images of water/thirst, darkness/light and death/life. The music would be the same, but varied texts could draw the assembly deeper into the desert of repentance as the season unfolds.

■ HYMNS: In the Liturgy of the Hours, the opening verse and response which begin each hour are followed immediately by a metrical hymn. During the eucharist, the preparation of the altar and gifts is a perfect place for the assembly to offer prayer in the form of a metrical hymn. The preparation rite is a fitting setting for the meditative reflection a hymn can afford, since the ritual moment comes midway between the liturgy of the word, probably with its initiatory rituals, and the liturgy of the eucharist with its more intensive style of attentive prayer.

Many fine metrical hymns grace the lenten season. Our own Latin tradition ought not to be neglected, and many of these hymns are available in modern Catholic hymnals and in the Episcopal *Hymnal 1982*. A number of them are rich in biblical and seasonal imagery, such as "Again we keep this solemn fast" and "O Sun of justice." See the *Lutheran Book of Worship* for some wonderful lenten and passion-oriented chorales of the German tradition. Look at the United Church of Christ's *New Century Hymnal* for some fine modern texts, like "Dust and ashes touch our face," and "An outcast among outcasts."

■ ACCLAMATIONS: Music for the acclamations that occur during the liturgy of the word and of the eucharist are considered below, in the section "The Eucharist."

The Rhythm of Lent

WHEN the Lord God summons an assembly and announces a fast, no one is exempted! Through the Prophet Joel, God is very specific, summoning people from all segments of the population: "The aged, the children, even infants at the breast . . . the bridegroom . . . the bride . . . the priests." For centuries this proclamation of scripture has opened the celebration of Lent as the first reading of the Ash Wednesday liturgy. Taking the call and the season seriously might involve a number of decisions:

- All organizations need to trim their calendars every year to the time and tone of this season.
- Religious education needs to be attuned to this season as the church's living catechism, whose "scope and sequence" embrace a lifetime of learning and living.
- Social events need to be planned carefully around the precious few days of festivity that mark an easing of lenten intensity. All through the centuries, almost every religious order and diocese worked in at least one mid-Lent holiday.
- Fund-raising needs to move beyond the parish to embrace the community and beyond that to cradle the world. Lent is our "tithe" of the year, in time and effort and income.
- Friday evening, as the culmination of a day of abstinence, might feature a meatless, fasting meal of soup and bread after the evening Mass and before Stations of the Cross.

Maybe this process has to begin in the spring or summer or whenever the main calendar is put together with dates fixed beyond changing. Planning Lent is a work that has to be done together, as seasons can only be kept together, and we can only be church together. To assist in the planning, LTP provides the *Paschal Mission* each year. It is a resource that has the potential to bring all the disciplines, days and disciples together.

- IN THE SCHOOL: See *Preparing Liturgy for Children and Children for Liturgy* (81 – 92) for models of weekday liturgy with children.

The Word of God

Each of the lenten Sunday lectionary's three cycles are constructed according to the same outline:

- the first readings, from the Hebrew Bible, present passages that chart the course of salvation history;
- the second readings, from the letters of the apostles, "have been selected to fit the gospel and the Old Testament readings and, to the extent possible, to provide a connection between them." (*Introduction to the Lectionary for Mass*, 97)

In Year B this outline is fleshed out to tell the story of God's continuing invitation to us to enter more deeply into a relationship of covenantal love with God. Each Sunday the first reading presents a different event in God's covenant-making with the people, while the second reading reflects on God's covenant in light of the Christ-event.

SUNDAYS' FIRST AND SECOND READINGS

- FIRST SUNDAY: THE BEGINNING: Each year, this Sunday's first reading tells stories of humankind's earliest relationship with God. This year, the story is the covenant with Noah: "See, I am now establishing my covenant with you . . . and with every living creature." The author of 1 Peter looks at Noah's family, saved in the ark, and concludes that "this prefigured baptism, which saves you now."

- SECOND SUNDAY: ABRAHAM: Each year the stories are of the relationship between God and "our father in faith." In Year B we hear of the covenant with Abraham: "I will bless you abundantly . . . because you obeyed my command." In Romans 8, Paul marvels that God would do what, in the end, he had not asked of Abraham: "He who did not spare his own Son, but handed him over for us all."

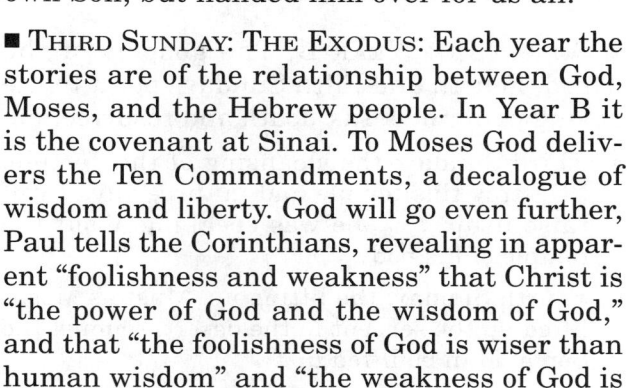

- THIRD SUNDAY: THE EXODUS: Each year the stories are of the relationship between God, Moses, and the Hebrew people. In Year B it is the covenant at Sinai. To Moses God delivers the Ten Commandments, a decalogue of wisdom and liberty. God will go even further, Paul tells the Corinthians, revealing in apparent "foolishness and weakness" that Christ is "the power of God and the wisdom of God," and that "the foolishness of God is wiser than human wisdom" and "the weakness of God is stronger than human strength."

- FOURTH SUNDAY: THE NATION: Each year the stories are of the relationship between God and nation if Israel. In Year B the story is of the covenant renewed through exile. In response to human infidelity, God's design is fulfilled in ways and through people we would not have imagined, through the humiliation of exile, through the intervention of a pagan king. Thus, in the matter of salvation, both the Jewish and Christian communities can concur with the author of Ephesians: "by grace you have been saved through faith; and this is not from you; it is the gift of God."

- FIFTH SUNDAY: THE PROMISE: Each year prophecies are read regarding history's fulfillment in a new, definitive, redemptive intervention by God. In Year B, the topic is the New Covenant. To a people whose experience is the humiliation of defeat and the hopelessness of exile, God promises a new covenant when "I will place my law within them and write it upon their hearts; I will be their God and they shall be my people." Everyone will be included "from the least to the greatest," a whole new generation of sons and daughters. The author of Hebrews paints a portrait of such a son who "learned obedience from what he suffered" and who, "when he was made perfect, became the source of eternal salvation for all."

SUNDAY GOSPELS

Each of the lectionary's three cycles begin with the synoptic gospel stories of the temptation of Jesus in the wilderness (First Sunday of Lent) and the transfiguration of Jesus on the mountain (Second Sunday of Lent). A pastoral decision must be made about which selections from the Gospel of John will be proclaimed to the assembly.

- **GOSPELS OF YEAR B:** The gospels of the Third, Fourth and Fifth Sundays point to the saving power of Jesus' death and resurrection.
  - Third Sunday: the cleansing of the Temple. "'Destroy this temple and in three days I will raise it up' . . . he was speaking about the temple of his body."
  - Fourth Sunday: the lifting up. "Just as Moses lifted up the serpent in the desert, so must the Son of Man be lifted up."
  - Fifth Sunday: the grain fallen to the earth. "The hour has come . . . unless a grain of wheat falls to the ground and dies, it remains just a grain of wheat; but if it dies, it produces much fruit."

- **GOSPELS OF YEAR A:** These magnificent Johannine gospels are, in the opinion of many liturgists, too beautiful to be replaced by the other years' texts or to be abbreviated, as even the Year A lectionary permits. The lectionary introduction notes:

  > Because these gospels are of major importance in regard to Christian initiation, they may also be read in Year B and Year C, *especially* in places where there are catechumens. (97, italics added)

Especially, but not *only*, where there are catechumens. The progression of these readings is clear and powerful both in theme and symbol. From glory to glory they lead toward the baptismal font:

  - Third Sunday: the Samaritan woman at the well (living water)
  - Fourth Sunday: the man born blind (light of faith)
  - Fifth Sunday: the raising of Lazarus (new life)

Moreover, they prepare for the heart of the Johannine gospel, the Passion according to John, a central feature of every year's principal Good Friday liturgy. Heard Sunday by Sunday for the major part of Lent, these texts sound a theme of paschal victory that will be heard clearly on Good Friday, when, in the red vestments proclaiming Jesus "the faithful witness [martyr] and firstborn from the dead," the presider will lift the cross high as what the classic Latin passion hymns call the "royal banner" ("Vexilla regis") and the "trophy of victory" ("Pange, lingua").

Reflections on these gospel readings appear in the calendar entries for each Sunday of Lent.

THE WEEKDAY SCRIPTURES

The calendar entries offer brief reflections on the daily readings. Their arrangement is straightforward:

- Ash Wednesday through the following Saturday: scriptural references and reflections on the principal disciplines of Lent.
- Weeks 1 through 3: Hebrew scriptures and gospel passages paired by themes, with elements proper to a catechesis designed to foster baptismal renewal and penitential reconciliation.
- Week 4 through Holy Week: semi-continuous selection from the gospel of John, with thematically paired first readings leading toward the celebration of the Triduum.

The Eucharist

ENTERING LENTEN WORSHIP

THE principal Mass on the First Sunday of Lent ought to begin with a penitential procession originating in a place apart from where the eucharist will be celebrated (Congregation for Divine Worship, *Circular Letter Concerning the Preparation and Celebration of the Easter Feasts*. Rome, January 1988; English translation, *Origins,* 17, #40 [March 17, 1988], United States Catholic Conference [1-800-235-8722], publication 219-5). This procession is accompanied by the litany of the saints. In the *Ceremonial of Bishops,* #261, this gathering and procession mark not just the First Sunday but any celebration of the eucharist during Lent at which the bishop gathers with a community of the faithful. Each community will have to decide whether such a procession is practical before the principal Mass on the First Sunday, or every Sunday, of Lent.

The official provision for a penitential procession shows us the mind of the church on the character of lenten worship. There is the sense that we are on a journey (not alone, of course, hence the litany of the saints) which mirrors that of the Israelites in the desert and Jesus in the wilderness. Processions bespeak focus, purpose, single-minded attention to the task at hand — very much what lenten fasting is meant to achieve. Every entrance during Lent, therefore, ought to establish the same purposeful presence and focused attention the penitential procession. Good order, deliberate pace and the consciously reverent bearing of all who take part will help even the smallest procession of ministers (and elect?) gather the rest of the assembly into the mood and mystery of worship during Lent.

THE INTRODUCTORY RITES

■ GREETING: The sign of the cross and greeting conclude what may have already been an extensive rite of gathering. Words here are best kept brief and formal, the introduction unnecessary if one preceded the procession and minimal even if one did not! Choose one special greeting for use throughout the season. Or perhaps one text for the first four weeks and a second for use toward the end of Lent and through Holy Week.

■ PENITENTIAL RITE: Although it may always replace the penitential rite, the sprinkling with water would hardly be appropriate during Lent as we look forward to Easter baptism and baptismal renewal. The "I confess" form of the penitential rite provides a kind of communal "act of contrition" that is appropriate during this season, and in some parishes this is prayed with the whole assembly kneeling. A sung Kyrie may follow; then, "Let us pray," a brief silence, and the opening prayer. If the kneeling posture is used, remember that it is the deacon (or in the deacon's absence, the presider) who intones, "Let us kneel." This directive to a posture for prayer will be heard again at the Good Friday liturgy.

For Kyrie chants, consider Richard Proulx's "Three Plainsong Kyries" with tropes from the sacramentary (GIA, G-3162) with choral companion (G-3161). In the present sacramentary's form C of the penitential rite, invocations IV and V seem to be lenten in tone.

The Gloria is omitted during Lent, except on the feast of the Chair of Peter and on the solemnities of Saint Joseph and the Annunciation.

THE LITURGY OF THE WORD

■ SEASONAL PSALMS FOR LENT: Psalm 51 is appointed for Ash Wednesday and at least three other times in the lenten weekday lectionary. It is also used each Friday at Morning Prayer. Traditionally known as the Miserere (from the first word in the Latin version), settings of this classic penitential psalm have been composed in every style and appear in every major hymnal. If the parish already has a standard setting that helps identify the season for the assembly, by all means retain it. Some newer settings of Psalm 51 include:

- "Be merciful, O Lord" by John Karl Hirten (GIA, G-3318); Steven Janco (GIA, G-3518); Joseph B. Smith (GIA, G-3494); Michael Joncas (GIA, G-3433); John Schiavone (GIA, G-2845); Thomas M. Cosley (*Six Psalms for Sundays and Seasons,* WLP, 6208); James Chepponis (*Ostinato Psalm Responses,* WLP, 8536)
- "Psalm for Lent" by Robert Verdi (GIA, G-2629)
- Psalm 51 by Michael Ward (WLP, 8568); Michael Bedford (from *Sing Out! A Children's Psalter,* WLP, 7190)
- 2 settings titled "Create in me" by Bob Hurd (OCP, 10251 and 8792)
- "Give me a new heart" by Christopher Walker (*Singing the Psalms,* vol.3, OCP, keyboard: 10253; guitar: 10254)

Psalms 91 and 130 are also seasonal lenten psalms. Settings include:

Psalm 91

- "Be with me, Lord" by James Chepponis (*Ostinato Psalm Responses,* WLP, 8536); William Ferris (WLP, 6221); Dolores Hruby (*Seasonal Psalms for Children,* WLP 7102); Bob Hurd (OCP, 10250); Michael Joncas (OCP, 10053)
- Psalm 91 by Steven Warner (*Psaltery,* GIA, G-3445); John Bell (*Psalms of Patience, Protest and Praise,* GIA, G-4047)
- "My God in whom I trust" by Fran O'Brien (GIA, G-4516)

Psalm 130

- "Out of the depths" by Mike Hay (*Three Psalms,* WLP, 8583)
- "The Lord will bring mercy" by Michael Bogdan (WLP, 6214)
- "With the Lord" by Michael Joncas (*Singing the Psalms,* vol. 2, OCP, keyboard: 10078; guitar: 10077)
- "From the depths" by Andrew Witchger (GIA, G-3482)

- "De profundis" by Alexander Peloquin (GIA, G-2044)
- "Out of the depths" by Fran O'Brien (GIA, G-4521)

■ GOSPEL ACCLAMATION: One of Lent's oldest and most distinctive traditions directs us to fast from the singing of the alleluia, even on solemnities and feasts and at ritual Masses that happen to fall in Lent. A number of acclamations substitute for the alleluia. These appear in a variety of styles in every major hymnal. Choose one or two settings and use them for the entire season. World Library offers Charles Gardner's "Praise to you, Word of God" (WLP, 8560), a practical setting with easy-to-learn verses for cantor or choir; and Paul French's "Praise and honor to you, Lord Jesus Christ," a slightly more challenging piece.

■ GOSPEL CEREMONIAL AND PROCLAMATION: Highlight the gospels of Lent ritually by honoring their proclamation with a formal gospel procession: incense, candles, lectors (if the gospel will be proclaimed in parts), deacon or presider with gospel book. All of us have experienced and participated in the "parts" approach to the passion gospels of Palm Sunday and Good Friday. LTP recently published *The Passion of Our Lord Jesus Christ,* which contains all four passion gospels divided into sections that make sense according to each unique narrative; suggestions for including music in the proclamation are given.

Older Catholics may remember three clerics chanting the passion during Holy Weeks past, and some will remember the ornate chants that could be used on certain days. Adaptations of the ancient chants with English texts are available ("Passion Gospels and Chants for the Readings" GIA). Opinion varies on the suitability of proclamation of the passion gospels in parts. Some feel that one good reader ought to be able to carry the whole narrative, signaling the varying characters in the story by the subtle changes of inflection and movement that anyone well-trained in public reading would use. Some fear an overdramatization or an entertainment orientation being inflicted on a sacred text that is, after all, a liturgical proclamation. Yet as Aelred Rosser has pointed out regarding the passion narrative in LTP's *Workbook for Lectors and Gospel Readers, 1996:*

> Liturgical practice through the ages, however, has preferred a group — not only because it adds variety but because it adds dynamism and power. (140)

The principle might be extended to include the Johannine gospels for the Third, Fourth and Fifth Sundays of Year A. David Haas and Victoria Tufano have prepared arrangements of these gospels, faithful to the biblical texts, the narrative line kept intact but punctuated with acclamations sung by the assembly at appropriate places (GIA, G-3662). Of course, musicians could search the parish repertoire of well-known hymns to find musical fragments to serve as acclamation, also.

■ DISMISSAL OF CATECHUMENS AND ELECT: Throughout the year, the catechumens are dismissed each Sunday after the homily. During Lent, the catechumens and those among them who have been elected for Easter baptism are dismissed. Alternative forms of the dismissal for specific occasions during Lent are in the *Rite of Christian Initiation of Adults.* Two texts for dismissing catechumens (#67) make the spirit of the dismissal clear. Other words may be used, but any dismissal should convey concern and affection.

■ PROFESSION OF FAITH: The profession of faith is prescribed for Sundays, and for the solemnities of Saint Joseph on March 19 and of the Annunciation on March 25. On the Annunciation, as on Christmas, because of the focus of that feast on the incarnation, a genuflection is prescribed in the profession of faith. See the note about alerting the assembly to this under our Christmas reflections (page 35).

Be aware that initiation rites change the order of concluding the liturgy of the word: After the rite of sending, rite of election, penitential rite for candidates for reception and scrutinies, the catechumens and elect are dismissed. The general intercessions and the profession of faith follow (see RCIA, 156, for example).

■ GENERAL INTERCESSIONS: When catechumenal rites take place on the Sundays of the scrutinies, two different kinds of intercession happen close together. Be sure to keep them distinct. Intercessions for the elect could be chanted with a sung response. Bilingual communities will want to do the intercessions for the elect in various languages, a sung refrain following each intention. After the dismissal, use a more familiar format for the general intercessions by the faithful, and see the suggested scripturally oriented petitions and concluding collects in LTP's *Prayers for Sundays and Seasons,* Year B (or Year A if those gospels are proclaimed instead).

LITURGY OF THE EUCHARIST

■ PREPARATION OF THE GIFTS: See the notes on the suitability of metrical hymns at this moment in the liturgy (page 88).

■ LENTEN PREFACES: Until its replacement by the Vatican II missal in 1970, the Tridentine missal had only one lenten preface, whose focus was entirely on bodily fasting. The current sacramentary provides twelve (P-8–19), drawn from the universal church's rich treasury of liturgical texts and patristic homilies. As is always the danger with the abundance of liturgical riches provided by Vatican II, these prefaces can be chosen by the presider at random and at the last minute! As befits Vatican II's careful provision for solid theology and pastoral variety, particular texts should be carefully and thoughtfully chosen.

Special care needs to be taken with regard to the Third, Fourth and Fifth Sundays of Lent. The prefaces that bear those titles are for use *only* when the Year A gospels are proclaimed! The calendar entries offer reminders and suggestions about this.

■ "LENTEN" EUCHARISTIC PRAYERS: As with the prefaces, thought should go into choosing a eucharistic prayer for Lent. Forgoing the over-used Eucharistic Prayer II should be a foregone conclusion! Time should never be a factor in this holy season, even when initiatory rites are being celebrated, and even at weekday Mass. A brief, carefully prepared homily will balance the use of a eucharistic prayer that may be slightly longer than Eucharistic Prayer II.

- *Eucharistic Prayer for Reconciliation I and II:* These prayers are also appropriate for use during Lent, though there is no provision in them for inserts regarding the elect.

Reconciliation II is especially appropriate for the first four weeks of Lent. It celebrates Christ as "the Word that brings salvation [Sundays 1 and 2], the hand you stretch out to sinners [Sunday 3] [and] the way that leads to your peace" [Sundays 4 and 5].

Reconciliation I is especially appropriate during the fifth week of Lent and Holy Week. Hear the beautiful echoes of the Lord's passion: "When we were lost and could not find the way to you. . . . Before he stretched out his arms between heaven and earth. . . . He desired to celebrate the paschal feast in the company of his disciples. . . . Knowing that he was to reconcile all things in himself by the blood of his cross. . . ."

- *Eucharistic Prayer I:* Two interpolations for Masses at which the scrutinies are celebrated: at the first "Memento" ("Remember, Lord") and at the "Hanc Igitur" ("Father, accept this offering"). See the sacramentary, "Ritual Masses," I. Christian Initiation, 2. The Scrutinies.

■ EUCHARISTIC PRAYER ACCLAMATIONS: Let the sung acclamations during the eucharistic prayer remain constant for the season, at least for Ash Wednesday and the first four Sundays. The lenten sound should echo in whatever setting is chosen. Many of the old chant-style settings work well, especially adaptations of Mass XVIII. When a modern setting is chosen, some parishes signify the unity of the full ninety-day season in an aural way, by using the same acclamations, keeping them in unison (and even a cappella) during Lent, then adding choral and instrumental embellishments for the Triduum and Easter's Fifty Days.

■ THE COMMUNION RITE: See LTP's *Prayers for Sundays and Seasons, Year B* for sample texts to use for the introduction to the Lord's Prayer and the invitation to holy communion.

■ SIGN OF PEACE: We baptized may take for granted or, even worse, trivialize this liturgical gesture and sign. It ought to be celebrated with new meaning and sincerity during this holy season. One option recently approved by the United States bishops (awaiting confirmation from Rome) follows the lead of the Ambrosian rite. In this option, the sign of peace takes place after the general intercessions and before the gifts are brought forward from the assembly. This would be a particularly striking place to have the sign of peace, if the catechumens and elect have just been dismissed. They, after all, will first share in that sign during their initiation at the Easter Vigil, and the most ancient texts describing adult initiation saw this "holy kiss," together with the eucharist, as the culmination of the neophytes' incorporation into the community.

■ Music during communion: The Roman rite's preference for this moment and the most practical arrangement for people moving forward is an antiphon sung by the congregation with psalm verses by a cantor or choirs. When a common psalm is used consistently at the liturgy of the word, the communion procession provides an opportunity to sing the appointed psalms for the Sundays of Lent. Some may already be known to the parish. The learning load is light for the assembly, which has to learn only the refrain.

CONCLUDING RITES

■ Blessing and dismissal: These should have a distinctive style during Lent, to mirror the purposeful entrance ritual. Avoid the solemn blessing that the editors of the current U.S. sacramentary have placed randomly on the First and Third Sundays of Lent. This is a passion oriented text more appropriate to the latter part of the season. In the absence of a solemn blessing for Lent in the current sacramentary, take the text provided in the *Book of Blessings,* number 5 at #2047. This is a translation from an original text in the Italian sacramentary and is a fine choice for the first four Sundays. Alternately, during the first four weeks, choose from among the Prayers over the People: #6 ("a complete change of heart") or #16 ("care for your people and purify them") or #24 ("strengthen [your children] against the attacks of the devil"). For the fifth week of Lent and for Holy Week, #17 is a traditional, passion-oriented prayer ("the love which our Lord Jesus Christ showed us when he delivered himself . . . and suffered the agony of the cross"). Whichever is chosen may be used on weekdays as well. Sample dismissal texts appear in LTP's *Prayers for Sundays and Seasons, Year B.*

■ The recessional: People are generally surprised to find that the Order of Mass does not prescribe a recessional hymn! We have become used to singing as we end the liturgy, and it is true that the final hymn can serve well as a kind of musical sending-forth or commissioning for witness. But the very "usual-ness" of singing a recessional might well be a good reason to omit one during Lent. Although official directives argue against instrumental music during Lent, absolute silence at this point may quickly degenerate into loud conversation (which would set no kind of mood at all). An alternative would be a blessing and dismissal and then the exit of presider and ministers while the organ (or other instrument) quietly plays one of the plaintive lenten chants, for example, "Audi, benigne conditor" or "Vexilla regis prodeunt," or "Parce, Domine."

Other Celebrations

MORNING AND EVENING PRAYER

An increasing number of parishes have begun celebrating vespers on Sunday evenings of Lent. This can be the basis for a tradition of regular celebration of Morning and Evening Prayer throughout the year. It may be very easy to interest at least a part of the regular weekday assembly in gathering a bit earlier or staying a bit later around the morning and/or evening Mass times to celebrate this form of liturgical prayer. See LTP's *Morning and Evening* booklets for assembly and presider/cantor, along with the orientation book, *Morning and Evening: A Parish Celebration* for a thoroughly informative and very convenient way to begin or to improve upon this official form of communal liturgical prayer.

VIGILS

Parishes that have grown familiar with the Liturgy of the Hours may find the later hours of Saturday night conducive to extended praise and reflection. The Lent-Easter volume (II) of the full *Liturgy of the Hours* contains all the material necessary for an Office of Readings—Vigils celebration.

COMMUNAL PENANCE

Since lenten penance is not only individual but also social, Lent is an appropriate time for communal penance services. One approach is to schedule one service early in Lent and a second closer to or at the beginning of Holy Week. The earlier service could be primarily an opportunity to hear the word of God and a directed meditation on it, leading to an examination of conscience and the undertaking of a penance to be lived throughout Lent. The later service then becomes the occasion for confession and absolution in preparation for the Triduum.

Resources for planning an order of service appear in the *Rite of Penance,* appendix II. Unfortunately, by suggesting the use of water and the veneration of the cross, these rites anticipate ritual elements best left to the Triduum. Instead, the chanting of a litany while kneeling is a traditional form of penitential prayer. For a fine text, see the *Book of Common Prayer,* page 267.

COMMUNAL ANOINTING OF THE SICK

The celebration of anointing is a sacramental way of joining the sick even more closely to the Lord's paschal mystery. Ritual Mass texts should not replace proper texts on Sundays of Lent or on March 19 or 25. The rite, however, may be celebrated within Mass even on those days. One reading from the ritual lectionary may be substituted for a Sunday scripture passage.

FUNERALS

Funeral Masses are not permitted on Sundays of Lent. The spirit of Lent can be maintained and the celebration of Christian death enhanced on weekdays by using the day's scriptures, if appropriate.

MARRIAGES

With the pastoral sensitivity that marks Vatican II, liturgical norms permit marriages during the lenten season. But we are also required to explain to couples why the nature of Lent makes it an inappropriate season for such celebrations (*Rite of Marriage,* #11; *Ceremonial of Bishops,* #604). The ban on flowers and instrumental music seems to apply to these celebrations as well. Pastorally, all policies need to be arrived at with broad discussion and free exchange of ideas, and implemented with charity and understanding.

BAPTISMS AND CONFIRMATIONS

The *Circular Letter Concerning the Preparation and Celebration of the Easter Feasts* (#27) emphasizes the inappropriateness of baptism and confirmation during Holy Week. That observation goes for Lent as well. Pastorally sensitive policy should defer baptisms, ordinarily, until the Easter Vigil, Easter Day or Eastertime.

STATIONS OF THE CROSS

Stations of the Cross on Fridays is a time-honored tradition in many parishes and a newly revived custom in many others. Recent publications offer a variety of formats and emphases for this devotion. While venerable and fitting, the "Stabat Mater" is not mandatory at Stations. The "Vexilla regis" is available in a number of modern translations set to the ancient chant (for example, *Worship,* #435), and is a powerful hymn celebrating the triumph of the cross. Another option is the chanted Agnus Dei of Mass XVIII.

At Home

PRAYER AT TABLE

Always the first and best way to pray as a household or alone, mealtime calls us to fulfill a bodily need and, it is to be hoped, nourishes our spirits as well. Prayer at these natural moments is a custom to revive or intensify during Lent especially. The easiest aids to this goal, in every season of the year, are the series of *Mealtime Prayercards.* The lenten ones have Lent on one side and Eastertime on the reverse. They combine easily celebrated prayer with optional scripture and song. On the table, too, should be some simple reminder of the season — cross, bare branches, violet candle.

SPECIAL DAYS AND BLESSINGS

Catholic Household Blessings and Prayers is always a rich resource. For this season of the year it offers the following celebrations for use or adaptation by every household:

- Ash Wednesday: Blessing the Season and a Place of Prayer, page 132
- Blessings of the Lenten Disciplines: Fasting and Almsgiving, page 137
- Passion Sunday: Placing the Branches in the Home, page 140
- Prayers of the Triduum, page 143

PRAYER ALONE

Lectio divina, "holy reading," is a custom embraced by many Christians as an oasis of peace in a too-busy world. Lent is the perfect time to begin or revive this custom. The Office of Readings excerpted from the *Liturgy of the Hours* is published by the Daughters of Saint Paul. It is filled with fine patristic and sanctoral writings from across the centuries and has a year's cycle of scripture as well. The two-volume *Lent Sourcebook* from LTP is a remarkable compendium of lenten scripture, homilies, poetry, reflections and prayers. A helpful introduction to the discipline of *lectio divina* can be found in the front of *Prayers for Sundays and Seasons, Year B.*

CALENDAR

March

WED 8 — #219 (LMC, #176–184) violet
Ash Wednesday

ORIENTATION

Day of fast and abstinence. • In planning the Ash Wednesday schedule and preparing the day's liturgies, consider this: Ash Wednesday is not a holy day of obligation and people usually are very busy in midweek. Moreover, the lenten discipline has undergone so many changes over the decades, with extensive revision even since Vatican II, that keeping up with all the rules and regulations is quite a challenge.

All the more amazing, then, that such a remarkable number of people flock to Ash Wednesday celebrations, seeking to participate in at least its most distinctive ritual. Let all who plan and preside at liturgy, and all who cherish the power of liturgy, rejoice on Ash Wednesday, especially in this Jubilee year! Motivation and faith are not ours to judge. Trusting that the same Spirit who led Jesus into the desert will lead to our liturgies all who need to be with us on this day, let our gift to them be well-prepared and faith-filled celebrations.

Consider a full schedule and keep some details in mind:

- Morning Prayer should include the famous lenten sermon of Pope Leo the Great (see the Office of Readings for the Thursday after Ash Wednesday)
- Mass has a unique introductory rite today.
- Ashes may be distributed at liturgies of the word any time during the day.
- Consider crowning the observance with sung Evening Prayer.
- Because today is a day of fast and abstinence, provide a fasting community meal after evening Mass or vespers. This would be most appreciated by parishioners who come directly from work precisely to make a good beginning to this special season.

ASH WEDNESDAY MASS

Before Beginning

Ashes are the focus for today's worship. Give them prominence by placing them on a pedestal in the sanctuary, in the midst of the assembly, or near the font or entrance if all can turn and face it. Dignified vessels should be reserved exclusively for this once-a-year purpose. The ashes may remain visible as part of the seasonal decor or in a seasonal corner. See notes for Ash Wednesday in *The Sacristy Manual* (G. Thomas Ryan, LTP, 1993), pages 19–95. There should be no burning of palms as part of today's liturgy. In fact, nothing extra should be added to this liturgy, whose symbol is ashes, not fire, and whose tone is solemn simplicity. Traditionally, ashes are placed on our foreheads in the form of a cross, branding us again with the sign of baptism, reminding us that Lent is a time of baptismal renewal.

Introductory Rites

Strong, stately and perhaps a capella, the entrance song should set a good beginning to this season. "Attende Domine," in Latin or any of its many English translations, is a good choice. Like the official introit chant of the sacramentary, it extols God's mercy. Some Taizé Kyries are appropriate as well.

Today the opening prayer follows the greeting immediately. Both may be chanted. The penitential rite is omitted, since the ritual with ashes functions as a solemn penitential rite.

Liturgy of the Word

Psalm 51, the Miserere, today's responsorial psalm, has always been the community's chant as we move toward Easter. The gospel acclamation verse, from Psalm 95, is the invitatory from the Liturgy of the Hours. Like Psalm 51, it is one of Lent's time-honored songs: "If today you hear God's voice, harden not your hearts."

Today's liturgy of the word and the dramatic penitential rite provide the homilist with an interesting paradox. Almost as soon as we hear Jesus' exhortation to wash our face and groom our hair when fasting, we begin a ritual that seems to ignore what he said! However, received in penitence as a mark of our mortality and in hope as a promise of resurrection, the ashes are an inspiration to evangelization. We do need the cautionary note in today's scriptures, especially the gospel. Otherwise, the imposition of ashes — indeed the keeping of the whole season — can become empty formalism, or worse, prideful elitism. Consult the Office of Readings in the *Liturgy of the Hours* for homiletic help.

MARCH

Blessing and Giving of Ashes

Unlike for the blessing rites for Candlemas and Palm Sunday, the sacramentary provides no formal introduction. Perhaps it was felt that the homily that immediately precedes the blessing would provide the necessary introduction. Homilists might adapt the brief words found in the *Book of Blessings* (#1663) or the introduction in the *Book of Common Prayer* (page 26) to conclude the homily, then follow this exhortation with the invitation to prayer found in the sacramentary.

- MUSIC: For the distribution of ashes, choose music that does not require hymnal or worship aid. Hymns are generally not useful here. Lucien Deiss' (World Library, *People's Mass Book*) "My soul is longing for your peace" (Psalm 131) or "Grant to us, O Lord," (Ezekiel and Jeremiah) would work well. The refrain of "Give us, Lord, a new heart" by Bernadette Farrell (OCP, #710) goes well with verses of any psalm that speaks of trust and conversion (Psalms 25, 62 and 130) chanted to Tone 1 by Joseph Smith (*Lead Me, Guide Me*).

- GENERAL INTERCESSIONS: Conclude the rite by linking the community's prayer, fasting and almsgiving to the needs of the wider human family. Sample texts are in *Prayers for Sundays and Seasons, Year B*. See below the notes on the observance of the Jubilee Request for Pardon.

Liturgy of the Eucharist

The suggested preface for this day is Lent IV, but Lent III is also suitable, since it speaks of self-denial as a form of expressing thanks and incorporates the social dimension of penitence. The preface of Reconciliation I strikes a familiar chord: "Now is the time for your people to turn back to you and to be renewed in Christ your Son, a time of grace and reconciliation." Eucharistic Prayers for Reconciliation I or II are good choices for this season.

DISTRIBUTION OF ASHES OUTSIDE MASS

See the *Book of Blessings* (chapter 52) for the complete order for blessing and distributing ashes apart from Mass. This may be done in church or with a gathering as in a nursing home, and may be led by a priest, deacon or layperson (a layperson uses ashes already blessed). There is no provision for distribution of ashes apart from communal prayer and the proclamation of some scripture. For liturgies celebrated with children, consult *Preparing Liturgy for Children and Children for Liturgy*, 81.

JUBILEE OBSERVANCE

In Rome today there is a penitential procession in the morning and the Pope is scheduled to proclaim at some time today a solemn Request for Pardon. This text is expected to acknowledge the failures of Christians over the past millennium, especially those in communion with Rome, and to ask pardon of God and of the whole human race for these sins and failures — ours and those of our forebears. Local communities may wish to enter into the spirit of this extraordinary public act of contrition, either by incorporating a similar penitential text into the liturgies of Ash Wednesday or as a separate celebration. If an official text is not provided by the national or diocesan Jubilee office, consider using or adapting the Litany of Penitence found in the *Book of Common Prayer* (pages 267 – 269). That litany follows the imposition of ashes and the chanting of Psalm 51 and is recited kneeling, a posture of humility and repentance.

THU 9 #220 (LMC, #176–184) violet
Thursday after Ash Wednesday

Frances of Rome, married woman, religious founder, optional memorial. • The weekdays preceding the First Sunday of Lent may be thought of as an orientation to the observance of Lent. The scripture readings reflect on the disciplines and attitudes that should form our approach to life from now until Easter. Today both passages sound the note of choice: the way of life (Deuteronomy), the way of the cross (the gospel).

Frances, a busy wife and mother, cared for the poor and the sick while the plague and civil war raged through Rome in the late fourteenth and early fifteenth century.

FRI 10 #221 (LMC, #176–184) violet
Friday after Ash Wednesday

Day of abstinence. • Isaiah's God describes the kind of fast acceptable to the Lord: a fast from self-centeredness to become more attuned to the needs of others. Today's scriptures are perfect for the first of Lent's Fridays. All Fridays of Lent are days of abstinence, all tinged with grief and gladness as they point toward Good Friday, to Jesus' Sabbath rest in the tomb, and to the first day of the week.

SAT 11 #222 (LMC, #176–184) violet
Friday after Ash Wednesday

Isaiah's call to conversion continues to move our attention from self to others. The call of Levi parallels this, making the

MARCH

social nature of conversion clear. Levi invited all his friends — his fellow sinners, that is — to meet the Lord. Is there a missionary outreach to our lenten observance, or do we think of Lent as a time for personal spirituality only? How do Christians in this community seek out alienated or apathetic neighbors? Parishes without catechumens or elect or candidates seeking full communion need to reflect on why that is, and what might make next Lent different.

12 #23 (LMC, #19) violet
First Sunday of Lent

ORIENTATION

In the centuries before the addition of Ash Wednesday and the weekdays that follow it, this Sunday was the beginning of Lent; in fact, it still is in the calendar of the Ambrosian rite of Milan. On this first Lord's Day of Lent, today's principal eucharist ought to feature at least two distinctive elements:

- PENITENTIAL PROCESSION: This procession is the recommended opening rite at the principal eucharist in all communities today (*Circular Letter on Lent, Triduum and Eastertime,* #23, and the *Ceremonial of Bishops,* #261). Consult LTP's *The Sacristy Manual,* 196–198.

- RITE OF SENDING: Most dioceses celebrate the rite of election at the cathedral, and perhaps at an additional location if the diocese covers a lot of territory. The parish rite is the Rite of Sending the Catechumens for Election and Candidates for the Call to Continuing Conversion. See *Rite of Christian Initiation of Adults,* #111, for catechumens, both adults and children; #38 for baptized candidates; and #536 for catechumens and candidates together. See the notes in *The Sacristy Manual,* pages 199–200.

The godparents' testimony should express to the assembly what God has done in the lives of the elect. If not using the formulary in the rite, godparents should avoid listing achievements and focus on God's action in the lives of the elect during their initiation journey. Asking the godparents to write out their testimony and go over it with the initiation director may help focus what they are going to say.

For appropriate music see David Haas' *Who Calls You by Name,* volume 1 (GIA). Contact diocesan planners for information on the cathedral program so that the parish's music can link the celebrations.

LECTIONARY

See the Lectionary Overview and "The Word of God," page 89. Year B presents Mark's succinct version of the Temptation of Jesus. At first reading, it may be a disappointment to hearers — and homilists — who recall the more familiar, richly detailed versions of Matthew (Year A) and Luke (Year C). This is the beauty of Vatican II's three-year lectionary! We can hear each evangelist's unique perspective on Jesus. We also benefit from the insights of the Protestant adaptation of Vatican II's work, *Revised Common Lectionary* (RCL). Both benefits can come together this Sunday.

First, let the powerful simplicity of Mark's account be the focus of liturgical preaching, leaving aside Matthew and Luke. Then look at what RCL adds to the Roman lectionary. To our Mark 1:12–15, the ecumenical lectionary adds verses 9–11, Mark's baptism scene. The homilist may wish to call attention to this. By adding the baptism, RCL emphasizes the link between Jesus' baptism, his temptation in the wilderness and his announcement of God's kingdom. At the baptism the Spirit descends, and then *at once* (Greek: *euthus,* immediately), the same Spirit drives out (a dramatic phrase) the one who was just baptized into the desert. There is urgency here that links the mission of Jesus to that of Israel. Moreover, it links Jesus to the experience of his disciples in every age. Baptism did not lead Jesus into peaceful prayer at a woodsy retreat. The word "immediately" (omitted in the Roman lectionary) makes clear that Jesus, after his baptism, like Israel after its Red Sea passage, like Christians after baptism, must experience wilderness testing before bearing witness, whether that witness be Israel among the Gentiles, Jesus before the nation, or us in our own corner of the world.

SACRAMENTARY

A special preface is appointed for the First Sunday in Lent (P-12). Avoid the solemn blessing in most U.S. editions of the sacramentary. The editors chose the blessing entitled, "Passion of the Lord," which is not the focus of this first phase of Lent. The sacramentaries of the other language groups have added a solemn blessing for Lent. An

LENT: MARCH 99

MARCH

English translation of this text appears in the *Book of Blessings,* blessing 5 at #2047. The "prayer over the people" is a style of collect-blessing unique to the Roman rite, prescribed before Vatican II for daily use during Lent. Suggested choices for this prayer appear in "The Eucharist" section of the introduction to this season. Suggested texts for general intercessions, introduction to the Lord's Prayer, invitation to holy communion and dismissal of the assembly are in *Prayers for Sundays and Seasons, Year B* (use the Year A volume on the Third, Fourth and Fifth Sundays if the scriptures of that year are used).

THE WEEK AHEAD

Because this is the first full week of the season, presiders will want to announce personally any lenten gatherings that begin this week: Bible study, the Liturgy of the Hours, fasting meals, paschal mission or the Way of the Cross.

MON 13 — Monday of the First Week of Lent
#224 (LMC, #176–184) violet

Today's Leviticus passage lists the demands of justice toward one's neighbor. This reading from Israel's Torah is linked to Matthew's story in which Jesus, whom Matthew presents as the giver of the new Torah, teaches that the judgment we will receive hinges on our care for those in need.

TUE 14 — Tuesday of the First Week of Lent
#225 (LMC, #176–184) violet

The beautiful passage from Isaiah pictures a heaven-sent spring: God's word descends as rain and then flowers in an abundant harvest of holiness. What is the choicest fruit that word has brought forth? The gospel presents it at the very beginning of Lent. It is the Lord's Prayer, formed in the heart of God's own Son and heard on the lips of his disciples in every age. The gospel also presents the condition without which even the Lord's Prayer will not be acceptable to God: mutual forgiveness.

WED 15 — Wednesday of the First Week of Lent
#226 (LMC, #176–184) violet

The honest Jonah appears in both readings: in the first, as a prophet heeded by sinners; in the gospel, as a warning to us to heed a prophet even greater than Jonah. Only the briefest portion of Jonah is prescribed, but read the whole thing — it isn't very long. We do well to rejoice that God's love has found us, especially the God whose love embraces the multitude "who do not know their right hand from their left — not to mention all the animals!" (Jonah 4:11)

THU 16 — Thursday of the First Week of Lent
#227 (LMC, #176–184) violet

Once a year we read from the book of Esther, basis for the Jewish feast of Purim. The wicked Haman's plot to exterminate the Jewish people is no mere biblical memory but a horror made real in the Holocaust of our own century. May we never forget! But Israel's stronghold then and now is that radical trust in God's power to save, to which Esther bears unflinching witness.

FRI 17 — Friday of the First Week of Lent
#228 (LMC, #176–184) violet

Patrick, bishop, missionary, optional memorial. Day of abstinence. • The penitential discipline of Fridays in Lent makes today's scripture message particularly appropriate. Jesus tells us to take the initiative toward reconciliation — not only when we have something against someone, but whenever someone has an issue with us. Here is the unique formula of Jesus' teaching, repeated tomorrow: "You have heard it said before... but I say to you...."

Lent and Saint Patrick's Day are easily celebrated together. There is even a tie-in to Christian initiation. Patrick's legendary first liturgical action brought the Celtic May Day bonfire into Christian life as part of the service of light for the Easter Vigil. The shamrock was a helpful visual aid for teaching about the Trinity. Driving the snakes out of Ireland was a dramatic form of exorcism. Green became the ritual color of penitents returning to the church at Easter, as white is associated with the newly baptized.

SAT 18 — Saturday of the First Week of Lent
#229 (LMC, #176–184) violet

Cyril of Jerusalem, bishop and doctor of the church, optional memorial. • Not only is the disciple forbidden to hate the enemy, we are commanded to love and pray for the enemy.

■ SAINT FOR THE ELECT: See Cyril's writing in the Office of Readings. Cyril is one of many master catechists and mystagogues. Ambrose, John Chrysostom, Augustine, Chromatius of Aquileia and Cyril have much to teach the elect and us, the penitent faithful, journeying with them to the font; and, thanks to Vatican II, their homilies are available to us in the Office of Readings of the *Liturgy of the Hours.*

MARCH

19 Second Sunday of Lent
#26 (LMC, #22) violet

ORIENTATION

The Transfiguration is celebrated annually on August 6, but liturgical instinct wants to celebrate the mystery closer to Easter. Most Protestant churches observe the Transfiguration on the Sunday before Lent, thus bracketing the time after Christmas with two manifestations of the Lord. Roman custom waits until just after Lent begins to celebrate the event. Florists sometimes force flowers to bloom that would wait a few more weeks if left to themselves. So the church catches a glimpse of glory in the Transfiguration as "preparation for the Lord's approaching passion" and a promise and foretaste of "the glory of the Lord's resurrection" (Preface, Second Sunday of Lent).

PENITENTIAL RITE FOR CANDIDATES

A special penitential rite may be celebrated today with candidates, similar to the scrutinies for the elect that take place on the next three Sundays. This rite (see RCIA, 59) is for baptized but uncatechized Catholics and people baptized in other Christian communities now joining the Catholic church. For discussion of the importance of distinguishing between baptized candidates and the elect, see Ron Oakham's *One at the Table* (LTP, 1996).

LECTIONARY

See the Lectionary Overview and "The Word of God," page 89. "Gospel writers," writes Fred B. Craddock, "reveal their intent either in how a story is told or in when a story is told; that is, where it is located in the narrative" (*Preaching through the Christian Year B*. Trinity Press International, 1993, 126). Mark places the Transfiguration of Christ almost at the midpoint of his gospel, at the center of Mark 8:22 — 10:52. That section opens and closes with the healing of a blind man, and three times during that section Jesus foretells his passion and death. Throughout the whole section, however, the disciples themselves remain unable to see who Jesus really is and fail to understand what his predictions mean. The Transfiguration occurs after the first prediction of the passion. No sooner have they enjoyed that glimpse, however, than they are arguing over who is the greatest, after the second prediction, and jockeying for seats of honor, after the third prediction.

The linking of the Transfiguration to the springtime shared by nature and the church makes good sense. Many icons depicting this event carry the Greek title *metamorphosis*, the same word we use to describe the phenomenon in nature at this time of year. Today's liturgy reminds us that the way to resurrection is through suffering and death. We, like the disciples in Mark's gospel, are often blind to who Jesus is and to what that demands of us. For us, as well as these first disciples, the invitation is frightening, confusing, transfiguring and glorious.

SACRAMENTARY

Ritual patterns and texts used last week continue throughout this first phase of Lent. Today's preface (P-13) echoes the gospel reading and the orientation of today's liturgy to lenten observance.

THE WEEK AHEAD

Two solemnities occur this week, the transferred observance of Saint Joseph and the annual solemnity of the Annunciation. Next Sunday the First Scrutiny is celebrated and the long Johannine gospels begin, continuing on the following two Sundays. If the initiatory rite of *traditio*, the "handing on" of the Creed next week and the Lord's Prayer during the fifth week are to be celebrated, now is the time to obtain worthy copies of these texts, perhaps on parchment, in calligraphy.

MON 20 Joseph, Husband of the Virgin Mary
#543 (LMC, #272) white
SOLEMNITY

ORIENTATION

"A righteous man, unwilling to expose Mary to public disgrace," is how Matthew describes Joseph. Not a spoken word of his

LENT: MARCH 101

MARCH

do we have, but we can see faith-filled obedience and courage in his deeds! Joseph was a descendant of the royal house of David so that Jesus could fulfill God's promises to that dynasty, and a carpenter by trade. From the fourth century on, he was venerated in the East; his popularity flourished in the Western church especially during the fifteenth century. No doubt the widespread adoption of Francis of Assisi's manger scene as well as the medieval nativity plays augmented this devotion. Craftsman, provider and guardian of Mary and Jesus, Joseph is venerated as patron of the universal church, of fathers, of workers and of a happy death. The insertion of his name into the canon of the Mass (Eucharistic Prayer I) by Pope John XXIII was the first formal alteration of that text in centuries.

LECTIONARY

The solemnity's proper readings fit well with Lent's themes. The first reading is God's promise to David to establish and uphold his family's house. By baptism we too are descendants of Abraham, whose faith Paul praises. Abraham, "hoping against hope, believed that he would become 'the father of many nations.'" Joseph acted in faith to receive Mary as his wife.

SACRAMENTARY

A thoughtful celebration can keep Lent's solemn tone even as the community rightly exalts Joseph and feasts in his honor.

- Lenten elements: sung acclamations, most of the décor, passion chant or hymn
- Festal elements: white vesture (perhaps the Christmas set), floral arrangements, instrumental music, the Gloria and suitable decoration or lighting for Joseph's window, statue or shrine. Good hymns in honor of Joseph are few. "By all your saints still striving" (*Worship*, #706) has a verse in his honor, and G.W. Williams's "Come now, and praise the humble saint" is matched to the well-known American tune, LAND OF REST. The *Collegeville Hymnal* also has selections for this solemnity.

SAINT JOSEPH'S TABLE

This Italian tradition began as a meal to which all, especially the poor, were welcomed. It was often given in gratitude to Saint Joseph for a favor received. This is a perfect lenten custom, since it combines prayer, fasting and almsgiving. Prayer and song, both for Joseph and Lent, are customary. The table features meatless dishes, and a collection is taken for the poor. See *Book of Blessings,* "Order for the Blessing of St. Joseph's Table" (chapter 53) and *Catholic Household Blessings and Prayers* for domestic prayer (165) and Saint Joseph's litany (36).

JUBILEE CELEBRATION

Today in Rome the Jubilee celebration of craftspeople is observed. Communities may wish to give a special place in an evening celebration of the eucharist or Hours to those who enrich the parish in the various crafts and trades, as well as to workers in general, and perhaps honor them afterwards with a festive collation.

TUE 21 — #231 (LMC, #176–184) violet
Tuesday of the Second Week of Lent

Hypocrisy is the first deadly sin for religiously observant people. Both readings castigate pious observance devoid of practical consequences. If we would see our scarlet sins become white as snow, says Isaiah, then come to the aid of the community's least powerful: Justice for widows and orphans is the biblical way of putting it. Jesus points to the frequent link between ostentation in religious practice and neglect of others. Away with obsession with titles and status! The humility of knowing how much we need to learn can keep us open to serving those who can reveal God's face to us.

WED 22 — #232 (LMC, #176–184) violet
Wednesday of the Second Week of Lent

Rejection and unjust suffering often await true prophets, including Jeremiah and Jesus. Thus a twofold challenge emerges from today's readings, and the challenge confronts each of us as well: Are we willing to share the prophets' fate as part of our baptism into Christ? How do we respond to prophetic voices that trouble our certainties?

THU 23 — #233 (LMC, #176–184) violet
Thursday of the Second Week of Lent

Toribio de Mongrovejo, bishop, optional memorial. • The target audience: religiously observant people "who loved money." The setting: a Jeremiah reading about human instability, unreliability and deviousness. Part of our lenten journey involves a serious assessment of our principles. The frightening point of today's gospel, for us who are busy minding our business, is

MARCH

that the rich man was condemned not for doing something wrong, but for doing nothing.

Today's saint began his ecclesiastical career as a professor of law and a judge in the Spanish Inquisition. Still a layman, he was appointed Archbishop of Lima, where he opposed both ecclesiastical abuses and colonial exploitation of the native peoples. Toribio was a model bishop, tirelessly visiting his far-flung parishes and presenting the faith to the peoples of the "new world" in their own languages. He died in Peru on this day in 1606.

FRI 24 — Friday of the Second Week of Lent
#234 (LMC, #176–184) violet

Day of abstinence. • The story of Jacob's son Joseph, one of the Bible's greatest, is told in the first reading and psalm today. It is a tale of treachery and sin transformed by God's providence into salvation for the brothers who betrayed their own flesh and blood. Christ's rejection and execution will become, in God's saving purpose, a harvest beyond anything the appointed tenants could have produced.

On this day in 1980, Archbishop Oscar Romero of San Salvador was martyred as he presided at the eucharist, repeating a sacrilege that is part of our history, for example, Stanislaus of Cracow (+ 1079) and Thomas Becket of Canterbury (+ 1170). Those bishops were canonized almost immediately, but the official church has yet to honor Romero in this way. His people do not forget, however, and Romero's icon is venerated throughout the Americas. Pray for justice and peace in El Salvador.

SAT 25 — The Annunciation of the Lord
#545 (LMC, #274) white
SOLEMNITY

ORIENTATION

Nine months before Christmas, this ancient (sixth century) feast marks the day when the archangel Gabriel hailed the virgin of Nazareth. The proximity of this day to the beginning of spring (in the Northern Hemisphere), as well as its liturgical rank (no fasting allowed!), make it a welcome day off from the rigors of Lent.

LECTIONARY

To relate this solemnity to the lenten season, look to the second reading, Hebrews 10:4–10. It links the incarnation of Christ to his sacrificial life and death. Burnt offerings and animal sacrifices are superseded by his proclamation of vocation: "I have come to do your will." His doing of God's will is linked, in turn, to our "sanctification through the offering of the body of Jesus Christ once for all."

SACRAMENTARY

As on the solemnity of Saint Joseph, thoughtful choices can maintain the spirit of Lent while appropriately celebrating Annunciation:

- Lenten elements: introduction to the Lord's Prayer, invitation to communion, final blessing and dismissal.
- Festal elements: the Gloria is sung today, and white vestments are worn. Suitable decoration or lighting is appropriate for any representations of the annunciation or of Mary or the archangel Gabriel. There is a special preface (P-44), which means that a eucharistic prayer for reconciliation may not be used.

FESTIVE EVENING PRAYER

Every religious order and nation seems to have a feast in Lent that suspends fasting for that day. Here is a solemnity for all of us! Why not have a vespers service with a little feasting afterwards? A custom common to France and Scandinavia was the preparation of yeast-raised waffles served with whipped cream. Special pastries after evening prayer might help usher in spring without detracting too much from the focused intensity of Lent.

JUBILEE CELEBRATION

The Jubilee calendar calls for a celebration at Nazareth today which will be linked to the Basilica of Saint Mary Major in Rome and to the world's great Marian shrines. The purpose of the celebration is "to underscore the dignity of women in the light of Mary's mission." Local communities may wish to plan similar celebrations to honor the women who minister in our midst, or to explore expanded roles for women in church and society.

26 Third Sunday of Lent

#29 or 28 (LMC, #25)
violet

ORIENTATION

The Third Sunday of Lent is the Sunday of the First Scrutiny. This initiatory rite should take place at the principal celebration. This Sunday thus marks an intensification of observance for the elect. Careful preparation will allow the liturgy to deliver its message with the eloquent simplicity that is traditional of the Roman rite.

FIRST SCRUTINY

Paragraph numbers refer to the *Rite of Christian Initiation of Adults*:

- *Invitation to Prayer (152):* After the homily, the elect and godparents gather facing the congregation, with presider in center aisle; or pairs of elect and sponsors may be positioned throughout the assembly. Presider directs elect to bow their heads or kneel and pray. A period of silence is observed.

- *Intercessions for the elect (153):* Godparents place right hands on the shoulders of the elect during the intercessions. These are prayers for the elect, not the usual general intercessions. Some parishes adapt them to pray for the power of Christ to overcome what is sinful in the elect and in the community.

- *Exorcism (154):* Presider, with hands joined, offers first prayer, then lays both hands on head of each of the elect in silence (in many parishes, catechists and godparents also lay on hands). The silence is unhurried and complete, not covered by instrumental music or congregational singing. Presider, with hands outstretched over all the elect, offers second prayer (in some parishes, the whole assembly joins in this gesture).

  The exorcism may conclude with a psalm or song. Select one and sing it at each scrutiny. Since the scrutinies are meant to uncover and heal what is weak and sinful, a hymn that speaks of healing might be appropriate. Some suggestions: for first scrutiny: "O Healing River," arranged by J. Michael Joncas (GIA, G-259); for second scrutiny: "Amazing Grace" ("blind but now I see"); Marty Haugen's "Awake, O sleeper" (text echoes second reading, Year A); for third scrutiny: refrain of "I am the Bread of Life" (Susanne Toolan), repeated several times; "God is our fortress and our rock" (translation by Michael Perry in Worship); "Now the green blade rises."

- *Dismissal (155):* An optional text is provided if the elect are not dismissed, but this by way of concession. The dismissal should take place.

  Throughout this Lent of the Jubilee Year, the official papal calendar of events prescribes the full observance of the scrutinies as well as the rite of giving the creed and the Lord's Prayer to the catechumens.

LECTIONARY

■ YEAR A READINGS: Moses strikes the rock in the desert and water flows for the people (first reading). The love of God has been poured into our hearts through the Holy Spirit (second reading). The water Jesus gives is living water (gospel). An important element in the Year A gospels for the Third, Fourth and Fifth Sundays is the progression in the main character's understanding of who Jesus is as the story unfolds. This week the Samaritan woman is represents each catechumen's journey to faith; therefore, her manner of addressing Jesus is significant. She begins by calling him, politely but not perceptively, "Sir" (4:11, 15, 19a). Later she advances to, "You are a prophet" (4:9b). Then she opens the way for Jesus to announce who he is really is. "When the Messiah comes he will teach us everything," the woman says, and Jesus responds, "I who speak with you am he" (4:25–26). The passage ends with the townspeople acknowledging Jesus as "Savior of the world" (4:42). We, too, are growing in our appreciation of who Jesus really is, and, like the townspeople, we make our own decision about who Jesus is for us. Mark W. G. Stibbe points out a further dimension of today's gospel, a nuptial motif:

> [The Samaritan woman] has been married five times and is now living with a sixth man. This makes Jesus the seventh and therefore perfect man in her life. A symbolic betrothal is now suggested. The woman of Samaria becomes the eschatological bride. At the same well where Jacob was betrothed to Rachel, the woman of Samaria becomes the "bride" in the long-awaited marriage between God and his people. The surprise, of course, is that she is not Jewish; she is a Samaritan, and "Jews do not associate with Samaritans" (4:9). This indicates that the new era inaugurated by the Messiah will be universal rather than narrowly nationalistic. All who follow Jesus can be part of this new age, whether they are Jews, Greeks, Samaritans or any other race. No longer is Israel alone the bride of Yahweh. (*John's Gospel,* New York: Routledge, 1994, 67–68)

■ YEAR B READINGS: See the Lectionary Overview and, for notes on the first two readings, see "The Word of God," page 89. On

MARCH

the Third, Fourth and Fifth Sundays of Lent, the Year B lectionary presents passages from John that anticipate the death and resurrection of Jesus. In today's passage Jesus cleanses the temple. The most striking difference between the synoptic gospels and John's version is where the story falls within John's narrative. Matthew, Mark and Luke all place Jesus' cleansing of the temple after his triumphant entrance into Jerusalem; that is, at the end of his ministry. In fact, the incident is the immediate cause of the authorities' hostility. But in the Fourth Gospel, the cleansing takes place just after the wedding feast at Cana, in chapter 2. For John, the cleansing of the temple is not the end of Jesus' ministry but a sign that proclaims the deepest meaning of Jesus' ministry: Jesus does not simply cleanse the temple, Jesus becomes the new temple. The event takes place during the first of the three Passovers in Jerusalem that John's gospel records, as Jesus becomes the new Passover. Until now, God has dwelt among his people in a place; after the temple of Jesus' body is raised up (John changes Mark's Greek word for *build up* to a word that has more the sense of *raise up*), God will dwell among his people in the person of Jesus.

SACRAMENTARY

In preparing for this Sunday's liturgy, be aware of these elements proper to it:

- Year A scriptures: preface of the Third Sunday of Lent (P-14)
- Year B scriptures: preface for Lent I (P-8) or II (P-9)
- Celebration without scrutiny: all texts from Third Sunday of Lent
- Celebration with scrutiny: opening prayer, prayer over the gifts, prayer after communion and insert for Eucharistic Prayer I from the ritual Masses in the back of the sacramentary
- The position of the general intercessions and Creed is reversed after the scrutiny (RCIA, 156). The introduction to the general intercessions might link them to the prior prayers for the elect. ("We now continue our ministry of intercession, praying for the needs of all.") Resist the rubric that permits omission of these elements

See *The Sacristy Manual,* pages 201–202, for additional notes on today's liturgy.

THE WEEK AHEAD

The RCIA (#157) provides for the ancient *traditio,* or handing on, of two of the community's treasures to the elect: the Creed this week and the Lord's Prayer in the fifth week. If the Presentation of the Creed is to be observed this week, it should be announced, perhaps before the dismissal of the elect, and the whole community should be invited to it.

#237 (LMC, #176–184)
violet

MON 27 Monday of the Third Week of Lent

Beyond politics and personalities, what lay at the heart of the sixteenth-century Reformation was the assertion that salvation is a gift received, not a reward achieved. Neither the waters of the Jordan nor the waters of the parish font seem extraordinary enough to work miracles, yet that is what happened for the Syrian commander and what is about to happen for the community's elect. Meanwhile, Christ in present in his word, in the eucharist, in the elect of the community. Can we hear what Christ is telling us through these several voices?

#238 (LMC, #176–184)
violet

TUE 28 Tuesday of the Third Week of Lent

Peter thinks he is being generous by doubling the threefold forgiveness recommended by the rabbis of his day, and adding one more for good measure. But Jesus makes it clear: We can stop forgiving others only when we want God to stop forgiving us. Whenever the first reading in Lent pleads for God's mercy, forgiveness of our sins or acceptance of our offering, the gospel always challenges us to offer forgiveness to others.

#239 (LMC, #176–184)
violet

WED 29 Wednesday of the Third Week of Lent

Today's Mass was once part of a scrutiny in which the elect were examined on the Ten Commandments. The First Testament reminds us that the Commandments are the gift of the God who has chosen to come near his people. Jesus reminds his disciples that far from abolishing the Law or the prophets, he has come to make them complete.

#240 (LMC, #176–184)
violet

THU 30 Thursday of the Third Week of Lent

By some reckonings today is Lent's midpoint. The opening prayer captures the anticipation of the elect and the penitent baptized: "Help us, O God, to be ready to celebrate the great paschal mystery. Make our love grow each day as we approach the feast of our salvation."

MARCH

FRI 31 — Friday of the Third Week of Lent
#241 (LMC, #176–184) violet

Day of abstinence. ▪ God's tender love for an often unlovable people: This theme is dear to Hosea, whose prophecy we hear today and tomorrow. "I will heal; I will love; they shall blossom; they shall flourish." The scribe in today's gospel hears from the lips of Jesus himself, "You are not far from the kingdom of God."

April

SAT 1 — Saturday of the Third Week of Lent
#242 (LMC, #176–184) violet

"Be brief, be blunt, be gone." Apocryphal or not, this is the advice that the renowned preacher and translator Ronald Knox was said to have offered those who asked how to go to confession. While the new rite of penance would not agree with that, as one of the desert fathers said, "both the tax collector and the penitent thief were reconciled by a single phrase." Love, not sacrifice, is what God desires. But often our love is as insubstantial as the morning dew, in Hosea's words, and our prayer is prideful. Today's scriptures summon us to better things.

2 — Fourth Sunday of Lent
#32 or 31 (LMC, #28) violet/rose

ORIENTATION

Laetare, Jerusalem! The ancient entrance chant gives this Sunday its title and its mood:

Rejoice, Jerusalem and all who love her;
mourners, rejoice and be consoled,
blissful as babies at the breast.
(see Isaiah 66:10–11)

The custom of bringing the first roses of spring to church on this day may have led to the alternative vestment color, rose. Floral arrangements may be added to the church decor today and instrumental music as well, perhaps with rose-scented incense as a crowning delight. These signs of festivity, repeated yearly, distinguish Laetare Sunday in the parish's liturgical life and make it a welcome sign of the paschal spring.

SECOND SCRUTINY

See the outline for last week's first scrutiny (page 104).

LECTIONARY

■ YEAR A READINGS: Some see a parallel between the anointing of David (first reading) and the Lord's anointing of the blind man's eyes with mud (gospel). The reference to initiation's anointings is obvious. Others see the mud as a reference to Genesis: Jesus patterns his "re-creation" of the man born blind on God's creation of the first man from the dust of earth. A more obvious parallel is the Lord's caution to Samuel, "the Lord does not see as mortals see; they look on the outward appearance, but the Lord looks on the heart" (1 Samuel 16:7). Ephesians invites us to see the gospel's miracle in the baptized by reminding us that "once you were darkness but now light in the Lord." In the gospel there is, as there was last week, a progression; or more accurately, progression and regression! The progression of the titles by which the man born blind addresses Jesus parallels the titles used by the Samaritan woman in last week's gospel.

What John has been describing speaks directly to his own situation and that of his church. The man healed of blindness represents the genuine believer coming to faith in spite of those who would prevent him from doing so. The religious leaders, on the other hand, represent the members of the synagogue in John's city who fail to see in Christ the continuation of God's redemptive work in Israel. The tragic conclusion of the chapter finds the reality of unbelief even in the presence of genuine faith and discipleship. The reader has once again (cf. chap. 8) been warned of the human tendency to cling to its self-constructed security, a tendency which blinds those who think that they can see to the light of the manifestation of God in their midst. (Robert Kysar, *John*. Augsburg, 1986, 158)

■ YEAR B READINGS: See the Lectionary Overview and, for notes on the first two readings, see "The Word of God," page 89. In the Gospel of John, *lifting up* is an image not only of crucifixion but of exaltation; or better, exaltation through crucifixion. The gospels proclaimed on the Third, Fourth and Fifth Sundays of Year A and Year B lead us not to the synoptic Passion gospel read on Palm Sunday but to the Passion of Glory, the Passion according to John, proclaimed every year on Good Friday. "No one takes my life from me," the Jesus of John's Gospel proclaims. "I lay it down on my own. I have the power to lay it down and to take it up again" (John 10:18). As with the serpent in the desert (Numbers 21:4–9), what could have been a sign of condemnation for sin and the guarantee of death

APRIL

becomes a cause of faith and the source of eternal life. God's will is clear: not condemnation but salvation.

SACRAMENTARY

See *The Sacristy Manual,* pages 201–202. If an a cappella chant ("Attende, Domine") has begun the liturgy so far this Lent, the glorious hymn "Lift high the cross" (CRUCIFER) makes a distinctive opening today. For instrumental and choral parts see settings by Carl Schalk (Concordia) and Richard Hillert (GIA). This anthem provides a foretaste of the Triduum; it is a perfect entrance song for Holy Thursday and even for Good Friday's veneration. Note also:

- Year A scriptures: preface of the Fourth Sunday of Lent (P-15)
- Year B scriptures: preface for Lent I (P-8) or II (P-9), although the preface of the Sacred Heart (P-45) quotes the Year B gospel
- Celebration without scrutiny: all texts from Fourth Sunday of Lent
- Celebration with scrutiny: opening prayer, prayer over the gifts, prayer after communion and insert for Eucharistic Prayer I from the ritual Masses in the back of the sacramentary
- See last week's notes on the intercessions and Creed.

See *The Sacristy Manual,* 201–202, for additional notes on today's liturgy.

MON 3 — #244 (LMC, #176–184) violet
Monday of the Fourth Week of Lent

Today begins a semicontinuous proclamation of John's gospel, leading through Wednesday of Holy Week into the Passion according to John on Good Friday. These passages involve treachery, pain, the passion. But this is a life-giving passion; the first two days celebrate the gift of new life in the healing of the Gentile's child and of the paralyzed man by the pool of Bethsaida. The prophecy of Isaiah celebrates the imminent creation of a new heaven and a new earth. The church's longing intensifies as we draw near to the sacraments of initiation.

TUE 4 — #245 (LMC, #176–184) violet
Tuesday of the Fourth Week of Lent

Isidore of Seville, bishop and doctor of the church, optional memorial. • *Vidi aquam,* "I saw water flowing forth from the Temple." Ezekiel's vision has given the church an age-old Eastertime chant that may accompany the sprinkling with water at Sunday eucharist. The healing of the paralyzed man in Bethsaida's water was long ago seen as an image of the risen life given in baptism or restored in penance, as a number of ancient baptistry mosaics testify.

Today's saint served as Archbishop of Seville in Spain at the beginning of the seventh century. He was noted for his theological brilliance, pastoral dedication and liturgical scholarship. The recently restored Mozarabic rite, unique to the Iberian Peninsula, received its principal codification at Isidore's hand.

WED 5 — #246 (LMC, #176–184) violet
Wednesday of the Fourth Week of Lent

Vincent Ferrer, priest, optional memorial. • "Can a woman forget her nursing child, or show no compassion for the child of her womb?" Isaiah offers a tender image of God's abiding love for each one of us. The late Pope John Paul I commented on this text during one of the general audience talks of his month-long reign. "We see from these words," said the Pope, "that God is not only our Father — God is also, in a real sense, our Mother as well."

The Dominican friar and preacher Vincent Ferrer was responsible for innumerable conversions throughout early fifteenth-century Europe. He also worked tirelessly to end a scandal that not only kept nonbelievers out of the church but drove out a good number of believers: the schism between the rival popes of Avignon and Rome.

THU 6 — #247 (LMC, #176–184) violet
Thursday of the Fourth Week of Lent

Moses appears in the first reading in several roles: Israel's lawgiver, the national liberator and the great priest who intercedes to turn God's wrath away from the people. Jesus invokes the witness of John and the authority of Moses as a joint witness on his own behalf.

FRI 7 — #248 (LMC, #176–184) violet
Friday of the Fourth Week of Lent

John Baptist de la Salle, priest, optional memorial. Day of abstinence. • With Good Friday two weeks away, both scripture passages point to the passion. For every disciple in every age, Jesus must be "the reproof of our thoughts," the reproach to our established prejudices, our cherished sins. His prophetic challenge can echo in the voices of those who, in our own day, challenge the established order, only to be rejected just as he was.

Like almost every religious founder, today's saint knew opposition, from outside and within the household of the faith — sadly, even within the brotherhood. Undaunted, he pioneered schools for the poor and working classes, care for children with special needs, and quality education for teachers. His work lives on in the innumerable schools and communities that bear the name La Salle.

SAT 8 #249 (LMC, #176–184) violet
Saturday of the Fourth Week of Lent

Jeremiah's reflections on rejection and betrayal have long been applied to the experience of Jesus. The gospel shows good, religious people trying to determine the truth by interpreting the scriptures. Little do they know they don't have all the facts. Nicodemus appeals in vain to reason and justice. The Catholic approach enlists revelation and reason in searching out the ways of God. But we still fail — and not only with theologians centuries ago! Reflecting on a friend's suffering at the hands of fellow believers, Saint Paulinus of Nola wrote: "Christ suffers his passion over and over again in everyone who has suffered, from the beginning of time until now."

9 #35 or 34 (LMC, #31) violet
Fifth Sunday of Lent

ORIENTATION

Today the Passion phase of Lent begins. Although Passiontide was suppressed by Vatican II's calendar reform, the liturgy's mood changes now as Holy Week draws near. The passion of the Lord comes into clearer focus, but this is still the season of baptismal preparation and penitential discipline. For the two weeks ahead, in scripture and in prayer, both appear more clearly as a participation in the paschal mystery.

THIRD SCRUTINY

See the outline for the first scrutiny (March 26, page 104).

LECTIONARY

- YEAR A READINGS: Today's first reading omits completely the dramatic vision of Ezekiel and gives only the three-verse conclusion. It is difficult to see how this minimal excerpt makes any sense on its own, let alone provide a coherent preliminary to the raising of Lazarus. The *Revised Common Lectionary,* in use among most of the Protestant churches, assigns the full text: Ezekiel 37:1–14. Paul's Letter to the Romans sees a future for us far more glorious than Ezekiel's vision dared hope for: "the One who raised Christ from the dead will give life to [our] mortal bodies also, through his Spirit dwelling in [us]." The gospel story for today is rich indeed. Any fruitful homiletic preparation will require some time with a commentary. The raising of Lazarus is the seventh sign Jesus performs in the Gospel of John. Since seven is the number of perfection in Judaism, this is the crowning of Jesus' wondrous deeds, the immediate cause of his death, and the final preparation for the resurrection. One detail is important for communities with catechumens. When Lazarus at last comes out of the tomb, raised by God's power and summoned by Jesus, there is still work for the community to do — "'Unbind him,' Jesus told them, 'and let him go free!'" (11:44)

- YEAR B READINGS: See the Lectionary Overview and, for notes on the first two readings, see "The Word of God," page 89. The Gospel of John began at Cana with Jesus informing his mother that "my hour has not yet come" (John 2:4). Now the world, in the person of the Greek visitors, is drawing near, and Jesus announces, "The hour has come for the Son of Man to be glorified." But the path to glorification must be clearly understood. So Jesus invokes the image of the grain of wheat, which only by its death can produce much fruit. This is both a prediction of Jesus' own future and an invitation to discipleship, for "whoever serves me must follow me." In John's gospel, suffering is never separated from glory. And what is true of John's Christ is true for the disciples as well. This is our invitation to enter into the final weeks of Lent and the Triduum with a sense of our own sin and trust in the power of Christ to draw us and the whole world to himself.

SACRAMENTARY

Preparation notes are in *The Sacristy Manual,* 201–202. The official entrance chant in the sacramentary signals the mood of this liturgy: Psalm 42, "Give me justice, O God! Defend my cause against the wicked! Rescue me!" Last week's "Lift high the cross" is again an excellent gathering song. More passion-oriented hymns might make an appearance today. Additional considerations:

- Year A scriptures: preface of the Fifth Sunday of Lent (P-16)

A P R I L

- Year B scriptures: preface for Lent I (P-8) or II (P-9), although, as last week, the preface of the Sacred Heart (P-45) quotes the Year B gospel
- Celebration without scrutiny: all texts from Fifth Sunday of Lent
- Celebration with scrutiny: opening prayer, prayer over the gifts, prayer after communion and insert for Eucharistic Prayer I from the ritual Masses in the back of the sacramentary
- See the notes on the intercession and Creed on pages 92–93.

THE WEEK AHEAD

The RCIA (178) has a rite for celebrating the ancient *traditio,* handing on, of the Lord's Prayer during the fifth week. If this rite is to be observed this week, announcement of it should be made, perhaps before the dismissal of the elect, and the whole community invited to participate in it.

MON 10 — #251 (LMC, #176–184) violet
Monday of the Fifth Week of Lent

In a beautiful couplet, the lectionary presents the story of Susanna as the first reading and Christ's encounter with the adulterous woman as the gospel. Susanna's story is too good to be omitted and too interesting to be abbreviated. Bring out the Bible and read the whole story (or see the Canadian edition of the weekday lectionary for two coherently edited versions).

Beginning today the preface of the Passion of the Lord I is used.

TUE 11 — #252 (LMC, #176–184) violet
Tuesday of the Fifth Week of Lent

Stanislaus, bishop and martyr, optional memorial. ▪ In both passages there is a "lifting up" that results in healing for all who behold and believe: the serpent in the desert and the Son of Man on the cross. In both testaments, the path to healing and to glory leads through suffering. But never alone: the Lord God accompanies the Israelites, never deserts Jesus and, in the presence of the Spirit, stays forever with the community. As our celebration of the passion draws near, keep in mind the Johannine perspective that never loses sight of the glory.

The memorial of Stanislaus is an optional commemoration during Lent, but when it falls outside this season it is obligatory — a recent change. Before becoming Bishop of Rome, John Paul II was Stanislaus' successor as Archbishop of Cracow. He felt, with good reason, that the whole church should celebrate Stanislaus' example of preaching the truth, no matter how powerful the target or how perilous the consequences. Stanislaus was killed at the altar, during the liturgy, on orders of the king on this day in 1079.

WED 12 — #253 (LMC, #176–184) violet
Wednesday of the Fifth Week of Lent

The story of Shadrach, Meshach and Abednego is the first reading today. The United States edition of the lectionary presents it in a fragmented version, but the Canadian lectionary, by the judicious addition of a couple of verses, puts together a coherent edition. Consider using that arrangement: Daniel 3:13–20, 24, 49–50, 91–95. Jesus has already invoked the memory of Moses, and now he calls on Israel's "father in faith," the patriarch Abraham, to bear witness to his authority.

THU 13 — #254 (LMC, #176–184) violet
Thursday of the Fifth Week of Lent

Martin I, pope and martyr, optional memorial. ▪ In the first reading God makes covenant with Abraham. As that covenant had to be lived out in testing and trial before it could issue in glory, so Jesus' renewal of that covenant will involve the passion and cross before it issues in the glory of resurrection.

From deacon ambassador to Constantinople, Martin was elected Bishop of Rome. As Pope Martin I, he called a council to condemn the error that Christ did not have a human will and to protest the Emperor's support of this heresy. For this he was imprisoned and died in exile about 655, the last pope to be venerated as a martyr.

FRI 14 — #255 (LMC, #176–184) violet
Friday of the Fifth Week of Lent

Day of abstinence. ▪ Today, one week before Good Friday, Jeremiah appears again, forsaken by mortals but accompanied by God, in whose abiding care the prophet trusts and exults. The gospel's ending is poignant: As many people do when anticipating death, Jesus returns to the Jordan where John had been baptizing, where Jesus was anointed with the Spirit for the mission he is now about to accomplish.

SAT 15 — #256 (LMC, #176–184) violet
Saturday of the Fifth Week of Lent

At this final Mass before Holy Week, the lectionary features a prophecy of Ezekiel: Gathered from its exile is a nation now united as a covenant people in a land restored. The nation's sin is cleansed; its age-old wounds are healed; David is re-established as the shepherd of the reconstituted, faith-filled and obedient flock. Jesus is at Bethany, scene of the raising of Lazarus, which prefigures his own resurrection. A new prophecy is pronounced by an unlikely spokesman: Jesus will die and gather into a covenanted people not only his own nation but the dispersed of every land.

16 Palm Sunday of the Lord's Passion
#37 or 38 (LMC, #34)   red

ORIENTATION

Holy Week is the name given by our ancestors to this one week of all the year. This ancient designation should lead us to enter this week with reverence, embrace its demands with delight, and celebrate its rites with all the care, devotion and energy they deserve. To celebrate Holy Week is, after all, to celebrate who we have become through Christ's paschal mystery. Those who serve the community's prayer must now lay aside all other cares. All parish activities should cease, all regular business be suspended and the community's efforts and attention be focused entirely on these "days of salvation."

THE COMMEMORATION OF THE LORD'S ENTRANCE INTO JERUSALEM

This commemoration takes place at every Mass on this day. There is to be a procession (presider, ministers, at least some of the faithful) from the door of the church, where the palms are blessed, to the sanctuary. At the principal Mass, a solemn blessing in a separate place ends in a great procession to the church. Rubrics restrict this procession to the principal Mass, not to restrict the parishioners' experience of the rite, but to call for one grand liturgy for all parish members — just as during the Triduum (for preparation notes for Palm Sunday, see *The Sacristy Manual*, pages 203–204).

■ GATHERING: Quotes without reference are from the sacramentary; others from the *Ceremonial of Bishops* (CB).

- Assembly gathers in a place "distinct from the church to which the procession will move."
- Branches of sufficient size are distributed in generous quantity. They are already in the hands of the assembly before the presider and other ministers arrive.
- Red vesture: the color of Christ as "the faithful witness (martyr) and firstborn from the dead." Presider wears cope or chasuble; deacon wears dalmatic.
- Traditional antiphon at ministers' entrance: "Hosanna to the Son of David" (mode VII, adapted by Richard Proulx, *Worship*. See Proulx's choral setting titled "Fanfare for Palm Sunday," GIA, G-2829).

■ BLESSING OF THE BRANCHES:

- Sign of the cross (CB, #266)
- Greeting: Use the same greeting that was chosen for the other lenten Sundays.
- Introduction: The sacramentary text is concise. It may be given by the deacon or by a concelebrant (CB, #266).
- Blessing: Presider offers prayer of blessing (present sacramentary says "with hands joined")
- Sprinkling: Presider silently sprinkles branches held by the people. This should be distinct from the Sunday sprinkling of the assembly with holy water. People should be invited to hold their palm branches up and outstretched.
- Presider and other ministers who have not carried branches from the beginning take them from table or pedestal. Incense is placed in the censer. The deacon who is to proclaim the gospel is blessed.
- Gospel: Deacon, concelebrant or presider proclaims the gospel of the entry into Jerusalem.
- A *brief* homily may be given.

■ PROCESSION:

- Invitation to procession: Deacon (or presider) invites assembly to join procession.
- Order of procession: thurifer, cross bearer (with cross "suitably adorned") flanked by two candle bearers, deacon with book of gospels, lectors, concelebrants, presider and assistants, choir, assembly.
- The procession moves directly to the church, or may take a longer route around the parish property. Be sure that thurifer and cross bearer walk slowly enough to keep the procession together. A longer route may require a permit from the municipality or the cooperation of the police. Some cities require permission for the use of audio systems outdoors, even on private property. Walk the processional route beforehand, looking for trouble spots as you go: Will banners and cross fit through tight places? Will the head of the procession (cross and its decorations) be clearly visible? Are there places where part of the procession can be delayed,

APRIL

where people can trip easily, become confused or take shortcuts?

■ PROCESSIONAL MUSIC: "All glory, laud and honor" was written for this procession by Bishop Theodulph of Orleans about the year 800, and translated beautifully by John Mason Neale in the mid-1800s.

LITURGY OF THE WORD

■ THE SCRIPTURES: The heart of today's liturgy of the word is the proclamation of the Lord's passion, read in its entirety from one of the three synoptic versions. This year it is Mark's account, and a brief reflection on his version may be found in Lectionary Overview, page 000. To lead the assembly into the verbal sacrament of the reading of the passion, two other passages are read, a psalm and acclamation sung, and silence kept. Isaiah's text celebrates the mysterious "suffering servant of the Lord God," while Paul's text is the canticle of Christ's self-emptying love and of God's glorious vindication.

Everything is to focus on the proclaimed word. The marks of reverence customarily accorded the gospel are omitted this day: no candles, no incense to honor the book, no greeting and no signs of the cross on the book, forehead, lips or breast at the beginning of the passion, no kissing of the book at the end.

If every word of the Lord requires careful preparation for public proclamation, how much more so the passion! Traditionally, this long text is read or chanted in three parts: the words of Christ, the narrator, and the other persons who figure in the narrative. Contemporary arrangements make the assembly a fourth part, the crowd. But the narrative could be divided into sections, proclaimed by different readers, with some variation in the posture of the assembly for each section. Between sections there could be periods of reflection and sung acclamations or hymns. Especially suitable would be "O sacred head surrounded," "My song is love unknown" and "What wondrous love is this." LTP's *Passion of Our Lord Jesus Christ* divides the passion readings (all four of them) into sections and suggests placement for music. Remember that despite this quasi-dramatic presentation, the passion is not a play. It is the word of God proclaimed solemnly yet simply, in an engaging but not affected way.

■ PSALM 22 is available in a variety of settings:

- C. Alexander Peloquin, *Songs of Israel* (GIA, G-1666)
- Christopher Willcock, *Psalms for Feasts and Seasons* (Liturgical Press)
- Marty Haugen, *Gather*
- David Isele, *Psalms for the Church Year* (GIA, G-2262)
- Christopher Walker in *Out of Darkness* (OCP)

■ GOSPEL ACCLAMATION: Whatever acclamation is chosen, make sure that the traditional verse, "Christ became obedient for us," is sung, perhaps by a cantor using a simple chant formula (the *tonus peregrinus* and tone IV are both appropriate).

■ BRIEF HOMILY: That today's homily should be brief is understandable, because the passion says so much. That the homily should be omitted is unconscionable, in light of the sacred days about to unfold. Gabe Huck has a fine model of such a homily in *The Three Days* (LTP, 1992 [revised edition], appendix: part three). Raymond Brown provides a moving insight into Mark's gospel and into the diversity among the passion narratives in *A Crucified Christ in Holy Week* (Liturgical Press, 1986). If anti-Semitism is a danger in the hearing of Holy Week's texts, consult the Bishops' Committee on the Liturgy's *God's Mercy Endures Forever,* #21 – 25.

■ DISMISSAL OF CATECHUMENS AND ELECT: Continue to use a lenten dismissal formulas.

■ PROFESSION OF FAITH AND GENERAL INTERCESSIONS: These follow in the usual way. In the sacramentary's appendix, the intercessions for Monday, Tuesday and Wednesday of Holy Week are suitable also for today, or see LTP's *Prayers for Sundays and Seasons Year B.*

LITURGY OF THE EUCHARIST AND CONCLUDING RITES

■ EUCHARISTIC PRAYER: Special texts for today:

- Preface for Passion (Palm) Sunday (P-19)
- Eucharistic Prayer for Reconciliation I is especially appropriate.

■ CONCLUDING RITE:

- The solemn blessing "Passion of the Lord" is appropriate.

Some parishes end the celebration on a great note of triumph with a rousing recessional hymn as people bear their palms homeward. Other communities chant the blessing and dismissal but then have the ministers leave quietly to the "Vexilla regis" chant, a melody at once triumphant and reflective.

APRIL

AT HOME

■ DOMESTIC PRAYER: *Catholic Household Blessings and Prayers* provides prayers for Placing of Branches in the Home on Palm Sunday (page 140) and Prayers of the Triduum (page 143).

MON 17 #257 (LMC, #176–184) violet
Monday of Holy Week

From Isaiah's canticle-like "Songs of the Suffering Servant" come the lines about the compassionate servant of the Lord God who "will not break the bruised reed or extinguish the dimly flickering flame." Jesus graciously receives the anointing of Mary and gently deflects Judas' criticism.

For special general intercessions, see the appendix to the sacramentary. The Preface of the Passion II (P-18) is specific to these days. For the Prayer over the People see the traditional Holy Week text (17).

TUE 18 #258 (LMC, #176–184) violet
Tuesday of Holy Week

The suffering servant's mission is the ingathering of the dispersed children of God. The canticles of praise accompany the sacred meal among friends at the table of the Last Supper while Judas goes to do what he is to do. "And it is night." See the Office of Readings for Basil's meditation on our baptism into Christ's death and resurrection.

WED 19 #259 (LMC, #176–184) violet
Wednesday of Holy Week

Today is traditionally called "Spy Wednesday," and was known to Christians as early as 250 as the "day of betrayal." Our lectionary continues this custom in its choices. The servant of God sets his face like flint, defying his adversaries. In the gospel, the price of betrayal is set and paid. It is almost the Triduum.

THU 20 Chrism Mass #260 white
Holy Thursday

From the moment dawn breaks, there are signals that something is different today: the Triduum is at hand!

■ NO MORNING MASS: Only for the most grave pastoral necessity, with the explicit permission of the diocesan bishop, may a Mass other than the Evening Mass of the Lord's Supper be offered. That concession given, sacramentary and lectionary provide no texts. The texts used could certainly not be those of Thursday evening, for anticipating the Triduum is specifically forbidden. Nor are funeral Masses permitted. These prohibitions have a positive purpose: Everyone, including mourners, senior citizens, schoolchildren — the whole assembly — is to be present this evening for the solemn inauguration of the Christian Passover.

■ MORNING PRAYER: At the time in the morning that daily Mass has been held, why not celebrate Morning Prayer, perhaps with augmented readings? Try the Letter to the Hebrews on the high priesthood of Jesus and the Easter homily of Melito of Sardis, both in the *Liturgy of the Hours*.

■ NO COMMUNION CALLS: While communion may be brought to the sick at any hour of the day if necessary, the 1988 *Circular Letter of the Congregation for Divine Worship* correctly suggests that communion be borne to such persons directly after the celebration of the Lord's Supper. Viaticum may be brought at any time.

■ SCHOOL PRAYER: Catholic schools are often still in session today, and various prayer customs have developed for the students. Mass is out of the question, but a prayer service that is a prelude or call to worship for the Triduum would be fitting. Students should be encouraged to attend the Triduum liturgies. These liturgies will help form them in the Catholic way of life, and most young people respond movingly to the beauty of these sacred rites. See an outline of ideas for prayer today in *Preparing Liturgy for Children and Children for Liturgy* (page 90).

■ CHRISM MASS: This celebration should draw representatives from every area, even every parish of the diocese. The *Sacramentary Supplement* (1994) considers it appropriate that the oils be formally received by the parish at the Evening Mass of the Lord's Supper, especially since these will be used at the Easter Vigil's celebration of initiation.

TRIDUUM

The Season
The Setting of the Triduum / 115
A Sense of the Triduum / 116
The Look of the Triduum / 118
The Sounds of the Triduum / 119
The Rhythm of the Triduum / 120
The Word of God / 120
The Eucharist / 120
Other Celebrations / 121
At Home / 121
The Calendar
April 20 – 23 / 122
Holy Thursday / 122
Good Friday / 126
Holy Saturday / 130
Easter Vigil / 132
Easter Sunday / 140

The Setting of the Triduum

In spring all creatures came into being and the first parent was formed from the clay of the earth.

In spring Jacob was called from Mesopotamia to his own land.

In spring the children of Israel were led out of the land of Egypt, the blood of the lamb turned the destroyer of Egypt away, and they entered the promised land after crossing the Jordan.

In spring Christ our Redeemer, ascending by the example of his death from the valley of tears to the mountain of Paradise, summons the church, saying:

"Arise, hasten, my love, my lovely one, and come, for winter is past!"

(Apponius, fourth century)

THE setting of the Triduum is the springtime of nature, at least in the Northern Hemisphere where the liturgical texts and rites of the Three Days of the Lord's Pasch originated and developed. Writing in the mid-1950s, a pioneering liturgist wrote, "Springtime is nature executing her Easter liturgy" (Pius Parsch, *The Church's Year of Grace*). That is the setting of the Triduum: In the spring of the year; at the heart of the church's liturgical calendar; at the heart of the individual's conversion and of the catechumen's participation in Christian initiation, and at the heart of the penitent believer's annual renewal of the baptismal covenant.

But we who celebrate the Triduum in this first year of the new millennium need to recall that by the mid-twentieth century, the Triduum had all but disappeared from the church's consciousness and experience. There were no catechumens; adult baptism was celebrated privately whenever "converts" completed individual instructions. There was barely a congregation at sparsely attended services, conducted in Latin, at hours completely out of synch with the mysteries celebrated. In fact, the word Triduum itself did not exist! These three days were simply the last three days of Holy Week, indeed, the last three days of Lent. When the church bells rang at noon on Holy Saturday, as the priest recited the Gloria by himself, in Latin, at this strange midday "Easter Vigil," the non-attendant majority of parishioners knew that Lent was over, though they would not really celebrate Easter until the next day's Sunday morning Mass.

Pius XII changed all this by publishing the *Restored Order of Holy Week,* which went into effect in March 1956. Read in light of what happened a decade later, after Vatican II, the official instructions of 1955 preparing for the restored Holy Week sound prophetic indeed. Regarding the relationship between the liturgy and the laity, there are phrases like "restored to hours that are suitable and at the same time convenient," "to be attended by the faithful more easily, more devoutly, more fruitfully," "to receive richer fruits from a living participation." Those presiding are challenged to have a grasp of the liturgy "not only concerning the ritual celebration" of the restored Triduum, "but also concerning its liturgical meaning and pastoral purpose" (*Instruction,* November 1955).

The first liturgical reform in four hundred years began at the Triduum, at the heart of it all!

Setting the Triduum at the heart of the whole church's life and of this local church's life requires that the Triduum be celebrated with all our hearts. A heartfelt commitment makes sure that these basic considerations form the foundation of the general setting of the Triduum celebration:

- *Sufficient numbers of well-prepared ministers:* Besides presiders and deacons, the assembly will need lectors who can translate skillfully the awe-inspiring words of these days from page to sound; cantors who can exalt the chant of the psalms and draw the assembly into the church's song; choirs and servers and sacristans, too.
- *Good eucharistic practices:* What should be normative all year must be normative at this time of the year: eucharist consecrated at and for each celebration (except Good Friday, of course); bread that can be broken; the cup offered to all.
- *Good music:* To add solemnity and beauty to the celebrations and to facilitate participation of the whole assembly: This is the goal of the music ministry during the Triduum. Specific hymns are prescribed at various points in the Triduum liturgies, in contrast to the Roman rite's usual preference for antiphons. The assembly should be prepared for these and provided with materials to assure their participation.
- *One church, one celebration.* This is the norm throughout the Triduum. Religious and lay communities should take part in the worship of the local parish. Like smaller families among the Israelites who gather with larger families to observe the seder, smaller parishes might consider teaming up with larger ones to keep the Three Days well. Those considering the scheduling of multiple celebrations of a particular Triduum liturgy must never let convenience be the deciding factor, nor should the quality of a liturgical celebration suffer on account of its being repeated.

A Sense of the Triduum

Individuals and communities who engage themselves wholeheartedly in living the entire paschal cycle — Lent, Triduum and Easter's Fifty Days — discover, not that they have taken hold of the pasch, but that the pasch has seized them and changed them forever! This is especially true of the Triduum which, standing at the heart of the paschal cycle, is an intense immersion in the fundamental mystery of what it is to be Christian and to be church. Year after year, those who keep the Triduum hunger in fasting and rejoice in feasting, share in death and resurrected life, contemplate cross-unto-glory, tell and hear the great stories of salvation, emerge fresh-robed from the waters into light and fragrant anointing, sing songs of victory and taste of the wedding banquet of heaven and earth. In these most human and yet most divine of actions, the old passes into the radically new. (Joan Halmo, *A Triduum Sourcebook* I, vii)

TRIDUUM: the most accurate translation of this singular noun is the paradoxical one that adds a definite article to make a unity out of what seems to be a plural: *The Three Days.* Sundown on Holy Thursday through sundown on Easter Sunday is one celebration played out in three movements:

> The Triduum is a single celebration of the paschal mystery presented, over three days, under different aspects. Christian remembering is more than retracing the Lord's steps during his last days in Jerusalem. At the Holy Thursday eucharist, the church is already drawn into the whole event of Jesus' death and resurrection. The Good Friday celebration of the Lord's passion is austere but never sad, for the risen Lord already reigns triumphant. On Holy Saturday the church waits for the celebration of Christ's resurrection and its own at the Easter Vigil, when the Spirit hovers over the waters of the font and the community of faith drinks deeply again of the mystery of Jesus' passage from death to life. (Roman Missal, quoted in *Triduum Sourcebook* I, 10)

Any planning that separates the three movements into individual pieces, each a celebration unto itself, has gone off the rails. In fact, as Gabe Huck reminds us, the Triduum has been "planned" already. Our task is to prepare what has been planned:

> The tradition, taking shape in our sacramentary and lectionary and RCIA, has an order, a

plan, of liturgy. What is left for us is exactly this work of preparing. To prepare the liturgy is to make the church's liturgy accessible to the church, this church, right here. To prepare the liturgy is to make it possible for this assembly of baptized people to do what baptism has made their work, their duty and their privilege. (LTP, *The Three Days,* 9)

■ SOURCES: One gathers a sense of what the Triduum is all about by turning to three principal sources:

- *Lectionary:* What passages are prescribed for each movement of the Triduum?
- *Sacramentary:* What are the choices of antiphons, prayers and hymns telling us? What does the "choreography" of each day communicate? Black text (prayers) and red text (rubrics) must be looked at together.
- *Rite of Christian Initiation of Adults:* How are we intimately involved in the mystery happening to the elect during these three days?

■ RESOURCES: LTP has prepared three useful resources that correspond roughly to the three official sources listed above:

Workbook for Lectors and Gospel Readers: It contains the complete Triduum lectionary (NRSV and RNAB translations).

The Three Days: Parish Prayer in the Paschal Triduum (revised edition, 1992): Over 200 pages of commentary and suggestion, pastoral and practical in nature, for translating sacramentary rubrics into a lived experience of the Triduum.

A Triduum Sourcebook (revised, three-volume edition, 1996). A treasury of texts from Jewish and Christian sources, translations, lectionary references from all the Christian churches, the perfect prayer book to accompany the elect and baptized alike through the long and beautiful hours of a fully celebrated Triduum.

■ WARNING SIGNALS: These recommended sources and resources alert us to signs that we may be off course, and contain the correctives we may need. Here are some liturgical warning signals:

■ HOLY THURSDAY:

- "Lord, who at that first eucharist," or any eucharistic hymn as the gathering song, is a sure sign that this opening movement of the Triduum has been disconnected from the whole and turned into a celebration focused only on the eucharist's institution. The official entrance chant from the sacramentary for that night comes from Galatians 6:14: "We should glory in the cross of our Lord Jesus Christ, in whom is our salvation, life and resurrection."
- Bowls for handwashing (Pilate's action!) to replace the footwashing mandated by Jesus.
- Mass turned into a reenactment of the Last Supper, complete with table for twelve in the sanctuary. Parish "seders" or agape meals after the Mass — when the paschal fast has begun!

■ GOOD FRIDAY:

- Sound effects, for instance, a distant hammer coldly pounding a nail, before, during or after the liturgy, indicating that this celebration of the Lord's triumphant witness is being approached as a kind of passion play or funeral service for "the late Jesus Christ."
- Mournful sounds of "Were you there?" as the congregation comes forward to venerate the cross, when the sacramentary prescribes the triumphant "Pange, lingua" (the Venantius Fortunatus text that calls the "faithful cross" the "tree of glory." See *Worship,* #437).

■ HOLY SATURDAY:

- A church filled all day with people loudly and busily decorating for Easter: sure sign that keeping a quiet vigil, the mood for the day according to the sacramentary, has simply been bypassed for the feverish activity of getting things ready for the Vigil.

■ EASTER DAY:

- The church locked up by noon on Easter; a sign that, here at least, the Triduum is over before the sun has even set, and that paschal vespers with community and neophytes will not be held.

None of these warning signals indicate bad will or an intentional decision not to do the right thing. Often, they signal just the opposite: a sincere desire to make the Triduum special, an attempt to be creative with what can seem to be a disconnected series of complex ceremonies. Even so, these mistakes can empty the paschal mystery of much of its power by turning living sacrament into dead history, ritual celebration into dramatic reenactment, and Christ's saving presence among us here and now into an attempt to create an emotional rush.

The Look of the Triduum

OVERVIEW FOR DECORATING

Early in Lent, draw up a chart of priorities, necessities and a wish list. Essential information for the decorating and sacristy teams is in *To Crown the Year* (pages 74 – 119) and *The Sacristy Manual* (pages 207 – 219). Some items that need early and detailed planning:

- **VESTURE:** What will be needed for presiders, ministers, the elect?

- **FLOWERS:** How much to be spent, how many needed, when to be delivered?

- **LIGHTS AND SOUND:** Replace all burned-out bulbs, realign spot and track lighting, take care of any bugs in the sound system.

- **GROUNDS AND CHURCH:** Before Palm Sunday, clean up and spruce up all places of gathering and processional routes.

VESSELS AND OTHER OBJECTS

- **HOLY THURSDAY**
  - Processional materials: cross, banners, incense, candles
  - Altar materials: cloths, purificators, corporals, festive paraments
  - Communion vessels: distribution, procession, reservation
  - Oil vessels: containers, ambry
  - Footwashing items: pitchers, bowls, towels

- **GOOD FRIDAY**
  - Cross for veneration, incense vessels

- **EASTER VIGIL**
  - Fire and light: paschal candle, assembly candles, material for the fire, baptismal candles
  - Initiation materials: baptismal needs, chrism vessels, towels, robes

VESTURE

- **HOLY THURSDAY**
  - Simple white Mass vestments; humeral veil(s)

- **GOOD FRIDAY**
  - Red as on Palm Sunday, Holy Cross, feasts of martyrs; not Pentecost

- **HOLY SATURDAY**
  - Violet for Liturgy of the Hours and preparatory rites for initiation

- **EASTER VIGIL AND ONWARD**
  - Finest paschal vesture, used only during the Fifty Days
  - Albs for singer of Exsultet, neophytes, lectors and cantors (for greater solemnity).

LITURGICAL BOOKS

- Usual books: sacramentary or special presider's book, lectionary, book of gospels
- Book or scroll of the Exsultet
- Ritual books for Liturgy of the Hours

Coordinate cues for lighting, movement and song with musicians, ministers and servers. These cues might be gathered in books for those who prepare and those who lead the celebrations, and kept for those who will prepare next year.

SPECIAL TIMES

- **THURSDAY EVENING (BEFORE MASS)**
  - Tabernacle empty, veil removed, vigil light removed, doors left open
  - Church stripped and cleaned, only materials needed for the eucharist present

- **THURSDAY EVENING**
  - When elect and catechumens are dismissed, they go to the catechumeneon, a space apart conducive to gathering and prayer
  - Chapel of reservation, not a side altar or the usual tabernacle (Bishops' Committee on the Liturgy *Newsletter*, March 1993), suitably decorated, conducive to prayer (Circular Letter, #49)

- **THURSDAY EVENING (AFTER MASS)**
  - Stripping of altar and church carried out in an orderly and reverent way
  - Furniture not part of the building removed: credence table, kneelers, chairs, and so on
  - Rugs rolled up and removed
  - Crosses removed from church or veiled
  - Holy water removed from fonts

- **THURSDAY MIDNIGHT (AFTER NIGHT PRAYER)**
  - All candles extinguished, except one near the tabernacle in chapel of reservation
  - All other decorations taken from eucharistic chapel before first hour of prayer on Friday

- **Friday (before the Celebration of the Passion)**
  - Only furniture needed for the rite is set out
  - Candles ready near cross for solemn entrance
  - Altar cloth kept to side for later use
  - All else bare

- **Friday (after communion rite)**
  - Remaining eucharist brought to separate, private place to be kept for viaticum (not eucharistic chapel; reservation is not provided for visitation or private prayer)

- **Friday (after the celebration)**
  - Altar and sanctuary again completely stripped, except perhaps for the cross
  - Cross carried in during the celebration is placed with lighted candles in a place conducive to quiet prayer and veneration. The Circular Letter (#71) suggests the now-empty eucharistic chapel. If the cross is stationary, candles or spotlight might grace it

- **Saturday in general**
  - Church is bare for Liturgy of the Hours, preparatory rites, any other assembly
  - Cross, enshrined, remains in its place of honor
  - Church should be decorated for the Vigil as late as possible (see Mazar, page 127)

- **Saturday morning**

Circular Letter (#74) suggests that an image or two be introduced into the space for the day:

  - Image of Christ crucified or lying in the tomb (see catalog from Monastery Icons, 1482 Rango Way, Borrego Springs, CA 92004; 800-729-4952; website: www.monasteryicons.com for veneration cloth of the Byzantine rite and the icons the Letter suggests)
  - Icon of the descent into (or "harrowing of") hell, which mystery Holy Saturday recalls in the Office of Readings
  - Image of the sorrowful Virgin Mary

- **Saturday night (Vigil)**
  - *Ceremonial of Bishops* (#48) bans flowers from "Ash Wednesday until the Gloria at the Easter Vigil"
  - Immersion font is called for. A temporary font large enough for an adult to kneel in while water is poured over the head, a graceful position for baptism, is devised easily. See the article "Testing the Waters," *Environment & Art Letter* (LTP, April 1992).

The Sounds of the Triduum

See the Calendar section for specific suggestions regarding each day. Note that, for the Triduum alone, the sacramentary prescribes distinctive antiphons, certain hymns, and even sounds:

- **Holy Thursday**
  - Entrance chant: cross, salvation, life, resurrection, saved, set free (Galatians 6:14 or similar)
  - Gloria: church bells are rung and then remain silent until the Easter Vigil
  - Footwashing: antiphons based on gospel story and 1 Corinthians 13:13
  - Procession of gifts for the poor: "Ubi caritas," Where charity and love are found
  - Communion: the body given, the cup of the blood of the covenant (1 Corinthians 11:24–25 or similar)
  - Procession: "Pange lingua" (Aquinas' eucharistic text) or another eucharistic hymn

- **Good Friday**
  - Solemn intercessions: optional acclamations by the assembly
  - Veneration of the cross: worship Christ, venerate cross, praise the resurrection, through the cross comes joy to the whole world (and Psalm 66:2); or the "Reproaches," (some countries and other churches have rewritten or replaced these); "Pange lingua" (passion text by Venantius Fortunatus: "Sing, my tongue, the song of triumph" *Worship*, #437)

- **Easter Vigil**
  - Liturgy of light: "Christ our Light," "Thanks be to God"; "preface" responses at the Exsultet and optional acclamations during it; Amen at its conclusion
  - Liturgy of the word: responsorial psalms; Gloria (with ringing of church bells); solemn alleluia repeated three times, with verses from Psalm 118
  - Liturgy of baptism: litany of the saints; "Springs of water" (optionally during, but certainly at the conclusion of the blessing of the font); "I saw water flowing" (Ezekiel 47:1–2, 9) or a chant with similar theme during sprinkling of assembly
  - Liturgy of the eucharist: "Christ our passover is sacrificed for us" (1 Corinthians 5:7–8) or

similar chant at communion; solemn dismissal and response with double alleluia

- EASTER DAY
  - Liturgy of the word: the Easter sequence: "Victimae Paschali laudes" (*Worship,* #837)
  - Renewal of baptismal vows: "I saw water" or chant with similar baptismal theme during sprinkling of assembly
  - Solemn dismissal and response with double alleluia.

Consider pieces from an ever-expanding ecumenical repertoire. From *Wonder, Love and Praise,* the supplement to the Episcopal *Hymnal 1982,* comes a hymn suitable for use throughout the Triduum: "Three holy days enfold us now" (#731–732). In the same source are two fine texts for the footwashing at the evening Mass of the Lord's Supper: "As in that upper room you left your seat" (#729-730) and "You laid aside your rightful reputation" (#734). From the Lutheran supplement, *With One Voice:* "When twilight comes" (#663) which uses Jesus' own image of himself, the mother hen gathering her young. From the same collection a hymn for the veneration of the cross: "There in God's garden stands the tree of wisdom" (#668).

experience of the Triduum results from a sudden breakdown of worship that generally goes right week by week.

PARISH STAFF AND MINISTRIES

There is no substitute for prayerful study together. This *Sourcebook* provides some study materials. Also see Gabe Huck's *The Three Days* (LTP), Kenneth Stevenson, *Jerusalem Revisited: The Liturgical Meaning of Holy Week* (Pastoral Press, 1988) and Raymond Brown, *A Crucified Christ in Holy Week* (Liturgical Press, 1986).

PARISHIONERS IN GENERAL

Why not supplement Bible study with liturgical study? Ministers are frequently surprised at the number of people who will make this kind of lenten commitment, whether for a series or one session of concentrated study, perhaps on Palm Sunday before or after Evening Prayer. The texts of the rites are the primary workbook, and perhaps the music that weaves these days together. From their own study, parish ministers can bring biblical and historical insights to these sessions.

The Rhythm of the Triduum

THE Easter Triduum and the rest of the liturgical year mutually affect each other. A powerful experience of celebrating—not watching or attending—the Three Days can draw the marginally active worshiper back to recapture something of the grace of those moments. A parish whose Sunday liturgies feature well-prepared ministers, a strong tradition of sung liturgy, good communion practice, thoughtful presiding and sensitive preaching is likely to find that all these efforts blossom—and all that prayer comes to fruition—in a moving celebration of the Triduum. It is unlikely that a parish careless about its Sunday liturgy, or negligent of its ministries year round, will have the commitment and energy to celebrate a very prayerful Triduum. Nor is it likely that a poor

The Word of God

THE *Workbook for Lectors and Gospel Readers* is an essential resource. See LTP's revised *Triduum Sourcebook,* volume II, pages 252–253, for a chart of the Easter Vigil readings in all the traditions, including the Byzantine, and the *Revised Common Lectionary,* in increasing use among Protestant Christians.

The Eucharist

THE main liturgy for each movement of the Triduum, as well as the other services that might be celebrated during the Three Days, appear under each date's entry in the Calendar section of this *Sourcebook.*

Other Celebrations

According to the church's ancient tradition, the sacraments are not celebrated today or tomorrow. (Sacramentary, Good Friday rubric)

PENANCE

Penance may be celebrated, but it properly belongs in Lent as a preparation for the Triduum. Penance services should not be scheduled during the Triduum; in the Vatican's Jubilee Year calendar, the communal celebration of penance with individual absolution to be presided over by the pope is scheduled for Tuesday of Holy Week rather than during the Triduum.

ANOINTING OF THE SICK

Anointing of the sick may be celebrated in cases of emergency, but normally would not be scheduled during the Triduum.

COMMUNION TO THE HOMEBOUND

The directives of the Circular Letter (1988) are not mere fussy canonical prescriptions but, in fact, decisions based on sound liturgical insight. Exceptions may always be made in cases of genuine emergency, but these norms are the ideal:

- Holy Thursday: communion may be brought to the sick in the evening, following the parish's celebration of the Mass of the Lord's Supper
- Good Friday: communion outside the Celebration of the Lord's Passion may be given only to the sick; no communion, for instance, at Stations of the Cross
- Holy Saturday: communion may be given only as viaticum.

FUNERALS

Funeral Masses are not celebrated during the Triduum. Funerals that cannot be delayed until Monday are to be conducted without Mass, music or flowers. The *Order of Christian Funerals* (179) allows for funeral rites to take place at sites other than church. The rite used during the Triduum begins at 183.

WEDDINGS

Weddings are not celebrated from Holy Thursday through Easter. Weddings are allowed on Easter (with the texts of the day) but are clearly inappropriate.

At Home

PASCHAL FAST

Steady catechesis helps people to embrace this new, though old, discipline. In the recent past, our juridical, "Roman" view of fasting has been reinforced by the lack of any meaningful practice of this discipline: What do I *have* to do? That is, what is the *minimum* required? But our tradition is so much richer than legalistic minimalism! This fast is an intimate part of keeping the Triduum and coming to the Easter Vigil with enthusiasm and delight.

EASTER CANDLES

Some parishes encourage families to make or decorate their own Easter candles. These candles are brought to church and used during the Vigil in place of individual tapers, then brought home and lighted during prayer through the Fifty Days of Easter.

CALENDAR

April

20 Holy Thursday
#39 white

The Easter Triduum begins with the evening Mass of the Lord's Supper, reaches its high point in the Easter Vigil and closes with Evening Prayer on Easter Sunday. (*General Norms for the Liturgical Year and Calendar*, 19)

ORIENTATION

Entering into the Triduum

With this evening's liturgy (all the documents make clear that this evening's Mass is to be the only one celebrated today), we enter into the Triduum. Lent — and, ideally, all parish "business as usual" — has already ended quietly sometime before this liturgy. If there is to be any community agapé or love feast, that happens first. Indeed, any meals are taken before this liturgy, whether communal or by individuals or households at home. And that is the last full meal for the duration of the Triduum. With this evening's liturgy, the time for feasting together has yielded to the time for keeping the paschal fast together — all of us as one community in union with the elect, who are keeping the most intense fast of their lives as they prepare to descend into the saving waters. After this evening liturgy of the Lord's Supper, the community's time will be spent in quiet, watchful prayer, all feasting suspended until after the Easter Vigil.

The Evening of Unity

■ THE MASS OF THE LORD'S SUPPER: ". . . that they may all be one. As you, Father, are in me and I am in you, may they also be in us, so that the world may believe" (John 17:21). "According to the church's ancient tradition," says the sacramentary, there is one liturgy in each community on this day; that liturgy is celebrated in the evening; that liturgy assembles the whole parish, all its various groups gathered as one church, to enter as one community into this first movement of the Easter Triduum.

The evening liturgy is celebrated, therefore, with the full participation of all the various ministries of the community. Presbyters concelebrate and deacons proclaim the gospel and the general intercessions. Readers and cantors and choir fulfill their roles. Servers in sufficient numbers assist with the footwashing. Those involved in the catechumenal ministries and the pastoral care of the sick bear the holy oils in procession. Eucharistic ministers will bring communion to the sick and homebound at the liturgy's end. Communion may be distributed to the sick at any time of the day, but the Vatican's Circular Letter rightly urges that these visits come after the evening liturgy — a dramatic way of helping even those separated from the assembly to experience their bond with us and of drawing them more deeply into the rhythm of the Triduum.

The Evening of Mutual and Self-sacrificing Love

■ FOOTWASHING AND GIFTS FOR THE POOR: "For I have set you an example, that you also should do as I have done to you" (John 13:15). Two once-a-year signs of mutual love and service mark this evening's liturgy: footwashing and a procession with gifts for the poor.

What is the footwashing meant to be? Among the Seventh Day Adventists, footwashing is celebrated whenever the eucharist is celebrated. They reason that the washing of feet is, no less than the eucharist, a fulfillment of Jesus' clear command: after washing the disciples' feet, "As I have done, so you must do"; after sharing the bread and cup, "Do this in memory of me." Once a year, as we enter most intensely into the mystery of the Lord's death and resurrection for us and in us, we do this, foregoing explanatory words and accompanying the action only with song, because in its humility, intimacy, and total self-surrender.

Close upon the footwashing, there follows a procession in which the assembly comes forward with gifts for the poor. This, again, is a once-a-year directive. It is as if by this procession the church wished to extend the gesture of footwashing in a practical way to embrace all those in need, at the same time prefiguring the procession with the eucharist that will bring this evening's liturgy to a close.

The Evening without Ending

"Father, the hour has come. Glorify your Son so that the Son may glorify you" (John 17:1).

With the solemn transfer of the eucharist to a place apart from the main church, the Lord's Supper liturgy ends simply, silently, without a formal dismissal.

Remember that processions go somewhere! The idea is not to carry the eucharist around the church only to bring it back to its usual place, but to take it somewhere. If there is no blessed sacrament chapel, a special place of prayer apart from the main church should be set up and suitably decorated.

Then, quietly, reverently, thoroughly, the altar is stripped, the sanctuary cleared of all that is moveable, crosses are removed from the church or covered, and votive lights are extinguished. If it has not already been done, the baptismal font and holy water fonts are emptied.

HOLY THURSDAY CHECKLIST

Sacristans and planners may find a list similar to the following helpful from year to year:

- Get holy oils
- Prepare pitcher(s), bowl(s), towels
- Clean censer, fill boat with incense
- Clean cups for communion under both species
- Measure enough wine for all to receive
- Prepare enough bread for Thursday and Friday
- Prepare baskets or other receptacles for gifts for the poor at Mass
- Use white altar paraments and vestments
- Prepare humeral veil(s)
- Prepare place of reservation
- Empty tabernacle, doors open
- Tell those responsible about bells during Gloria: servers for small bells indoors; maintenance personnel about tower bells
- Train servers for procession
- Prepare inserts for eucharistic prayer
- Arrange for stripping of altar and church after Mass
- Announce adoration until midnight

MASS OF THE LORD'S SUPPER

Introductory Rites

■ OPENING HYMN: The sacramentary's official entrance antiphon sounds the keynote of the whole Triduum and signals the unity of the Three Days:

> We should glory in the cross of our Lord Jesus Christ, in whom is our resurrection, our salvation and our life. (Galatians 6:14)

Any alternative should likewise reflect the unity of the paschal mystery. Most suitable is the ancient text by Venantius Fortunatus, "Sing my tongue" — not the eucharistic "Pange lingua" (which Aquinas based on Fortunatus) — but the passion-oriented one prescribed for the veneration of the cross on Good Friday (*Worship,* #437; *Hymnal 1982,* #166). Other gathering songs: "Lift high the cross," "Praise to you, O Christ our Savior" (Farrell, OCP, 7126).

■ RECEPTION OF HOLY OILS: In the dioceses of the United States, the rite prescribed in the *Sacramentary Supplement* (Catholic Book, 1994), pages 31–32, is observed.

In the dioceses of Canada, the rite takes place as outlined below. Its celebration "should not resemble the blessing of oils and does not recall the Chrism Mass but emphasizes the beginning of the Paschal Triduum and the community's celebration of the paschal mystery."

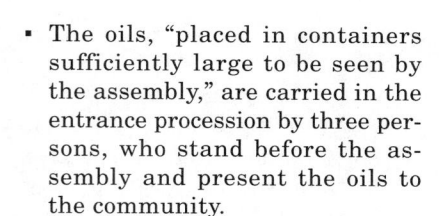

- The oils, "placed in containers sufficiently large to be seen by the assembly," are carried in the entrance procession by three persons, who stand before the assembly and present the oils to the community.
- Sign of the Cross and Greeting
- Presider's Address (in these or similar words):

> My brothers and sisters,
> we have completed
>   our lenten observance
> and now have begun
>   the solemn celebration
>   of the Easter feast.
> On these great days
>   it is our duty
> to glory in the cross
>   of our Lord Jesus Christ
> in whom we have salvation,
>   life and resurrection.
>
> These oils we receive tonight
>   were blessed and consecrated
> at the Chrism Mass by N.,
>   our bishop,
> for use throughout the year.
> With them the sick will
>   be anointed,
> those awaiting the waters of
>   rebirth will be strengthened,
> and those who are baptized
>   and confirmed
> will share the mission of
>   Christ, the Anointed One.
>
> By the outpouring
>   of the Holy Spirit,
> who fills these holy oils
>   with life and grace,
> the saving work of Jesus Christ
>   is continued in the Church.

- The person carrying the vessel of the oil of the sick faces the assembly and holds up the vessel of oil. A cantor sings:

> Behold the oil of the sick:
>   receive God's grace
>   and healing.
> R. Thanks be to God.

- The person carrying the vessel of the oil of catechumens faces the assembly and holds up the vessel of oil. A cantor sings:

> Behold the oil of catechumens:
>   receive God's strength
>   and wisdom.
> R. Thanks be to God.

- The person carrying the vessel of the sacred chrism faces the assembly and holds up the vessel of oil. A cantor sings:

  Behold the sacred chrism: give thanks, O priestly people.
  R. Thanks be to God.

- The "Glory to God" is sung by all. The priest may use the following words to introduce the "Glory to God:"

  Let us sing the praises of the Lord,
  the God who made us,
  those glory is from age to age.

- All join in the singing of the "Glory to God." While the community sings, the oils are brought in procession to their place at the baptistry.

  Copyright © Concacan, Inc., 1999. All rights reserved.

■ GLORIA: Either of Richard Proulx's "Two Plainsong Gloria Settings with Handbells" (GIA, G-3638) is suitable, since neither will overshadow the festivity of the Vigil's version. The first is a setting of John Lee's "Gloria" *(Worship),* the other from Chant Mass VIII ("Missa de Angelis"). If the parish's Gloria has a refrain, consider a random handbell ring during the refrain. Tradition calls for church bells to be rung during tonight's Gloria.

Liturgy of the Word

■ CHILDREN'S LITURGY OF THE WORD: Tonight the whole community gathers at the only eucharist permitted. Since this liturgy celebrates our unity in Christ, children should not be sent to a separate liturgy of the word (see the introduction to the *Lectionary for Masses with Children,* 30). The readings are straightforward, and the washing of feet is a powerful ritual in which children should be included. It is for the homilist to preach in a manner accessible to all on this special night.

■ FOR PSALM 116: The setting by Michael Joncas (NALR, JO 07-JON-SM) is a wonderful choice, though material for some verses is taken from outside the psalm. Marty Haugen's setting in *Gather* is also a fine choice, as is Marcy Weckler's "Our blessing cup" (WLP, 6201). A skilled cantor is needed for Charles Conley's setting with the refrain "What return can I make to the Lord?" (GIA, G-2528) and for Stephen Dean's "How can I repay the Lord" (OCP, 7119).

Washing of Feet

■ THE MANDATUM: What "serious pastoral reasons" could justify disobeying this command, ignoring this example of the Lord? What discomfort could justify replacing this imitation of Jesus with a handwashing — Pontius Pilate's gesture. The footwashing is a powerful symbol of our identity as a servant people. It calls for humility on the part of those who do it and those who have it done to them. Peter, remember, was the first to find it a bit too much.

No words of introduction are provided in the ritual, so the homily should lead naturally into the washing of feet (see the Episcopal Church's *Book of Occasional Services* for eloquent words). If not carried in the entrance procession, washbasins, pitchers of warm water and towels can be brought from the sacristy as the singing begins and as participants move to their places. This singing continues throughout the washing and during any follow-up washing of the hands of the ministers, ending just before the intercessions. Note several points about this rite:

- First, the presider should not be alone but assisted by other leaders of the community. This is a recommitment to ministerial service more powerful than words.

- Second, "twelve" is not specified but only "a representative group" of the faithful. This reminds us that this is not historical reenactment, but sacramental-liturgical ritual. There is nothing to prevent a larger number or even the whole assembly taking part. Parishes might invite the poor, the homeless or people with AIDS to have their feet washed as a sign of the community's commitment to serve.

- Third, visual participation by the assembly requires careful positioning, perhaps at various points throughout the church.

■ MUSIC: Music for the mandatum should be chosen carefully. The entire assembly should be able to watch or participate in the foot-washing. A hymn, by its complexity of text, may force the assembly to choose between participating in singing or participating in the ritual action. These are some good responsorial pieces: Steve Janco's "Whenever you serve me" (WLP, 6210); Taizé's "Mandatum novum" (GIA, G-2433); Michael Ward's "A new commandment" (WLP, 7579); Steve Warner's "The garment of love" (WLP, 7211); Chrysogonus Waddell's "Jesus took a towel" *(Worship,* #432). "Jesu, Jesu" *(Worship,* #431) is a song from Ghana that speaks of our "mandatum" to serve as Jesus did. Christopher Walker's "Faith, hope and love" is based on the mandatum text with alternate verses derived from "Ubi caritas" (OCP, 7149).

■ DISMISSAL OF CATECHUMENS AND ELECT: Catechumens and elect are sent forth after the washing of feet. The elect and catechumens may continue reflection and discussion on their own, perhaps with some prepared questions as a guide. This would allow the catechists to stay for the entire liturgy. However, a catechist may view accompanying the elect and catechumens as another way of following the Lord's command to wash feet.

- GENERAL INTERCESSIONS: See the texts in *Prayers for Sundays and Seasons,* or the intercessions from tonight's Evening Prayer in the *Liturgy of the Hours* (recast these as invitations to pray to the Father rather than to Christ).

Liturgy of the Eucharist

- PREPARATION RITES: "At the beginning of the liturgy of the eucharist, there may be a procession of the faithful with gifts for the poor" (sacramentary). Canned goods for a food bank, "rice bowls" for Catholic Relief Services or similar gifts could be collected in this procession, which ends with those bringing up the bread and wine for the eucharist.

In a rare directive, the church prescribes the song for this moment. "Ubi caritas" (c. the year 800) is accessible to every congregation in many chant adaptations. Few hymns have such a venerable history. Do not let another Triduum planning season go by without this chant. Richard Proulx offers two versions, one in *Worship* (#598) and a second, "God is love" (GIA, G-3010) for unison choir, cantor and congregation. Taizé's mantra "Ubi caritas" (*Worship*, #604) establishes a calm, prayerful environment. It may be embellished for use throughout the ritual. A well-known survivor from the 1960s is "Where charity and love prevail," now with inclusive language in the *People's Mass Book* and *Gather.* Musicians may call on flute or oboe for interludes between verses. World Library offers a new setting of "Where charity and love prevail" by Mark Hill (WLP, 8593).

- EUCHARISTIC PRAYER:
- Preface: Holy Eucharist I is prescribed.
- Three special inserts are provided for tonight.

- ACCLAMATIONS: Richard Proulx's "Corpus Christi Mass" (for unaccompanied choir, cantor and congregation), based on the familiar "Adoro Te," suits this evening perfectly. The familiar tune provides for participation by the assembly.

- BREAKING OF BREAD: Even if the parish does not yet use loaves large enough to break for the community at every Mass, tonight truly requires such bread. Breaking the one bread is an important symbol. Bread for tomorrow is also broken tonight. See LTP's *The Three Days* for a good recipe.

- COMMUNION PROCESSION: Psalm 34 is most appropriate. Settings include James Moore's "Taste and see" (GIA, G-2802), which needs a cantor who can do justice to the wonderful gospel-style verses; Stephen Dean's "Taste and see" (OCP, 7114); Michael Joncas' "Take and eat" (GIA, G-3435); J. Gerald Phillips' "O taste and see" (WLP, 8613); Richard Hillert's "Taste and see" (in *Service Music for the Mass,* vol. 1; WLP, 6611); and Alan Hommerding's "Taste and see," which uses the "Adoro te devote" melody (in *Sing Out! A Children's Psalter,* WLP, 7910). Robert Hutmacher's "Love is his word" (*Worship,* #599) gathers the evening's several images in a graceful musical setting. Lucien Deiss' "Song of my love" (WLP, 2561) contains beautiful language about the eucharist. Alan Hommerding's "Litany for the Holy Eucharist" (*We Celebrate,* #29) is based on the Agnus Dei from the "Jubilate Deo" Mass. Musicians might repeat tonight's song for the communion procession at the Vigil.

- DISMISSAL OF EUCHARISTIC MINISTERS: The Circular Letter (#53) reminds us that the hospitality of the Lord's table should be extended to the homebound by bringing them communion directly from this evening's celebration.

- AFTER COMMUNION: The vessel with eucharistic bread for Good Friday's communion is left on the altar. After a period of silence, the prayer after communion is sung or said. The procession follows immediately.

Transfer of the Holy Eucharist

- PREPARATION: The presider stands before the altar and places incense in the thurible. Kneeling, he incenses the eucharist three times. Assisting ministers and all others kneel. Presider then puts on humeral veil, takes vessel with eucharist and covers it with the ends of the veil. Meanwhile, ministers who will lead the procession gather in order. If the largest vessel available cannot contain the bread for Good Friday, a second vessel should be carried by a deacon or concelebrant also wearing a humeral veil.

- PROCESSION: The cross bearer and two acolytes lead the procession. Deacons, concelebrants, two censer bearers and presider with eucharist follow. Other ministers and members of assembly follow presider to reservation chapel, if room permits.

APRIL

"Pange lingua/Sing my tongue" (Aquinas' eucharistic text) is the classic chant for this ritual. Verses may be sung in Latin, English or alternate between the two. Musicians should coordinate with planners so that the first four verses may be repeated or so that the procession lasts until the final two verses ("Tantum ergo").

■ CONCLUSION OF PROCESSION: The presider sets vessel down in tabernacle (leaving door open) or just in front of it. He then removes the humeral veil, kneels and incenses vessel with one of the thuribles. All then sing the last two verses of the "Pange lingua" ("Tantum ergo"). The deacon places eucharist in tabernacle (if the presider did not) and closes the door. A period of silent adoration follows. Then altar is stripped in silence. People may stay for prayer and leave when they choose. Note that there is no dismissal, no real ending of this liturgy, which thus forms one movement of a liturgy that ends only at the Vigil. People simply disperse to continue their prayer and fasting at home.

EUCHARISTIC ADORATION

From the transfer of the eucharist to midnight, all should be encouraged to continue in prayer. The Circular Letter (#56) calls for John 13 – 17 to be read as part of this prayer time. Many parishes encourage participation by involving different groups in vocal prayer and song — religious communities, prayer groups, Bible-study groups or others. With coordination and division of time, the chapel can be filled for hours with public prayer (it should be parish prayer, not the devotions of any particular group or of individuals). See *To Crown the Year,* pages 94 – 97, for ideas on preparing the place of reservation.

NIGHT PRAYER

Many parishes conclude the period of adoration by singing Night Prayer together just before midnight, then quietly extinguishing the candles and dispersing in silence. In place of the usual responsory, "Into your hands," the church uses "Christ became obedient" throughout the hours of the Triduum, adding a phrase each day.

21 #40 red
Good Friday

ORIENTATION

On this day "when Christ became our paschal sacrifice," the church reflects on the Passion of its Lord and Spouse, adores his cross, commemorates its own origin from the side of the dead Christ on the cross, and intercedes for the salvation of the entire world. (Circular Letter, #58)

A Day to Celebrate the Passion

What is the mood of this day? The title of the principal liturgy holds the key: the Celebration of the Lord's Passion. The passion according to John, proclaimed as the heart of the celebration, expresses beautifully the dominant motif of the day. This is the passion whose keynote is glory:

> John's passion narrative presents a sovereign Jesus who has defiantly announced, "I lay down my life and I take it up again; no one takes it from me. . . . He does not cry out, "My God, my God, why have you forsaken me?" because the Father is always with him (16:32). Rather, his final words are a solemn decision, "It is finished." (Raymond E. Brown, *A Crucified Christ in Holy Week,* Liturgical Press, 1986, 69 – 70)

Even before John's passion, the other scriptures sound the note of ultimate victory. Isaiah's Servant of the Lord, though "wounded for our transgressions and crushed for our iniquities," "shall see light . . . shall make many righteous . . . shall divide the spoil with the strong." The community's response is the Lord's own confident prayer from Psalm 31, "Into your hands I commend my spirit." The author of the Letter to the Hebrews introduces Jesus as "a great high priest," a Son who "learned obedience through what he suffered;" because of him we can "approach the throne of grace with boldness," confident that we shall "receive mercy and find grace" in our time of need.

Thus the veneration of the cross, which follows the great intercessory prayer, is best accompanied by glorious passion hymns like the "Vexilla regis" ("The royal banners forward go") and the "Pange lingua" ("Sing, my tongue, the song of triumph"). The focus is not so much on Christ crucified as on the cross itself, held aloft between two candles, the community's sign and assurance of victory and salvation. There should be only one cross for all to kiss or touch. The sense of this gesture is not "Look at what my sins have done," but rather "Look at how much I am worth, that while I was yet dead in my sins, Christ did this for me!" (Romans 5:8). After the liturgy, the glorious cross remains in church — the focus of quiet reflection and grateful prayer.

A fine orientation to the spirit of the Roman rite on this day comes from the official prayers that bracket the celebration. In the Good Friday liturgy of some churches, for instance, the opening prayer asks God "graciously to behold this your family, for whom our Lord Jesus Christ was willing to be betrayed, and given into the hands of sinners, and to suffer death upon the cross." But the Roman prayer speaks of the suffering and death of Christ as "saving us all from the death we inherited," and asks that we be "reshaped in the likeness of Christ to bear the stamp of his heavenly glory through the sanctifying power of your grace." The closing prayer used by some churches asks Jesus "to set your passion, cross and death between your judgment and our souls." But the Roman prayer ends the liturgy on the same note of victory with which it began: "Send down your abundant blessing upon your people who have devoutly recalled the death of your Son in the sure hope of the resurrection. . . . May their faith grow stronger and their eternal salvation be assured."

According to the church's most ancient tradition, the eucharist is not celebrated today. Penance is better celebrated before the Triduum and as a preparation for it. Communion may be brought to the sick any time today, and, depending on the condition of each communicant, the ministers will want to read part of the passion of John to them and lead them in intercessory prayer.

A Day to Keep the Paschal Fast

So much of what we say and do not say in our liturgy, do and do not do, use and do not use is based on the paschal fast. The term *paschal fast* first appears in the *Constitution on the Sacred Liturgy* (1963): "Let the paschal fast be kept sacred. Let it be observed everywhere on Good Friday and, where possible, prolonged through Holy Saturday, as a way of coming to the joys of the Sunday of the resurrection with uplifted and welcoming heart." The calendar norms of 1969 reaffirm this (#20), and the Circular Letter (1988) says that "the fast on the first two days of the Triduum is especially sacred" (#39). Clearly more is here than the Friday fast and abstinence required by church law. What? A whole attitude of mind and heart. The elect, for example, with whom the fast places us in solidarity are to fast from more than food: "They should refrain from their usual activities, spend their time in prayer and reflection, and . . . observe a fast" (#185).

We can't live these days well unless we change our schedule of meals, their content and their quantity. Business as usual, entertainment as usual, chatter, shopping, diversion, dining — these must be radically altered if we want the darkness before Easter dawn to be filled for us.

A Day of Intercessory Prayer

After the proclamation of the glorious passion according to John, the church stretches out its arms, as Christ does forever "between heaven and earth, in the everlasting sign of the covenant" (Eucharistic Prayer for Reconciliation II), to make intercession for the needs of the whole world. It is as if the church wishes only the image of Christ the eternal high priest (second reading) to shine forth, and for the church to stand with Christ in this priestly prayer.

The Liturgy of the Hours is also to be celebrated: the Office of Readings and Morning Prayer at the day's opening; perhaps Midday Prayer at noon; and Compline at the close of day.

OFFICE OF READINGS AND MORNING PRAYER: TENEBRAE

Tenebrae, the "Office of Shadows" or "Darkness," was the title used before Vatican II for the Office of Readings combined with Morning Prayer, during which candles on an elaborate triangular "hearse" were extinguished one by one as the liturgy progressed and the morning light came in. In recent centuries, despite the early-morning images, this was sometimes moved to Wednesday night as a sort of prelude to the Triduum, which led to various explanations of the diminishing candles. The *Ceremonial of Bishops* (#296), the *Liturgy of the Hours* (#210) and the Circular Letter (#40, 62) all call for a return of the original Tenebrae. While more permanent rites are prepared, parishes may choose between the Office of Readings and Morning Prayer, or combine the two liturgies using the General Instruction of the Liturgy of the Hours (#99) for structural guidance. The combined office follows this outline:

- Invitatory antiphon and psalm (Office of Readings [OR]); chant these "recto tono" (on one note)
- Hymn: Fortunatus' "Pange lingua" is prescribed
- antiphons and psalms (OR)
- verse (OR)
- scripture: Hebrews 9:11 – 28
- silent reflection and responsory (OR)
- patristic reading: from *Catecheses* of John Chrysostom: "The power of Christ's blood"
- silent reflection and responsory follows (OR)
- antiphons, psalms and Old Testament canticle: Morning Prayer (MP)
- scripture: Isaiah 52:13 – 15
- response: Triduum antiphon: "Christ became obedient for us even unto death," adding today, "even unto death on a cross": MP; see note for Thursday Night Prayer, page 126
- antiphon and Canticle of Zechariah (MP)
- intercessions, Lord's Prayer and concluding prayer (MP)
- blessing and dismissal.

CHILDREN AND THE TRIDUUM

Those who prepare the Triduum liturgy must consider how best to include the community's children. Child care should be provided for the youngest ones, at least for the main celebrations. Ways to involve preschool and older children should be planned carefully. Possibilities include:

- Midday Prayer (or Stations of the Cross) with music learned in religious education classes
- References to the faith life of children in the Triduum homilies
- Participation of children in preparing the church building for the Triduum
- Catechetical assemblies for all parish children on Good Friday and Holy Saturday mornings.

■ CATECHETICAL ASSEMBLIES: One way to encourage the active participation of young people may be to hold catechetical assemblies on Good Friday and Holy Saturday mornings. Parents will appreciate this effort to draw their children into the great mystery of faith, and children will enjoy the gatherings if they are planned well. Such events could involve youth from preschool through grade six or so. They would gather each day for an hour-long event organized more or less as a celebration of the word. What distinguishes this from a children's liturgy that competes with the principal liturgy is that it must clearly point to the parish assembly — a kind of rehearsal and orientation to enable children to participate fully in the principal liturgies.

Good Friday's catechetical assembly might include:

- Music that speaks of the passion and cross, and will be used at the celebration of the Lord's passion
- A reading or two from the day's Liturgy of the Hours, using images with which children can identify
- Instructions by one or more catechists, introducing the liturgy that the children will take part in later today. Instructions may be given in smaller groups by age level
- Rehearsal and explanation of the solemn actions they will perform with the adults later on
- Some preparation of the physical requirements for the principal liturgy: For example, children can see the stripped-down church and reflect on it, help prepare a resting place for the cross, or get the cross out of storage and bring it to the place from which it will be carried in solemn entrance
- Some of the intercessions from the celebration of the passion.

GOOD FRIDAY CHECKLIST

A list similar to what follows may be helpful for sacristans and planners:

- Practice singing intercessions
- Arrange microphones for passion
- Cross, candles, matches in back (incense materials, too, if used for veneration)
- Altar cloth and corporal on credence table
- Arrange for collection for Holy Land
- Be sure holy water fonts are emptied
- Prepare red vestments
- Prepare a private place for reservation of any remaining consecrated bread after service
- Prepare a place for enshrinement of the cross after the service

CELEBRATION OF THE LORD'S PASSION

Introductory Rites

■ SILENCE: Silence plays a significant role in this liturgy. The liturgy begins in silence and ends in silence. No cross, no candles, no great procession. No gathering song. No solo instruments. Only those ministers necessary for the liturgy sit in the sanctuary. Except for a book-bearer, even the servers could be seated with the assembly, with the lectors and ministers of communion coming forward only when needed.

■ PROSTRATION: Presider and assistants reverence the bare altar, then fully prostrate themselves. The Circular Letter (#65) stresses the importance of this ritual gesture:

APRIL

This act of prostration, which is proper to the rite of the day, should be strictly observed, for it signifies both the abasement of "earthly man" [sic] and also the grief and sorrow of the church.

The assembly kneels while the few in the sanctuary lie prostrate. All pray silently, as the sacramentary suggests "for a while," which means long enough for the power of this gesture to sink in and long enough for this silence to evolve into prayer.

- OPENING PRAYER: At the chair, the presider omits both greeting and "Let us pray." This signals that today's liturgy is a continuation of the liturgy we began last night. With hands extended, the presider offers the opening prayer and sits down for the liturgy of the word.

LITURGY OF THE WORD

- LITURGY OF THE WORD FOR CHILDREN: Today, let the children remain with the main assembly rather than leave for a separate liturgy of the word.

Psalm 31 is the first music of this liturgy. Let it be sung a cappella. The absence of musical instrumentation throughout this celebration can be a powerful experience. Choose music that is easy to sing without accompaniment. Chant always serves well. Notice that Psalm 31, rather than last Sunday's Psalm 22, has been chosen for today. This is in keeping with the majestic image of Christ that shines through the Johannine passion. *Worship*'s setting (#814) is effective. Francis V. Strahan's simple refrain, "Father, Father" *(People's Mass Book)* is a fine alternative.

- PASSION ACCORDING TO JOHN: Several approaches are possible for this proclamation. It may be chanted by three strong singers to the time-honored melody of the Roman rite (GIA, G-1795). Deacons, presbyters, cantors or capable lectors chant the parts of Christ, narrator, speaker. Or, a single well-prepared lector may provide a strong proclamation. Or, several lectors may each take a section of the story, with musical refrain by assembly between sections. An appropriate refrain would be the parish's usual setting of the memorial acclamation "Lord, by your cross." This text is fitting, since John's passion focuses on the triumph of the cross.

However it is proclaimed, the passion is read in an atmosphere of simple austerity:

- No incense or candles
- No greeting or signs of the cross
- After the verse of the Lord's death, all kneel and silence is observed.

- HOMILY: Today's homily should avoid any language that even hints at blaming the Jewish people for Christ's death. In fact, the homily should correct any such impression left by the text of John's passion.

- DISMISSAL OF ELECT AND CATECHUMENS: The general intercessions are prayers of the baptized faithful, so the elect and catechumens are dismissed before they begin. They may leave with a catechist or on their own to continue reflection on the passion, perhaps returning to venerate the cross.

- GENERAL INTERCESSIONS: These are an important part of the ministry of the baptized on this day. The ancient form of the prayers at this liturgy can help all of us see these prayers as part of a priestly ministry through which we share in the high priestly role of Christ.

Veneration of the Cross

- THE CROSS: The object of veneration is not the figure of the crucified, but the cross as a symbol of victory and salvation. Therefore, the cross should be large and well-crafted. Only one cross should be used. Processions may approach the cross simultaneously from several directions, as ushers direct the flow. Using several small crosses is absurd after bringing one large cross in with solemn reverence. The other alternative, holding the cross up for communal worship by a silent assembly in place, loses all the power of the ritual.

Peter Mazar provides a fine treatment of the subject of the cross and its veneration (*To Crown the Year,* pages 98–103).

- BEHOLD THE WOOD OF THE CROSS: Two options are given in the sacramentary for the introduction of the cross into the worship space: "uncovering" and "bringing in." The "uncovering" form is necessary if the cross is suspended or otherwise stationary. Architects or designers should have planned for lowering it for this rite. Note what the rubrics say: The veiled cross is not carried in and unveiled in stages along the way. Rather, the gradual unveiling occurs entirely in one place.

- VENERATING THE CROSS: See Mazar for interesting ideas on how to place the cross for veneration. Some parishes make sure the cross is always held by people during the veneration. Some parishes simply lay it flat or on the steps before the altar (make sure the elderly and infirm can approach easily). The

TRIDUUM: GOOD FRIDAY

cross should never be propped up on furniture, much less on the altar.

An ancient custom calls for all ministers — indeed all the people — to come to the cross barefoot or in stocking feet. While this custom is not mentioned in the sacramentary, the *Ceremonial of Bishops* (#322) tells the presider to leave his chasuble and shoes at the chair. They should be taken off before the entrance of the cross, so that the procession flows into the veneration. This tradition, still observed by many monastic orders and frequently mentioned by ancient homilists, catches on quickly if the presider and other ministers handle it with grace. Announce it in the participation booklet. If the presider is seen taking his shoes off while other ministers in the sanctuary do the same, other members of the assembly may feel comfortable removing theirs.

■ Music for the veneration: When selecting music, keep in mind the unity of the Triduum. Today is a celebration of the Lord's passion, austere but never sad. One way to establish this mood is an invitation to come and adore sung by the cantor near the cross followed by a strong proclamation of praise such as the traditional Good Friday trisagion, "Holy is God." Three settings, by Howard Hughes, David Isele and Michael Joncas, appear in *Praise God in Song* (GIA, G-2270).

The veneration will take time and cannot be rushed. Prepare plenty of music. Vary styles and participants, congregational singing and pieces by the choir. Cantor or soloist can add further variety. Begin and end with music that involves the assembly. "Sing, my tongue" (the passion "Pange, lingua") is most ancient and appropriate. Marty Haugen's, "Tree of life" (GIA, G-2944) is suitable throughout the Triduum, as are the Taizé (GIA, G-3719) "Crucem tuam," "Adoramus te Domine I" (*Gather,* #221) and "Jesus, remember me" (*Gather,* #167). Owen Alstott's "Wood of the cross" for choir and congregation (OCP, 8826) combines the refrain "Behold the wood of the cross" with Psalm 22. The "Lamentations of Jeremiah" are coupled with a haunting chant melody in *The Three Days* (LTP). The refrain "Jerusalem, Jerusalem, return to the Lord your God" can be sung by the assembly after the cantor without any rehearsal.

The Reproaches still appear as an option in the official Roman books and in many missalettes. Their danger is the potential of misreading texts as directed toward all the Jewish people of Jesus' time — or our own. A striking revision of the verses, clearly directed to the church of today, appears in the United Methodist *Book of Worship,* with the trisagion ("Holy is God") mentioned above.

Communion Rite

■ Communion: A simple transfer rite brings the eucharist to the altar, where altar cloth, corporal and book have been placed. Candles carried with the cross are arranged near the altar. The order is simple: Lord's Prayer, embolism, invitation to communion. The music from last night may be repeated. Haas' "Now we remain" (*Gather,* GIA) is also appropriate.

■ After communion: Any remaining eucharist (for Holy Saturday viaticum) is carried without ceremony by an assisting minister to a suitable place outside the main worship space. Then the prayer after communion is said.

■ Prayer over the people: The traditional greeting is omitted. The presider extends hands over the assembly and offers this prayer, which, like all the official texts, is focused on eternal life and glory. This liturgy has no dismissal or formal ending. All depart in silence.

NIGHT PRAYER

This liturgical prayer, perhaps celebrated after a fasting meal, follows the same format as last night's prayer and includes the same proper antiphon, with the addition that was added this morning: Christ became obedient for us even unto death, even unto death on a cross.

22 violet
Holy Saturday

ORIENTATION

On Holy Saturday the church waits at the Lord's tomb, meditating on his suffering and death. The altar is left bare, and the sacrifice of the Mass is not celebrated. Only after the solemn vigil during the night, held in anticipation of the resurrection, does the Easter celebration begin, with a spirit of joy that overflows into the following period of fifty days. (Sacramentary, rubric for Holy Saturday)

APRIL

Day of Waiting

Waiting for what? For the Vigil, and for initiation. For the elect, it is a day of intensive retreat, and also for many of the faithful who join them. For as many of us as possible, today is a day for all other concerns to be set aside. Even much church business is set aside on this day. The church fasts from the eucharist: no communion calls today. Viaticum for the dying is the only eucharistic event permitted. No one gets married today, when the great marriage feast of heaven and earth is about to break upon us. Penance and anointing of the sick may be celebrated if truly necessary, but these are better celebrated before the Easter Triduum.

The paschal fast continues; who could think any substantial meal when the banquet of love is to be shared with the neophytes for the first time in just a few hours?

With growing anticipation, we gather with the elect to celebrate some or all of the preparation rites: the presentation of the Lord's Prayer, the "return" or recitation of the Creed, which was presented solemnly during Lent, the ephphetha rite and the choosing of a baptismal name.

Day of Prayer

As on Good Friday, the Office of Readings and Morning Prayer should be celebrated with the assembly. The patristic text for today from the Office of Readings celebrate Christ's descent among the dead and his liberation of the souls of the just.

Midday Prayer may be celebrated on its own or with some of the preparation rites. There may be catechetical assemblies for the children of the parish. Although there will be no blessed water to sprinkle, some ethnic groups may wish to make preparations for the blessing of foods that will be used to break the paschal fast once the Vigil is over. Evening Prayer, as the sun sets, is the last celebration before the great work of the Easter Vigil begins, and its final antiphon sets the stage for that Vigil: "Now is the Son of Man glorified, and God is glorified in him!"

Day of Growing Anticipation

Late Saturday afternoon, perhaps even before Evening Prayer, as the hour of the Vigil draws near, anticipation is growing among the elect, their sponsors and all who have come this far with them. Like all the liturgies of the Triduum, the Vigil does not really begin, it continues. How do we experience that? Some of the scriptures that have been associated with the Vigil at various times in history but are not now included in the Roman lectionary might be proclaimed quietly as the hours draw toward the Vigil.

Among the "lost" scriptures that this time could reclaim: selections from the Noah stories (Genesis 5 – 9); Ezekiel's vision of the valley of the dry bones; the entire Jonah story; Daniel's story of the young men in the fiery furnace; the story of Elisha and the Shunammite woman.

OFFICE OF READINGS AND MORNING PRAYER: TENEBRAE

The outline on page 127 is used. Even if the Office of Readings is not combined with Morning Prayer, be sure to read the patristic homily assigned today. It paints a beautiful picture of Christ's triumphant entrance into Sheol, his meeting with our first parents, and the beginning of the great victory procession by which the souls of the just are liberated by the conquering savior, King Jesus.

After the scripture reading of Morning Prayer, the special Triduum antiphon is chanted again, "Christ became obedient for us even unto death, even unto death on a cross," with the final phrase of glorification added: "Therefore God raised him on high and gave him the name above all other names."

Many parishes combine Morning Prayer with the preparation rites for the elect or the rite of reception of children (before infant baptism) on this day. Notes are given in the next section.

PREPARATION FOR INITIATION

Preparation Rites for the Elect

The *Rite of Christian Initiation of Adults* (starting at #185) describes the preparation rites on Holy Saturday: song and greeting, reading the word of God and homily, certain rites (presentation of the Lord's Prayer, the return of the Creed, and/or the ephphetha rite).

These rites can be celebrated on their own, with participation by the parish community encouraged. They could also be joined to an hour of prayer from the Liturgy of the Hours. In this case, the preparation rites follow the proper psalmody and scripture reading (and perhaps the patristic homily).

Note that anointing with the oil of catechumens is no longer part of these preparation rites. The current edition of the rite prescribes this anointing as a repeatable rite during the period of the catechumenate.

APRIL

Rite of Reception of Children

If infants will be baptized at the Vigil, the *Rite of Baptism for Children* (#28) calls for preparatory rites with infants, parents, sponsors and community. A preparatory rite for the infants to be baptized involves receiving the children at the door, the prayer of exorcism and anointing with the oil of catechumens. This may be celebrated before a fasting lunch or in conjunction with one of the hours of the Liturgy of the Hours.

Combined Preparation Rite

A service combining reception of infants with preparation of the elect is possible, uniting in one assembly the prayers and expectations of the elect, the parents, the sponsors and the catechists. The format is as follows:

- Gathering hymn, with entire assembly at the entrance. An appropriate text is found on page 170 of the *Triduum Sourcebook*
- Reception of infants (*Rite of Baptism for Children* [RBC], 35 – 41)
- Procession of all to seating near ambo; refrain or hymn sung by all
- Liturgy of the Hours option: psalms, antiphon, scripture of the appropriate hour

  or

  Liturgy of the word option:
- reading(s) related to preparatory rites, followed by psalm (possible rites listed in RCIA, 185.2; readings at #179 – 180, 194, 198)
- Homily
- Preparation rites for infants: exorcism (RBC, 49), anointing with oil of catechumens (RBC, 50)
- One or more preparation rites for adults and children of catechetical age: presentation of Lord's Prayer (RCIA, 180), recitation of Creed (RCIA, 195) or ephphetha (RCIA, 199)
- Hymn or gospel canticle (if part of Morning or Evening Prayer)
- Intercessions from Morning or Evening Prayer of Holy Saturday, supplemented with prayers for baptized candidates for full communion
- Prayer of blessing (RCIA, 204)
- Dismissal (RCIA, 205)

CATECHETICAL ASSEMBLY FOR CHILDREN

See the introduction under this heading on Good Friday, page 128. Today's catechetical session may include any of these items:

- Participation of children in preparation of the elect, especially if children of catechetical age will be prepared
- Participation in any of the hours of the Liturgy of the Hours
- Painting of Easter eggs to be distributed to all after the Vigil
- Hearing (and dramatizing) scriptures from the Vigil
- Preparing the worship space for the Vigil

These activities are meant to prepare the children for participating in the Vigil.

EVENING PRAYER

Depending on the time of the Vigil, this hour may be best for the preparatory rites for the elect. It also may be the best hour to link to a fasting meal. If the Vigil is very late or just before dawn, those in the habit of coming to church for early evening Mass may appreciate Evening Prayer at that time. The official hymn for this hour recapitulates the focus of the day: "Devoted friends laid you to rest/within the tomb's tranquility,/But you descended to the dead/to grant their longed for liberty."

22–23

#41 white
Easter Vigil

ORIENTATION

Just as our faith, thanks to Christ's resurrection, is made strong enough to keep us awake and watchful, so by our Easter vigil let us make this night blaze with light. Then we shall be one in mind with the universal church on this Easter day, instead of being left in darkness. How many congregations are gathered together in Christ's name throughout the world for this solemn celebration! And not one of them is left in the dark. The sun may have set, but in its stead the earth is ablaze with a light of its own. . . . Christ to whom we say: "You will enlighten my darkness" is even now flooding our hearts with his radiance, so that not only do our eyes enjoy the splendor of these shining candles, but our minds are enlightened and given the power to understand the significance of this glorious night. (Saint Augustine)

Fire in Darkness

The only place we can begin is in the dark, the dark of a Saturday night and Sunday morning. People are quietly assembling. They may be many or few. They come as individuals, couples, households, friends. Some of them are

132 TRIDUUM: HOLY SATURDAY

light-headed from 48 hours of a strict fast; they are hungry to be in this assembly tonight. In the darkness outside, a bonfire is burning and from it a great candle is lighted. All move inside and by the light of that candle a member of the assembly sings a summons to rejoicing: Angels, earth, church, everyone here: Rejoice! The singer proclaims that this is our passover, that this — tonight, if you would believe it — is the night when the slaves were delivered to freedom and safety, the night when God raised up Jesus and broke death's hold on us. This night (the song continues) will see evil driven away, the proud humbled, mourners rejoicing, hatred take flight and peace settle in.

Words around the Fire

Then for a long time in the darkness, the assembled people listen to what perhaps are their most sacred scriptures. On this one night of all the year, the book is opened to its first page. Only on this night do the people hear the wonderful and amazing words that are written on that page: "In the beginning . . . " Over and over again come the words that both judge and direct everyday life: "God saw how good it was!" And when that page has been read and pondered, readers turn to the story of God's promise to Abraham; to the story of how the slaves escaped right through the sea; to the poems of Isaiah where God woos a people "afflicted, storm-battered and unconsoled," and where the penniless are summoned to feast in a realm where the tables are turned; to Baruch's summons to search our God's ways for "she has appeared on earth and moved among us"; to Ezekiel's promise of a new heart; to Paul's dazzling and right question: "Are you not aware that we who were baptized in Christ Jesus were baptized into his death?" (into his death?); and last, to the page of the gospel that tells the story of the empty tomb.

Take Me to the River

When all of these scriptures have been heard with silences and psalms between them, a chant begins. The singer calls out the names of the ancestors; saints of all times and places are summoned now to stand with this generation, to stand around a font full of water. Here, beside the waters, the elect (who were chosen 40 days ago and told to make final preparations to do battle with evil and fix their hearts on good, to pray and fast so as to come ready this night) are left in no doubt about the stakes. They are asked to make renunciations, asked to say publicly that they will turn away from an entire way of life. One by one they do this, then profess eagerly that which will bind them to this people: a life lived by faith in God who is Creator, Redeemer and Holy Spirit.

Then each one enters a pool of water and is baptized, poured over or dipped three times. The point is drowning. The point, quite simply, is death. For to be baptized in Christ is to be "dead and have one's life hid with Christ in God" (Colossians 3:3). All this really has not changed since it was described by Augustine and Cyril and Ambrose 1,600 years ago. After the waters comes the perfumed oil called chrism, poured on each newly baptized head, sealing the baptism as the sweet odor fills the hall. Then all join in making intercession to God for the world's needs.

The Welcome Table

Bread and wine are brought to the holy table where with prayer and acclamation they are blessed; after sharing the kiss of peace, all eat of the one bread and drink from the one cup. All alike are members of Christ whose body and blood are their nourishment, peace and bond.

The Big Question

Who in the world would give up a Saturday night for this? Yet for those who gather, this is the most worldly Saturday night of the year. It is the night of all nights most about this world. The life that is affirmed and embraced this night is not merely some afterlife of bliss. The death that we proclaim defeated is not merely the death that each of us must die. This is the most worldly of nights because what is defeated — so we hear and so we mean, though the news is traveling slowly — is death in life, that death that masquerades as life: the death that dwells in economic and political systems when any human being is without food or dignity, the death that dwells in our very selves when we live at ease with bounty and allow the balance to grow more and more lopsided while we continue beating our children's plowshares into a sword. Defeated is that death which dwells in homes and nations when we learn and teach that any color is better, any sex, any age, any nationality, any status.

This night we affirm the death of all that death, for we know — just hear those scriptures, just look at that woman entering the waters, just smell that chrism, just taste that cup — what is passing away and what abides. This is our passover, that paschal mystery that we proclaim.

Preparation

It is clear that no one gets up from the dinner table on this Saturday night and strolls over to the church for such a Vigil. Nor does anyone walk out afterwards expecting a typical Sunday. The Vigil can exist only within its own time, the Triduum, and the Triduum prepared by Lent and overflowing into Eastertime. (Gabe Huck, *The Three Days,* 111–114)

EASTER VIGIL CHECKLIST

This list is offered to help with the Vigil's ceremonial complexities. It needs adaptation to the local situation and should be used with *The Sacristy Manual* (pages 215–217) and *To Crown the Year* (pages 104–117).

Items to be prepared and put in place:

- Fire, matches, wood
- Paschal candle, stylus, nails, incense
- Censer, charcoal (one or two pieces at base of fire), incense, tongs
- Wooden tapers to light paschal candle from fire
- Sacramentary or presider's book
- Small flashlight
- People's candles (bobeches, windguards)
- Water container, for emergency
- Aspergillum and bucket (or branches and bowls)
- Containers for filling holy water fonts
- Chrism
- Baptismal candles
- Towels for baptized and for floor around font
- Baptismal garments
- Exsultet music in suitably decorated book or on scroll
- Hymnals where needed
- Bells for the Gloria
- Wine, chalice, cups for assembly's communion, purificators
- Bread and additional patens for distribution
- Music for eucharistic prayer; sheet for concelebrant

SERVICE OF LIGHT

Darkness

The liturgical books emphasize that the Easter Vigil takes place at night: after nightfall, before daybreak. In fact, the Circular Letter reserves some of its strongest language for this requirement:

> This rule is to be taken according to its strictest sense. Reprehensible are those abuses and practices which have crept in many places in violation of this ruling, whereby the Easter Vigil is celebrated at the time of day that it is customary to celebrate anticipated Sunday Masses.

The power of darkness must be felt before the light of the Risen One can be truly experienced in the Easter candle. Consult almanac tables and weather services to determine the earliest time to begin the Vigil.

Easter Fire

■ WHAT: *Rogus,* in Latin. A precise translation would be "bonfire."

■ WHY: To draw the assembly together in its warmth and light.

■ WHERE: On a lawn, if a thick tarp is put down with ten inches of sand on it, *or* a trough as for watering livestock can be used, with sand or cinder blocks underneath for insulation.

■ WHO: Everyone meets around the fire, which may be lighted before most arrive. Bad weather (short of a blizzard or downpour) should not deter us. Those who do not gather outside should be asked to move to the sides of the church so as not to impede the procession in the center aisle. The church remains in total darkness.

■ SAFETY CONSIDERATIONS: Dried hardwood is safer than pine or other softwoods. Consult the fire department or fire marshal's office. Many municipalities have regulations about fires, even on private property. Officials are generally respectful of religious customs. No responsible pastor would allow any official to rule out one of the central symbols in this service of light: the lighted candle in every person's hand. Ushers should be alert and prepared to smother stray sparks with a thick blanket. One should be kept on hand along with fire extinguishers.

■ BLESSING THE FIRE AND LIGHTING THE CANDLE: A large new paschal candle of wax is mandatory, according to the Circular Letter. Artificial candles are specifically prohibited.
Order:

- No cross or other candles are carried
- Unlit paschal candle is carried by acolyte or deacon. Deacon may also read introduction, so this may determine who serves as candle bearer
- Censer bearer has empty censer
- According to the most ancient usage, no greeting is given; we have been in the Triduum liturgy since Thursday night. The liturgy begins with the presider's or deacon's words of introduction, spoken when all are ready
- Deacon, presider or concelebrant gives instruction, using sacramentary text or similar words
- Fire is blessed
- Paschal candle is prepared and lit.

Procession

The censer is prepared at this point with coals from the fire and adding incense. Because it takes time for the coals to be ready for incense, the charcoal should be placed in the fire before the liturgy begins. Use tongs to retrieve the coals.

The deacon carries the candle high, preceded only by censer bearer, followed by presider: These three lead the whole procession into church.

APRIL

Everyone's candles should be lit early in this procession. Careful planning with several acolytes passing the flame avoids delays.

The one who will chant the Exsultet (perhaps wearing a cope) carries a beautiful book or scroll with the text and music. If the deacon is to sing the Exsultet, an assisting minister will serve as book or scroll bearer.

If the fire is some distance from the church, use a glass windguard for the Easter candle. People's candles may be lit before the procession if windguards are provided. Paper cones are available; Orthodox church goods stores offer red plastic windguards designed for the substantial candles used in their processions. "Light of Christ! Thanks be to God!" is the processional song. It may be augmented by acclamations in honor of Christ. One recommendation is to intersperse verses of the evening hymn "O Radiant Light" (Phos hilaron) set to the chant "Jesu, dulcis memoria" between acclamations.

Coordination of movement, music and ministers cannot be left to chance. Be sure the acclamation pitch is clear and matches the key of the hymn. If each acclamation or hymn verse will be sung at a higher pitch, carefully prepare and rehearse transitions.

The candle is honored with incense when placed in the stand, normally near the ambo where the Exsultet is sung. The censer bearer stands nearby. If the deacon sings the Exsultet, he asks for and receives the presider's blessing in a low voice.

Easter Proclamation

Despite the suggestion in the sacramentary, do not turn on the electric lights until after the Exsultet. Some parishes, in fact, conduct the whole liturgy of the word by candlelight, turning the lights on only at the Gloria.

Robert Batastini's adaptation of the Exsultet (GIA, G-2351) is a smooth working of the English text to the traditional chant melody for single cantor. Christopher Walker has a setting for cantor and SATB choir, with assembly's concluding Amens (St. Thomas More, OCP, 7175). J. Michael Thompson's arrangement of the sacramentary setting is available from World Library (#5716). Everett Frese's setting (Pastoral Press) respects the integrity of the text for cantor and incorporates the assembly in the opening and closing sections.

LITURGY OF THE WORD

The Circular Letter sees the liturgy of the word as "the fundamental element of the Easter Vigil." The clear message of the whole tradition of the church, East and West, Roman and reformed, in all the service books that have evolved over the last three decades, is that on this most holy night time is *not* of the essence, any haste would be irreverent, and any abbreviation of the liturgy of the word undesirable.

Readings

To sustain the assembly's attention through the long Vigil, try a variety of ways of proclaiming the lessons and singing the responses. Though the proclamation of a long reading by one well-prepared lector is effective, consider the approach suggested for Lent's Johannine gospels. The Genesis and Exodus readings lend themselves to reading by several lectors stationed throughout the worship space, accompanied by acolytes if the liturgy of the word is conducted by candlelight. If the long form of the creation story is chosen, chant "Evening came and morning followed, and God saw that all this was good" after the proclamation of each day of creation.

See LTP's *Triduum Sourcebook* (pages 252–253) for Easter Vigil readings from the various Christian traditions, if your parish is ready to add to the nine readings in the lectionary (for instance, Noah and the flood, omitted from the current Roman lectionary). If the parish has done minimal readings in the past, gradually restore the full celebration by adding one reading each year until the parish regains the riches of this full liturgy of the word, by which the character of this night as a vigil is demonstrated clearly.

■ PSALMODY: The assembly's response to the proclamation of the word takes several forms. Reflection on each reading is aided by the silence that follows the reading, by the singing of the responsorial psalm after that silence, and finally by listening and responding to the prayer proclaimed by the presider. A variety of settings are available.

The canticle response to Exodus is incorporated into the reading. The lector could end the reading with the previous line: "Then Moses and the Israelites sang this song to the Lord." The lector turns, at this point, in the direction of the cantor. This great song of the Israelites must be rhythmic and lively, and may be accompanied by percussion instruments. A tambourine lends an Eastern flair. See *Worship,* #821, *Gather Comprehensive,* #143, and *Praise God in Song* for settings.

For the response to Isaiah 55, see Robert Batastini's "You will draw water" (GIA, G-2443), with a handbell accompaniment that suggests water imagery.

Gloria

The sung Gloria points toward the proclamation of the gospel of the resurrection and, therefore, should not be so elaborate that it overshadows what it is meant to introduce. A Gloria with a repeated refrain is a good choice, especially where there are many visitors. Some of these are: Peter Jones, "Glory to God" (OCP); Richard Proulx, "Gloria for Eastertime," based on "O filii et filiae" (GIA, G-3086 or choral version G-3087); C. Alexander Peloquin, "Gloria of the bells" (*Worship,* #258).

■ DURING THE GLORIA: Candles on or near the altar are lit. If all the lights in the church were not turned on after the Exsultet, they are turned on now. Church bells are rung now, as on Holy Thursday. The procedure of the two nights should be parallel, as a public announcement of good news to the neighborhood.

The worship space may be decorated at this point. (See Mazar, pages 111–112). A "decoration procession" of flowers and other items is the most orderly way. Ask volunteers, perhaps also certain groups (confirmation class or altar guild) to come to a brief rehearsal on Holy Saturday after the flowers are delivered. Assign clusters of volunteers to zones of the space. Participants can place the flowers where they should end up after the Gloria. After the rehearsal bring the materials to a side room or rear pew. During the last reading and psalm before the Gloria, the "ministers of decoration" quietly join their clusters near their materials, pick up the items and form double lines. As the Gloria begins, the groups go in procession to place their decorations.

Gospel Acclamation

An ancient custom, revived in the *Ceremonial of Bishops,* says that before the gospel acclamation, "the deacon or the reader goes to the bishop [presbyter] and says to him, "[Most] Reverend Father, I bring you a message of great joy, the message of 'Alleluia'" (*Ceremonial of Bishops,* #352). If this ancient custom is followed, it must be proclaimed clearly and well. The minister may chant recto tono and then intone the solemn, once-a-year only, triple alleluia (see the official Mode VIII chant, *Worship,* #826). All repeat the alleluia each time on a higher pitch. The cantor then sings the verses of Psalm 118. All sing the same alleluia after each verse.

Other possibilities for the reintroduction of the alleluia include "Celtic Alleluia" (*Gather;* OCP, 7106) with handbells, if possible; "Easter Alleluia" (*Gather*), based on "O filii et filiae," verse by Marty Haugen; Richard Proulx's "Alleluia and Psalm for Easter" (GIA, G-1965), specifically written for this night, with familiar threefold Mode VI Alleluia (congregation, choir, cantor, organ and handbells) and Donald Reagan's "Fanfare and Alleluia" (WLP, 7959).

The gospel acclamation must match tonight's full procession: incense, perhaps banners, gospel book held high. No candles are carried tonight because the Easter candle is the symbol of light, enthroned near the ambo from which the Exsultet and gospel are proclaimed. Choir, bells, brass, organ, with music that does not require the assembly to have heads in hymnals, will best welcome the alleluia back into our worship.

The gospel passage, or at least the greeting and conclusion, may be chanted.

Homily

Any preacher would be overwhelmed at the thought of offering reflections in a context as awesome as the Vigil. See the paschal homilies in the Office of Readings through the Easter octave. Look also at LTP's *Triduum Sourcebook* for John Chrysostom's Vigil homily and other excellent reflections, as well as at its companion volume, *Easter Sourcebook.*

Children and the Liturgy of the Word

Tonight's assembly is the gathering of the whole church, including children and the parents of infants to be baptized. No separation of age groups is desirable.

INITIATION AT THE VIGIL

The liturgy of baptism takes one of several forms, depending on the situation.

- *Parishes with elect to be baptized and candidates to be received into the full communion of the Catholic church:* This outline is followed in the commentary that follows and in the *Rite of Christian Initiation of Adults* (RCIA), appendix I, 4. Some parishes with elect and candidates also baptize infants at the same assembly.

- *Parishes with elect to be baptized but without candidates for reception into full communion:* Follow RCIA, part I and the elements discussed in the following section. Note that these are arranged in a different order. See the note on page 139. Some of these parishes also baptize infants at the Vigil.
- *Parishes with only infants to be baptized and candidates for full communion:* Same outline as for parishes with both elect and candidates. Note rubrics for infant baptism at the Vigil at #28 of the Rite of Baptism for Children (RBC).
- *Parishes with only infants to be baptized and no candidates to be received into full communion:* Follow the RBC, noting the rubric at #28. Although that rubric notes that the presentation of the lighted candle is omitted, it may be appropriate to keep it.
- *Parishes without baptisms but with candidates to be received into full communion:* Use RCIA, appendix I, 4, beginning with #580.
- *No one to be baptized or received:* Follow the order in the sacramentary. The renewal of baptismal promises may be enhanced with some of the following elements of the rite of baptism.

Initiation: Celebration of Baptism

■ PRESENTATION: The RCIA outlines three methods of presentation for those to be baptized (#219, 568). This presentation is connected with the procession to the baptistry. Almost every parish can use form B, regardless of the location of the font. The summoning of the elect and godparents (infants and parents) is done solemnly, with names called out loudly and slowly.

■ PROCESSION TO THE BAPTISTRY: Those to be baptized process to the baptistry behind the paschal candle carried by the deacon or an acolyte. The elect, godparents and parents of infants are followed by the deacon, presider and assisting ministers. If the baptistry is outside the main assembly area, others may process as well. This procession should take a long route through the church to the baptismal font.

■ LITANY OF THE SAINTS: This chant accompanies the procession, calling those gone before us to accompany this most important part of the community's pilgrimage. Names may be added to the standard litany (see RCIA, #221, 570; sacramentary, #41): the titular of the church (if saint or blessed), patron saints of the area (diocese, city), patrons of those to be baptized and received.

Several settings of the litany are available: John Becker's "Litany of the Saints" (OCP); David Haas' "Litany of the Saints" in *Who Calls You by Name,* vol. I; Matthew Nagi's setting, #A40 in *We Celebrate,* vol. 2, cycle A; and Paul Page's setting (#165) in volume 1 of the same resource.

■ INVITATION TO PRAYER: In form B (RCIA, #219 or 568), when all are at the font and the litany is done, the invitatory (RCIA, #220 or 569) follows.

■ BLESSING OF WATER: This blessing may include repeated sung acclamations, even alleluias. David Haas' "Blessing of the Water" (*Who Calls You by Name,* vol. II (GIA) with the "Springs of water" refrain that concludes it, is set to the familiar "O filii et filiae" chant.

By tradition, the candle is plunged into the font once or three times, an archetypal symbol that needs no explanation. If the font is visible from the assembly area, keep the sight lines clear.

The blessing ends with an acclamation by the people. The suggested text is "Springs of water." Suitable music at this point includes:

- Thomas Savory, "Springs of water" (GIA, G-2549); cantor verses use Psalm 118
- Donald Fellows, "Springs of water" (GIA, G-3639); cantor verses use text from the sprinkling rite, "I saw water flowing . . ."
- Mike Hay, "Springs of water" (#108, *We Celebrate,* volume 1)
- Richard Proulx, "Rite of sprinkling" (GIA, G-3097)

■ PROFESSION OF FAITH: This profession of faith is at the heart of baptism, the immediate prelude to the water bath.

Follow the rite closely; ignore the options given "if there are a great many to be baptized." While the rite may be done with a group or individually, the questions of profession of faith are asked of each individual, who is then baptized immediately. Parents and godparents of infants to be baptized are then addressed and questioned as in the RBC (#58, 60 – 61).

■ BAPTISM: Immersion is the preferred method of baptism in the Roman Catholic church. If the permanent font does not allow for that, consider temporary arrangements until full renovation is possible.

As each person rises from the waters, the acclamation is sung by the assembly. Keep the assembly free to watch the ritual and sing the acclamation by using the call-and-response form: cantor sings the line, assembly repeats it. Some suggestions:

- Howard Hughes, "You have put on Christ" (GIA, G-2283)
- Arthur Hutchings, "Rejoice, you newly baptized" (*ICEL Resource Collection,* GIA, G-2514)

APRIL

- Marty Haugen, "Song over the waters" *(Gather)*
- Lynn Trapp, "Rite of Christian Initiation of Adults" (Morning Star MSM-80-907A)
- John Olivier, "You have put on Christ" *(People's Mass Book)*

A lively sung alleluia also works well. Whatever is chosen should be the parish's standard baptismal acclamation, used whenever the community celebrates baptism throughout the year.

■ EXPLANATORY RITES: Infants are anointed with chrism after the prayer (RCIA, #228 or 577; or RBC, #62).

The newly baptized (adults and children) are dressed in their baptismal garments. A room for parents to diaper and dress infants should be prepared with as many dressing tables as there are babies (diapers, powder, lotions could be left there by parents before the liturgy). Separate rooms for adult men and women should be prepared, with more towels.

Godparents assist adult neophytes in drying off as they emerge from the font and in robing while other professions of faith and baptisms continue. The words at the robing (RCIA, #229 or 578) may be omitted, or said by parents and godparents as the newly baptized are clothed.

The presentation of the baptismal candle is described in the RCIA, #230 or 579. The presider and godparents pass light to the neophytes. Plain, small paschal candles with followers make good baptismal candles, if the parish paschal candle is sufficiently larger. Some candlemakers offer smaller versions of their paschal candle designs for this purpose (for instance, Marklin Candle Design, PO Box 1001, Nashua NH 03061; 603-595-2981).

■ NOTE: Ministers in parishes that will celebrate baptisms at the Vigil but no receptions into full communion should read "Initiation: Rites after Baptism when There Are No Receptions," page 139, before reading the next three sections.

INITIATION: RENEWAL OF BAPTISMAL PROMISES

Renewal

Baptismal promises are spoken from the font, and the water for the sprinkling comes from the font. If the font is in a separate place, process to the front of the main worship space for the renewal of promises. Candidates for reception join in the renewal at this point (RCIA, #580), so that their reception flows from it.

All stand. The candles of the assembly are relit (neophytes may share the flame from their baptismal candles). The renewal formula may be sung to avoid an anticlimactic mumbled "I do" to momentous questions.

When renewal is completed, water is drawn from the font (if it has not already been brought from the font). During the sprinkling or signing, parents and godparents of newly baptized infants bring them back to their places in the assembly.

Sprinkling

The important ritual gesture of sprinkling should be as full as possible. People should feel the water. Assisting ministers may sprinkle side aisles while the presider takes the main section of the assembly. Branches from evergreen bushes or trees make excellent sprinkling implements. Tie several together to form a generous surface. Tape the stems at the bottom to form a handle and to keep sap off ministers' hands. Colorful ribbons may be added. Each person who sprinkles might be accompanied by an assistant who carries the bowl of water.

During the sprinkling, acolytes take water to all the holy water fonts in church.

■ SIGNING: Instead of sprinkling, everyone may come to the font (if it is in the worship space) or to bowls filled with water drawn from the font. People may approach the font or bowls in lines from all sides and sign themselves or others with water.

■ MUSIC FOR SPRINKLING OR SIGNING: Music used at end of blessing of water (see page 137) may be repeated here, unifying the use of water tonight. Richard Hillert's "Lord Jesus, from your wounded side" *(Worship)* and Michael Joncas' adaptation of the Baptist hymn "O healing river" (GIA) would serve well.

INITIATION: CELEBRATION OF RECEPTION

Procession

If the font is in a separate building, the procession occured before the renewal of promises. If neophytes and ministers are in the main church building, they now return in procession from the font to the front of the main worship space. The neophytes carry their lit baptismal candles in procession behind the paschal candle.

RCIA, #584, suggests a hymn at this time. The *Ceremonial of Bishops* (#366) suggests "You have put on Christ." Another appropriate text is Michael Saward's "Baptized in water" found in *Worship*. The Taizé ostinato "Beati in domo Domini," is another good choice, particularly if the procession is short.

Act of Reception

The rite of reception (RCIA, #584) is brief but solemn and deliberate. Neophytes and godparents should be nearby but not blocking the assembly's vision of this act. Those being received and their sponsors stand so that the congregation can see their faces. Consider concluding the receptions with a repeat of an earlier acclamation. An alleluia is appropriate.

INITIATION: CELEBRATION OF CONFIRMATION

If there are both neophytes and newly received to be confirmed, use the introduction at RCIA, #589. Confirmation is the same for newly baptized and those received into the church. They are not anointed in any particular order.

(Note: Those who are received into the Catholic church from Eastern Christian churches were confirmed at the time of their baptism. Because the Catholic church recognizes the validity of the sacraments of the Eastern churches, these people are not confirmed when they are received into the Catholic church. Those who were confirmed in Protestant churches are confirmed when they are received into the Catholic church. See chapter 3 of John Huels' *The Catechumenate and the Law* [LTP, 1994] or consult with your diocese's canon lawyer or ecumenical office.)

The music to be sung during the laying-on of hands, prayer and chrismation must be chosen carefully. A Taizé ostinato ("Veni, Sancte Spiritus" or "Confitemini Domino") serves well; the song may be continued quietly or hummed during prayer. Christopher Walker's "Veni, Sancte Spiritus" (St. Thomas More/OCP, 7116) also is effective. The refrain repeats the text several times and is easily singable; omit overlaid cantor verses for this occasion, unless the number to be confirmed is large. The traditional "Come, Holy Ghost" may be used.

INITIATION: RITES AFTER BAPTISM WHEN THERE ARE NO RECEPTIONS

If there are baptisms but no receptions, the procession from the font to the front of the church takes place after the explanatory rites (RCIA, #231). Confirmation follows (#233), using the music suggested above. The renewal of baptismal promises (#237) leads to signing or sprinkling of all, as described above. During the signing or sprinkling, the neophytes return to their places in the assembly.

General Intercessions

For the first time, the neophytes, now members of the order of the faithful, join in the church's priestly ministry of intercession for the needs to the world. All the languages of the community should be represented in the petitions.

LITURGY OF THE EUCHARIST

Preparation Rites

The neophytes bring up the bread and wine for the eucharistic meal in which they will share for the first time.

After the lengthy rites of initiation, the choir and musicians may offer the community any selection from the wide array of Easter anthems and instrumental music, with full instrumentation restored for Easter.

Eucharistic Prayer

Preface of Easter I includes the words "on this Easter night." Eucharistic Prayer I has several inclusions:

- "Remember . . ." from ritual Mass of baptism if there were baptisms (post godparents' names into the sacramentary)
- "In union . . ." for Vigil and octave (printed under the prayer in the sacramentary)
- "Father, accept . . ." from the ritual Mass of baptism if there were baptisms, or for the Vigil and octave (printed under the prayer in the sacramentary) if there were no baptisms. The two versions of this insert start the same, but the initiation text is richer.

Communion Rite

"Before saying 'This is the Lamb of God,' the presider may briefly remind the neophytes of the preeminence of the eucharist, which is the climax of their initiation and the center of the whole Christian life" (RCIA, #243). A similar note for the newly received appears at #594.

Music for the communion procession might include Tom Parker's "Praise the Lord, my soul" (GIA, Gather or G-2395); a setting of Psalm 34 with the refrain "Taste and see the goodness of the Lord"; Paul Hillenbrand's "Eucharistic litany" (WLP, 5200); "I received the living God" (*Worship* and GIA, G-3071; choral setting is one step higher than hymnal) by Richard Proulx (a beautiful concertato version, by Ellen Doerrfeld-Coman, is available from World Library, #7215); Taizé's "Eat this bread" (GIA, G-2840); Michael Joncas' "Take and eat" (GIA), especially if it was sung on Thursday evening.

Concluding Rite

The dismissal with double alleluia might be sung to the Gregorian melody associated with it from time immemorial. Note that this distinctive dismissal is sung every day of the octave, at Mass and at the Liturgy of the Hours, including next Sunday and again on Pentecost. The Episcopal church prescribes this dismissal throughout the entire Fifty Days of Easter, a tradition Roman Catholics might consider adopting.

BLESSING OF FOOD AND FOOD FOR ALL

The blessing of food on Holy Saturday is no longer practiced, because it predates the revision of Holy Week and hearkens back to a time when Lent ended at noon on Holy Saturday. The *Book of Blessings* (chapter 54) provides texts and outlines for tonight's blessing of food for the first meal of Easter. See the discussion of this custom on page 141.

If Easter eggs are distributed or a parish Easter breakfast held tonight, include these foods in the blessing. This breakfast, a hallowed tradition among the Orthodox and many ethnic groups, is a grand celebration for all the baptized, and a kind of reception that welcomes the neophytes to share Easter joy for the first time as fully initiated members of the household of faith. See the recipe for "Pascha" in the revised *Triduum Sourcebook,* page 477.

Easter water should be available for people to take home tonight and tomorrow. Easter eggs (and fresh flowers) may be given to all as they leave or during breakfast. The eggs may have been colored at the catechetical assembly of children earlier or prepared and distributed by the candidates who will be confirmed during Easter's Fifty Days.

23 Easter Sunday
#42; afternoon, #46 white

ORIENTATION

We might hope that someday a whole parish will attend their Vigil. When the great breakfast ends and the sun is up (and perhaps Morning Prayer has been sung), it is time to rest and then to gather again in the late afternoon around the font to celebrate the paschal Vespers. Morning Masses are not then necessary. What will be necessary in large parishes is a place where everyone can gather for such a Vigil; that will be a pleasant problem to have.

For now, we might look on the Easter Sunday morning Masses as the first Masses of the Easter season. They are not to be abbreviated versions of the Vigil for those who didn't make it. The room (not just the area in front) is filled with the Easter flowers. The paschal candle burns continuously (until the completion of Evening Prayer on Sunday) and the font somehow invites all

to approach and take some of the water. (*The Three Days,* 161)

MORNING PRAYER

This is the Catholic version of the sunrise service popular among Protestant churches that have yet to recover the Easter Vigil. A growing number of parishes have found that a surprising number of people welcome the opportunity to greet Easter dawn with Morning Prayer. This early morning celebration may be a good ecumenical prayer, if the community would like to join with non-Catholics in celebrating the risen Christ who is Lord of us all. See GIA's *Worship: Liturgy of the Hours,* leader's edition or LTP's *Morning and Evening.*

MORNING MASS

Introductory Rites

Throughout the Fifty Days, the standard greeting among Orthodox and Eastern-rite Catholic Christians, both inside and outside church, is the joyous acclamation, "Christ is risen!" and the response, "He is truly risen!" The forthcoming revision of the sacramentary suggests the Episcopal church's version of this:

V. Alleluia, Christ is risen.
R. The Lord is risen indeed. Alleluia.

If this would require practice or an announcement (a real mood-breaker after a joyous gathering anthem!) the presider could simply add an Easter touch to the standard greeting: "Alleluia! The Lord is truly risen! His grace and peace be with you all!"

Because the sacramentary places the sprinkling at the renewal of baptismal promises that comes after the homily, water is not used in the introductory rites on Easter morning. Some parishes begin all the Easter morning liturgies at the baptismal font, and place the renunciations and professions immediately after the greeting, followed by a generous sprinkling with water from the font. Their reasoning is that since the sprinkling with water will be part of the introductory rites throughout the Sundays of Easter, the ritual on Easter morning ought to be here too, to link all the Sundays of Easter with this introductory rite. The uniqueness of Easter morning comes from the whole liturgy beginning there at the font, rather than at the chair. Some parishes follow the same procedure throughout Eastertime, beginning all the Sunday liturgies beside the waters.

Liturgy of the Word

Throughout the Fifty Days, the Acts of the Apostles replaces the readings from the First Testament scriptures.

- PSALM: The Eastertime responsorial psalm may be used this morning. Throughout Eastertime the antiphon for the responsorial psalm can always be alleluia.
- SEQUENCE: The beloved sequence hymn, "Victimae Paschali Laudes," follows the reading from Paul. Some settings: chant, Mode I, in Latin and English translation by Peter Scagnelli (*Worship*, #837); Richard Proulx (arr.), "Easter sequence" (GIA, G-3088), a lively setting of chant with congregational refrain. Ann Colleen Dohns has set both Easter and Pentecost sequences with responses for the assembly (WLP, 5718).
- GOSPEL ACCLAMATION AND PROCESSION: Today's gospel procession should be in proportion to the day's solemnity and the greater-than-usual assembly.
- HOMILY: Gracious hospitality and a real desire to share the community's joy with everyone who has joined us at worship: This was John Chrysostom's approach.

> Come you all: Enter into the joy of our Lord. You the first and you the last, receive alike your reward. You rich and you poor, dance together. You strong and you weak, celebrate the day. You who have kept the fast, and you who have not kept the fast, rejoice today. (See *Triduum Sourcebook*, 335)

Renewal of Baptismal Promises

Repeat the Vigil's procedure: several buckets and sprinklers, or instead of sprinkling, the entire congregation can come to the font for ritual signing with the Easter water. Buckets or bowls (if used) should be filled from the font for this rite.

Liturgy of the Eucharist

Preface of Easter I is prescribed. Eucharistic Prayer I has two inserts. Use the Eastertime acclamations, which were first heard at the Vigil and will be heard at every liturgy until Pentecost.

Concluding Rite

As on Christmas, beware of seasonal greetings and gratitude that make it sound as if "the priests and staff thank you for helping them with Mass!"

Use the distinctive Easter dismissal with its double paschal alleluia, sung to the time-honored Gregorian melody we share now with other Christian churches. See note on page 140.

Hospitality

A spring flower may be given to all as they leave Mass today. Easter eggs are a traditional gift with sacred significance. Parishes that have a weekly coffee hour should keep the custom today, despite the crowds and even if many will be going out for an Easter brunch.

An Easter egg hunt can be held for adults and children either after Mass or in the afternoon before paschal vespers.

BLESSING FOODS AT THE END OF MASS

Blessing Easter food is a custom that should be revived or initiated in every community. It is not simply a pious custom among some ethnic groups. It is, in reality, a Christian tradition that provides a prayerful link between the Lord's table and the household meal. Remind people toward the end of Lent to bring baskets of food as well as children's Easter baskets to any Mass on Easter, including the Vigil. Tables may be set up for the baskets, and ushers should be prepared to direct people to place their baskets on these tables, especially at the Vigil when people arrive in the dark. Or household members may keep baskets with them in their places and raise them up for the blessing prayer and sprinkling.

According to the *Book of Blessings*, the Order of the Blessing of Food for the First Meal of Easter takes place after the prayer after communion (#1723) or before post-Mass refreshments. The water sprinkled on the food baskets is drawn from the font.

MIDDAY PRAYER AND EASTER DINNER

Midday Prayer helps the parish observe the entire Triduum ritually, sustaining the spirit of celebration that marks this whole solemnity. Some suggestions:

- Introduction: V. Christ our Light. R. Thanks be to God.
- Hymn (perhaps the one that closed the Easter Vigil or the morning Mass)
- Psalmody: Psalm 118
- Scripture: Ephesians 2:4–6
- Response: "This is the day the Lord has made" (in a version the community knows already)
- Prayer: of Easter Day in sacramentary or conclude with blessing of food

Alternatively, the blessing of food may be celebrated on its own (*Book of Blessings*, #1707–1719). This blessing is especially meaningful if the parish holds a festive Easter dinner.

AFTERNOON MASS

Parishes with a regular Sunday afternoon or evening Mass should have one today, too. There is a special gospel for this evening, at #46 in the lectionary (#47, in the new lectionary). There is a hymn based on the Emmaus gospel in *Worship*, "Daylight fades" (#448), which may be appropriate.

PASCHAL VESPERS

Restoration of paschal or "baptismal" vespers to complete the Triduum is recommended in several official documents: the Circular Letter (#98), the *Ceremonial of Bishops* (#371) and the *General Instruction of the Liturgy of the Hours* (#213). This is the traditional way for the community and its neophytes to continue the joy of the Vigil, a kind of reconvening to celebrate after catching our breath.

This liturgy is stational: The various components are celebrated in different locations ("stations") in the church complex. The pattern follows that of early and medieval Christians who, celebrating this vespers at their cathedrals, went from the eucharistic space to the baptismal space to the chrismation space. A suggested order:

- Gathering: Assembly gathers near the paschal candle
- Service of light: Assembly's candles and all church candles are lit from the paschal candle
- Opening dialogue: V. Christ our light. R. Thanks be to God.
- Hymn: "At the Lamb's high feast"
- Thanksgiving for light, sung by cantor or presider. For Easter texts: see GIA's *Praise God in Song* or *Worship: Liturgy of the Hours* (leader's edition) or LTP's *Morning and Evening* (edition for cantor and presider). The assembly's candles may be extinguished as the lights needed for the psalmody are turned on
- Psalms: Sunday, Evening Prayer II, Week I. The psalms should be sung
- During the canticle from Revelation, the congregational alleluia is repeated as cantors sing verses, and the assembly processes to the font: incense bearer, minister with paschal candle and presider lead. Take the longest route, preferably the same one used to and from the font last night
- Depending on the size and location of the baptistry, all remain there until after the baptismal commemoration or until the end of the service
- Reading: Hebrews 10:12–14 or Emmaus gospel
- A patristic selection from the Easter octave texts in the *Liturgy of the Hours* may be read, or a brief homily on symbols of Easter; or omit preaching anything beyond the patristic words, and enjoy silent prayer and reflection
- Sung response to reading as at Morning Prayer: "This is the day"
- Prayer over blessed Easter water (adapt RCIA, #222 D or E); or rite of sprinkling, form C, sacramentary
- All approach the font to sign themselves or each other while singing the antiphon, as at the blessing of water at the Vigil
- Canticle of Mary (Magnificat): sung with proper antiphon while all are honored with incense. Procession to the altar may take place during this canticle
- Intercessions from *Liturgy of the Hours*
- Lord's Prayer
- Concluding prayer of Easter Day
- Solemn blessing
- Dismissal: Easter tone with traditional double alleluia
- Closing hymn suggestion: "Come ye faithful, raise the strain" (*Worship*, #456) or "The day of resurrection" (*Hymnal 1982*, #210)

EASTER

The Season
The Setting of Eastertime / 145
A Sense of Eastertime / 146
The Look of Eastertime / 147
The Sounds of Eastertime / 148
The Rhythm of Eastertime / 150
The Word of God / 150
The Eucharist / 151
Other Celebrations / 152
At Home / 154
The Calendar
April 24 – June 11, 2000 / 155

The Setting of Eastertime

THE setting of the Easter season — its origins, imagery, themes and theology — is entirely springtime. How fitting, then, that the first Easter of the new millennium should occur at almost the latest date Easter can possibly be, so that all of the Fifty Days of Eastertime will unfold as springtime is in full bloom!

To a degree unparalleled by any other liturgical observance, Easter's motifs are related to the astronomical phenomena that surround the spring equinox. The Christmas season, for instance, is anchored to a fixed date, but December 25 is not widely regarded as a date determined by historical computation. The centerpiece of the Christmas celebration is as much a theological concept as a historical fact. Every age and every area, therefore, has been able to assimilate the mystery of the incarnation and to tell the story in a way that incorporates its own culture and climate.

In contrast to Christmas, however, the execution of Jesus at the time of the celebration of Passover is generally accepted as a historical fact. The date of the Easter, like the Jewish Passover from which it derives, depends on a natural phenomenon, namely, the full moon that comes as the earth's orbit tilts our Northern Hemisphere more fully toward the sun. Now the days, whose hours of sunlight have been lengthening almost imperceptibly since the winter solstice, are noticeably longer. They are brighter and warmer, too. The Easter season's scriptural passages, its liturgical texts, and especially the words of its hymnody — a treasury that spans the centuries — all bear the stamp of an origin of the Northern Hemisphere.

For example, from the mid-sixth century comes this text by the most famous of the classic Latin Christian poets, Venantius Honorius Fortunatus:

> Earth her joy confesses, clothing her for spring,
> all fresh gifts returned with her returning King:
> Bloom in every meadow, leaves on every bough,
> speak his sorrow ended, hail his triumph now.
>   (tr. John Ellerton, 1826 – 1893)

From the Middle Ages come two anonymous odes to spring. The first was sung to the tune we use now for "Good King Wenceslaus":

> Spring has now unwrapped the flowers,
> Day is fast reviving,
> Life in all her growing powers
> Towards the light is striving:
> Gone the iron touch of cold,
> Winter time and frost time,
> Seedlings working through the mould,
> Now make up for lost time.
>   (tr. *Oxford Book of Carols,* 1928)

The last century added this song of the springtime work of the Creator:

Out from snowdrifts chilly,
   Roused from drowsy hours,
Bluebell wakes, and lily;
   God calls up the flowers!
Into life he raises
   All the sleeping buds;
Meadows weave his praises,
   And the spangled woods.
            (*Oxford Book of Carols,* 1928)

All this nature imagery faithfully reflects what most likely was the core of the original paschal celebration. The primitive observance seems to have been an agricultural festival celebrating two of springtime's most important gifts:

- new life in the animal world, sheep and cattle bringing forth their young, the precious livestock refreshing and repopulating its ranks
- new life springing up from the earth, the stirrings of life in the luxuriant growth of burgeoning fields

The meaning of this springtime festival, which came to be called "the pasch," deepened as the communities celebrating it reflected on God's interventions in the Exodus, in Jesus, in the church, and in the individual believer. Thus we inherit a long faith-filled heritage that enriches the feast with several dimensions. Easter is now:

- the pasch of Israel: a liberation festival. The people of Israel stream forth from slavery, through the sea to a new land flowing with milk and honey.
- the pasch of Jesus: a redemption festival. Jesus emerges victorious from the slavery of death and the grave, to a place of honor at the Father's right hand.
- the pasch of the catechumens: a regeneration festival. The neophytes, newly initiated into Christ's death and resurrection, pass through saving waters of baptism to feast in their new home, the church.
- the pasch of penitents and faithful: a reconciliation festival. By the light of the Easter candle, at the font where our new sisters and brothers have been baptized, we renew our baptismal covenant at the Easter Vigil.

From every perspective, Easter is indeed springtime!

   'Tis the spring of souls today:
      Christ hath burst his prison,
   and from three days' sleep in death
      as a sun hath risen;
   all the winter of our sins,
      long and dark, is flying
from his light, to whom we give laud
   and praise undying.
      (John of Damascus, eighth century;
      tr. John Mason Neale, 1818 – 1866)

A Sense of Eastertime

A TIME FOR MYSTAGOGY

Eastertime's special sacramental identity and liturgical character spring from the experience of the risen Christ and the gift of the Spirit in the initiation rites of baptism, confirmation and eucharist at the Easter Vigil. The neophytes are present now in the midst of the assembly as living icons of the resurrection feast, the human face, as it were, of the paschal mystery.

The *Rite of Christian Initiation of Adults* uses the esoteric term *mystagogical catechesis* to mean the "unpacking" of the mystery of Christ's death and resurrection, not as something remembered but as something experienced, shared in and lived out. The custom is ancient. The fourth-century pilgrim to the Holy Land, Egeria, attended the Easter-octave mystagogy given to the neophytes and faithful in Jerusalem's Church of the Holy Sepulcher. She describes it:

> The newly baptized come into the Anastasis [church of the resurrection], and any of the faithful who wish to hear the mysteries. . . . The bishop relates all that has been done [at the Easter Vigil] and interprets it, and, as he does so, the applause is so loud that it can be heard outside the church. Indeed the way he expounds the mysteries and interprets them cannot fail to move his hearers. (quoted in *Preaching about the Mass,* LTP, 1992, xv – xvi)

Imagine that kind of response!

In this "school of the Lord," our textbook is the Sunday and weekday lectionary, compiled by the reformers of Vatican II according to the traditions of East and West. From this same source comes another treasury, the Office of Readings of the *Liturgy of the Hours* (volume II). Here we find teachers without peer: Melito of Sardis, Cyril of Jerusalem (and the others who first preached the Jerusalem Catecheses), Augustine of Hippo, Ambrose of Milan, John Chrysostom, Justin, Bede and a host of others.

True mystagogy quickly moves beyond the text to the sacramental choreography of this dance of life: the rites we have celebrated. Other focal points are the elements that have mediated Christ to us: water and oil, bread and wine, the touch of hands laid upon us, shining garments and myriad candles alight.

Eastertime's mystagogy is not something done *to* or *for* the neophytes. It is something done by the community and the neophytes together, as we strive to deepen our grasp of the paschal mystery and to make it part of our lives. There is action and contemplation here: meditation and personal experience. The community of faith helps the neophytes and, in turn, is inspired by the fervor of these newest sisters and brothers.

A TIME FOR INITIATION

Eastertime's Fifty Days are an especially appropriate time for the celebration of other rites associated with initiation: infant baptism, confirmation of children baptized as infants, first reception of the eucharist. In most communities it ought to be easy, over the course of a couple of years, and with sensitivity to local feelings, to establish or redirect parish custom in this direction.

- Diocesan confirmation scheduling focuses frequently on either fall or spring, according to parish request and episcopal availability. An early enough request ought to secure a date within Eastertime.

- First communion may already be associated with a Saturday in May or with Mother's Day. Homilies, bulletin announcements and musical selections, together with the renewal of baptismal vows around the font, can link the liturgical celebration to Easter. Scheduling should aim toward a principal Lord's Day Mass, making the event a community-wide celebration rather than a semiprivate ceremony. Just as this year's catechumens, elect and candidates have been the object of the parish's prayerful attention, so might the parish's prayers now include the names of the youngsters preparing for these initiatory rites and their families and sponsors.

The Look of Eastertime

OUTDOORS, DOORWAYS, VESTIBULE

To those arriving for worship or business and to neighbors who may never come inside, the house of God's people should proclaim visually our most solemn season of joy. Bunting and banners, maypoles and streamers: There are all kinds of possibilities. Eastertime wreaths adorning every doorway will communicate our celebration of the springtime of nature and grace.

INSIDE THE CHURCH

For Eastertime's decorations, see page 220 of G. Thomas Ryan's *The Sacristy Manual* and Peter Mazar's *To Crown the Year* (pages 122–152).

■ THE EASTER CANDLE: The Easter candle needs to be large enough for its function as the symbol of the risen Christ in our midst, and for the worship space in which it is displayed. The candle stand needs to be proportionate to both candle and room. To ensure the Easter candle's effectiveness at every liturgical gathering:

- Light the Easter candle for every service held during the Fifty Days
- Light it before the first worshipers arrive
- If other candles need to be lighted for a service, light them from the flame of the Easter candle once the worshipers have arrived. Let it be obvious to the whole assembly
- Never extinguish the Easter candle until every worshiper has left.

The Easter candle is enthroned near the ambo so that the Exsultet can be sung and the Vigil scriptures proclaimed in its light. This is its proper place throughout Eastertime. Leave it there even during funerals and move it only after Evening Prayer of Pentecost, when its proper place for the rest of the year is the baptistry.

■ THE FONT: Making the font a focal point for Eastertime can be a challenge, depending on its location, construction and appearance. Newer (or newly renovated) churches ought to have an easy time of it, especially if the font is large enough for adult baptism and alive with flowing water.

Constructing a whole new area for a temporary font is tempting if the parish's real font is not in clear view.

Old fonts that are not works of art or that are clearly too small even for infant baptism may be renewable only by replacement. This may need to be a parish priority for the coming year. Some parishes have found it possible to construct new fonts and to recycle the older fonts.

Beware of using moveable punch bowls in Easter "displays" in the sanctuary or ugly electric water circulators in make-believe fountains. Better to decorate and honor the real font wherever it is located.

■ THE NEOPHYTES: Attend to the living symbols of Eastertime, the neophytes baptized at the Vigil. In them the Lord's death and resurrection is clearly visible this year. According to the RCIA, they, "their godparents and those who have assisted them in their preparation" have a special place reserved for them in the Sunday assemblies of Eastertime. Specifics will depend on the architecture of the worship space, but perhaps there is room near the ambo and Easter candle, or near the font. If this cannot be done, honor their reserved places with floral decorations and honor them with incense.

■ FLOWERS: "Discouraged in Lent, demanded by Easter," is the way Mazar begins "Easter Flowers" in *To Crown the Year* (pages 149–152). This is an area which has not always reflected Eastertime as one great fifty-day celebration. A common practice was to blanket the altar and sanctuary area (and perhaps the paschal candle) with lilies on Easter Sunday. Usually by the fourth week of Eastertide, all that remained of Easter's splendor were a few pots of sadly wilting, slowly browning lilies.

Many parishes plan their floral displays and adjust their flower budgets to cover the entire season. Mazar mentions a number of suitable plants for the church's Eastertide decor: forsythia, flowering plum, apple and pear blossom, for instance. The mood to create is sustained festivity and steadily growing anticipation.

The latter part of the Easter season falls in May this year, the month traditionally dedicated to Mary. This, too, should be relected in the church's floral decorations.

■ ALTAR, VESSELS, VESTURE: While the noble simplicity of the altar table is rightly emphasized during most of the year, for the Fifty Days a full covering of fine fabric or tapestry might be appropriate. If the altar has a resurrection motif carved into it there might be a way to highlight this, encircling it with a wreath, for instance.

The Sounds of Eastertime

ALLELUIA! is the sound of Eastertime, and across the centuries musicians have given their best efforts to providing a feast for ear and voice and heart. The fast is over; now let us delight in the rich fare their talent provides!

■ PRELUDES: Eastertime is a season when our gatherings can be blessed with an abundance of instrumental riches. In preparation for the Fifty Days, all church musicians should review their repertoire of preludes and postludes. This music is participatory in its own way: setting a festive mood as the assembly gathers, sending the community forth on its mission of witness with joyful praise.

The Episcopal and Lutheran churches, with their rich traditions of instrumental music, offer helpful resources; write to the Church Hymnal Corporation (Episcopal), 800 Second Avenue, New York NY 10017; and Augsburg/Fortress (Lutheran), Box 1209, Minneapolis MN 55440, for catalogs.

■ DURING THE SPRINKLING WITH HOLY WATER: This rite is the most suitable way to begin the principal Mass on all the Sundays of Eastertime. Choose a strong setting, melodic and interesting enough to be the parish's Eastertime theme song. Among the possibilities: Howard Hughes' "You have put on Christ" (GIA, G-2283); David Hurd's "Vidi aquam" (in English; GIA, G-2512); Michael Ward's "I saw water flowing" (WLP, 8548). Also, see the music suggested for the blessing of the water at the Vigil.

■ GLORIA: The Gloria should be sung on all Eastertime Sundays, and each day of the octave. A simple, festive unison setting could be used for most Masses; a more ornate version for Masses when the choir participates. Some simple versions have choral enhancement, thus permittin both continuity and embellishment. See the suggestions for the Gloria at the Vigil. Other suggestions: Christopher Walker, "St. Augustine's Gloria" (OCP, 7107); Marty Haugen, "Mass of Creation" Gloria (Gather); John Rutter, "Gloria" (Worship, #276).

■ RESPONSORIAL PSALM: Psalm 118 is the Eastertime psalm, the core of the Easter Vigil gospel procession, the proper psalm for Easter Sunday and its octave. Numerous settings make it an easy addition to every community's repertoire. Michael Joncas' setting in *Psalms for the Cantor,* volume 1 (World Library) is delightful for cantor and congregation. Richard Proulx has a joyful setting, embellished easily by canonic singing of refrain and descant (GIA G-1964). Christopher Willcock's composition in *Psalms for Feasts and Seasons* (Liturgical Press) has 7/8 time refrain and lively verses for cantor. Christopher Walker's "This day was made by the Lord" is dance-like; the assembly's "echo" within the verses is delightful. Scott Soper's "This is the day" (OCP) is easily sung. Hal H. Hopson's "Psalm 118" in *10 Psalms* (Hope, HH 3930) is for SATB, congregation, organ. Bob Hurd's "This is the day" (OCP, 9458) is arranged for SATB, congregation, piano, guitar and two trumpets.

■ SEQUENCE HYMNS: Eastertime begins and ends by enhancing the liturgy of the word with *sequence hymns.* Do not let these be recited! A variety of English adaptations of the traditional Gregorian settings are available (see, for instance, *Worship,* #837 and 857).

■ GOSPEL ACCLAMATION: Eastertime should feature an exuberant alleluia chant for the gospel acclamation. The threefold alleluia refrain of "O filii et filiae" ("Ye sons and daughters") is particularly appropriate for Eastertime; see John Schiavone's version for Easter, Ascension, Pentecost (GIA G-2162). Robert Hutmacher's "Gospel processional" (GIA G-2450) is gently moving. J. Biery's arrangement of Vulpius' "Gelobt sei Gott" provides a "Gospel fanfare for Easter morning" (GIA G-2719), with option of trumpets, trombone, horn and timpani. Jeremy Young's "Easter alleluia" (GIA, G-3175) has verses for each Sunday of Easter.

■ EUCHARISTIC ACCLAMATIONS: For festive settings with brass and percussion parts available, see Richard Proulx's "Festival eucharist" (*Worship* or G-1960); Paul Inwood's "Coventry acclamations" (OCP, 7117); Christopher Walker's "Festival Mass" (OCP, 7154). Carrol T. Andrews' simpler "Easter carol Mass," (G-1398) offers settings for 2 equal or 4 mixed voices.

■ COMMUNION RITE: Where the Roman rite chants Lamb of God, the Episcopal eucharist chants "Christ our passover is sacrificed for us; therefore let us keep the feast." During Eastertime, alleluias are added to verse and response. This anthem may be useful as a communion processional during Eastertime. Other possibilities include Suzanne Toolan's "I am the bread of life" and Richard Hillert's "Worthy is Christ."

Some Taizé ostinato refrain settings include "Surrexit Christus" and "Christus Resurrexit" (*Music from Taizé,* volume II; GIA, G-2778), with segments of Psalm 118 by the cantor answered by short acclamations by the assembly. Bob Hurd's "In the breaking of the bread" (*Gather*) and Michael Ward's piece by the same name (WLP, 7950) recall the Emmaus appearance.

■ EASTERTIME HYMNS: Strong, familiar hymns, keynotes of the season, should be repeated each year. "The strife is o'er"; "Hail thee, festival day"; "Come, ye faithful, raise the strain"; and "At the Lamb's high feast," are found in many hymnals. To this familiar repertoire, add a few carol-style Easter hymns: "Now the green blade rises" (NOEL NOUVELET); "This joyful Eastertide" (VRUCHTEN); "That Easter Day with joy was bright" (PUER NOBIS).

In *With One Voice* (Augsburg/Fortress, 1995) are other possibilities: "There in God's garden," and a beautiful Kentucky Harmony tune with Charles Wesley's words "Come away to the skies, my beloved, arise." Both are appropriate Eastertide hymns. Also in this collection are Brian Wren's "Christ is risen! Shout hosanna!" and Herbert Brokering's "Alleluia! Jesus is risen." See the United

Church of Christ's *New Century Hymnal* for striking texts: "Because you live, O Christ, the garden of the world has come to flower" (#231), "These things did Thomas count as real" (#254), "At the font we start our journey, in the Easter faith baptized" (#308).

Two Emmaus hymns might be useful: In GIA's *Hymnal for the Hours,* find "Sing of one who walks beside us" (text by Ralph Wright, American folk melody HOLY MANNA) and "Daylight fades" (text: Peter Scagnelli, Gaelic melody DOMHNACH TRIONOIDE), also in *Worship.*

The Rhythm of Eastertime

THE STRUCTURE OF THE SEASON

In contrast to the incarnation cycle of the calendar, the paschal cycle is long! The "winter pascha" is almost the perfect length for sustaining the interest and enthusiasm of participants, but the "spring pascha" is more difficult because of its length. It may help to break it up a little. Consider these reflections on the structure of this long and beautiful season.

■ I. EASTER: THE SOLEMNITY OF SOLEMNITIES: "The Lord of life who died reigns glorified" (Easter sequence), walks in our midst and makes himself known in the scriptures we read, the bread we break and the companions with whom we share the journey.

■ II. EASTER OCTAVE: AN EIGHT-DAY SOLEMNITY: The church feasts on the community's finest stories of discipleship, the apostles' witness and our experience of the risen Lord — the heart of the Easter mystery.

■ III. FROM THE OCTAVE TO THE FORTIETH DAY: Christian life then is remembered, even as that memory becomes lived experience now. The church's experience of the risen Christ compels the believers to witness, which brings about development and expansion. It is a time of ministry and shepherding, of becoming an inclusive community that serves in mutual and self-sacrificing love.

■ IV. NINE DAYS FROM ASCENSION TO PENTECOST: Different places have different dates for Ascension, some keeping the feast on Ascension Thursday and others moving the solemnity to the Seventh Sunday of Easter. No matter; these nine days are the church's original novena. The Spirit, bestowed on the day of resurrection in John's gospel, is particularly associated with the fiftieth day in Luke's chronology (which gives the liturgical calendar its numbering system). Just as the season of intense resurrection celebration (octave) flowed into a season of joyful peace (the Forty Days), so these final days of Eastertime are appropriately marked by an intensification of prayer as the paschal mystery draws to its culmination.

■ V. PENTECOST: The whole cycle of Fifty Days is "the pentecost," but tradition gives the title in an entirely singular way. A vigil on Pentecost Eve appropriately marks the beginning of this solemnity.

The Word of God

THE Acts of the Apostles and the Gospel of John are the heart of the liturgy of the word throughout the Fifty Days of Eastertime. The Acts of the Apostles, which one translator subtitled "The Young Church in Action," a beautiful and realistic picture of the courage and conflicts of the first generation of believers. The presence of the risen Christ in the community's midst, the transforming power of the paschal mystery in the lives of the first believers, and the fruit of the Holy Spirit's gift are some of the recurring themes of this fifty days' worth of reading from Luke's second volume.

The Gospel of John, with its profoundly contemplative portrait of Christ, is the perfect gospel for this period of mystagogy. The Fourth Gospel provides a departure from the narrative style of the synoptic gospels and a more mystical orientation to the person of Jesus, the power of his paschal mystery, and the responsibilities of discipleship.

THE SUNDAY LECTIONARY

In each of the three lectionary cycles, the first readings come from the Acts of the Apostles and the gospel passages from John. In Year B, the second reading comes from the First Letter of John. The themes and imagery of these second readings are especially suited to the mystagogical character of Eastertime.

In *Scripture and Memory* (Collegeville, The Liturgical Press, 1997, 101–110), Fritz West suggests viewing the scriptures of the season in a specific structural arrangement:

■ ACTS OF THE APOSTLES: The Easter Sunday selection offers Peter's proclamation of the saving work of Jesus. The Seventh Sunday of Easter, when not observed as the Ascension, depicts the community on the brink of Pentecost. On the Sundays in between, the excerpts from Acts in each cycle of the lectionary trace the community's growth from its charismatic origins to a more structured organization:

- Second Sunday: the first Christians in Jerusalem
- Third Sunday: Peter as witness to the resurrection
- Fourth and Fifth Sundays: the growth of the early church
- Sixth Sunday: the authority of the church.

■ GOSPELS: West sees a twofold structure to the season's gospels: the first three Sundays focus on the resurrection and the risen Lord, the last four on our life in Christ:

- Easter Sunday: The beloved disciple sees and believes
- Second Sunday of Easter: The apostle Thomas doubts, then believes
- Third Sunday: We are invited to see and believe the risen Lord in the eucharist
- Fourth Sunday: Jesus the Good Shepherd is central to our relationship with God and with one another
- Fifth Sunday: Jesus is our way to relationship with the Father
- Sixth Sunday: the relationship of believers to Jesus, the Father and the Spirit
- Seventh Sunday: Jesus intercedes with his Father on behalf of believers

The Eucharist

ENTRANCE RITE

THE Triduum is the church's "entrance rite" into Fifty Days of celebration. Therefore, everything about the opening rites should signal that this gathering of the local church takes place within that wider gathering.

■ PROCESSION: The procession, with reverencing of focal points, might take on a special character for the Fifty Days. Some parishes carry in and ritually place the processional cross as in the other liturgical seasons, but for Eastertime the cross is festively adorned. Other communities leave the cross, suitably adorned, in place. Whatever ritual approach seems to work should become the parish's standard seasonal approach.

Incense, the special Easter scent, leads the procession throughout Eastertime. If the font is at some distance from the altar, the procession may pause there to reverence the font with incense and to draw water to carry to the chair for the blessing that will open the liturgy. Altar and paschal candle should also be reverenced with incense.

■ BLESSING AND SPRINKLING OF WATER: At least at the principal Sunday liturgies, the blessing and sprinkling of water should replace the penitential rite, using the special Eastertime prayer for the blessing of water. In the dioceses of Canada, Eastertime acclamations and responses may be found in *Sunday Celebrations of the Word and Hours*.

■ GLORIA: Suggested Eastertime versions are mentioned on page 149. The Gloria can be too much of a good thing when it follows both a strongly engaging entrance song and a powerful sprinkling chant. Some communities sing the Gloria during the sprinkling.

LITURGY OF THE WORD

■ RESPONSORIAL PSALM AND GOSPEL ACCLAMATION: See notes under "Sounds of Eastertime," page 149.

■ HOMILY: Since the mystagogy of Eastertime is to assist the renewal of all, keep in mind the RCIA's point: The homily "should take into account the presence and needs of the neophytes" (#248). Scan the texts in the Office of Readings. Those great fourth-century preachers took their communities back to the water, the oil and the table, and unpacked the words and actions that had happened. Next, they challenged their listeners' perceptions of the world and its "wisdom" in the light of the sacramental encounter with the risen Christ. Finally, they pointed the assembly toward the kingdom's dawning yet to be, not only in the world to come but in this world, progressively transformed by Christ's gospel incarnated in the lives of his disciples.

■ DISMISSAL OF THE CATECHUMENS: While the community rejoices in the presence of the neophytes in its midst, there may yet be catechumens who will be among next Lent's elect, next Easter's neophytes. These should still be dismissed after the homily to continue their prayer and reflection on the word.

■ GENERAL INTERCESSIONS: Reflect the scriptural words and images of the season, and don't forget the sacraments of initiation. Examples may be found in *Prayers for Sundays and Seasons, Year B.*

LITURGY OF THE EUCHARIST

■ PREFACES: Five prefaces bear the designation "Easter." The former prescription that Easter I alone be used throughout the octave has been removed. Each preface has a title, which suggests a thoughtful rotation of prefaces according to the day's readings or the part of Eastertime being celebrated.

For Ascension, two prefaces are provided. The second is brief. The first is longer and richer theologically and poetically. There is an almost litanic celebration of the exalted Christ's titles: Lord, King of glory, mediator between God and humankind, judge of the world, Lord of heavenly powers, beginning and head.

■ EUCHARISTIC PRAYER: For Eucharistic Prayer I, the sacramentary provides three inserts: Easter and its octave, Ascension and Pentecost.

■ EUCHARISTIC PRAYER ACCLAMATIONS: See notes under "Sounds of Eastertime," page 149.

■ COMMUNION RITE: Thoughtful variations in the communion rite can help sustain the assembly's Eastertime spirit. As ritual texts designed to form a community in prayer, these should not be ad-libbed; neither should they be new every week. The best variations parallel the official texts in style and spirit.

For musical suggestions, see notes under "Sounds of Eastertime," page 149.

CONCLUDING RITE

■ BLESSING: The current sacramentary alternates the threefold solemn blessing with a randomly chosen prayer over the people on all the Sundays of Eastertime. This editorial decision might not represent the best solution. Would it not be better to use (sing?) a threefold solemn blessing throughout the season? The following schema might be a good example:

Blessing 6: Easter Sunday, throughout the octave, Second Sunday of Easter

Blessing 7: Sundays 3 – 6

Blessing 8: Ascension and Sunday 7 (changing the reference to "on this day")

Blessing 9: Pentecost

If the prayer over the people is used on the weekdays of Eastertime, the most appropriate seem to be #3, 14 and 18 in early Eastertime; #20, 23 and 24 in later Eastertime.

■ DISMISSAL: The double alleluia in its beautiful Gregorian melody graces the deacon's dismissal and the assembly's response: on Easter, throughout the octave (including the Second Sunday of Easter), on Pentecost (Mass and Evening Prayer). Some traditions continue the practice for all Fifty Days.

Other Celebrations

LITURGY OF THE HOURS

EASTERTIME'S seven Sundays provide a perfect opportunity to keep alive the communal celebration of Evening Prayer or the other Hours which may have been prayed during Lent or the Triduum. Here is another lenten custom that can find an exuberant counterpart in the Easter season, if not the rest of the year. In a simple and prayerful way this says that Eastertime is at least as important as Lent. Begin with the lighting of the assembly's candles from the paschal candle, perhaps repeating the Vigil's "Light of Christ"/"Thanks be to God."

A vigil on the eve of Pentecost should usher in the season's completion. This celebration parallels the Easter Vigil, though its character is not baptismal, but evocative of the prayerful expectancy of Mary and the Apostles at the first Pentecost. See special texts on page 166.

ANOINTING OF THE SICK

Rites celebrated with the community's sick, that is, anointing or holy communion for the homebound, use scriptural passages from the Acts of the Apostles or the Johannine selection on the Good Shepherd. If offered communally on an Eastertime Sunday, the scriptures of the Sunday should be used.

MARRIAGES

On the Sundays of Eastertime one of the scripture selections offered in the marriage rite may be substituted for the Eastertime readings, but on Easter Sunday, Ascension and Pentecost, no such substitution is permitted—the church's polite way of suggesting that no rite, not even one as important as marriage, should distract from solemnities as important as these.

FUNERALS

In many parishes, people who buried their loved ones at noneucharistic services during the Triduum will return to celebrate Mass during the octave. On these days it is appropriate to use the Acts readings and gospels already assigned, perhaps choosing a second reading from the New Testament selections of the funeral lectionary. Remember that the presidential prayers of the funeral Mass, form C, are for use in the Easter season. Because these liturgies are not concluded by a procession to the cemetery, the parish should offer food and hospitality following the liturgy.

At funeral Masses after the octave, the first reading may be chosen from among the Acts of the Apostles selections in the funeral lectionary or from Revelation. The Emmaus gospel is also appropriate. Funeral Masses are not celebrated on Sundays of the season or on Ascension Thursday.

HOUSE BLESSINGS

The *Book of Blessings* (chapter 50) speaks of Christmas and Easter as traditional times for blessing homes. Despite the work involved in coordinating such an effort, the results can be wonderful in terms of community-building and faith-sharing. The texts place "visitation" in the context of prayer, the minister's presence as evangelization, sharing the good news. All pastoral ministers may be involved and forms for blessings offered by lay ministers are provided.

NATURE BLESSINGS

Springtime has always been blessing time in agricultural Christian communities. In the medieval and post-Tridentine church, rogation days (April 25 and the three days before Ascension Thursday) were set apart for prayer for growth and fruitfulness. The *Book of Blessings* contains orders of blessing for fields and flocks (chapter 26) and for seeds at planting time (chapter 27). For other materials contact the National Catholic Rural Life Conference, 4625 N.W. Beaver Drive, Des Moines IA 50310.

MARIAN DEVOTION

The month of May begins this year almost as soon as Eastertime does. In this "fairest of seasons" as the old hymn says, the church traditionally honors the Virgin, whom the angel hailed as "fairest among women." With careful planning and sensitive coordination, there need be no conflict between Eastertime's focus on the risen Lord and the community's veneration of the mother of the Lord.

■ THE MARIAN SHRINE: Most Catholic churches reserve a special space for a statue or icon of the Virgin Mary. Moving the image front and center is hardly ever the best approach: Such a setup can compete with the Easter candle for attention. Better to honor the image of Mary wherever it happens to be. If the parish's Easter finery has been kept up, surely an appropriate decoration of Our Lady's image will not detract from the font or Easter candle.

Most sanctoral devotions do not mix with the eucharistic liturgy very well. Simply inserting Marian devotions such as the litany or a decade of the rosary after the homily or after communion does not do justice to the eucharist or to Our Lady! But these prayers can serve as the core of a noneucharistic devotional gathering. Recent recordings of the pope praying the rosary demonstrate how easy and beautiful it is to enhance this devotion with scripture and song. The traditional May crowning can be a service unto itself, or offered in connection with Evening Prayer, or even after Mass, with a procession to the Lady shrine to carry out this ritual, beloved in many communities.

The Common of the Blessed Virgin Mary in the *Liturgy of the Hours* provides good resources. Explore the *Collection of Masses of the Blessed Virgin Mary:* volume I, sacramentary (Catholic Book and Liturgical Press). None of these Mass formularies may replace the proper Masses of Eastertime (introduction, #21, 28).

At Home

SEE *Catholic Household Blessings and Prayers* for a blessing at table (page 84), blessing of the home (page 153), blessing of children before confirmation (page 230) or first eucharist (page 231), blessing for Mother's Day (page 197), intercessory prayers for the blessing of fields and gardens (page 166), and a prayer to complete Eastertime on the Solemnity of Pentecost (page 157).

Liturgy Training Publications' resources *Take Me Home* and *Take Me Home, Too* both contain pages for each week of the season through Pentecost.

CALENDAR

April

OCTAVE OF EASTER

An octave, an honor reserved for the solemnities of Christmas and Easter, is the eight-day prolongation of a liturgical feast. The incarnation and the paschal mystery are too deep for explanation, too precious for analysis, too special for anything but celebration. So the church keeps celebrating Christmas and Easter for a full week. Then, to crown that number, which has symbolized completion since the creation, the church adds an eighth day, as if to say that in Christ's incarnation and paschal mystery, a new creation has begun.

All week long, until Evening Prayer next Sunday night, everything should look and sound and feel and even smell like Easter Sunday:

- All eight days are solemnities of the Lord, the highest rank possible, equal to an observance of Sunday
- The white-robed neophytes, with their sponsors, should have a place of honor.

■ THE EUCHARIST: Every eucharist is celebrated just as on Easter Day, omitting, however, the profession of faith.

MON 24 — #261 (LMC, #185–192) white
Easter Monday
SOLEMNITY

Almost 1600 years ago, Saint Augustine opened an Easter octave homily with this exuberant salutation:

> My little children in Christ, new offspring of the church, gift of the Father, proof of Mother Church's fertility, a holy seed, a new colony of bees, the very flower of our ministry, the fruit of our toil, my joy and my crown!

In his church, they gathered each day of the octave for mystagogical catechesis. Perhaps language was more florid then and the pace more leisurely. Still, we need to show our neophytes how glad we are to have them with us, and we need to to make the octave special for the whole community:

- Celebrate eucharist on one or several evenings of the week, with mystagogical sharing.
- Follow one of these with refreshments and socializing. Many people like to watch videos of big moments. What could be more important than rebirth? If initiation was videotaped at the Vigil, put that up on the screen of the parish hall and ybe give a tape to each neophyte as a remembrance.
- Invite the neophytes to dinner with the staff, or with families in different parts of the parish. This is a perfect time for gifts.
- Invite this year's neophytes to celebrate with those of previous years.

Even in parishes without neophytes, this is a week of rejoicing. The octave is perfect for gathering those involved in the planning and celebration of the liturgies of Lent and the Triduum to swap stories, constructively critique the experience, make notes for next year, sing Easter songs and treat each other to Easter feasting.

TUE 25 — #262 (LMC, #185–192) white
Easter Tuesday
SOLEMNITY

Peter's sermon in Acts is a model for preachers today. Having experienced forgiveness himself, Peter helps his listeners toward a new direction. Jesus' encounter with Mary reminds us that we, too, are known by name to Jesus.

WED 26 — #263 (LMC, #185–192) white
Easter Wednesday
SOLEMNITY

Time and movement are featured in both readings today. At three o'clock Peter and John go up to the Temple for midday prayer. Late in the day, after a journey with a heart-warming stranger, two disciples sit at table in Emmaus. Each time, Jesus is manifested: in the making whole of a sick man and in the breaking of the bread. Christ is visible everywhere to the eyes of faith: in the sacred space of worship and along the busy roads of our lives; in all of our breaking and in the making whole again.

THU 27 — #264 (LMC, #185–192) white
Easter Thursday
SOLEMNITY

In the Acts of the Apostles, Peter's words are a model of Christlike approach to past mistakes: "I know you acted in ignorance." Jesus sends the disciples to be preachers of repentance and ministers of forgiveness.

FRI 28 — #265 (LMC, #185–192) white
Easter Friday
SOLEMNITY

Psalm 118, heard before the gospel at the Easter Vigil, is appointed for today and tomorrow. Peter quotes it in the first reading, and it recurs throughout Eastertime. Jesus manifests himself on the lake shore and provides in abundance for the community when they give their fishing one more try. There is a lesson here for neophytes and baptized alike. Jesus always pushes us just beyond what we think we're capable of.

APRIL

SAT 29 — Easter Saturday, SOLEMNITY
#266 (LMC, #185–192) white

From disbelief to faith to bearing witness: Today's gospel summarizes three post-resurrection appearances. The selection from Acts reminds us to whom we owe our first allegiance.

Saturday for Catholics always carries a remembrance of Our Lady. A fine Easter Marian hymn is "Regina coeli, laetare," widely available in English matched to the ancient chant (see *Worship*, #443).

- WEDDINGS IN THE OCTAVE: Because today is a solemnity, the Mass of the day is used at wedding celebrations.

30 — Second Sunday of Easter
#44 (LMC, #38) white

ORIENTATION

- DOMINICA IN ALBIS [DEPONENDIS]: "Sunday when the white robes are removed" — This was today's name in the old liturgical books, because the neophytes finally laid their baptismal garments aside today after Evening Prayer. Eastern Christians call this octave "Bright Week." In East and West, the Easter octave culminates in this "Sunday of Thomas." The gospel of Thomas' doubting and believing is proclaimed, always in the context of the risen Lord's word of peace and gift of reconciliation.

- HOLY SUPPER: Parishes with certain ethnic traditions observe the Second Sunday of Easter as a day for a parish potluck supper, called in some traditions "the holy supper." Ethnic specialty dishes chase away the last memories of the lenten fast and recall that several of the Lord's resurrection appearances took place at a meal.

- FIRST HOLY COMMUNION: In many parts of the world, this is the traditional day for children to receive their first communion.

LECTIONARY

The reading from the Acts of the Apostles portrays the inner life of the young church. This is the basis of the community's public witness and is an important in attracting converts. Those who joined the community had not seen Jesus "in person," but they had seen him in *persons*, the disciples whose lives had been transformed. The selection in Year B celebrates the early community's oneness in Christ that manifested itself in the economic reality of their everyday lives. "No one claimed private ownership of any possessions . . . everything they owned was held in common . . . there was not a needy person among them" (Acts 4:32, 34).

The second reading throughout the Sundays of Eastertime in Year B is from the First Letter of John. The excerpts for the Sundays of Eastertime read as a kind of postbaptismal exhortation. Today's begins by associating the believer's new birth with Christ's own victory.

Forgiveness and reconciliation strengthened the community and drew others to it. The risen Christ confronts the disciples with the wounds their cowardice helped inflict upon him, not to submerge those disciples in guilt but to transform them with a word: "Peace!" Whether "doubting" Thomas took the Lord up on his offer to touch the wounds, the text is not clear. But "believing" Thomas' profession of faith closes the circle opened in John 1:1. The Word who was with God, and who was God, is acknowledged by the disciple to be "My Lord and my God!" Jesus blesses all of us "who have not seen and yet have come to believe."

SACRAMENTARY

Today is still the *today* of Easter day. Let it be heard in the antiphons and acclamations: "*This is the day the Lord has made!*" Chant it in the preface, "on this Easter *day* (not "in this Easter season") when Christ became our paschal sacrifice." Reinforce the sense of today as Easter Day by chanting the sequence one last time, and by adding the double alleluia at the dismissal.

May

MON 1 — Easter Weekday
#559 (LMC, #185–192) white

Joseph the Worker, optional memorial. - Today the dialogue between Nicodemus and Jesus begins. If they seem to be talking past one another from time to time, remember the technique John uses to communicate the truth of Christ: statement by Jesus, misunderstanding by listener, clarification by Jesus. The reading from Acts presents a model for liturgical prayer. Apparently God also thought the prayer was powerful: The Spirit came and the people witnessed with boldness.

Today's memorial was instituted during the Cold War to "baptize" workers' celebrations sponsored by groups or governments hostile to the church.

MAY

From Leo XIII's *Rerum Novarum* (1898) on, the church has been a champion of working people. In the United States, Labor Day in September may be a better occasion to celebrate a votive Mass for the blessing of labor.

TUE 2 — #268 (LMC, #185–192) white
Athanasius, bishop and doctor of the church
MEMORIAL

Today's saint was no stranger to persecution. Athanasius was sent into exile several times because of his loyalty to the teaching of the Council of Nicea, the council that defined the church's belief in the divinity of Christ. To the Arians of his time, the concept of God becoming our brother in the flesh was too difficult. Athanasius stood firm in this faith, which is still ours: Jesus Christ, truly God, truly human.

WED 3 — #561 (LMC, #185–192) red
Philip and James, apostles
FEAST

Today's celebration of apostles fits in naturally with the Easter season. The first reading reminds us that our faith is none other than the faith of the first disciples, handed down faithfully from generation to generation. In the gospel, Jesus counsels Philip to see the Father in him; we must see and serve the living God in the neighbor who is before us.

THU 4 — #270 (LMC, #185–192) white
Easter Weekday

To obey God rather than human authority: This principle, asserted by Peter and the apostles today in Acts, sounds simple enough, but what happens when human authority claims to speak for God? What the church really does and does not teach, who speaks definitively and when: These are important topics. We can rest secure in the promise Jesus gives Nicodemus: "The Father loves the Son and has placed all things in his hands" — and that includes us!

FRI 5 — #271 (LMC, #185–192) white
Easter Weekday

Gamaliel's wisdom has much to teach religious leaders in every age. The gospel story of the loaves and fishes points toward the eucharist.

SAT 6 — #272 (LMC, #185–192) white
Easter Weekday

It took barely four chapters for the idyllic picture of "all things in common" to change to a scene of complaint — over food! Human nature hasn't changed much. The gospel story confirms our trust in Christ: With Jesus in the boat (boats are often a symbol of the church), we will survive the storms and reach shore.

7 — #47 (LMC, #41) white
Third Sunday of Easter

LECTIONARY

The Third Sunday of Easter presents the preaching of Peter in the reading from Acts and, in the gospel, a "meal appearance" of Jesus, a text that leads homilists and hearers to reflection on the eucharist. Peter begins by rooting the paschal mystery of Jesus in the liberation experience of Israel. He invokes "the God of Abraham, the God of Isaac, and the God of Jacob, the God of our ancestors." Those who rejected Jesus are his "brothers," and Peter attributes their actions not to malice but to ignorance; and, through everything, God brings his saving plan to fulfillment.

The gospel passage also makes the link with Judaism specific: "Everything written about me in the law of Moses, the prophets, *and the psalms* must be fulfilled." Note the parallels between today's gospel and the Emmaus story. There is a meal, the opening of the disciples' minds to understand the scriptures, and the affirmation of the Messiah's role as suffering servant. As at Emmaus, the encounter leads the disciples to witness.

The second reading is a perfect link between Acts and the gospel. In Acts, Peter tells the crowd to repent "that your sins may be wiped out." In the gospel, Jesus says that "repentance and forgiveness of sins" are to be proclaimed to all nations. 1 John draws these together in its affirmation of who Jesus is: "the atoning sacrifice for . . . the sins of the whole world."

SACRAMENTARY

The rite of blessing and sprinkling with water is the best way to begin the Sunday eucharist throughout the Great Fifty Days. If the penitential rite is used, and at weekday eucharist this week, choose invocations C *v* or *vi*.

The prefaces Easter III or V might be good choices. Because today's gospel is the follow-up to the story of Emmaus, keep in mind the new eucharistic prayer for Masses for Various Needs and Occasions. All four forms of this prayer refer to Emmaus: "As once he did for his disciples

MAY

(at Emmaus), Christ now opens the scriptures for us and breaks the bread." Although its rubrics seem to restrict its use on Sundays, Pope John Paul II used this prayer at Sunday Mass during his historic visit to Cuba.

Today would be the day to switch to the Easter Season blessing (#7), which should continue in use through Ascension Day. The solemn blessings and prayers over the people at the end of each Sunday Mass formulary in the sacramentary are there by the editorial decision of the publisher. Planners and presiders are free to make their own choices.

MON 8 — #273 (LMC, #185–192) white
Easter Weekday

The passages from Acts today and tomorrow give a brief summary of Stephen's witness before the Jewish authorities. Unlike him, we often prefer to sugarcoat the gospel. Today's gospel asks us to reflect on what we hope to find as we follow Jesus. Which of our goals are perishable and which will endure.

TUE 9 — #274 (LMC, #185–192) white
Easter Weekday

Confident trust and unconditional forgiveness: Stephen manifests these gospel values at the hour of his death. The gospel reminds us that only in Jesus, the living bread come down from heaven, can we find the strength so to live and so to die.

WED 10 — #275 (LMC, #185–192) white
Easter Weekday

Acts presents Stephen's martyrdom as the beginning of a time of trial for the early church in Jerusalem, and a time of expansion far beyond that small beginning. Even Saul's appearance yesterday and today brings joy to us who know how his story ends.

THU 11 — #276 (LMC, #185–192) white
Easter Weekday

The story of Philip and the Ethiopian eunuch reminds us that for the disciple of Jesus, no encounter is a chance meeting. The most unlikely settings may present an unexpected opportunity for evangelization. The gospel continues our meditation on the bread of life, with passages that lead beautifully to eucharist-centered mystagogy.

FRI 12 — #277 (LMC, #185–192) white
Easter Weekday

Nereus and Achilleus, martyrs; Pancras, martyr; optional memorials/red. ▪ Philip finds an unlikely place for evangelization, while Ananias meets the world's most unlikely candidate.

Nereus and Achilleus are traditionally counted among the innumerable Christians who were soldiers when converted and refused further military service after baptism. Of Pancras, little is known, beyond a tradition that numbers him among several heroic teenaged martyrs who died in the persecution of the Roman church under Diocletian.

SAT 13 — #278 (LMC, #185–192) white
Easter Weekday

In Acts, persecution has yielded to peace, though trials will surely come again. Acts is wonderful for the detail of its living history of the young community. In the gospel, Jesus, instead of backing away from the hard words of his teaching, invites the disciples to go away if they want to. Peter's words are our own, "Lord, to whom shall we go?"

14 — #50 (LMC, #44) white
Fourth Sunday of Easter

LECTIONARY

The Fourth Sunday of Easter every year depicts Jesus as the Good Shepherd. Popular religious art often distorts this biblical image by suggesting a meek herdsman carrying a limp lamb. The shepherd in the gospel text is just the opposite. The strong and self-assured gospel shepherd is committed to his mission and in command of his destiny. He defends his sheep to the death, because he knows them as intimately as the Father knows him. The shepherd of John's gospel foresees a time when there will be one flock, one shepherd. When death comes to the shepherd at last, it comes only because he, Jesus, has decided to lay down his life, a life he will take up again.

The community can be reminded that this is the background to the glorious passion we heard on Good Friday. Across the centuries, the image of the Good Shepherd has been a source of strength and comfort for Christians.

On the Fourth and Fifth Sundays of Easter, in all three years, the lectionary shows the young church growing. Peter and John bear witness to the healing power of Jesus' name, a power flowing from his resurrection. The selection from 1 John reflects on another aspect of our new life in Christ: who we are already and what we are yet to be.

MAY

SACRAMENTARY

Good Shepherd Sunday is traditionally "World Day of Prayer for Vocations." Use the Fourth Sunday texts and maintain the ritual patterns established for the Easter season. Prayers and readings for vocations in the back of the liturgical books are not to be used today; the intention has a natural place in the general intercessions. The assembly should neither ignore the church's need for ordained and religious servants nor devalue lay ministries or the vocation of marriage. The preface Easter II pictures Christ as a good shepherd leading his people back into the kingdom. If there is no sprinkling rite, use form C vii for the penitential rite.

MOTHER'S DAY AND MARY'S MONTH

This weekend is Mother's Day, a traditional first communion day in many communities. The motif of the liturgy remains paschal joy, and The clear focus is on the scriptures. The words to "The church's one foundation" summarize the theology of the church as bride and mother. The homily could link the Vigil's initiation rites to the first communion celebration, and recall the importance of Mary as an image of the church: virgin, bride and mother. Sample general intercessions that bring Mother's Day into the assembly's prayer are in the *Book of Blessings* (#1727); a Prayer over the People for use at the end of Mass follows at #1728. If the traditional May Crowning takes place today, this is best done apart from the eucharist, perhaps after a final hymn ("Ye watchers and ye holy ones"). Look in these resources for texts: *Book of Blessings,* #1277 ff., and *Collection of Masses of the Virgin Mary,* formularies for the Easter season, #15 – 18. A blessing of mothers could be done at Our Lady's shrine or image at the end of the Marian devotion. As always with such blessings, liturgical planning should be sensitive to those who may not have or be mothers, and who may feel a special sorrow on this day.

This year's Easter season occupies most of May, when Catholics traditionally honor Mary. It is possible to incorporate Marian hymns while keeping the focus of the liturgy primarily on the risen Lord and Eastertime. Some are: "Be joyful, Mary, heav'nly queen"; "Regina coeli"; "Ye watchers and ye holy ones."

MON 15 — #279 (LMC, #185–192) white
Easter Weekday

Isidore the farmer, married man, and his wife Maria, optional memorial/white. ▪ Today's liturgy of the word celebrates the inclusivity of Jesus' mission. Acts recounts Peter's development in appreciating how boundary-less the Christian community is meant to be. Today's gospel continues yesterday's Good Shepherd imagery, emphasizing that Jesus is the gate of salvation for all.

Isidore and Maria were poor farmers in sixteenth-century Spain. They are remembered for their generosity to those even poorer than they and for their fidelity to prayer. Isidore's optional memorial was placed on the U.S. calendar at the request of the National Catholic Rural Life Conference in the 1950s. More recently, his wife Maria, who has always been venerated in Spain, was included.

TUE 16 — #280 (LMC, #185–192) white
Easter Weekday

Today's reading from Acts should not fail to move us: "It was in Antioch that the disciples were called 'Christians' for the first time." The gospel keeps Sunday's reflection on the Good Shepherd in mind. Do we who bear the name "Christian" truly follow the shepherd's voice? Spirituals found in many hymnals work very well when festivity calls for music but resources dictate that the music be a cappella. "Lord, I want to be a Christian in my heart" and "I have decided to follow Jesus" would be perfect complements for today's scriptures.

WED 17 — #281 (LMC, #185–192) white
Easter Weekday

The selection from Acts shows the disciples guided by the Spirit as they choose people for ministry. The gospel presents Jesus' testimony that he has come "not to judge the world but to save it."

THU 18 — #282 (LMC, #185–192) white
Easter Weekday

John I, pope and martyr, optional memorial/red. ▪ Through the rest of the week, the first reading presents Paul's "history of salvation" delivered in the synagogue at Antioch in Pisidia. Paul takes his listeners from Exodus to Jesus. The gospel reminds us that our imitation of Christ expresses itself in self-sacrificing service of our brothers and sisters.

In these days of conflict between Eastern-rite Catholics and Orthodox Christians, today's saint is a reminder that communion between the churches has never been easily maintained. Pope John I, renowned

MAY

as a peacemaker, died on this day in 526, a prisoner of the emperor who thought his sympathy toward the Eastern church excessive.

FRI 19 #283 (LMC, #185–192)   white
Easter Weekday

"My brothers, children of the family of Abraham and you others who reverence our God." Paul begins by addressing his audience with a respect that can be a model for us when we meet people of other faiths. Malice is not imputed to those responsible for Christ's death: "[They] failed to recognize him. . . ." and the good that ensued is acknowledged to be part of a wider plan: "They fulfilled the words of the prophets . . . [and] brought about all that had been written of him." The outcome is "good news" of what "God has fulfilled for us, our ancestors' children."

SAT 20 #284 (LMC, #185–192)   white
Easter Weekday

Bernardine of Siena, presbyter, religious, missionary, optional memorial/white. ▪ Today's selection from Acts reminds us of the conflict between the early Christians and the Jewish community as the gospel spread to the Gentiles. Jesus speaks of his unity with the Father and of his disciples' unity with him in doing the work of God, part of which is to promote reconciliation and mutual respect among people of all faiths. His words are spoken as "the hour was at hand for him to depart."

The theme of East and West comes up again today in the memorial of Bernardine. This popular Franciscan preacher worked at the fifteenth-century Council of Florence toward unity between the Eastern and Western churches, a gift that eludes us still.

☼ 21 #53 (LMC, #47)   white
Fifth Sunday of Easter

LECTIONARY

This week's first reading continues the theme of the early church's growth. The community grows as it learns to receive as gifts from the Spirit the varied people drawn to the Lord. The former chief persecutor, Saul, gets off to a shaky start with the disciples. 1 John continues its exhortation to living the new life in Christ. In the gospel, Jesus invites the disciples and us: "Abide in me." First John defines what abiding in Christ looks like: "Let us love, not in word or speech, but in truth and action." To love one another is to abide in Christ and to let Christ abide in us.

SACRAMENTARY

Let the liturgical patterns of Eastertime continue and, perhaps, the texts used in last weekend's liturgy. The scriptures show new members being added to the community and repeat the need for abiding in Christ. Easter Preface IV echoes these themes, speaking of a broken world being renewed and the human race being made whole. The Preface for Christian Unity (P-76) sounds a similar theme, as does the preface that is part of Reconciliation II. A traditional couplet added to any preface during Eastertime is, "We praise you with greater joy than ever in this Easter season, when Christ became our paschal sacrifice." Some presiders add this to the preface at marriage and funeral Masses.

MON 22 #285 (LMC, #185–192)   white
Easter Weekday

Paul and Barnabas have an experience familiar to missionaries in every age: They preach one thing, but their listeners hear something else. The Lycaonians rename the pair after Greek gods, amusingly to us. In the gospel, Jesus promises that the community will always be assisted by the Paraclete in its growth in the truth. For the next two weeks, the Canadian lectionary uses an approved option. Each day's passage is introduced by a brief text designed to make the gospel's context clear. Today's opening is: "Before the festival of the Passover, Jesus knew that his hour had come to depart from this world and go to the Father. During the supper, Jesus said to his disciples:" This is important for keeping the subsequent words of Jesus in their context: his last earthly prayer for his community.

TUE 23 #286 (LMC, #185–192)   white
Easter Weekday

Peace is Jesus' bequest and promise in today's gospel — but not the peace the world gives. The first reading from Acts illustrates the truth of that promise.

WED 24 #287 (LMC, #185–192)   white
Easter Weekday

The next three selections from Acts chronicle a crisis of interpretation in the early church and its peaceful resolution. This reminds us that disagreement is normal in the church and that anything and anyone who is alive is by definition growing and changing.

MAY

THU 25 — #288 (LMC, #185–192) white
Easter Weekday

Bede the Venerable, presbyter, religious, doctor of the church; Gregory VII, pope; Mary Magdalene de Pazzi, virgin, religious; optional memorials/white. ▪ Today's first reading recounts the discussion at the first council of the church in Jerusalem. Despite strong feelings on both sides of the issue, the council made a courageous and far-sighted decision to move beyond the Judaism in which the majority of the participants had been raised so as not to burden Gentile converts with more than was truly necessary for shared faith. In its finest hours, often in council, the church has been guided by the Spirit along similar paths of courage and foresight.

Today's optional saints gave generously of themselves to the church and the world. Bede offered historical narration and scriptural commentary in the eighth century. Hildebrand (Gregory VII) reformed the church and secured its freedom from secular authorities in the eleventh century. In the turbulent decades after the Reformation, the Carmelite Mary Magdalen de'Pazzi bore witness in ecstatic prayer and in physical suffering she offered for the renewal of the church.

FRI 26 — #289 (LMC, #185–192) white
Philip Neri, presbyter, religious founder
MEMORIAL

Acts shows that the decision of the community's elders partakes of the Spirit's presence in a special way: "It is the decision of the Holy Spirit, and ours too. . . ." The result is joy among the Gentiles awaiting word. Surely the decision to suppress customs that were part of the religious heritage of many at the council was a true "laying down of one's life for one's friends," as Jesus counsels in the gospel.

In the church of Philip Neri's day, things were far from ideal. Various Reformations, Protestant and Catholic, had exacerbated factions and divisions within the church. But Philip Neri dared to confront the situation with faith, hope, love and a sense of humor. His principal work was among the young in the slums of Rome. The numbers he evangelized were extraordinary. Is anyone attracted to our community by the witness of our love and joy?

SAT 27 — #290 (LMC, #185–192) white
Easter Weekday

Augustine of Canterbury, bishop, religious, missionary, optional memorial/white. ▪ A moving transition happens in today's first reading. All through the reading the subjects are Paul, Silas, Timothy and, presumably, those traveling with them. But in the last verse, the author of Acts shows himself: "*We* immediately tried to cross over to Macedonia, being convinced that God had called *us*." In the gospel, Jesus identifies us with himself in a way that makes us less comfortable: "If they persecuted me, they will persecute you also."

Around the year 600, Pope Gregory the Great wrote to Augustine about unity in diversity, offering advice that heartens all who work in liturgy:

> Your brotherhood is familiar with the usage of the Roman church since you have very pleasant memories of being raised and nurtured in that usage. But it seems to me that you should carefully select for the English church, which is still new to the faith and developing as a distinct community, whatever can best please almighty God, whether you discover it in the Roman church or among the Gauls, or anywhere else. For customs are not to be revered for their place of origin; rather those places are to be respected for the good customs they produce. From each individual church, therefore, choose whatever is holy, whatever is awe-inspiring, whatever is right; then arrange what you have collected as if in a little bouquet according to the English disposition and thus establish them as custom. (quoted in James F. White, *A Brief History of Christian Worship,* Abingdon, 1993, 44)

28 — #56 (LMC, #50) white
Sixth Sunday of Easter

In the dioceses of Canada and of the states of Alaska, California, Hawaii, Idaho, Montana, Nevada, Oregon, Utah and Washington, the Ascension of the Lord is transferred to next Sunday, June 4. In those places, the second reading and gospel of the Seventh Sunday of Easter (#60) may be read on the Sixth Sunday of Easter.

LECTIONARY

The Sixth Sunday of Easter shifts gently toward the Pentecost mystery. The abiding presence of the Lord in the midst of the community, always the same yet ever new, is manifest in the ways authority in the church evolves. Each year on this Sunday, the lectionary presents a passage from Acts that reflects the development of church authority. In today's selection, Peter grows in his appreciation of God's reaching out beyond

EASTER: MAY **161**

the boundaries of Judaism. In Cornelius and his household, the Gentiles become part of the community. Indeed, the Spirit can act even apart from the liturgy. "While Peter was still speaking, the Holy Spirit fell upon all who were listening." First came the Spirit, *then* the new converts were baptized! This reading highlights the work of the Spirit in initiation from the earliest days of the church. The passage from the First Letter of John links the passage from Acts to the gospel of John. The Spirit poured out upon us engenders love, for God is love. That love is first of all a gift to us, and then becomes the gift we share with one another, the gift that defines the Christian community.

SACRAMENTARY

The Roman liturgy's chants for this weekend (entrance and communion antiphons) manifest the twofold spirit of this weekend's liturgy: the joy of Easter ("the Lord has set his people free, alleluia") and the promise of the Spirit ("the Father will send you the Spirit to be with you forever, alleluia.")

The music should combine both motifs, signaling the coming fulfillment of Eastertime in the celebration of Pentecost. The general intercessions should include petitions for the coming of the Spirit's transforming power in the church, the world, the local community. Announce any special times of prayer in preparation for the end of the Easter season.

ROGATION DAYS AND PENTECOST NOVENA

The three days before Ascension were formerly designated for *rogare,* communal prayer and supplication. Monday, Tuesday and Wednesday of the Sixth Week of Easter were marked by processions through fields and gardens, accompanied by litanies and the sprinkling of Easter's blessed water on behalf of the fruits of the earth. In some places, there was intercession for those preparing for orders. These days culminated in the celebration of the Ascension and led into a replication of the "first novena" of prayer in preparation for Pentecost. Communities may reflect on renewing these traditions as a way of crowning the Eastertime observance.

MON 29 — #291 (LMC, #185–192) white
Easter Weekday

Luke is still writing in the first person: "We went outside the city gate by the river, where we thought we would find a place for prayer." Haven't we all sought out a place designed by nature for prayer? Lydia, a local businesswoman, accepts the gospel and opens her home to the missionaries. These golden moments of communion strengthen us for less shining times: The gospel answers the inevitability of persecution with the firm assurance of the Spirit's unfailing presence.

■ MEMORIAL DAY: Many parishes celebrate Mass in the cemetery on this day. Alternatively, today's liturgy might conclude with a procession to the cemetery. The *Book of Blessings,* chapter 57, provides a formal rite; *Catholic Household Blessings and Prayers* has a simpler prayer (pages 178, 280).

TUE 30 — #292 (LMC, #185–192) white
Easter Weekday

Another of the Spirit's gifts is celebrated in today's selection from Acts: reconciliation through the witness of self-sacrificing charity. An all-night vigil of song and prayer doesn't convert the jailer. But the concern of the Christian prisoners for the jailer's plight makes their witness authentic to the distraught man. As Jesus says in the gospel, when it comes to sin and righteousness and judgment, worldly standards yield to the Spirit's truth.

WED 31 — #572 (LMC, #302) white
The Visitation of the Blessed Virgin Mary
FEAST

ORIENTATION

The origins of this feast are rooted in the Franciscan charisms of peace and reconciliation. Saint Bonaventure (July 15) introduced it into that order's calendar in the thirteenth century; it was extended in 1389 to the entire Western church as an observance of prayer to heal the divisions afflicting the church in that age.

LECTIONARY

The lectionary provides two options for the first reading. Zephaniah matches the gospel canticle in joy and expectancy. The Romans text calls us to imitate Mary's concern for others. As Raymond Brown demonstrates in *The Birth of the Messiah* (2nd edition, 330–366), the Visitation episode is enormously rich in meaning. However, these richer meanings may be more appropriately preached when the Visitation appears in the lectionary on the Fourth Sunday of Advent, Year C. Today's observance seems to have a more devotional approach: Mary, filled with Christ and overshadowed by the Spirit, hastens to be of

JUNE

assistance to Elizabeth. Unlike on the Advent Sunday, today's passage contains the entire Magnificat, and its themes always suggest an abundance of homiletic reflection.

SACRAMENTARY

There are three Prefaces of Mary in the sacramentary (two in place and a newer one in the appendix), and fifty in the *Collection of Masses of the Blessed Virgin Mary*. The Preface of the Visitation (P-3) in that resource echoes not only the scriptures of the feast but the lesson of Mary's selfless love. In fact, the rich prayer texts of that formulary (*Collection,* #3) are particularly appropriate if the homilist is emphasizing Mary's example of charity and service. The Canticle of Mary, the Magnificat, would be a fine hymn of thanksgiving after communion.

June

THU #58 (LMC, #53) white
The Ascension of the Lord
SOLEMNITY

In the dioceses of Canada and of the states of Alaska, California, Hawaii, Idaho, Montana, Nevada, Oregon, Utah and Washington, the Ascension of the Lord is transferred to next Sunday, June 4. In those places, June 1 is kept as an Easter weekday. Readings are found at #294 in the lectionary.

ORIENTATION

Liturgical history suggests that originally, the solemnity of Pentecost celebrated both the Lord's ascension into heaven and the giving of the Holy Spirit, perhaps as a parallel to Moses' ascent of Mount Sinai and the giving of the Law (and see John 20:17, 22). Toward the end of the fourth century, the Ascension began to be observed as a separate feast on the fortieth day of Eastertime, reflecting Luke's chronology (see Acts 1:3). Leo the Great preached about the importance of this feast for the transformation of believers' lives in Christ:

> The Lord's resurrection filled us with joy on Easter Day; so too his ascension into heaven is the cause of our gladness now, as we commemorate and solemnize the day on which our lowly nature was raised up in Christ above all the hosts of heaven, above all the ranks of angels, beyond the height of all the heavenly powers, to the throne of God the Father. . . . Though everything that seemed to move us to due reverence is removed from our sight, our faith remains constant, our hope firm and our charity warm. (*Office of Readings,* Easter Week 6, Friday)

LECTIONARY

Luke's prologue to the Acts of the Apostles, addressed to Theophilus ("you who love God"), sets forth the story of today's feast. As Luke's gospel has led Jesus to Jerusalem and to his passion and death, volume II of Luke's work leads the church, Christ's presence in the world, from Jerusalem to the ends of the earth and to Rome, the heart of the empire. The responsorial psalm (Psalm 47) should be used from Ascension to the Saturday before Pentecost. Fine settings abound; choose one and use it every year. Proulx's setting in *Worship* is a good choice. Other possibilities: Hal Hopson's "Sing out your praise to God" in *Psalms for All Seasons* (NPM); Angelo della Pica's setting in *Psalms for the Cantor,* vol. V (WLP); Christopher Willcock's "God mounts his throne" in *Psalms for Feasts and Seasons* (Liturgical Press); and Marty Haugen's "God mounts his throne" *(Gather).*

The Ascension is one of the solemnities for which the new U.S. edition of the lectionary provides optional second readings for Years B and C. Lectors using some editions will need to be careful. The suite entitled "Ascension of the Lord B," contains the designation, "Second Reading A" (which is the standard Year A reading, Ephesians 1:17 – 23) followed by "or B Longer Form" (Ephesians 4:1 – 13), followed by "or C Shorter Form" (Ephesians 4:1 – 7, 11 – 13). Despite these confusing designations, both B and C forms are the alternate readings for Year B.

One Lord, one faith, one baptism is the theme of this year's second reading. For the gospel of Year B, the lectionary turns to the Longer Ending of Mark. The unique message resounds in the final lines: "the Lord worked with them," and he works with us still.

SACRAMENTARY

The eucharist on the Ascension is an Eastertime Mass. Keep the Eastertime patterns, with

JUNE

the changes of text required by the liturgy and modifications of decor suggested by the feast (see Mazar, *To Crown the Year*, pages 143–144). In former times the paschal candle was extinguished after today's gospel, but now it stays in its Easter location and is lighted until the Fifty Days are completed. Set the tone with a strong opening hymn such as "Hail the day that sees him rise" (LLANFAIR) or "A hymn of glory let us sing" (LASS UN EFREUEN). Use the Easter vesture and repeat the Eastertime Gloria. Ascension I is the richer preface. It could be included in the bulletin the week before. Eucharistic Prayer I has its proper insert in the sacramentary.

FRI 2 — #295 (LMC, #185–192) white
Easter Weekday

Marcellinus, presbyter, and Peter, exorcist, martyrs, optional memorial / red. • "Do not be afraid; speak; do not be silent: there are many of my people in this city." These words are spoken by the Lord to Paul in today's first reading. In the face of his own death, Jesus invokes the image of birth. The anguish of the disciples may be likened to the pain of labor, for in the paschal mystery of Christ a new creation is forever coming to birth.

Of today's saints, nothing certain is known except the honor in which the early Roman church held them: a basilica over their tombs and inclusion in Eucharistic Prayer I (the Roman Canon).

SAT 3 — #296 (LMC, #185–192) red
Charles Lwanga and his companions, martyrs
MEMORIAL

Acts relates Paul's journeys to proclaim the gospel and Apollos' eloquence in the service of the gospel. The gospel's promise that God will provide the community with what it needs is fulfilled in every generation through those who offer their time and talent for the building up of the body.

Others in every generation are willing to lay down their lives. Today's saint, Charles Llwanga, a catechist, and his young friends, Catholics and Anglicans, offered their lives for the sake of the kingdom (1885–1887). In the spirit of ecumenism, Pope Paul VI traveled to Uganda to canonize these martyrs in 1964, and asked that the Anglican archbishop be present to honor the martyrs of that church as well. That archbishop, Janai Luwum, was himself martyred by another tyrant, Idi Amin. History repeats itself.

"In my window," wrote Angelo Roncalli in his diary, "a little light must always shine, so that anyone may knock and enter and find a friend." That light one day shone over Saint Peter's Square and the whole world found a friend in "Good Pope John." Today is the 37th anniversary of the death of Pope John XXIII, whose pontificate of only five years (1958–1963) gave the church Vatican II and transformed our liturgical and ecclesial life.

4 — #60 (LMC, #56) white
Seventh Sunday of Easter

In the dioceses of Canada and of the states of Alaska, California, Hawaii, Idaho, Montana, Nevada, Oregon, Utah and Washington, the Ascension of the Lord is celebrated on the Seventh Sunday of Easter. The readings and prayers used there are those of that solemnity. This discussion focuses on the celebration of the Eastertime Sunday.

LECTIONARY

"I am not asking you to take them out of the world." Today's gospel assures us that we are exactly where Jesus wants us to be. The Seventh Sunday of Easter is always the Sunday of Jesus the High Priest, Jesus the Intercessor. Each of the lectionary's three cycles presents a portion of his "high priestly prayer" for the disciples from John 17. As Jesus stands with hands outstretched between heaven and earth, so this Sunday stands between Ascension and Pentecost to remind us of our spiritual location. We still live between the "already" of the kingdom's announcement and the "not yet" of the kingdom's fulfillment. Jesus does not ask the Father to take us from this difficult place, but to protect us from the evil one and equip us to bear witness. The second reading takes us back to the first encounter of the first disciples. *Abide* (NRSV) or *remain* (RNAB) with Jesus is what they had done the first day they met him. Now the word recurs: God is love, and those who abide in love abide in God, and God abides in them. It is love for one another that renders God visible in our midst.

SACRAMENTARY

This Sunday's music should point us toward Pentecost. While keeping the Eastertime patterns, use a new gathering song, Psalm 47 from Ascension, and perhaps both "Alleluia, sing to Jesus" (a reference to Christ's Ascension and to his promise to remain with us) and "Come down, O Love divine" or the par-

JUNE

ish's favorite Holy Spirit hymn. The new sacramentary will have a preface adapted from the Italian sacramentary for these days between Ascension and Pentecost. It pictures the assembly gathered as Mary and the first disciples were, awaiting the Spirit, and celebrates Christ as the high priest who has entered the sanctuary of heaven to plead for the continual outpouring of that Spirit on the community of his people. Since neither Ascension preface mentions the gift of the Spirit, it might be good to use Holy Spirit I (P-54), since it does mention both Ascension and Pentecost.

MON 5 — #297 (LMC, #185–192) red
Boniface, bishop, religious, missionary and martyr
MEMORIAL

Baptism and the gift of the Holy Spirit through the laying on of hands: the selection from Acts to begin this week before Pentecost. Christ predicts persecution and dispersal, but the courage needed will be the Spirit's gift.

Today is the anniversary of the martyrdom of Boniface, apostle of Germany and a giant in church history, who faced persecution and death in the mission of evangelization (+ 754).

TUE 6 — #298 (LMC, #185–192) white
Easter Weekday

Norbert, bishop, religious founder, optional memorial/white. ▪ The reading from Acts tells of Paul hurrying to get to Jerusalem for his Pentecost. His ministry is a model of tireless preaching and practical service. For him the Spirit was not a theological concept but an abiding friend. This gives courage to us, whose place, according to Christ's gospel word, is not in detached contemplation, but in the midst of the world with his work to do.

In the twelfth century, as the winds of reform began to blow through an increasingly comfortable church, Norbert gave up a life of ease to embrace evangelical poverty. He died on this date in 1134. His spiritual brothers carry on the mission and are known as the Norbertines (or more formally, the Praemonstratensions).

WED 7 — #299 (LMC, #185–192) white
Easter Weekday

The farewell scene on the beach is vivid. Paul's departure speech offers guidance for us all: vigilance and self-sacrificing service. Jesus' prayer in the gospel is also for us: Our vocation is not to escape the world but to immerse ourselves in its service.

THU 8 — #300 (LMC, #185–192) white
Easter Weekday

Acts is a wonderfully human document. Paul gives a good account of himself in today's first reading, reducing his accusers to argument with each other. Always a masterful ploy! But in the midst of the humanity, the Spirit is present: Paul must go on to Rome. Today's gospel reminds us that we, too, are to be evangelizers, and that the Lord's farewell prayer is not only for us but also for those who will come to believe through our word.

FRI 9 — #307 (LMC, #185–192) white
Easter Weekday

Ephrem of Syria, deacon and doctor of the church, optional memorial/white. ▪ Today's passage from Acts explains the legalities by which the Spirit's will was accomplished, and Paul is sent to Rome. If there is no morning Mass tomorrow, add tomorrow's reading to this one, thus bringing the reading of Acts to completion. In Rome, Peter and Paul will offer their lives in answer to Jesus' question in today's gospel: "Do you love me?"

The Syrian deacon Ephrem (+ 373) is a poet whose hymns are still a treasured part of the church's repertoire. Some of these appear in LTP's revised *Triduum Sourcebook*. A beautiful text filled with references to the gospel is in the Episcopal *Hymnal 1982* (#443).

SAT 10 — #302 (LMC, #185–192) white
Easter Weekday

This morning's reading from Acts concludes Eastertime's presentation of the young church alive in the Spirit. John's gospel ends with the reminder that our call is to proclaim Christ faithfully to the end. Though the written canon of scripture is finished, the story of Christ continues in the living pages of disciples' lives.

SUN 11 — #63, day; 62, vigil (LMC, #58) red
Pentecost Sunday
SOLEMNITY

ORIENTATION

Not just a single day, the Pentecost is the great Fifty Days, that "most joyful span of time" (Tertullian) which we have been celebrating as a single continuous feast of the risen Christ. In a "week of weeks" (7 × 7) plus a festival day, the Jewish people celebrated the harvest, which came to be associated also with Moses' ascent of Mount Sinai to receive the Law and, later, with the covenants with Abraham and Noah as well. Thus various themes enter into the Christian celebration of the day:

- the harvest of the nations in the inauguration of the messianic community, as the gift of tongues reverses the confusion of Babel
- the coming of the Spirit as Christ ascends like Moses to bestow the law of the new covenant to be written in the hearts of believers
- the missioning of the disciples to proclaim the good news to all creation ("As the Father has sent me, so I send you. . . . Receive the Holy Spirit")

LECTIONARY

The richness of the feast is manifest in the array of scripture selections provided for the day. The new lectionary for use in the United States presents four Old Testament readings from which one is to be selected, but the Roman *Circular Letter* (1988) makes it clear that an extended vigil is preferred. The new Canadian lectionary provides a valuable resource. See the notes under each celebration below. Be careful using the new U.S. lectionary. Some editions repeat the Year A readings each year just before the new optional readings designated "B" in both Years B and C. Double-check the heading before marking the place.

SACRAMENTARY

Pentecost is the day to recapitulate all that Eastertime has been for this community. The gift of the Spirit has been celebrated unceasingly since the Easter Vigil, beginning with what the Byzantine liturgy calls "the awe-inspiring rites" of baptism, chrismation and eucharist. The intimate relationship of Pentecost to Easter should be manifested ritually:

- Easter's resplendent vesture
- the sprinkling of the assembly with water
- Eastertime's fragrant incense
- the music of the Eastertime Gloria, the special sequence ("Veni, Sancte Spiritus," the golden sequence), resounding alleluias at the gospel acclamation, and the unique dismissal melody with its double alleluia that closes Mass and echoes in the final verse and response of Evening Prayer.

NEOPHYTES

The neophytes, dressed for the last time in their white robes, should be present in their special places. They may be honored in the homily and by incensation before the rest of the assembly in the preparation rite, prayed for by name in the general intercessions, and feasted in hospitality.

Babies baptized at Easter and throughout the past year can be brought to church in their baptismal gowns, accompanied by parents, godparents, families and friends.

Those received into full communion should be included in the intercessions and might also have reserved seating.

The newly confirmed and first communicants should also be in our prayers. They, too, might have special seating and wear what they wore at confirmation or first communion.

DECORATIONS

Peter Mazar (*To Crown the Year*, pages 145–148) derives suggestions from the link of this day to the Jewish titles of Shavuout (harvest) and Yom Habikkurim (day of first fruits).

SATURDAY VIGIL MASS

The vigil described below is the preferred form of celebration this evening. If the regular Saturday vigil Mass is celebrated, use the special texts in the sacramentary and lectionary.

EXTENDED PENTECOST VIGIL

As with all solemnities, the church taps into its Jewish roots, computing time from sundown to sundown. The *Circular Letter* (1988) from the Vatican's Congregation for Divine Worship urges an extended vigil whose character is not baptismal, but one of intensive common prayer modeled on Acts 1. Using the Old Testament readings in the lectionary, this vigil is a suitable way to end the period of postbaptismal catechesis.

MASS DURING THE DAY

Introductory Rites

An expectant atmosphere can be established with special instrumental music or the Taizé ostinato "Veni, Sancte Spiritus." Once the actual liturgy begins, continue the Eastertime ritual patterns.

JUNE

Liturgy of the Word

On this last day of Eastertime, the assembly responds to the proclamation of the Pentecost event in Acts with Psalm 104. Three settings are offered by GIA: C. Alexander Peloquin (GIA, G-1662) and Robert Edward Smith's (G-2122) "Lord, send out your Spirit"; and Paul Lisicky's "Psalm 104," in Gather. World Library offers several settings of this psalm: Angelo della Pica's in *Psalms for the Cantor,* vol. V; Vern Pat Nelson's "Spirit psalm" (#2616) which has more elaborate verses for the cantor; Dan Tucker's fine "Lord, send out your Spirit" (#7994); and two bilingual settings, "Renueve la Tierra Madre" by Charlotte Struckhoff, and "Ven, O Espiritu" by Lorenzo Florián, which is particularly good for children.

Don't fail to sing the sequence. The traditional chant melody, called the golden sequence, with Latin or English text, can be found in *Worship* (#857), and this is the translation that appears in the Canadian lectionary. Be careful trying to sing (or recite) the text in the new U.S. lectionary. The rhythm and rhyme scheme are tricky. The sequence hymn does not end with alleluia; the gospel acclamation is begun immediately. An alternate setting of the sequence is Ann Colleen Dohn's version with responses for the assembly (WLP, 5718). The text might appear beforehand in a bulletin insert orienting the community toward Pentecost, and maybe in a take-home brochure for the novena of prayer between Ascension and Pentecost.

LITURGY OF THE EUCHARIST

See today's proper preface and the inserts for Eucharistic Prayer I. Repeat the acclamations used throughout the Fifty Days, perhaps enhancing them with more instrumentation and harmonies.

CONCLUDING RITE

There is a solemn blessing for today which may be repeated at Evening Prayer II. Today's dismissal includes the double alleluia chanted to its unique melody, a final reminder (at Mass and vespers) that this is still the Easter feast.

HYMNODY

The hymn of the day, in addition to the golden sequence, is "Veni Creator Spiritus," found in many forms, including Richard Wojcik's "O Holy Spirit, by whose breath" (*Worship,* #475), Ralph Wright's translation in *Hymnal for the Hours* (GIA), which can be sung to the traditional chant or to an 88.88 meter tune (e.g., PUER NOBIS); and Mike Hay's "Holy Spirit, Creator's breath" (*We Celebrate,* #940). For a hymn that sings specifically of the Pentecost event, see Jane Parker Huber's "On Pentecost they gathered" in *The New Century Hymnal* (#272). Newer hymns for Pentecost incorporate the biblical images in an explicit way. See Carl P. Daw Jr.'s "Like the murmur of the dove's song" in *Hymnal 1982* (#513); Thomas H. Troeger's "Wind who makes all winds that blow" in *The New Century Hymnal* (#271). Communities ready to blend traditional descriptions of the Holy Spirit with alternative images may like Shirley Erena Murray's "Loving Spirit" in both the Lutheran church's supplement, *With One Voice* (#683), and the Episcopal church's new supplement to *Hymnal 1982, Wonder, Love and Praise* (#742).

DOMESTIC PRAYER

Today's mealtime prayer might be celebrated at a dining table graced with an assortment of spring's brightest blossoms, and perhaps red dinner candles. Prayers for home use are in *Catholic Household Blessings and Prayers* (page 157), and the outline for Eastertime table prayer still is appropriate today (page 84).

EVENING PRAYER II

This liturgical hour marks the end of Eastertime and merits attention and celebration. The double alleluia dismissal signifies the formal end of the Fifty Days. A procession accompanies the transfer of the Easter candle from its place of honor near the ambo to its year-round place of importance at the font. Use the best of Easter's songs for the procession or one with plenty of alleluia refrains for people to sing by heart (maybe the alleluia from the Easter Vigil gospel). As when entering the church at the Easter Vigil, the assembly follows the candle — this time to the font. As the candle is placed there, let the music continue, while all come to the font to sign themselves with the living and life-giving waters.

SUMMER AND FALL ORDINARY TIME

The Season
The Setting of Summer/Fall Ordinary Time / 171
A Sense of Summer/Fall Ordinary Time / 172
The Look of Summer/Fall Ordinary Time / 173
The Sounds of Summer/Fall Ordinary Time / 174
The Rhythm of Summer/Fall Ordinary Time / 174
The Eucharist / 176
At Home / 177
The Calendar
June 12 – December 2, 2000 / 178

The Setting of Summer/Fall Ordinary Time

Even though we return to Ordinary Time quite late this year — in the third week of June! — the Christian liturgical assembly still faces an almost six-month stretch of Sundays that are simply and gloriously only Sunday, the Lord's Day. But as we have seen in *Dies Domini,* far from being bereft of meaning, Sunday in Ordinary Time is filled with meaning in and of itself.

The length of Ordinary Time in any year depends on the date of Easter. This year, for instance, because Easter is so late, we lose only four days from Ordinary Time. The last four weekdays in the Ninth Week in Ordinary Time are replaced by the weekdays after Ash Wednesday. When Ordinary Time resumes, on the day after Pentecost, June 12, 2000, we reckon it as Monday of the Tenth Week in Ordinary Time.

At Sunday liturgy the resumption of Ordinary Time is not immediately obvious, because two solemnities always supersede the Sundays just as Ordinary Time resumes. The Sunday after Pentecost is the Solemnity of the Holy Trinity, and the Sunday after that is the Solemnity of the Body and Blood of Christ (formerly called Corpus Christi). These Sundays are celebrated in white vestments rather than in green, and the scriptures are not from the sequential reading of Mark but are specially selected for their relationship to the feasts.

Once the Sundays in Ordinary Time resume, this year with the Thirteenth Sunday in Ordinary Time, we will already be in July! The Sundays in Ordinary Time continue until the week before Advent, and this year there is only one interruption. The Eighteenth Sunday in Ordinary Time is replaced by the Feast of the Transfiguration of the Lord (August 6). The last Sunday in November is the Thirty-fourth and final Sunday in Ordinary Time, celebrated as the Solemnity of Christ the King. A final week of Ordinary Time leads us to the eve of a new liturgical year. The first Sunday of December is the First Sunday of Advent, the beginning of the liturgical year 2001.

As noted in the introduction to Winter Ordinary Time, planners and presiders would do well to let three letters be their companions on the journey that will take us from mid June to early December: Pope John Paul II's *Dies Domini: On Keeping the Lord's Day Holy;* the late Cardinal Joseph Bernardin's *Guide for the Assembly;* and Cardinal Roger Mahony's *Guide for Sunday Mass: Gather Faithfully Together,* with an accompanying video that shows the letter's insights and principles being put into practice.

These letters take seriously Vatican II's challenge that we "realize that something more is required than the mere observance of laws governing valid and lawful celebration" (*Constitution on the Sacred Liturgy,* 11). By analogy we could say that, in preparing the liturgy for Ordinary Time, "something more" is required than simply noting the passage of months in the civil calendar.

In every local church, and in ways unique to each local church, these 25 weeks of Ordinary Time witness the unfolding life of a living community. Whatever their age and gender, their economic or educational background, whatever their ethnic heritage or country of origin, the individuals who form the liturgical assembly live and work in the real world. In that world, the world "God so loved so much as to send the only Son," several calendars intersect, sometimes complementing each other, sometimes challenging each other, sometimes conflicting with one another. But "to Christ all time belongs and all the ages," as we pray at the Easter Vigil. His are the seasons and the centuries, and so our Christian forebears saw no conflict in adorning their churches not only with icons of Christ, Mary and the saints, but with the signs of the zodiac as well. Our goal is to prepare worship that is both faithful to the tradition and appropriate for the contemporary assembly.

SCRIPTURAL CALENDAR

Sourcebook has already examined the lectionary arrangement for Year B and summarized some of the critical insights of recent scripture scholarship (see Lectionary Overview). As noted in that overview, there is more than one way of analyzing the Gospel of Mark, but the lectionary pattern for Summer/Fall Ordinary Time of Year B looks like this:

- *Early Summer: Ordinary Time, Weeks 10 through 14 (Sundays 13 and 14).* Mark's gospel reaches a turning point here with the decisive misunderstanding and rejection of Jesus by his own townspeople.
- *High to Late Summer: Ordinary Sundays 15 through 23.* A mission of preaching and stories of healing bracket a prolonged excursus into the Gospel of John on the Bread of Life, Jesus' compassion made incarnate in food that satisfies physical hunger and teaching that nourishes the inner person.
- *Autumn: Ordinary Sundays 24 through 30.* The nature of discipleship is explored throughout these Sundays, with challenges for each of us in every walk of life.
- *November: Ordinary Sundays 31 through 34.* The Gospel of Mark takes us to Jerusalem for the ending of Jesus' teaching and Jesus' teaching about the end. The lectionary of the Sundays in this month of all saints and all souls calls us to authentic gospel living while we have time and bids us be vigilant for the fulfillment of time in Jesus' return. For the last Sunday in Ordinary Time, the Solemnity of Christ the King, the Year B lectionary turns again to the Gospel of John and its presentation of Jesus before Pilate as a paradoxical portrait of our uncommon King.

A Sense of Summer/Fall Ordinary Time

PLANNERS and presiders should resist the temptation to divide Ordinary Time into several artificial or overly thematic mini-seasons, but the interaction of the scriptures with the seasons of nature and the culture's calendar will suggest shifts and shadings that permit planning for related celebrations, blessings, scripture study and so forth. A careful charting of these movements will prevent an unfocused drifting through these weeks, so that each Sunday may be celebrated as a feast of its own, yet related to the seasonal, social and scriptural context and to the Sundays before and after it.

What follows is one way of looking at Summer/Fall Ordinary Time 2000, taking into account the three calendars we have discussed. It is offered as a model for local planners to build on and modify.

■ EARLY SUMMER
Solemnities
June 18: Holy Trinity
 • Blessing of married couples
 • Father's Day intercession and blessing
June 25: Body and Blood of Christ
 • Parish eucharistic procession
 • Blessing of travelers

■ HIGH SUMMER
Sundays of Belief and Unbelief

July 2: Thirteenth Sunday
- U.S.: Independence Day (July 4)
- Civic blessings, prayers for peace

July 9: Fourteenth Sunday

Sundays of Mission, Compassion and the Bread of Life

July 16: Fifteenth Sunday
- Letter to the Ephesians begins: ecumenical motifs: unity within and beyond the community

July 23: Sixteenth Sunday

July 30: Seventeenth Sunday
- Gospel of John: Bread of Life discourse begins

August 6: Transfiguration of the Lord
- Prayers for peace

August 13: Nineteenth Sunday
- Assumption of Mary (August 15)
- Blessing of herbs, fruits and flowers

■ Late Summer

August 20: Twentieth Sunday

August 27: Twenty-first Sunday
- Gospel of John: Bread of Life discourse ends
- Blessing for departing parishioners
- Blessing for new parishioners

September 3: Twenty-second Sunday
- Letter of James begins: motifs of life in community and social justice
- U.S.: Labor Day (September 4)
- Blessing of human labor

■ Fall

September 10: Twenty-third Sunday
- Blessing of social justice ministries (James: poverty and wealth)

Sundays of Discipleship

September 17: Twenty-fourth Sunday
- Catechetical Sunday: blessing of catechists

September 24: Twenty-fifth Sunday
- Blessing of liturgical ministries (gospel: true greatness is service)

October 1: Twenty-sixth Sunday

October 8: Twenty-seventh Sunday
- Letter to the Hebrews begins: eschatological motif begins
- Canada: Thanksgiving (October 9)

October 15: Twenty-eighth Sunday
- World Mission Sunday

October 22: Twenty-ninth Sunday
- Alternative date for blessing social justice ministries (gospel: true greatness in service)

October 29: Thirtieth Sunday
- Anointing of the sick (gospel: healing of Bartimaeus)
- Reformation Sunday: prayers for unity
- Dedication Sunday, if date unknown
- Halloween, All Saints, All Souls

■ November

Eschatological Sundays: Jerusalem

November 5: Thirty-first Sunday
- Food collection for Thanksgiving begins

November 12: Thirty-second Sunday

November 19: Thirty-third Sunday
- U.S.: Thanksgiving (November 23)

November 26: Thirty-fourth Sunday

The Look of Summer/Fall Ordinary Time

VERDURE

THE array of nature, which Jesus considered to be finer than all the wardrobe that King Solomon possessed, surely should lend its beauty to the assembly's place of worship during the summer and fall months of Ordinary Time. Keep in mind the principle already articulated during the seasonal considerations elsewhere in this *Sourcebook:* The whole worship space deserves adornment. Not just the front of the church but the whole interior ought to figure in the planning of any decor. The place of the assembly, no less than the altar and ambo, ought to be honored with greens and flowers and the seasonal plant life indigenous to the locale. Let the natural progression in the area dictate the kind and quantity of what is used. Let the vessels these are put in reflect the shifting of the seasons as well: The clay pots and planters of early summer might yield to glass vases as summer progresses, just as metal vases and then woven baskets and cornucopia could come on the scene as the autumn approaches.

As saints' days come and go, images of those being honored in the liturgy might be honored in the decoration of their statues, windows or icons. Moving such images to front and center was popular in former days when the assembly's "participation" was largely passive and silent. With the renewed liturgy, this becomes a risky business: There is always the danger of detracting from the integrity and simplicity of the worship space or of taking attention from altar or ambo. Depending on their location, the images might be more fittingly honored by being kept in place and adorning that place in such a way as to draw attention to it apart from the celebration of the eucharist.

For a complete discussion of the possibilities of Summer/Fall Ordinary Time decoration see Peter Mazar, *To Crown the Year*, pages 154–197.

VESTURE

These are the green Sundays, the rationale behind this color choice often being explained as a choice for the color of growth, as in Ordinary Time we are to grow in our appreciation of the lessons learned during the festal seasons. There may be something to this, after all, but another explanation is simply that green was thought to be a neutral color and, therefore, appropriate to this season of nonthematic Sundays. In the Sarum rite, England's pre-Reformation variation on the Roman rite, the "ordinary time" color in summer appears to have been a kind of yellow or beige — a neutral color. Green is a color "umbrella" that shelters a wide variety of shades: Early summer's sprouting green is different from the lush greens of the high and humid summer weeks, different still from the darkening greens turning into the burnt oranges of autumn and the earth browns of late October and November. Without suggesting that the whole of Ordinary Time become a constant changing of the colors, it ought to be one of the community's goals to add to the collection of vestments that comprise the spectrum of this most prescribed color in the calendar.

The Sounds of Summer/Fall Ordinary Time

Specific suggestions for the various phases of Summer/Fall Ordinary Time will appear in the calendar entries. But review also the notes under Winter Ordinary Time. The ordinary Sundays invite the use of several kinds of music: seasonal, by which is meant, both attuned to the scriptures that unfold Sunday by Sunday and to the world of nature round about us; functional, ordered to the liturgical moment at which the hymn is sung; and Lord's Day hymns that celebrate the various motifs associated with Sunday: creation, redemption, sanctification, day of light, day of worship, day of recreation. The reduction of available musicians during summer ordinary time ought not mean the reduction of liturgical propriety: Simple responsorial psalms are readily available, and the common acclamations before the gospel and during the eucharistic prayer can be sung a cappella in their most familiar settings.

The Rhythm of Summer/Fall Ordinary Time

Summer/Fall Ordinary Time presents an opportunity for planners and presiders to take stock of where the assembly and its leaders actually are in terms of liturgical practice. Cardinal Mahony's letter spells out in specific detail what the liturgy of the word and the liturgy of the eucharist should look like in practice.

Here is what Cardinal Mahony's pastoral letter says about the elements of the liturgy of the word, interspersed with questions about implementing the Cardinal's vision.

■ Lectors "All the readers of Scripture know what they are there to do. They know that these readings could be read privately by each individual, but that this public reading is quite different. For two years now there have been no booklets for the assembly to follow the reading, although by the front doors there are Sunday Missals for the hearing impaired and for those whose language is different from the one used at this Mass. . . . These lectors have taken time to hear anew old words, to let the images of Scripture reflect against and mingle with their lives. Each has found something to cherish in a reading, something to be passionate about. But they also know how to communicate their passion without calling attention to themselves."

■ CANTORS "The cantor at this Mass . . . knows that the people want to hear the words. Good articulation is as important as a good voice."

■ ASSEMBLY "The assembly gives all its attention to the lector. . . . The assembly is hearing God's Word. You can tell that the main activity going on during these readings is good listening. And what a treasure that is! The liturgy — God's word proclaimed and God's word listened to — is being carried by the assembly and they mean it when they say, "Thanks be to God/*Demos gracias a Dios.*" Every Sunday the Sacred Scriptures have been opened and read aloud. God's Word proclaimed and listened to will be the foundation for all else that this Church does."

■ SILENCE "Silence follows the first and second readings . . . and again after the homily, lasting about a minute. People are used to it, and know what to do with it. They will tell you: Let that reading echo in your head, cling to a word or a phrase, savor it, stand under it. It becomes a very still time. Babies fuss, but people are not distracted."

■ PSALMODY "The psalm after the first reading is almost an extension of this silence. No one gets out a book because the parish uses a repertoire of perhaps a dozen psalms — and each year they learn one or two more — where all can sing the refrain by heart. . . . Sometimes the texts appear in the parish bulletin with the suggestion that these psalms be prayed at home. In these ways and more (seasonal evening prayer, for example), the people . . . are coming to know the Church's oldest prayer book, the Psalter."

- What programs do we have in place for training new lectors and cantors and for refresher courses for veterans?
- What is the ongoing process by which our community's lectors and cantors prepare for their ministry, either individually or as a group?
- What kind of participation aid do we provide for the Sunday assembly? What progress have we made toward the purchase of a parish hymnal or preparation of seasonal music resources?
- Have we incorporated the ongoing catechesis of the assembly into our liturgy planning and preparation? Specifically, have we attended to the three primary activities of the assembly during the liturgy of the word: active listening, silent reflecting, responsive psalmody?
- Do we provide advance notice of what the readings will be over the next block of Ordinary Time?
- Do we provide education about the scriptures that will be proclaimed during each season?
- Do our adult education programs and our children's and youth religious education programs incorporate material on the lectionary and liturgical practice?

■ GOSPEL PROCESSION AND PROCLAMATION "There is nothing half-hearted about the procession that now begins: The alleluia is singing to move with, to process with; it takes candle-bearing servers, incense bearer, and book-bearing [deacon or] presider through the assembly and to the place of proclamation."

- On what days, or in which seasons, does our community employ a solemn gospel procession?
- What does the Ordinary Time movement from the silence after the second reading to the gospel proclamation look like?
- Have the familiar gestures of signing the book, forehead, lips and breast become too familiar?

■ HOMILY "This Sunday and every Sunday . . . the expectation is that not only did the preacher work on this homily, but so did the ten or so people who meet every week on, say, Monday evenings to read, pray with and talk about the Scriptures for the coming weeks. The homilists are committed to being there and lectors often come as well."

Discussion questions for such a gathering might include:

- What is the bad news to be confronted by this week's homily?
- What good news will the homily propose in response to the bad news?
- What difference do we hope this will make in people's lives this week?

■ DIMISSAL OF CATECHUMENS "After a minute or so of silence, after the homily, catechumens . . . are dismissed to continue studying the Scriptures. Two catechists go with them."

- Is the RCIA in place as the standard way new members are initiated or received into our faith community?
- What is the liturgical dimension of our catechumenal formation? Do they have a place in our Sunday assembly? Are they reverently and

purposefully dismissed from the assembly at the appropriate moment?
- If our community does not have catechumens, what can be done?

■ CREED "The Creed is a loud, almost mighty sound, chant-like. Few need the text as the rhythm carries it along."
- The old Kyriale had some beautiful Gregorian melodies for this text. Are any of these known and appropriate today? What about some new musical versions? See Owen Burdick's "one note" version in the Episcopal church's new hymnal supplement *Wonder, Love and Praise* (#849) and a metrical version of the Apostles' Creed, "I believe in God Almighty" in the same collection (#768).

■ GENERAL INTERCESSIONS "No longer is there a dull reading of bland texts with a weak 'Lord hear our prayer/*Te lo pedimos Señor*' after each. Today the cantor chants the intercessions. The texts are short and strong. Only a few are written new each week, and these echo some image or notion from the day's Scriptures and the week's news. The assembly is engaged in this rhythmic exchange with the cantor."

The Eucharist

REFLECT on this checklist of the practices Cardinal Mahony proposed as normative for the liturgy of the eucharist in a liturgically renewed parish community.

■ THE EUCHARISTIC PRAYER "Great mystery is conveyed in the faces and postures, singing and silence, gesture and word. Everyone is attentive, bodies engaged as much as hearts. It is clearly the central moment of this Lord's Day gathering.... When we say 'Eucharist,' we mean this whole action of presider and assembly. That is the Eucharist whose grace and powerful mystery can transform us and, in us, the world (CCC: 1368).

"...The presider chants most of the Prayer and the refrains are the same most Sundays of the year, sung to music capable of carrying the liturgy week after week. The exchange between presider and assembly is seamless, as proclamation and acclamation are woven together. The Prayer takes only four or five minutes, but in its intensity it is clearly the center of this Sunday gathering.... No wonder that when the great 'Amen' is concluded, one can sense a collective sigh, a deep breath."

- The eucharistic prayer is the prayer of the gathered assembly, prayed by the presider. It should be clear to all by the intense participation of the assembly that this is the central moment of the Sunday liturgy.
- The eucharistic prayer should have a clear beginning (the preface dialogue set off from what went before) and ending (the Amen set off from the Lord's Prayer).
- The acclamations should be strong, as should the presider's proclamation. The flow of thanksgiving and praise, memorial, invocation of the Spirit and intercession should be chanted or spoken with great reverence and attention.

■ LORD'S PRAYER AND SIGN OF PEACE "The chanting of the Our Father then carries the assembly toward Holy Communion. The peace greeting is not long or protracted, but it is anything but perfunctory. People seem to look each other in the eye. They clasp hands firmly or embrace. As the presider raises a large piece of the consecrated bread to break it, the cantor begins the litany "Lamb of God/*Cordero de Dios*" that will carry us until the bread is all broken, the consecrated wine all poured into the communion cups."

- The *orans* position (standing with hands outstretched, not linked) is appropriate for all at the Lord's Prayer through "For the kingdom..."
- The Lamb of God is a litany to be sung all through the breaking of the bread and until the presider is ready to say, "This is the Lamb of God..."

■ COMMUNION PROCESSION "Here is a church partaking of the sacred banquet... the ordinary and extraordinary ministers of communion... represent the diversity of the community: women and men, young and old, of different races, backgrounds and circumstances. They are in no hurry and neither is the assembly. Yet there seem to be enough of them that the procession can keep moving while each individual is treated with reverence: Ministers look each person in the eye and say, without rushing, 'The Body of Christ/*El Cuerpo de Cristo*,' 'The Blood of Christ/*La*

Sangre de Cristo.' Each person has time to respond, 'Amen.'"

- The ministers of communion, including the presider, are to give great attention to each person coming to communion.
- The bread is to appear to the senses as bread (General Instruction of the Roman Missal: 283).
- The tabernacle is to be approached only when some misjudgment of the amount of bread needed has been made. Otherwise it is not used for communion at Mass.

■ SILENCE AFTER COMMUNION "We have come to learn that we all need the gift of silence throughout liturgy in order to help us enter more fully and deeply into the mystery of the death and resurrection of the Lord Jesus. The silence and the stillness in the church become a wondrous mixture of personal and communal prayer."

- An ample period of silence follows the communion procession.
- Announcements and other community activities follow the prayer after communion.

In one of the concluding paragraphs of his pastoral letter, Cardinal Mahony summarizes what must surely be the goal of any parish's liturgy planning team:

"People are intent on the hard work of liturgy, caught up in singing, procession and even silence. To be with them is to know deeply that we are the Body and Blood of Christ. To be with them is to learn how to be in this world with reverence, with a love of God that is incarnate in how we speak to others, how we move amidst the holiness of matter and of time."

Nussbaum) are lovely introductions to prayer at evening and morning for "ordinary" people. For those who wish to do more, *Psalms for Morning and Evening Prayer* and, indeed, the whole *Psalter,* are fine summer books with which to spend reflective time. All are available from LTP.

SUMMER READING AND FALL STUDY

A useful ministry is to assemble a lending library stocked with scripture commentary and liturgical materials. Next year's lectionary evangelist is Luke. Here are some helpful resources.

Brown, Raymond E. *Introduction to the New Testament.* Sections on Luke and Acts. New York: Doubleday, 1997.

_____. *Christ in the Gospels of Ordinary Time.* Collegeville: The Liturgical Press, 1998.

Danker, Frederick W. *Luke.* Proclamation Commentaries. Second Edition, Revised and Enlarged. Minneapolis: Fortress, 1987.

Green, Joel B. *The Gospel of Luke.* The New International Commentary on the New Testament. Grand Rapids: Eerdmans, 1997.

Powell, Mark Allan. *What Are They Saying About Luke?* New York/Mahwah: Paulist Press, 1989.

_____. *What Are They Saying About Acts?* New York/Mahwah: Paulist Press, 1991.

Tiede, David L. *Luke.* Augsburg Commentary on the New Testament. Minneapolis: Augsburg, 1988.

At Home

MORNING AND EVENING PRAYER

ORDINARY Time frequently provides a bit more leisure for quiet prayer and even family prayer in common. Parishes would do a great service by making inexpensive resources available for summer reading and prayer. *I Will Lie Down This Night* and *I Will Arise This Day* (both are by Melissa Musick

CALENDAR

June

MON 12 — Weekday (Tenth Week in Ordinary Time)
#359 (LMC, #193–227) green

Lectionary

The Tenth Week in Ordinary Time marks a natural break in the arrangement of readings, the beginning of a new cycle of passages in both the first reading and the gospel.

■ FIRST READING: The tenth through the twentieth weeks of the Year II weekday lectionary are devoted to the Hebrew Bible. Now the lectionary turns to 1 and 2 Kings. This three-week cycle recounts the ministry of Elijah and his confrontation with Ahab, Jezebel and the priests of Baal, the succession of Elisha, the demise of Judah and, finally, the Babylonian conquest of Jerusalem. Beginning with the Thirteenth Week in Ordinary Time, the weekday lectionary presents selections from Amos, Hosea, Micah, Isaiah, Jeremiah, Nahum, Habakkuk and finally Ezekiel.

Today's first reading initiates a two-week "Elijah cycle" of readings, beginning with the prophet's announcement of a drought from which his word alone will bring relief. As God provided for his chosen people Israel in the wilderness, so now God provides food and drink for his chosen prophet.

■ GOSPEL: With the Tenth Week in Ordinary Time, the Gospel of Matthew begins. Beginning this year on Monday of the Twenty-second Week in Ordinary Time, the gospel passages are taken from Luke.

The selections from Matthew's gospel begin today with the Beatitudes. A standard approach structures the Gospel of Matthew around the five "great sermons" into which the evangelist has organized the teachings of Jesus. See Mark Allan Powell's *God with Us: A Pastoral Theology of Matthew's Gospel* (Minneapolis: Fortress, 1995) for an updated approach to Matthew. Powell suggests that the Beatitudes may be best viewed as two stanzas of four verses each. The first four present the reality of life apart from the reign of God: a spirit-deep poverty that has no hope and a sorrow that sees no cause for joy, the crushing of the meek and no righteousness for the lowly. The second four describe the reversal of such misfortune when the reign of God prevails. The "children of God" show God's own mercy to those described in the first four beatitudes. Single-heartedly they work for peace and are willing to suffer persecution in witness to God's reign. As the example of Jesus shows, to live the second four beatitudes is to count oneself among those described in the first four.

Sacramentary

The atmosphere of the liturgy should subtly signal the church's passage from Easter's high festivity to the gentler pace of Ordinary Time. Key to this spirit are unadorned ritual, simple acclamations, brief forms of greeting and invitation, intercessory and eucharistic prayer. Simplicity makes clear for the assembly the Roman liturgy's basic shape: word, silence, song; taking, blessing, breaking, sharing.

TUE 13 — Anthony of Padua, presbyter, religious, doctor of the church
#360 (LMC, #193–227) green
MEMORIAL

The pagan widow of Zerephath responds in faith and charity to Elijah's need and is duly rewarded. In Luke's version of the inaugural sermon at Nazareth, Jesus mentioned her as an example of God's all-embracing love and the possibility of goodness flowering in unexpected places and people.

Every Italian-American child learned early to call on Anthony (+ 1231) for help when things were lost. Perhaps he got that reputation by losing his first vocation in an Augustinian classroom, then finding his true vocation on the road with the Franciscans.

WED 14 — Weekday
#361 (LMC, #193–227) green

The long first reading presents Elijah's contest against the priests of Baal on Mount Carmel. The otherwise stern prophet derides the silent Baal: "Better cry louder, because he is a god, after all, and may be meditating or taking a nap!" But there was nothing funny about the stakes: idolatry or faith in the living God. Jesus presents his teaching as in continuity with Israel's law and prophets.

THU 15 — Weekday
#362 (LMC, #193–227) green

Perseverance and the willingness to suffer for the truth bear fruit in Elijah's prayer. As all who pray can testify, an answer can take time. On his seventh time looking, Elijah's servant sees the tiniest cloud, but then comes the mightiest rain! Jesus challenges us to renounce anger, insult and harsh language.

JUNE

FRI 16 #363 (LMC, #193–227) green
Weekday

The presence of the Lord is revealed to Elijah in what the NAB calls "a tiny whispering sound," which the NRSV translates as "a sound of sheer silence." Here is the God who always comes looking for us: "Adam, where are you?" and "While he was still a long way off, his father caught sight of him and ran out to greet him." Jesus lays down the law: "Judge not, lest you be judged."

SAT 17 #364 (LMC, #193–227) green
Weekday

Blessed Virgin Mary, optional memorial/white. • Continuity in the community: Elijah anoints Elisha, and the ministry of prophetic preaching continues. Jesus bids his disciples to be simple and straightforward. Transparent honesty and steadfast witness — these are the vocation of all the baptized.

If the Saturday memorial of Mary is observed, consider choosing from the lenten section of the *Collection of Masses of the Blessed Virgin Mary,* Mass #10, Mary, the Disciple of the Lord. The collect asks that God's saving word "speak to us in our daily lives and bring forth a rich harvest of holiness," and the prayer after communion asks that "we may be true disciples of Christ, eagerly hearing his words and putting them into practice."

☼ 18 #165 (LMC, #158) white
The Most Holy Trinity
SOLEMNITY

ORIENTATION

The Solemnity of the Most Holy Trinity came to be observed throughout the Western church during the fourteenth century. Some liturgists have labeled today's solemnity and others like it "idea" feasts or *credenda,* that is, observances of theological concepts. Other "idea" feasts are next Sunday's solemnity of the Body and Blood of Christ (originally Corpus Christi), the Sacred Heart of Jesus, the Immaculate Heart of Mary, the Holy Family and Christ the King. These observances are unlike more ancient feasts that celebrate events from salvation history or moments in the lives of Christ or Mary, feasts that could be said to form the liturgical year's *agenda.* Christmas, Epiphany and the Baptism of the Lord are examples of these, along with the Presentation, Transfiguration, Holy Week, the Triduum, Ascension and Pentecost.

Vatican II's liturgical reform enhanced the observance of these "idea" feasts immeasurably. The lectionary provides a rich array of readings that anchors doctrine and theology in a scriptural context. The Mass prayers and prefaces and the texts of the Liturgy of the Hours draw not only on scripture but on the vast corpus of patristic writing and preaching. Some devotional observances associated with these "idea" feasts have been renewed as well, and their piety transformed to communal and scriptural.

Festivity and Simplicity

It is Ordinary Time and should look and sound and feel that way. The observances of Holy Trinity and of the Body and Blood of Christ are "Solemnities of the Lord during Ordinary Time." Decorations, musical selections and ritual patterns should blend the festivity of a solemnity with the simplicity of Ordinary Time. Avoid giving the impression that this Sunday and next are a two-week extension of Eastertime. This may suggest omitting the sprinkling and incensations that were part of the Eastertime Sundays. The setting of the Gloria should not be the one used in Eastertime, and the gospel acclamation might be a simpler form of the alleluia.

LECTIONARY

In each year, the lectionary selections for Holy Trinity seek to proclaim who God is and to draw us deeper into friendship with God. The Year B motif: The God of love continually gathers a people together and forms that people as God's own. In Deuteronomy (first reading)

JUNE

Moses marvels at God's initiative and intimacy: "Has anything so great as this ever happened or has its like ever been heard of?" Paul's Letter to the Romans (second reading) celebrates the gift of adoption by which we are made "children of God, heirs of God, joint heirs with Christ" and by which we are given the privilege of calling God "Abba." The gospel reading comes from the conclusion of Matthew's gospel. Jesus gives the great commission to gather in a harvest from the nations so that Jesus and the church might form a new community. "Go, make disciples, baptize, teach." The one whom the angel had called Emmanuel, God-with-us, now departs on a note of intimacy, reminding them and us that he is not really leaving: "Remember, I am with you always."

SACRAMENTARY

Begin with the full apostolic greeting of Paul: "The grace of our Lord Jesus Christ, and the love of God, and the fellowship (communion) of the Holy Spirit be with you all." If Penitential Rite C is used, remember that the invocations are all addressed to Christ, and any mention of the other Persons of the Trinity should be conformed to this model. Here is an example that draws its images from the lectionary for today:

> Lord Jesus, you reveal the love of the Father who draws near to us to fashion us into a chosen people: Lord, have mercy.
>
> You send us forth to make disciples of all nations and to teach them your commandments: Christ, have mercy.
>
> You breathe upon your church the Spirit of adoption that makes us God's children and joint heirs with you: Lord, have mercy.

The Preface of the Holy Trinity must be proclaimed or chanted carefully if it is to be understood. Eucharistic Prayer III incorporates the mystery of the Trinity's saving work into its opening lines. Solemn Blessings 9 (Numbers 6:24–26) and 10 (Philippians 4:7) concluding with the trinitarian formula would be appropriate.

MUSIC

Add to the parish's repertoire of Trinity hymns by exploring the many new hymnals for texts that portray the ageless mystery in striking images. Trinitarian hymns can be used throughout Ordinary Time as songs that celebrate the Lord's Day. In GIA's *RitualSong* see Brian Wren's "How wonderful the Three-in-One" (#618) and "Stand up, friends" (#622: "Praise the God who changes places; praise the rabbi; praise the Breath of Love"). *With One Voice* from the Lutheran church provides "Creating God, your fingers trace" (#757) and, "Mothering God, you gave me birth" (#769), based on the revelations of Julian of Norwich. Ruth Duck's text, "Womb of Life, and Source of Being" in *The New Century Hymnal* (#274) presents the Trinity's life as a model for the life of the community. The Episcopal church's new supplement *Wonder, Love and Praise* provides two striking texts: "O threefold God of tender unity" (#743) and "God the sculptor of the mountains" (#747). Whether using standard or contemporary Trinitarian hymns, be sure not to omit the Holy Spirit by omitting the final verses.

■ BLESSING OF MARRIED COUPLES: *Book of Blessings*, chapter 1, III. Today's feast and doctrine celebrate God as a God of relationships. Today may be more appropriate for this blessing than Valentine's Day (sometimes in Lent) or the feast of the Holy Family (potentially painful at that time of year for families in difficulty).

MON 19 — Weekday (Eleventh Week in Ordinary Time)
#365 (LMC, #193–227) green

Romuald, abbot, optional memorial/white. ▪ The second week of the "Elijah cycle" of readings begins today. Elijah gives us a lesson in the justice God desires before going out in a blaze of glory. The readings juxtapose Ahab's and Jezebel's treachery with Jesus' command to "turn the other cheek." This might lead to an interesting homiletic reflection on injustice and the gospel response to it, as today and tomorrow Jesus outlines the self-sacrificing love that is the hallmark of his kingdom.

After witnessing a murder in his family, Romuald (+ 1027) turned to a life of strict solitude. Later, he founded the Camaldolese Order, in which one may live the solitary life of a hermit or a monastic community life according to the Rule of Benedict.

TUE 20 — Weekday
#366 (LMC, #193–227) green

The author of 1 Kings portrays evil Ahab's repentance, which causes even God to marvel! Practicing the love Jesus outlines will make his disciples "perfect as your heavenly Father is perfect." While the idea of being like God usually conjures up images of omnipotence and omniscience, Jesus teaches that being like God means loving the lovable and unlovable, the deserving and the least deserving.

WED 21
#367 (LMC, #193–227) white
Aloysius Gonzaga, religious
MEMORIAL

Elisha takes up the mantle of Elijah, whose prophetic spirit will fill the younger prophet's words and deeds from then on. At baptism we "put on" the Lord Jesus Christ, whose spirit should lead us to fulfill the counsel he proposes in today's gospel: unobtrusive piety, unremarked-upon charity, unobserved prayer.

Aloysius entered the Jesuit order against the wishes of his wealthy family. He demonstrated the courage of his convictions not only in choosing his way of life but in volunteering for a dangerous ministry. At the age of 23, Aloysius died of the plague, which he had contracted while caring for its victims (+ 1591). Pray today for those who devote themselves to the victims of modern-day plagues.

THU 22
#368 (LMC, #193–227) green
Weekday

Paulinus of Nola, bishop/white; John Fisher, bishop and martyr, and Thomas More, married man, martyr/red; optional memorials.
▪ In several places the weekday lectionary concludes its stories of a particular character from the Hebrew Bible by turning to the Book of Sirach for a canticle of praise in honor of that person. Today's passage summarizes Elijah's place in salvation history. From the lips of Jesus comes the model of perfect prayer, with the warning that without forgiveness of others, no prayer will be acceptable to the Father.

Two bishops and two married men are among the three saints who may be commemorated today. Paulinus (+ 431) and his wife gave their wealth to the poor, and he was subsequently elected bishop. John Fisher (+ 1535) stood alone among the bishops of England in his opposition to Henry VIII's divorce and repudiation of papal supremacy. In his youth, Thomas More (+ 1535) tried his vocation with the Carthusians, but married, was widowed and remarried, spending his life as a devoted husband and loving father of four. From all accounts the More home was a lively household — complete with a paid jester and a pet monkey! More joined Fisher in opposing Henry. Before his execution on the grounds of high treason, he who had once been Speaker of the House of Commons and respected Lord Chancellor, proclaimed himself "the King's good servant — but God's first." Today would be a good day to pray for courage and integrity for our ecclesiastical and political leaders.

FRI 23
#369 (LMC, #193–227) green
Weekday

Treason and treachery end with the death of the wicked Queen Athaliah, as the new king, Joash, works to renew the covenant with the Lord. The reform is short-lived, as tomorrow's first reading (superseded by the solemnity) demonstrates. Homilists may wish to summarize tomorrow's first reading. Because tomorrow's solemnity replaces the weekday lectionary, combine today's gospel text with tomorrow's passage: Both are a call to seek first the kingdom.

SAT 24
day: #587 vigil: #586 (LMC, #316) white
The Birth of John the Baptist
SOLEMNITY

ORIENTATION

This solemnity has been celebrated on this day since the fourth century. For most saints we celebrate their *dies natalis,* their heavenly birthday, that is, the day of their death. For only three persons does the calendar mark the date of birth into this life: the Lord Jesus, his mother Mary and the forerunner. The conceptions of these three are noted as well: Jesus on March 25, Mary on December 8 and John the Baptist on September 24, although the Western church no longer keeps this feast. Saint Augustine (+ 430) noted that the summer solstice coincides with today's feast. The daylight hours are as long as they ever get (in the Northern Hemisphere), and after today they begin to decrease. Augustine related this natural phenomenon to John's prophecy: "Christ must increase; I must decrease" (John 3:30).

Vigil Celebration

Today is a non-obligatory solemnity for which a vigil Mass formulary is provided. This testifies to the church's sense of the day's importance. Summer brings us

JUNE

two other vigils: Peter and Paul next week and Mary's Assumption in August. A gathering on the night of the 23rd for prayer and festivity would be a good way to honor John. Many ethnic groups have an evening cookout with bonfires or even fireworks to honor this shining light who blazed the way for the Messiah.

LECTIONARY

If either the vigil or day Mass is omitted, consider proclaiming both gospel passages at the Mass that is celebrated, so that the whole story can be heard.

SACRAMENTARY

If only one Mass is celebrated, use the collects for the Mass during the day, since they are the richer texts. The preface for John the Baptist is a twice-yearly text that might provide homilists with good material. Those who prepare the bulletin might print that preface with the schedule for today's worship and festivity.

Subtly connect this solemnity to Christmas by using the Christmas white vestments. If incense is used, bring out the Christmas scent. Sing the Canticle of Zechariah (Benedictus). The finest hymn for today is John Mason Neale's translation of an eighth-century poem by Venerable Bede: "The great forerunner of the morn," in both *Worship* and the Episcopal *Hymnal 1982*. Ralph Wright has provided a translation of a scripturally inspired Latin poem in the hymn "O Prophet John, O man of God," in GIA's *Hymnal for the Hours*.

25 The Body and Blood of Christ
#168 (LMC, #161)   white
SOLEMNITY

ORIENTATION

Known as Corpus Christi before the calendar reform of Vatican II, today's solemnity was first observed in several dioceses of Belgium before being extended to the universal church in 1264. It was originally kept on the Thursday after Trinity Sunday as a link to the Holy Thursday celebration, because, as it was said, the church's joy at the gift of the eucharist was overshadowed on Holy Thursday by the sorrow of Good Friday. The 1969 calendar reform combined the old observances of Corpus Christi and the Precious Blood (formerly July 1) into one solemnity that celebrates the mystery of the Lord's enduring presence in our midst through the gift of his body and blood given in the eucharistic liturgy. The solemnity is moved to Sunday in places where it is not a holy day of obligation. Today's solemnity also provides an opportunity for each community to examine its implementation of the General Instruction's directives on the nature of the bread used for the eucharist (#283) and the fullness of the eucharistic signs, that is, communion offered to all under both species at every liturgy (#240).

LECTIONARY

The covenant between God and the people of God is the unifying motif of the Year B lectionary readings. The Exodus reading shows Moses proclaiming God's word and committing it to writing in "the book of the covenant." Moses then seals the people's assent to the word by "the blood of the covenant." The Letter to the Hebrews portrays Christ as our high priest who enters the holy place "with his own blood" to mediate the new covenant that frees its participants from death. The account of the Last Supper from the Gospel of Mark has an eschatological emphasis. After giving his disciples the cup of "my blood of the covenant" to share, he tells them that he will "never again drink of the fruit of the vine until that day when I drink it new in the kingdom of God." Homilists will want to consult the latest bible dictionaries and commentaries (for instance, Raymond Brown's *Death of the Messiah*) for insights into the biblical understanding of blood and the shedding of blood in relation to covenant and salvation.

SACRAMENTARY

The Preface of the Eucharist II (P-48) stresses the effects of the eucharist in our lives and seems to be the preface of choice on this day (Eucharist I is oriented more toward Holy Thursday). Eucharistic Prayer I is rich in imagery that unites the church's earthly eucharist with the sacrifices gone before and with the eschatological liturgy of heaven. Eucharistic Prayer III is also a good choice today.

JUNE

MUSIC

Time-honored eucharistic hymns from the Latin tradition include these: "Pange lingua" ("Tantum ergo"), "Adoro te," "O salutaris." For a contemporary text that echoes the themes of manna and living bread, see GIA's *Ritual Song* (#845) for Sylvia G. Dunstan's "All who hunger, gather gladly." A hymn that captures Paul's eucharistic theology is Delores Dufner's "O wheat whose crushing was for bread" in the Episcopal church's *Wonder, Love and Praise* (#760). See the *New Century Hymnal* (#343) for Ruth Duck's "Jesus took the bread." Other additions to the church's treasury of eucharistic hymns include Omer Westendorf"s "Gift of finest wheat"; Jerry Brubaker's "O blessed Savior" (World Library); Robert Hutmacher's "Love is his word" (*Worship*, #599); J. Michael Joncas' "Song of the Lord's Supper" *(Gather)*; Christopher Walker's "There is something holy here" (OCP). Any of these hymns could be used throughout Ordinary Time, and refrains learned for this feast may be sung as communion processionals throughout the year.

The sequence hymn "Lauda Sion" should be sung by all, or by the assembly in alternation with the choir. Sections of it, in an English translation set to the original chant, are in the Episcopal *Hymnal 1982* (#320). The full text in a fine new translation is in the Canadian *Catholic Book of Worship III* (#693). This version will fit any "Tantum ergo" melody. Be careful of the translation in the new United States' lectionary. The rhythm can be tricky.

Communion under Both Species

Over twenty years ago (1978) Rome approved the request of the United States' bishops to permit communion under both species on Sundays and holy days as well as on weekdays. This should be the parish's standard eucharistic practice; this should certainly be done today.

Eucharistic Procession

See the order in *Holy Communion and Worship of the Eucharist outside Mass* (#101–108), including a form for solemn evening prayer on this day, and helpful notes in the *Ceremonial of Bishops* (#387–394).

Concluding Rites

If there is no procession, a solemn blessing may be given. Since there is no special text for this feast, signal the return to Ordinary Time by closing with the blessing that will be used throughout the next weeks.

MON 26 — Weekday (Twelfth Week in Ordinary Time)
#371 (LMC, #193–227) green

The first readings of the Twelfth Week in Ordinary Time begin with God's anger and with the tribe of Judah remaining faithful. Jesus commands us to refrain from judgment that we might be spared judgment.

TUE 27 — Weekday
#372 (LMC, #193–227) green

Cyril of Alexandria, bishop and doctor of the church, optional memorial/white. ▪ In response to earnest prayer, the Lord God manifests his faithfulness. Numbers count for nothing in God's plan; with a faithful remnant God can work wonders! In offering us the Golden Rule, Jesus counsels us not to be amazed if support seems thin.

Cyril (+ 444) was a rough and ready champion of the faith. In affirming Mary as Mother of God, he and the church were saying something profound about both Jesus and us. In Jesus we meet God-in-our-flesh. In Mary we see God's intimate bond with us.

WED 28 — Irenaeus, bishop and martyr
#373 (LMC, #193–227) red
MEMORIAL

The first reading recounts a powerful liturgy of the word. "I have found the book of the law in the house of the Lord!" The high priest Hilkiah rejoices at his find, but the king tears his garments in sorrow at the people's failure to uphold the covenant. The gospel passage ends with Jesus' criterion for authenticity, one we can paraphrase: "By *our* fruits others will know *us*."

The name Irenaeus (+ c. 200) comes from the Greek word for "peace." Today's saint is remembered for his theological writings on the incarnation, and for incarnating in his own ministry the gospel of peace. He worked tirelessly for reconciliation in the church of his age.

JUNE

THU 29 — Peter and Paul, apostles
SOLEMNITY

day: #591 vigil: #590 (LMC, #591) red

ORIENTATION

The church has set this day aside since the middle of the third century to honor the witness of the patrons of the Roman church, Peter and Paul, put to death during the persecution under Nero (64–67). Peter and Paul are always linked in liturgy, art and preaching. It is as if the church finds encouragement in this partnership of two great apostles: a relationship that in Christ formed the foundation of a worldwide communion. Traditionally, Peter represents the institutional church; Paul, the Spirit-inspired, charismatic side.

LECTIONARY

If only one Mass is celebrated for this solemnity, consider using the vigil's second reading from Galatians. Since both Mass formularies focus on Peter in the first and gospel readings, using the Galatians text will permit Paul to say something about his conversion and relationship to the church authorities. This would set the stage for a fruitful homiletic reflection on the complementary gifts that these two giants of faith brought to the early church.

SACRAMENTARY

This day was once marked by the celebration of three different liturgies: Peter was remembered in his basilica on the Vatican hill, Paul at his tomb on the road to Ostia, then everyone processed to a catacomb where the remains of both were concealed during persecution. Current liturgical books provide for one celebration on the solemnity itself and a vigil the night before.

The proper preface brings out the unity-in-diversity motif that these apostles portray. Eucharistic Prayer I (the Roman Canon) would be the logical choice. The solemn blessing printed at the day Mass is also appropriate for a vigil Mass and for the end of Evening Prayer. The hymn "By all your saints still striving" has a verse for Peter and Paul. "Two noble saints," in *Worship,* and "O Light of Lights" in *Hymnal for the Hours* are translations of Latin hymns for this feast.

FRI 30 — The Sacred Heart of Jesus
SOLEMNITY

#171 (LMC, #164) white

ORIENTATION

Devotion to the Sacred Heart became popular in the seventeenth century because of Margaret Mary Alacoque (October 16). A cloistered nun burdened with intense physical and emotional suffering, she described visions of Christ whose love though unrequited burned unceasingly: "Behold the heart that has loved people so, yet is loved so little in return." The devotion celebrates the love of God manifested in the heart of Jesus.

LECTIONARY

The Year B readings personalize the concepts of God's providence and compassion. Through Hosea, the "prophet of God's tenderness," God proclaims: "My compassion grows warm and tender. I will not execute my fierce anger." The Letter to the Ephesians celebrates the revelation of "the mystery hidden for ages," namely, "the boundless riches of Christ . . . the love of Christ that surpasses knowledge." The gospel for the solemnity is taken not from Mark but from John:

JULY

"One of the soldiers pierced his side with a spear, and at once blood and water came out." According to the patristic tradition, this represented God's creation of a new Eve. As the new Adam, Jesus, sleeps on the cross in death, blood and water come forth from his side, representing baptism and the eucharist, the two sacraments by which the new Eve, the church, is formed (see John Chrysostom, Good Friday, the Office of Readings). The Sacred Heart preface also draws on this imagery. Authentic devotion moves us from an individual experience of communion with God in Christ toward a deeper communion with one another in loving service. The Year B readings provide abundant material for homiletic reflections on life in the community and beyond it, our call to evangelize by reaching out as instruments of God's own unconditional and self-sacrificing love.

SACRAMENTARY

The preface for today is P-45. The liturgy points us toward God's initiative of love for us in Christ. Eucharistic Prayer III is standard for such solemnities, but the new Eucharistic Prayer for Masses for Various Needs and Occasions. Form D, Jesus, the Compassion of God, contains the beautiful lines:

> Open our eyes to the needs of all; inspire us with words and deeds to comfort those who labor and are burdened; keep our service of others faithful to the example and command of Christ. Let your church be a living witness to truth and freedom, to justice and peace, that all people may be lifted up by the hope of a world made new.

MUSIC

English-language Sacred Heart hymns have been notoriously awful, reflecting the sentimental piety of the late Victorian period. Latin texts, by contrast, are scriptural, relating the heart of Christ to the Ark of the Covenant containing the tablet of the new covenant of love. Current hymnals guide us to good choices, including "All you who seek a comfort sure" and "I heard the voice of Jesus say."

PRAYER OUTSIDE MASS

The beautiful scriptural Litany of the Sacred Heart in *Catholic Household Blessings and Prayers* (page 339) deserves to reenter our devotional prayer, perhaps as part of a period of prayer before the blessed sacrament or before the parish's image of the Sacred Heart.

July

SAT #573 (LMC, #193–227) white
The Immaculate Heart of Mary
MEMORIAL

Today's memorial is a partner to yesterday's solemnity of the Sacred Heart. The first reading is to be taken from the weekday lectionary. Lamentations makes a rare appearance. Christian piety has often applied this text to Mary's sorrows at the suffering of her Son: "O daughter Jerusalem! O virgin daughter Zion! Vast as the sea is your ruin; who can heal you?" The gospel is from the proper of saints, Luke's story of the finding of young Jesus in the Temple. Mary and Joseph share an experience common to many parents of twelve-year-olds: "They did not understand what he said."

There are proper texts in the sacramentary at the end of the May calendar for the observance of the Immaculate Heart, but see the *Collection of Masses of Blessed Virgin Mary*, #28, for a fuller formulary, complete with a proper preface, and far superior to the sacramentary texts.

2 #98 (LMC, #93) green
Thirteenth Sunday in Ordinary Time

SUMMER I: SUNDAYS 10–14

This year's liturgical calendar has only two post-Pentecost Ordinary Sundays. Thoughtful planning and preaching will make sense of the whole block.

First, refer to the detailed outline in the Lectionary Overview. Bracketing this block of Sundays are stories of misunderstanding and rejection. The Tenth Sunday's gospel begins with Jesus' family thinking he is insane and the religious authorities thinking him possessed. Next Sunday closes this block of Ordinary Time with the more of the same kind of rejection.

Between the stories of rejection were the Ordinary Sundays whose readings were superseded by Holy Trinity and the Body and Blood of Christ. The gospels of those Sundays present images as beautiful as early summer. Phenomenal growth is virtually unobservable while it is taking place. Jesus calms the storm and saves the ship. Faith when nothing seems to be happening and trust when all seems to be lost provide the background for this week's proclamation of the word.

LECTIONARY

"Righteousness is immortal" (NRSV) or "Justice is undying" (NAB): whichever translation you use, the point of today's first reading is in this line. Our God is the God of life. God's creation is wholesome. The person of faith believes this and lives the righteousness commanded by God. Wisdom sounds like the Gospel of John: to live God's righteousness in this mortal life is to begin living even now the immortal life for which we were made. "For God created us for incorruption, and made us in the image of his own eternity" (the NRSV is much clearer here than the NAB).

The gospel (in the longer version) presents two stories of healing. This exemplifies the "Markan sandwich" or intercalation. By telling a story within a story, Mark reinforces his message; in this case, several points. First, Jesus does not perform miracles in order to compel faith; rather, faith precedes healing in Mark's gospel. In the case of the woman with the hemorrhage, Jesus does not even consciously perform the healing. It is only after power goes out from him that he becomes aware that something has happened. Jesus makes it clear that the initiative for this healing had come from the woman's faith and that her healing is deeper than doctors could see: "Your faith has saved you." The passage concludes with a return to Jairus' daughter, who by now has died. Jesus encourages Jairus: "Do not be afraid; just have faith." Despite the crowd that has gathered to mourn the child's death, Jesus takes her by the hand and, in Aramaic (Mark quotes Jesus in Aramaic four times), bids the child "arise."

SACRAMENTARY

Let simplicity reign. The ancient Christian greeting, spoken with deliberation and reverent sincerity, should begin each liturgy of Ordinary Time: "The Lord be with you." For the penitential rite, establish one set of invocations for each block of Sundays, and let their words echo the gospels of that block. A suggestion for this year's first block of Summer/Fall Ordinary Time:

> Lord Jesus, divine physician, you bid us fear not but only have faith: Lord, have mercy.
>
> Christ Jesus, Lord of life, you grasp us by the hand and raise us up: Christ, have mercy.
>
> Lord Jesus, prophet sent from God, you impart wisdom to all who welcome you in faith: Lord, have mercy.

The general intercessions should be simple and direct. Some could be repeated throughout a block of Sundays whose scriptures are thematically similar, with one intercession each week changing to reflect the day's readings and current needs. The preparation of the gifts ought to be done simply and wordlessly, perhaps with instrumental music. Eucharistic Prayers II or IV, each with its own preface, would be appropriate. The preface Sundays in Ordinary Time III relates to the gospels in celebrating God's power and saving plan. The eucharistic prayer for Masses for Various Needs and Occasions, Form IV, Jesus, the Compassion of God, speaks of Jesus' "compassion for the poor and powerless, the sick and the sinner."

MUSIC

In singing the responsorial psalm, some parishes use the proper psalm each week, even when the assembly does not have the full text before them. Most newer antiphons are simple and melodic, easily repeated by an assembly after one instrumental playing and one sing-through by the cantor. Common psalms are always an option. See the lectionary, #175. Choose one common psalm for each block of Ordinary Time Sundays. In this block, Psalm 63 or 23, though not an official common psalm, is a versatile favorite.

Gospel acclamations should be simple and singable; one version can serve throughout the block of Sundays. Perhaps the cantor's verse might be chosen week by week to match the gospel. The same principle applies to the eucharistic prayer acclamations. Some parishes use one that is easily sung a cappella in case parish musicians take a break in the summer. For the communion processional, one or two refrain-style pieces might suffice. For general hymnody in this block of Sundays, focus on songs of discipleship and faith, healing and service.

JULY

MON 3
#593 (LMC, #193–227) red
Thomas, apostle
FEAST

The gospel records Jesus' invitation to Thomas, "Put your finger here and see. . . . Reach out your hand, and put it in my side," but there is no record of Thomas taking Jesus up on the offer. The only recorded response of Thomas is his act of faith: "My Lord and my God." Augustine says, we should be grateful to Thomas for the beatitude pronounced by Jesus on all generations of disciples: "Blessed are those who have not seen and yet have come to believe." Pray today for the peoples of India, whom Thomas is said to have evangelized, and for all for whom the act of faith is a challenge.

TUE 4
#378 (LMC, #193–227) green
Weekday

Elizabeth of Portugal, married woman, queen, religious, optional memorial/white; U.S.A.: Independence Day, civil observance.

LECTIONARY

Yesterday's first reading was superseded by the proper readings for the feast of Thomas. That selection from Amos presented a clear call to justice. It might be a perfect first reading for today's Independence Day liturgy! Planners may wish to skip the reading prescribed for today in the weekday lectionary and use Monday's instead, or combine the two.

In the gospel, Jesus at first sleeps through what the disciples fear is mortal danger. Jesus teaches them, and us, to pray not in panic but with faith. For Independence Day, Appendix X, Mass 6, lists optional scripture texts, all focused on peace.

SACRAMENTARY

There are two sets of liturgical texts in the 1985 edition of the U.S. sacramentary: one in July and a new set in appendix X, Mass 6. Note also two Prefaces for Independence Day and other Civic Observances, both dated by their exclusive language. Look for a new set of prayers in the revised sacramentary. Until that comes out, consider Eucharistic Prayer for Reconciliation II or the new Eucharistic Prayer for Various Needs and Occasions, especially form A (The Church on the Way to Unity) or D (Jesus, the Compassion of God).

National Songs

Some feel there is no place in the liturgy for national "hymns," others feel there are no boundaries. Catholic instinct is always to choose the middle ground on these issues: Choose "citizenship" music carefully. The verses of "America the Beautiful" are worth considering: "God mend thine every flaw,/confirm thy soul in self-control,/thy liberty in law," and "May God thy gold refine/till all success be nobleness/and every gain divine." A comprehensive selection appears in the "justice and peace" and "citizenship" sections of the United Church of Christ's *New Century Hymnal*.

Prayer at Home or at Civic Gatherings

See *Catholic Household Blessings and Prayers* (page 199) and *Book of Blessings* (#1965).

WED 5
#379 (LMC, #193–227) green
Weekday

Anthony Mary Zaccaria, priest, optional memorial/white. ▪ God despises the liturgies of the unjust, no matter how precise the ritual, how beautiful the music or how precious the offering. This is the word of the prophet Amos. The expulsion of demons inspires the neighborhood to invite Jesus to leave. Over the centuries, preaching the just word has often inspired hostility toward the church.

Just before the Reformation began in Europe, Anthony Zaccaria (+ 1539) left his medical practice and was ordained to the priesthood. Anthony took Saint Paul as his model in evangelization, and the eucharist and crucifixion as the focus of his preaching. For the renewal of the church in Milan, he gathered a group of priests who lived in community as pastoral servants of the people (the Barnabites). Before his death at age 37, he founded a similar community of women religious.

THU 6
#380 (LMC, #193–227) green
Weekday

Maria Goretti, virgin, martyr, optional memorial/red. ▪ Today Amos is invited to leave Bethel. It is the king's sanctuary, after all. Amos he gives the priest Amaziah his vocation story: He has been sent. Do we reflect on the prophetic anointing we received in baptism and confirmation?

JULY

Since her canonization, at which her elderly mother was present, Maria Goretti (+ 1902) has been presented as a model of steadfast chastity and of forgiveness because of her deathbed pardon of the man who had attacked her. At the age of eleven, just a few weeks after her first communion, she was stabbed to death during an attempted rape. She could serve as a challenge to violence and crime against children.

FRI 7 — #381 (LMC, #193–227) green
Weekday

Profit-making uninhibited by honest weights and measures, guaranteed by price fixing! This isn't a contemporary report, but an indictment almost 2,600 years old. The punishment God devises for that corrupt society is interesting: a famine over all the land; not for food, but for the word of the Lord. "But they shall not find it!" says the Lord. In the gospel, Jesus calls a civil servant away from a lucrative career into the inner circle of the Twelve. Matthew's job made him, if not a collaborator, at least a figure of scorn. The table fellowship at Matthew's house included tax collectors and sinners. Does our eucharistic table reflect the diversity and inclusivity of Matthew's table?

SAT 8 — #382 (LMC, #193–227) green
Weekday

Blessed Virgin Mary, optional memorial / white. • The selections from Amos end with comfort for the community, a Messianic promise, eschatological hope. Jesus works in continuity with the law and the prophets, but there is clearly something new going on — witness yesterday's table fellowship with tax collectors and sinners.

If the Saturday memorial of Mary is celebrated, consider Mass #20, Holy Mary, the New Eve from the *Collection of Masses of the Virgin Mary*. The texts resonate with Amos and Jesus in celebrating the life we have been called to live in obedience to God's covenant with us.

9 — #101 (LMC, #96) green
Fourteenth Sunday in Ordinary Time

The first block of Ordinary Sundays comes to a close with the rejection of Jesus, the prophet without honor in his hometown. We are told that the townspeople were "astounded," and "they took offense at him," and "Jesus could do no deed of power there." Mark's assertion that Jesus was powerless in the face of such disbelief may jar us. But remember last week's healing stories. Faith precedes healing, and it is the faith of the petitioner that saves, with Jesus acting as the instrument of God's power on behalf of someone who already believes. Joined to the Ezekiel reading, the message for the community today is challenging and comforting. We have been chosen and sent, entrusted with speaking God's word to a sometimes rebellious audience, and we need to be about our mission of evangelization. On the other hand, responsibility is placed also on those who hear the message. Theirs is the sovereign freedom to accept the word or reject it.

MON 10 — #383 (LMC, #193–227) green
Weekday

Comfort and challenge: a week of Hosea. These passages present the best in Israel's prophetic tradition: stern words, sure promise; wonderful material for homiletic reflection and meditation. Today Hosea gives us a beautiful image: The Lord "lures Israel into the desert to speak tenderly as in the days of youth's first love." In the gospel, two healings take place; the effective agent in both cases is faith.

TUE 11 — #384 (LMC, #193–227) white
Benedict, abbot, religious founder
MEMORIAL

"They sow the wind — and reap the whirlwind!" What a magnificent passage today's Hosea selection is. In Jesus, the God who punishes sin walks among us, full of compassion, healing and harvesting.

As a young man, Benedict (+ c. 547) at first fled the decadence of Rome to seek the Lord in solitude. But God used him to transform the society he had left by forming a whole new system of relationships. Benedict's solitude flowered into a communal life, Benedictine life, that still attracts many and to which the church owes much of its recent liturgical reform. Benedict's charism flourishes also among Benedictine lay oblates, women and men who live in the world, keeping Benedict's motto as their own, "pray and work," and offering the church's Liturgy of the Hours.

JULY

WED 12 #385 (LMC, #193–227) green
Weekday

In Hosea, yesterday's message comes back even more intensely. God promises the result: "Sow for yourselves righteousness; reap steadfast love." Jesus' choice of the Twelve carries foreboding: "and Judas Iscariot, who betrayed him."

THU 13 #386 (LMC, #193–227) green
Weekday

Henry, ruler, optional memorial / white. ▪ Today's first reading presents some of the most tender words in the Bible: God as a patient mother, a loving father, parents teaching their children to walk, lifting their infants to their cheeks. Infinite kindness mediated through human emotions. Jesus' instructions to his disciples are appropriate for us: What you have as a gift, give as a gift; and a blessing of peace upon all whom we meet.

Today's saint was a married man and a king. Henry (+ 1024) lived the scriptural messages of compassion and integrity, bringing joy to his people and throughout the church.

FRI 14 #387 (LMC, #193–227) white
Blessed Kateri Tekakwitha, virgin
MEMORIAL

In response to sincere prayer, God heals and loves, and summer seems to blossom in Hosea's text. Hosea adds: "Those who are wise understand; those who are discerning know." Not all are wise, Jesus warns us, painting a scene of division in political systems, religious institutions and even the family.

Blessed Kateri, the "Lily of the Mohawks," (+ 1680) was truly one whose powerful witness far transcended the simplicity of her person. A victim of misunderstanding and cultural clash, she stood firm in her faith and serene in her suffering. After her death at 24, the story of her exemplary life spread throughout the Native American missions of the United States and Canada and drew many to embrace the Christian faith.

SAT 15 #388 (LMC, #193–227) white
Bonaventure, bishop, religious and doctor of the church
MEMORIAL

The Saturday lectionary gives us Isaiah's vocation story. Jesus, too, gives a kind of vocation talk, explaining the cost and joy of discipleship.

Franciscan friar Bonaventure (+ 1274) was one of the most profound theologians of his age. When the Pope sent a delegation to bring him his cardinal's hat, Bonaventure was found taking his turn washing dishes. It is said that the papal delegation grew tired of waiting for him and left, hanging the red hat on a branch of a tree outside the friary door. To this day, the seal on the complete works of this theologian carries a tree in whose branches hangs the cardinal's hat, which the saintly Bonaventure wisely considered less important than finishing the dishes.

☀ 16 #104 (LMC, #99) green
Fifteenth Sunday in Ordinary Time

SACRAMENTARY

Simplicity is the motif of these Sundays. "The Lord be with you," spoken by the presider with reverence and the ritual embrace of the community (hands extended, then joined in a graceful gesture), says it all. Fashion the invocations of the penitential rite from the scriptures of this block of Sundays and let this litany be heard for all nine Sundays:

> Lord Jesus, you are moved with compassion for those who seek you: Lord, have mercy.
>
> Christ Jesus, you are the living bread come down from heaven: Christ, have mercy.
>
> Lord Jesus, you alone have the words of everlasting life: Lord, have mercy.

Consider a uniform set of general intercessions throughout this block of Sundays, changing one intercession each week.

The Preface of the Holy Eucharist II would be a fitting text for these Sundays, although the Eucharistic Prayer for Masses for Various Needs and Occasions speaks of God's love gathering us together and Christ repeating for us his gift to the disciples at Emmaus. Its fourth version, "Jesus, the Compassion of God," would resonate with these Sundays' portrayal of the compassionate Christ. If communion under both species is not yet the regular parish practice, these Sundays would be a good time to begin, since Jesus speaks explicitly of eating and drinking.

MUSIC

If the proper psalm for each week is not used, consider the refrain given as the first choice in the lectionary at #175: "Lord, you have the words of everlasting life." This would tie the whole block of Sundays together well. It is available in many settings. This refrain seems to be more appropriately matched to the verses of Psalm 34 (#175, choice 3) than Psalm 19.

JULY

For eucharistic prayer acclamations, see Richard Proulx's "Corpus Christi Mass" (GIA, G-3693), based on the familiar "Adoro Te" melody. This would work well a cappella.

The most likely communion processional is any version of "O Taste and See."

General hymnody in this block of Sundays may be drawn from the large repertoire of eucharistic hymnody. See the notes for the Solemnity of the Body and Blood of Christ (page 182). Check the indices of your hymnals.

MON 17 — #389 (LMC, #193–227) green
Weekday

This week of selections from the prophet Isaiah celebrates the Lord God's sovereignty and calling the people to conversion. Today the prophet reminds us that God does not hear the prayers of those whose hands are drenched in blood, not even the long ones! "Wash yourselves, and make yourselves clean!" says the Lord. What are we to do beyond that? "Even a cup of cold water" will gain a reward, says Jesus, and warns us that discipleship inevitably means division. Today would be a good time to reflect on our charity and patience with those who misunderstand us.

TUE 18 — #390 (LMC, #193–227) green
Weekday

"If you do not stand firm in faith, you shall not stand at all," the Lord tells Isaiah to warn us. Because they are proclaimed in the liturgical assembly, the words of Jesus are addressed to us, not to Jewish cities long ago. Woe to us! If the deeds of power done among us — the word, the eucharist, the healing and compassion of Jesus — were made known to non-believers, would they not change their lives?

WED 19 — #391 (LMC, #193–227) green
Weekday

The prophets urged Israel to develop spiritual wisdom to see the purifying hand of God in the devastation that history sometimes dealt them. Jesus praises his Father for revealing the mysteries of the kingdom not to the worldly-wise but to those with spirit-deep wisdom.

THU 20 — #392 (LMC, #193–227) green
Weekday

After the messages of devastation, Isaiah offers hope: "When your judgments are in the earth, the world's inhabitants learn justice." Not in thunder and lightning, but from the gentle heart of Jesus, God reveals the nature of the burden God imposes. The image of the farm animal's yoke is that of two creatures pulling the load side by side in partnership. The Lord who would one day bear the cross on his own shoulders promises us a yoke that is easy, a burden that is light.

FRI 21 — #393 (LMC, #193–227) green
Weekday

Lawrence of Brindisi, presbyter, religious, doctor of the church, optional memorial/white. • Isaiah shows God having compassion on those who have lived lives of compassion. Jesus reminds the religiously observant (that means us!) that God's first desire is not sacrifice but mercy. A heart filled with judgments on others has no room left to offer praises to God.

Lawrence of Brindisi (+ 1619) was a biblical scholar, a linguist and a preacher to the Lutherans. He was the right person for that work, for this Catholic preacher wrote of the scriptural word so cherished by the Reformers: "The word of God is a light to the mind and a fire to the will. It enables us to know God and to love God. It is bread and water, but a bread sweeter than honey, a water better than wine and milk."

SAT 22 — #394/603 (LMC, #193–227) white
Mary Magdalene, disciple of the Lord
MEMORIAL

Older calendars designated Mary Magdalene as "penitent" based on a long-standing but apparently erroneous identification of her with the sinful woman of Luke's gospel. The mistake is understandable in light of Mark 16:9's description of her as one "from whom Jesus had driven out seven demons." But this image of Mary Magdalene has kindled the devotion of countless generations. We all admire heroic sanctity — from a distance! In Magdalene we feel we have found a sympathetic friend, a struggling sister in whose example we find encouragement and on whose intercession we can count. Although the Roman Calendar of 1969 gave Mary Magdalene no special title, the revised sacramentary will restore an ancient designation: "disciple of the Lord." Just what all of us sinners hope to become! If the proper first reading is used, by all means use the Song of Songs selection. Mary's human devotion to Jesus can shine in that lovely love poem.

JULY

23 Sixteenth Sunday in Ordinary Time
#107 (LMC, #102) green

"Come away . . . and rest awhile." The opening words of today's gospel resonate at this time of the summer. Jesus' understandable wish for refreshment yields to a shepherd's heartfelt compassion. Jeremiah's picture of the good shepherd shines in Christ, who, as Ephesians says, gathers together those once far from God and at odds with each other. Jesus is our peace and reconciliation. Therefore, peace and reconciliation are not merely the result of our feasting together, they are the prerequisites for our partaking of this supper.

MON 24 Weekday
#395 (LMC, #193–227) green

To any of us who have ever wondered what gift to bring before the Lord God, Micah provides a simple answer. "Only this — to do justice, to love kindness and to walk humbly with your God." The living exemplar of that creed was Jesus.

TUE 25 James, apostle
#605 (LMC, #335) red
FEAST

"We have this treasure in clay vessels," says Paul, and the gospel shows us three of them: today's saint, his brother and their ambitious mother. Self-seeking comes naturally, Jesus warns the ten, who are probably angry because those Zebedee kids tried to beat them to the top. "It will not be so among you," says the Master, who came not to be served but to serve. As we look at patterns of leadership, an examination of conscience might ask: Has Jesus' wish been fulfilled? How *is* it among us?

WED 26 Joachim and Anne, parents of the Blessed Virgin Mary
#397 (LMC, #193–227) white
MEMORIAL

Beginning today we will be with the prophet Jeremiah for three weeks. "My eyes a fountain of tears," is this prophet's self-portrait. We sense his foreboding at the outset of his ministry. Isaiah had said, "Here I am, Lord, send me!" But Jeremiah says, "Not I, Lord! I do not know how to speak! I am too young!" Each call to discipleship is personal; each vocation is unique. Different, too, says Jesus, are the kinds of ground on which the Sower's seed falls. The point of the parable is not how little seed actually takes root, but how rich the harvest of the few seeds that do.

The parents of Mary are mentioned only in non-canonical writings, but they are venerated in long-standing tradition. The weekday lectionary is used today, although optional readings are given in the proper of saints for communities where this is the patronal observance.

THU 27 Weekday
#398 (LMC, #193–227) green

"Love makes time pass; time makes love pass," an old Italian proverb warns. Jeremiah points out the same thing to Israel, whose "fountain of living water" is now a dry cistern. In response to the disciples' question about Jesus' parables, he declares them blessed in being able to see and hear. Do we see? Do we hear? Do we drink deeply at this fountain of living water?

FRI 28 Weekday
#399 (LMC, #193–227) green

"It shall not come to mind, or be remembered, or missed; nor shall another one be made." How radical Jeremiah's word must have seemed to those who revered the ark in the midst of God's people. The Lord will be in our midst in a way that transcends symbols and signs: in the faith-filled and loving lives of the people. Today's gospel presents Jesus' homily on the parable we heard on Wednesday.

SAT 29 Martha, disciple of the Lord
#404/607 (LMC, #193–227) white
MEMORIAL

Martha, Mary and Lazarus of Bethany, hosts of the Lord: This is the beautiful title of this day's memorial in the monastic calendar. This is a summertime feast on which to celebrate hospitality; a day to remember the homeless and reflect on our community's service of them. The memorial of Martha reminds us that we always find the Lord in the guest: sometimes revealed, sometimes disguised. Nevertheless, the disciples of Jesus must offer a welcoming hand to all without exception. The text from Jeremiah fits this motif. What are the "deceptive words" Jeremiah warns against? "The temple of the Lord!" The first-created sacred places are our fellow human beings, created in the image of God. Justice, compassion and hospitality: This is the covenant love that forms the rock on which we stand.

JULY

#110 (LMC, #105)   green
30 Seventeenth Sunday in Ordinary Time

Today begins a five-Sunday reading of John 6. The readings from the Hebrew Scriptures have been chosen according to "correspondence." In today's passage about Elisha, for instance, there are barley leaves and food left over, after the prophet's word. Jesus' disciples echo Elisha's servant's questions, there is food left over, and the crowd calls Jesus "the prophet." Jesus is thus shown to be in continuity with Israel's prophetic tradition.

#401 (LMC, #193–227)   white
MON 31   **Ignatius of Loyola, presbyter, religious founder**
MEMORIAL

A brand-new pair of underwear! A week of readings from Jeremiah begins with the purchase of a linen loincloth — a simple visual aid that communicates a serious lesson. In the gospel, good things come from insignificant beginnings: a barely visible seed, yeast that disappears into the flour. As with the growth of the kingdom, so with the life of the disciples. Jesus had told them early on that they had to be salt: virtually invisible but noticeable when absent.

Pray today for the Jesuit descendants of Ignatius of Loyola (+ 1556). Remember among his spiritual sons those who have endured silencing for their creative thought (Teilhard de Chardin) and martyrdom for their fearless preaching of the just word (martyrs of El Salvador).

August

#402 (LMC, #193–227)   white
TUE 1   **Alphonsus Liguori, bishop and doctor of the church**
MEMORIAL

Jeremiah asks the people — and us — to reflect on where they place their trust: in idols or in the living God? Jesus explains the parable that was replaced last Saturday by the proper gospel for the feast of Martha. The preacher might want to prefix that parable to today's reading and use Jesus' explanation as the homily. To us, always too willing to weed the kingdom's garden, Jesus counsels patience, "Let them grow together." A polite way of telling us to mind our own business.

A lawyer who became a priest, Alphonsus Liguori (+ 1787) went on to found the Redemptorists and to serve as a diocesan bishop. Like many religious founders, Alphonsus had to cope with conflict within and opposition from without his religious family. Through it all, he continued to serve the people of God through preaching, writing and the ministry of reconciliation.

#403 (LMC, #193–227)   green
WED 2   **Weekday**

Eusebius of Vercelli, bishop; Peter Julian Eymard, priest; optional memorials/white. • Jeremiah articulates the pain of one who finds himself alone, alienated and ostracized. For him, it was for the sake of God's word. Jesus presents the kingdom of heaven in striking images: a hidden treasure, a pearl of great price. More striking still is the finder's reaction: sell everything to capture the prize.

Eusebius (+ 371) began his ministry as a lector and was elected first bishop of Vercelli. Preaching the orthodox Christian faith against the more popular Arianism brought Eusebius powerful political enemies. Peter Julian Eymard's (+ 1868) devotion to Christ present in the eucharist led him to found the Blessed Sacrament Fathers and the Servants of the Blessed Sacrament, an order of sisters devoted to perpetual adoration.

#404 (LMC, #193–227)   green
THU 3   **Weekday**

Clay in the potter's hand: a beautiful image. May we be shaped as a welcoming and reconciling community. The kingdom's net, says Jesus, takes in all kinds! Are we not the living proof of that? As one of the Desert Fathers said, "If there is room for me, then surely there is room for everyone!"

#405 (LMC, #193–227)   white
FRI 4   **John Mary Vianney, presbyter**
MEMORIAL

Who attacks Jeremiah for preaching God's word? Not unbelievers, but the priests and people gathered in the house of the Lord. Jesus' teaching in parables ends with his neighbors finding him offensive. Dostoyevsky noted that people "persecute their prophets and slay them, then pray to their martyrs and build shrines to those they have killed." How do we treat the prophets in our midst today?

When John Vianney (+ 1859) faced the unbelief in his village of Ars with faith and service, signs and wonders began to multiply. He dismissed an agnostic's fear that there might not be anything beyond the grave: "Ah, my child," Vianney smiled, "but then it would have been heaven

192   SUMMER AND FALL ORDINARY TIME: JULY

enough to have lived as a disciple of Jesus on earth!"

SAT 5 #406 (LMC, #193–227)   green
Weekday

Dedication of the Basilica of St. Mary in Rome; Blessed Virgin Mary; optional memorials/white. ▪ Jeremiah speaks the truth and is threatened for it, but spared in the end. John the Baptist is not so fortunate. The last line is ominous: "John's disciples came and took his body and buried it — then they went and told Jesus."

Today's memorial is an opportunity for every parish to research the date of its dedication and make plans to keep it as a local solemnity with grand liturgy and festivity. The dedication of the local cathedral should also be kept as a parish feast. These days link us to the bishop of Rome, to our diocese and to the Christ who lives in the midst of our own local church.

6 #614 (LMC, #344)   white
Transfiguration of the Lord
FEAST

ORIENTATION

Today celebrates the heights for which our human nature is destined and chronicles the depths to which we often prefer to descend.

Theologically, the feast celebrates the glory of divinity shining through the human person of the incarnate Lord, still shining in the world through the lives of Christ's disciples. The traditional icon of the Transfiguration pictures light cascading from Christ's robes onto the robes of the three apostles, sign and pledge of their share — and ours — in Christ's glory.

Historically, the feast points in less glorious directions. Its universal observance was mandated in the fifteenth century in thanksgiving for a Christian victory over Muslims on August 6 near Belgrade. In our own time, it was on August 6 that atomic weapons were used for the first time in the destruction of Hiroshima. Keep the prescribed liturgical texts, but include intercessions for peace in Mass and in the Liturgy of the Hours, and let homiletic reflections point out the feast's contrasts.

LECTIONARY

Today's gospel is the same as that of the Second Sunday of Lent, Mark's account of the transfiguration. On this feast, however, it is heard differently because the context is different. The accompanying readings from Daniel and 2 Peter and the chanting of Psalm 97 celebrate the "heavenly vision that will give us a share in Christ's radiance, renew our spiritual nature and transform us into Christ's own likeness" (Office of Readings).

SACRAMENTARY

Today should celebrate Christ's glory in a way similar in tone to Easter and Christ the King. The vestments of those solemnities should be used, along with candles and incense, at least at the principal celebration. The Gloria could be the Easter setting, if musical resources permit. There is a special preface, notably different from that of the Second Sunday of Lent, which applied the transfiguration mystery to the life of the church.

Hymns for the feast are in all major hymnals. Even if the melody given for a new text is unknown, the metrical indices found in all good hymnals often make it possible to sing a new text to a well-known tune.

A way of announcing the feast and setting a prayerful tone to the gathering would be to place the icon of the feast at the church entrance. A modest lectern can double as an icon stand. Place candles on either side, and in front of the stand a floral arrangement and bowl of fragrant incense. For contemporary re-creations of classic Eastern icons and a wide variety of incense, call Monastery Icons (800-729-4952).

KEEPING VIGIL

On the eve of the Transfiguration, revive the ancient Catholic tradition of keeping vigil with a celebration including incense, candlelight, scripture and intercession for peace.

MON 7 #407 (LMC, #193–227)   green
Weekday (Eighteenth Week in Ordinary Time)

Sixtus II, pope and martyr, and his companions, martyrs, optional memorial/red; Cajetan, presbyter, religious founder, optional memorial/white. ▪ The dispute between Jeremiah and Hananiah is neither ancient nor irrelevant. What criteria do we use for "the discernment of spirits"?

AUGUST

Note the gospel today: Matthew's account of the multiplication of the loaves and fishes.

Sixtus II was bishop of Rome during the persecution by the emperor Valerian and was martyred, together with four of his deacons, on August 6, 258. As the Reformation swept across the church and swept many out of the church, Cajetan worked to reform the church by gathering clergy and laity into confraternities to care for the sick and the poor.

TUE 8 #408 (LMC, #193–227) white
Dominic, presbyter, religious founder
MEMORIAL

After oracles of destruction and devastation comes the word of comfort: "You shall be my people, and I will be your God." Matthew enjoys presenting Peter in a human light. Even having seen so much, Peter still requests a sign. When the sign is given, Peter's faith falters again. Jesus is now in a place of faith, unlike his hometown, and healing can take place.

In an age when the papacy resorted to military force to expunge heresy, Dominic (+ 1221) and his followers wanted instead to become an "army of evangelizers," whose power was the truth of their preaching and the example of an apostolic life in common.

WED 9 #409 (LMC, #193–227) green
Weekday

Jeremiah announces more promises from the God who loves the people he has chastised: "I have loved you with an everlasting love." The conclusion to the Jeremiah cycle will be displaced tomorrow. That conclusion proclaims the "new covenant" which the Lord "will write in their hearts." It would be possible to replace today's Jeremiah reading with that one, as a way of bringing the Jeremiah cycle to a close. In the gospel, God's favor reaches beyond Israel to a woman whose faith opens the door for her daughter's healing.

THU 10 #618 (LMC, #348) red
Lawrence, deacon, martyr
FEAST

The texts for today's liturgy are a perfect match for Lawrence's story. "God loves a cheerful giver" (2 Corinthians 9:7); "Happy the merciful who give to those in need" (Psalm 112) and John 12's story of the grain of wheat. Four days after the martyrdom of Sixtus II (on August 6, observed on August 7), came that of his deacon, Lawrence (+ 258). The pope's memorial is optional, but his deacon's is a feast! Lawrence was well-known: the church's "money man," guardian of its treasury. Moreover, he was a comedian. According to legend, a local government official wanted Lawrence to inventory for confiscation all the treasures of the church. Lawrence gathered into one hall all the city's poor and homeless, sick and handicapped, abandoned by the government and sheltered by the Christians. Leading the official to the hall, Lawrence threw open the doors and exclaimed, "Here are the treasures of the church!" Alas, bureaucrats are not amused by jokes at their expense. Lawrence was sentenced to be burned on a gridiron (and is frequently pictured holding one). Courageous faith, unfailing humor: worthy of a feast of its own.

FRI 11 #411 (LMC, #193–227) white
Clare, virgin, religious founder
MEMORIAL

Nahum predicts joy for Judah and devastation for the enemies of God's city. Having rebuked Peter's mistaken notion of the path Jesus should walk, the Lord outlines the true journey for his disciples.

Clare of Assisi (+ 1253) and her friend Francis (+ 1226) were evangelical in their dedication to poverty and peace. Becoming one with the poor and homeless, making the Franciscan way of life flexible enough to embrace clergy and laypeople, celibates and married people, Clare and Francis helped who knows how many people to find their way home to the Father.

SAT 12 #412 (LMC, #193–227) green
Weekday

Blessed Virgin Mary, optional memorial/white. ▪ "I will stand at my watchpost . . . I will keep watch." Our only reading from Habakkuk celebrates fidelity. After coming down the mountain from the transfiguration, reality sets in immediately. "Your disciples were inadequate," says the father of a sick child. After the healing, the disciples ask Jesus, "Why could we not cast out the demon?" They are told that their faith is too small or, rather, that their faith can be small, but it must be real.

For the optional memorial of Mary, see the *Collection of Masses of the Blessed Virgin Mary*, #37, Mother of Divine Hope, or #44, Health of the Sick, for texts that relate to the scriptural themes of confident faith and divine healing.

AUGUST

13 — Nineteenth Sunday in Ordinary Time
#116 (LMC, #111) green

After last week's interruption by the Feast of the Transfiguration, the "Bread of Life" Sundays resume. Presiders should note the orientation of this block of Sundays in introductory remarks. Those who proclaim the gospel may wish to prefix today's passage with verse 35 from last Sunday's superseded gospel: "Jesus said to the crowds, 'I am the bread of life. Whoever comes to me will never be hungry, and whoever believes in me will never be thirsty.' The people began to complain. . . . "

Look to the first reading for inspiration: In the desert Elijah receives miraculous food, a gift from God, as strength for his long journey to God's mountain. As Christians journey through this world's desert to the kingdom, they should see in God's providential love an image of the eucharist. Because of God's gift, Elijah's discouragement is turned into strength for walking and witnessing. Because of the eucharist, Christians are meant to be pilgrims and preachers. In the gospel, the new Canadian lectionary, with Vatican approval, changes "Jews" to "people." Constant repetition of "the Jews" could distract from the point of the passage. A thoughtful rereading of LTP's *When Catholics Speak about Jews* may be useful for planners and homilists.

MON 14 — Maximilian Mary Kolbe, presbyter, religious, martyr
#413 (LMC, #193–227) red
MEMORIAL

Today we hear Ezekiel's vocation story, as we begin a two-week survey of his preaching. In every age, God calls forth prophets from every walk of life. Amos was a farmer, Jeremiah "a mere youth," and Ezekiel a priest. Because tomorrow's account of God's message to Ezekiel will be replaced by the Assumption readings, planners may wish to join it to today's. In the gospel, another prediction of the passion is followed by that strange money-bearing fish. Wishing not to offend unnecessarily, Jesus pays a tax to which he is not bound. There are times to bend and times to stand firm.

If ever there was a time to stand firm, it was in Europe in the 1940s. Yet tragically few had the courage. One who did was today's martyr, Franciscan friar Maximilian Kolbe (+ 1941), who volunteered to be executed in the place of a fellow prisoner, a married man. Perhaps when Kolbe spoke up to offer his life, some could hear an echo of the God who in Auschwitz seemed so deathly silent.

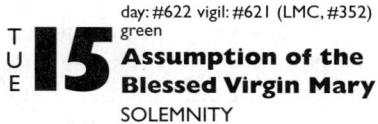

TUE 15 — Assumption of the Blessed Virgin Mary
day: #622 vigil: #621 (LMC, #352) green
SOLEMNITY

ORIENTATION

The earliest form of today's solemnity focused on Mary's death as a share in Christ's paschal mystery. Even before the fifth century, the church in Jerusalem commemorated the "Dormition" (falling asleep) of the Mother of God, a title the Eastern church retains. Later reflection made Mary's entrance into God's kingdom explicit, using scriptural images: victory celebration, bridal procession, Mary's being "lifted up." The feast came to be known in eighth-century Rome as the "Assumption." In 1950, Pius XII declared Mary's bodily assumption to be dogma and provided a new Mass formulary portraying Mary more clearly as an image of the church. Vatican II enriched the celebration with an extensive selection of biblical readings, prayers and a new preface.

LECTIONARY

The vigil texts present Mary as the Ark of God, and her sharing in Christ's victory over death as the reason for her bodily assumption. Jesus declares her blessed for hearing and doing the word of God. She is the model disciple who has already received the glory which is every disciple's destiny.

The first reading of the daytime Mass begins, like the liturgies of Eastertime, with the New Testament. The Book of Revelation depicts "the woman" threatened by the dragon, giving birth to a son and rescued with him by God. Evil is foiled, God's reign is established and Mary rejoices. Paul reminds us in the second reading that Mary's privilege will be shared by all who follow Christ. In a line omitted from last night's first reading, David leapt and danced before the Ark. In today's gospel, John the Baptist leaps with joy in Elizabeth's womb as Mary enters the room bearing Christ within her. All these scriptures celebrate God's mighty power at work among his people and in Mary as the model for all believers.

SACRAMENTARY

The assembly could be greeted as they arrive by an icon of the Dormition of Mary displayed on a suitably adorned stand in the vestibule or main entrance (see August 6). Try to lend an Easter character to the celebration, in keeping with the relationship of Mary's assumption to Christ's resurrection. The Easter vesture and incense, for instance, the Eastertime Gloria, alleluia and eucharistic prayer acclamations could all signal that relationship.

MUSIC

For a good setting of today's Psalm 45, see Howard Hughes' "Assumption psalm" (GIA, G-2028), and Diana Kodner's "The queen stands at your right hand" in *Gather*. First among Marian choices should be Mary's own words. Many settings of the Magnificat abound; Owen Alstott's "My soul rejoices" (OCP) is majestic and singable; James Chepponis' "Magnificat" (*Gather,* and octavo form) has a singable refrain and lilting verses. For a melodically pleasing metrical version, see the Lutheran Church's *With One Voice,* #730, "My soul proclaims your greatness," set to the lovely tune, KINGSFOLD. For hymnody, seek out the theologically sound. "Sing of Mary" has a verse that refers explicitly to the assumption; and GIA's *Hymnal for the Hours* has a text, "Blessed Virgin Mother," which paraphrases Dante's hymn of Saint Bernard from the "Paradiso" of the *Divine Comedy.*

■ BLESSING OF PRODUCE: For centuries, in many countries, the Assumption solemnity has been linked to the blessing of the earth's bounty. The full order of blessing is in the *Book of Blessings,* chapter 26 or 28; a simple order is in *Catholic Household Blessings and Prayers* (pages 170 – 171), with the Litany of Mary that can be chanted to a simple tone.

■ VIGIL OR EVENING CELEBRATION: Whether as a longer vigil on Saturday night or as vespers on the evening of the solemnity, a candlelight celebration could be held. See the *Liturgy of the Hours,* volume IV, for resources.

WED 16 — #415 (LMC, #193–227) green
Weekday

Stephen of Hungary, optional memorial / white. ▪ Some are in and some are out, in the Jerusalem of Ezekiel's vision. The judgment begins with the elders in the sanctuary. The gospel at first sounds like more of the same: Who's in, who's out. When Jesus outlines the community's approach to those who stray, his advice sounds harsh at first: "Let such a one be to you as a Gentile and a tax collector." Then we remember how Jesus treated Gentiles and tax collectors. He welcomed them to table, and he is welcoming us sinners still.

Today's saint, King Stephen (+ 1038), was beloved by his subjects because he showed himself subject to the gospel, seeking justice for the oppressed, charity for the poor.

THU 17 — #416 (LMC, #193–227) green
Weekday

Ezekiel proclaims God's message by word and by deed, in dramatic actions. We might think of them as staged demonstrations to provoke observers to serious reflection. The Canadian lectionary adds context by adding verses 13 through 16. In the gospel, Peter doubles the rabbinic prescription of threefold forgiveness and adds one for good measure. But he is speaking to Jesus, who multiplies Peter's "seven times" to infinity: seventy times seven.

AUGUST

FRI 18 — Weekday
#417 (LMC, #193–227) green

Jane Frances de Chantal, married woman, religious founder, optional memorial/white. • Alternate selections from Ezekiel are provided today. Perhaps the lectionary compilers felt that some communities might find the first selection too graphic. Both proclaim the promise of God's everlasting covenant with Israel. The gospel speaks of two ways in which members of the community can witness to God's faithful love: marriage and voluntary celibacy.

The optional memorial today is Jane Frances de Chantal (+ 1641), whose spiritual director, Francis de Sales (January 24), interpreted spirituality to enhance the vocations and ways of life of Christians. Together they founded the Congregation of the Visitation, which offered an alternative form of religious life for women.

SAT 19 — Weekday
#418 (LMC, #193–227) green

John Eudes, presbyter, religious founder, educator; Blessed Virgin Mary; optional memorials/white. • Through Ezekiel, God eliminates a proverb and raises the banner for personal responsibility. God's purpose in calling us to account for our own righteousness or sin is to call us to life, the ultimate plan for each of us. The gospel passage reminds us that children are too often without rights. Not so with Jesus, for whom children and the childlike are important citizens of the kingdom.

In his ministry to prostitutes, John Eudes (+ 1680) was a good shepherd to society's lost sheep. He founded a religious family of women who take the name and mission of shepherding seriously, the Sisters of the Good Shepherd. For the Saturday memorial of Mary see the *Collection of Masses of the Blessed Virgin Mary*, #32, Mother and Teacher in the Spirit or #39, Queen and Mother of Mercy.

20 — Twentieth Sunday in Ordinary Time
#119 (LMC, #114) green

Wisdom, who appears in today's first reading, is a complex figure. Who is she? Teacher, bride, mother, co-creator with God at the beginning and even divine playmate (Proverbs 8:30–31), the church, the soul of the individual believer: Commentators have seen many facets in this image. The Catholic heritage sees Wisdom's banquet as the eucharistic feast. The opening words of the reading once served as an antiphon for the feast of Corpus Christi; when the new Order of Mass was drawn up after Vatican II, they were paired with a verse from the *Didache* as a formula to be used at the preparation of the gifts.

Verse 51 of chapter 6 in the Gospel of John is so crucial that the verse ends last week's gospel and begins this week's gospel. Everyone planning or preaching during this block of Sundays needs to consult Raymond Brown's *Anchor Bible* commentary for its verse-by-verse analysis. Brown sees verses 51–58 as an explicitly eucharistic rewriting of verses 35–50:

No longer are we told that eternal life is the result of believing in Jesus; it comes from feeding on his flesh and drinking his blood (54). The Father's role in bringing [people] to Jesus or giving them to him is no longer in the limelight; Jesus himself dominates as the agent and source of salvation. Even though the verses in 51–58 are remarkably like those of 35–50, a new vocabulary runs through them: "eat," "feed," "drink," "flesh," "blood." (*Anchor Bible*, volume 29, 284)

Since there is no institution narrative in the Fourth Gospel's Last Supper scene, Brown thinks that this may be John's version of the institution, moved and rearranged to become part of the Bread of Life discourse.

MON 21 — Pius X, pope — MEMORIAL
#419 (LMC, #193–227) white

The weekday lectionary presents us with the most important passages from Ezekiel. The death of the prophet's wife, which he is not permitted to mourn, is a sign of Israel's desolation in exile. For many of us in affluent countries, the world is a playground, not our "valley of exile." The gospel's, "What do I still lack?" should be not only the rich young man's question but ours as well. Jesus takes our keeping of the commandments for granted. The way of perfection, is proclaimed so that each of us may examine what we cling to that would make us walk away sadly.

Pope Pius X (+ 1914) laid the groundwork for much of the liturgical reform that came to fruition in Vatican II. The centrality of the Lord's Day, the accessibility of the Lord's table, and a liturgy with full sung participation by the assembly were among his priorities. His will was the shortest in modern papal history: "I was born poor; I have lived poor; I die poor."

SUMMER AND FALL ORDINARY TIME: AUGUST 197

AUGUST

Among his last acts was his refusal to bless the troops assembled to defend Rome in World War I: "I bless peace, not war," he said.

TUE 22 — Queenship of the Blessed Virgin Mary
#420 (LMC, #193–227) white
MEMORIAL

"How shall I begin my spiritual journey?" the aspirant asked the desert father. "Go out into the desert," said the elder, "look up toward heaven and say over and over again, 'You are God, and I am not.'" Ezekiel presents the scriptural version of that story. It is important when we face the challenge of the gospel. Jesus agrees with Peter: Humanly speaking, discipleship is impossible, but not with God.

Originally celebrated on May 31, today's memorial was moved to this date to associate it more clearly with Mary's Assumption. See the *Collection of Masses of the Blessed Virgin Mary,* formulary #29, for an inclusive revision of the sacramentary Mass and a fine new preface to use today.

WED 23 — Weekday
#421 (LMC, #193–227) green

Rose of Lima, virgin, optional memorial/white. • The "sermon against the shepherds" has always provided an examination of conscience for the ordained ministry. Surely the expanding view of ministry suggests a broader application to all who exercise ministry and authority in the community. There is even more challenge in Jesus' images of the kingdom. What are our concepts of "right" and "fair"? The gap between our standards and God's is thrown into relief, for God's ultimate standard is love, a love that does not measure by expediency.

The first saint of the Americas to be canonized, Rose of Lima (+ 1617) was a Third Order Dominican. She is remembered for her intense love of God and for her persevering faith.

THU 24 — Bartholomew, apostle
#629 (LMC, #360) red
FEAST

Legend tells of Bartholomew preaching the gospel in India and Armenia, where he is said to have been martyred. Tradition also identifies him (as in today's gospel) with Nathaniel of Cana in Galilee. His reaction to Philip's enthusiasm is a snobbish skepticism: "Can anything good come out of Nazareth?" Far from being offended, Jesus praises Nathaniel's (Bartholomew's) authenticity: "Here is a true Israelite without any guile." Since Jesus chose all kinds of personalities, today may be a day to pray for the virtue of tempering our honesty with charity and our charity with honesty.

FRI 25 — Weekday
#423 (LMC, #193–227) green

Louis of France, married man, ruler; Joseph Calasanz, presbyter, religious founder, educator; optional memorials/white. • It is a shame that yesterday's proper first reading replaced the Ezekiel prophecy of a new heart and a new spirit, the ingathering of God's people and their sprinkling with clean water. Today's passage is too good to replace, but the presider might prefix its reading with a summary of yesterday's superseded reading. The message is one of overwhelming hope and promise. New life, new breath, new spirit: "I have spoken and I will act," says the Lord. In the gospel, Jesus points out the way to manifest this hope and life in flesh and blood: love of God and love of neighbor.

While reigning over a vast kingdom, Louis (+ 1270) and his wife raised eleven children. Joseph Calasanz (+ 1648) devoted his ministry to providing free education for the impoverished children of Rome.

SAT 26 — Weekday
#424 (LMC, #193–227) green

Blessed Virgin Mary, optional memorial/white. • Our "Ezekiel cycle" ends with a promise: God will dwell among his people Israel for ever! Jesus sets the stage for a new approach to teaching authority by counseling a humility and equality rarely found among religious hierarchies. His model of servanthood presumes an unceasing willingness to learn and an enduring openness to God's voice in one another.

For the Saturday memorial of Mary, see the *Collection of Masses of the Blessed Virgin Mary,* #24, Seat of Wisdom, #26, Image of the Church II, or #37, Mother of Divine Hope.

27 — Twenty-first Sunday in Ordinary Time
#122 (LMC, #117) green

This week it is not "the Jews" or even "the people" but rather the disciples who complain about Jesus' teaching and finally "turned back and no longer went about with him." Facing a decision and making a choice

198 SUMMER AND FALL ORDINARY TIME: AUGUST

A U G U S T

are nothing new in humankind's relationship with God. The lectionary matches to this gospel a first reading about Israel's covenant relationship with God. Joshua confronts the people with a life-or-death decision: to serve the living God or to follow alien gods. Some commentators suggest that the passage portrays a specific historical event, and that it also describes a liturgical rite. Questions and answers ritually announce and ratify the community's ongoing commitment. Jesus confronts the Twelve with a life-or-death decision: Do you also wish to go away?

The second reading is presented in the United States' lectionary as either Ephesians 5:21–32 or 25–32. The Canadian solution seems preferable: prefix 4:32 — 5:2 and see how much better 5:21–32 sounds! There is a mutuality in this longer text that is not apparent in the other editings.

■ BLESSING DEPARTING PARISHIONERS AND WELCOMING NEW PARISHIONERS: In many assemblies the final weekends of August and the first weekends in September are times of transition, as school and work take some people away from the community and bring new people to it. See the *Book of Blessings*, chapters 66 and 67, for commentary and texts.

MON 28
#425 (LMC, #193–227)
white
Augustine, bishop and doctor of the church
MEMORIAL

For the next three days the first reading presents a survey of 2 Thessalonians. In his *Introduction to the New Testament* (Doubleday, 1997), Raymond Brown notes the current scholarly division on authorship and date. One theory places the letter in the late first century "when increased apocalyptic fervor was manifest" (591). But before dealing with that issue (tomorrow), the author of the letter praises qualities that will always be in season: faith that is growing abundantly, mutual love, steadfastness. In the gospel, Jesus castigates religious leaders who are unworthy spiritual guides.

The calendar honors one of Christianity's most influential spiritual mentors. Augustine (+ 430) plumbs the depths of spiritual wisdom and psychological insight to exert an enduring influence on Christian thought. His conversion was a struggle of monumental proportions. For fifteen years he had lived with a woman whose name we do not know, and with her had a son whom he named "a gift from God" (Adeodatus). His conversion is a testimony to the power of several dimensions of liturgy: the dynamic preaching of Ambrose (December 7), the private prayer of his mother Monica (August 27), and the music of the church of Milan ("at the sound of your canticles I wept"). For more than three decades Augustine served as bishop of Hippo in Northern Africa, setting the example of a good shepherd in the community life he lived with his clergy, as well as in his tireless preaching to his people and service of the poor. The wonder of Augustine, and the hope for us, is that sin did abound in his life, but in the end grace triumphed. Yesterday's and today's Office of Readings tell the story in the saint's own words from his timeless masterpiece, *The Confessions*.

TUE 29
#426 or 634 (LMC, #193–227)
red
The Martyrdom of John the Baptist
MEMORIAL

As we move through 2 Thessalonians, homilists may wish to point out eschatological nature of this letter: Christ's return was presumed to be imminent. Note Paul's practical approach to the community's "millennium fever": Christ's disciples still have work to do!

Today's gospel is one appointed for the memorial of John the Baptist. Is there a more foolish waste than the silencing of that great preacher because of a two-bit despot's drunken promise to an exotic dancer whose mother bore a grudge? Yet the Baptist's voice echoes and his witness continues in all who dare to confront power with truth and to speak the truth without compromise.

WED 30
#427 (LMC, #193–227)   green
Weekday

Where are the Y2K survivalists of 1999? See how practical Paul is in dealing with a community who fully expected the Lord's imminent return: "No work, no food!" Christian waiting is not mere hanging around, but setting about the task of preparing the way of the Lord. Jesus' harsh words toward the religiously observant of his day are proclaimed in the church for our benefit, not their bashing. How do we respond to prophets in our own day?

THU 31
#428 (LMC, #193–227)   green
Weekday

Today we launch a three-week excursion through Paul's First Letter to the Corinthians. No one seriously disputes the authenticity of this document, which scholars date between

AUGUST

55 and 57 AD. It is written to a church composed of Jewish and Gentile converts established by Paul (Brown, 512). In today's passage Paul praises a community "not lacking in any spiritual gift" and promises them that God will "strengthen you to the end." Jesus admonishes his community not only to diligence in its work but to mutual love in its relationships. The day and hour of the Master's return may be a mystery, but what the Master expects of us when he arrives is not.

September

FRI 1 #429 (LMC, #193–227) green
Weekday

Corinth was a crossroads city familiar with a variety of philosophies and tolerant of a diversity of behavior. The weekday lectionary has skipped Paul's statement of the problem of factions within the community and the dangers of competing loyalties. Let all wisdom and cleverness yield, says Paul, to Jesus Christ crucified: foolishness to some, a stumbling block to others, but God's power and wisdom for those who believe. The cross will keep us focused, and keeping focused is a major concern of today's gospel.

SAT 2 #430 (LMC, #193–227) green
Weekday

Blessed Virgin Mary, optional memorial/white. ▪ How can there be factions in a community when everyone realizes that we are all alike? There cannot be, and so Paul reminds the Corinthians that they are all coming from the same place. Today's final weekday reading from Matthew's gospel points toward what will really matter in the final accounting: the economics of the kingdom Jesus announces are creativity and generosity, not selfishness and caution.

For the Saturday memorial of Mary consider #14, Mother of Reconciliation, or #33, Mother of Good Counsel, both in the *Collection of Masses of the Blessed Virgin Mary.*

3 #125 (LMC, #120) green
Twenty-second Sunday in Ordinary Time

The lectionary returns this Sunday to Year B's evangelist Mark. Although a number of arrangements are possible, *Sourcebook* groups this Sunday and next with the "Bread of Life Sundays" and the two Sundays before them (see Lectionary Overview). In this block of Sundays we have seen Jesus manifesting himself as "the Provider" (Juel, 96).

In the Deuteronomy reading, Moses commands that nothing be added to the Law nor subtracted from it. But various prescriptions in the Law had been reinterpreted and revised, even in the pages of Deuteronomy itself. Statutes for living communities must always have room for flexibility. Jesus suggests a new way to translate the letter of the Law into a vibrant way of life. Singleness of purpose and purity of heart will be the standard against which to measure ritual practices and the key to living the tradition of the ancestors. The history of the church has shown us that such an ideal is also a full-time challenge. It is always easier to perform rituals than to purify our inmost being.

A series of readings from the Letter of James begins today with an enumeration of commitments more challenging than the cleansing of hands and vessels: care for orphans and widows, and preservation from the world's corruption.

▪ GRANDPARENTS' DAY: It would be good today to gather in church or in a nursing home for a brief prayer service adapting texts from the Blessing of Elderly People (*Book of Blessings,* chapter 1, XII). Be mindful, especially in the church celebration, that people who become grandparents in their 40s and 50s might object to being called "elderly." At parish Masses, offer intercessions for grandparents living and deceased.

▪ BACK TO SCHOOL: Add to the Sunday intercessions some petitions adapted from the *Book of Blessings* (#527). The presider concludes by extending hands over students and teachers and using or adapting prayer #528 or #529. The first explicitly mentions the opening of school. Do include the wonderful phrase in the second prayer: "Let them take delight in new discoveries." The final blessing might draw from two other parts of the *Book of Blessings:* Prayer over the People (#543) or Solemn Blessing (#741).

MON 4 #431 (LMC, #193–227) green/white
Weekday

U.S.A.: Labor Day, civil observance; proper Mass: Blessing of Human Labor.

ORIENTATION

Today's observance is the modern equivalent of blessings on flocks and fields, seedtime and

200 SUMMER AND FALL ORDINARY TIME: AUGUST

SEPTEMBER

planting. The term "human labor" embraces an endless array of activities and commitments.

LECTIONARY

The weekday readings may be used. Corinth could be almost any parish on earth: a mixed bag of people with differing theologies, ethnicities and maturities, with strong opinions and, consequently, sometimes acrimonious divisions. Paul begins the week's readings with a bid to let the Spirit's power chart the course of the community's Christian life. Today we begin a weekday journey through the Gospel of Luke that will take us to the threshold of Advent. Jesus' hometown sermon brings down the house — on his head. In the examples this master homilist chooses, we glimpse the nature of the kingdom he proclaims and of the table he sets.

Whatever the individual Christian's field of labor, whether we are employed or not, the vocation bestowed by our baptism matches that of Paul and continues the work of Jesus. Our life's labor must be to proclaim the good news of God's reconciling love. Or, to put it another way, to embrace what Jesus proposed as the work of the Messiah: "to bring good news to the poor, to proclaim release to the captives and recovery of sight to the blind, to let the oppressed go free, to proclaim the year of the Lord's favor." Alternative readings appear in the lectionary, section #846–850, "Blessing of Human Labor" or #831–835, "For Peace and Justice."

SACRAMENTARY

Useful elements and their origin are given below:

- GREETING:

From Christ, the Son of God, who was pleased to be known as the carpenter's son: grace and peace be with you all.
(*Book of Blessings,* #925 adapt.)

- PENITENTIAL RITE:

Lord Jesus, to do the will of your Father was your work on earth: Lord, have mercy.

Christ Jesus, from a variety of occupations you called your first disciples: Christ, have mercy.

Lord Jesus, to those who labor and are heavy burdened you offer rest: Lord, have mercy.

- PRESIDENTIAL PRAYERS:

Various Needs and Occasions, Mass 25 (note the exclusive language); Mass 21: Progress of Peoples; Appendix X, Mass 6: Civic Occasions; May 1: Joseph the Worker.

- INTERCESSIONS:

Use BB #932 for inspiration, making sure that the petitions reach beyond the needs of the local community. Prayer to end these intercessions, #935.

- EUCHARISTIC PRAYER:

Eucharistic Prayer for Various Needs and Occasions: form C (Jesus, Way to the Father) or form D (Jesus, the Compassion of God).

Other Liturgies

See the *Book of Blessings* (chapter 24): "Order for Blessing Tools or Other Equipment for Work." An ecclesial or civil gathering for the holiday might be enhanced with these texts.

TUE 5 #432 (LMC, #193–227) green
Weekday

The issues Paul plans to deal with will be explored to the benefit of all, Paul reassures the Corinthians, because "we have received not the spirit of the world, but the Spirit that is from God," that is, "we have the mind of Christ." Jesus is recognized by the people in Capernaum — and a demon — as one who has authority.

WED 6 #433 (LMC, #193–227) green
Weekday

Various factions rally around different ministers of the same gospel: a familiar story! Our equality, says Paul, is attested to by our common servanthood. "One plants, another waters . . . only God gives the growth." The gospel shows Simon's mother-in-law using her restored health to be of service, while Jesus balances prayer in solitude with an active ministry of preaching and healing.

THU 7 #434 (LMC, #193–227) green
Weekday

Who has power and who has not, who belongs where and who does not — these questions do not exist for Christians. "All things are yours," says Paul, "and you belong to Christ, and Christ belongs to God." The gospel passage tells the story of the sweetest refusal ever made. When Peter asks Jesus to depart from him because Peter recognizes his own sinfulness, Jesus, who so often says yes, says no, and invites Peter to become part of a life-changing adventure.

FRI 8 #636 (LMC, #367) white
Birth of the Blessed Virgin Mary
FEAST

Today's readings celebrate God's loving providence in bringing the plan of salvation to fulfillment. For this reason, the Romans selection is fitting ("all things work together for good"). When proclaiming the gospel, read the whole thing. Matthew's genealogy of Jesus, often heard

SEPTEMBER

as a long list of mostly unknown names, is key to the saving gospel. For one thing, women are named, which is not customary in Jewish genealogies. And consider the women who precede Mary: Tamar, who seduced Judah; Rahab, the prostitute of Jericho; Ruth, the Gentile; and Bathsheba of the Uriah and David story. Those who first heard these words knew in the opening lines of the gospel that, in Jesus, down come the walls between Jew and Gentile, saint and sinner, male and female. God is making all things new!

SAT 9 #436 (LMC, #193–227)   white
Peter Claver, presbyter, religious, missionary
MEMORIAL

Paul breaks forth into a canticle in praise of the apostolic life to show his listeners why he feels so committed to the way of the gospel and so comforted by God's providential care for him — and them. In the gospel, Jesus asserts his authority as Lord of the Sabbath and Master of a community whose foundational law is practical love and compassion in action.

Today's saint, Jesuit Peter Claver (+ 1654), translated both readings into the lived witness of his heroic ministry among victims of the slave trade. The proper prayer for this American memorial notes that Peter's witness can help all of us overcome racial hatreds.

10 #128 (LMC, #123)   green
Twenty-third Sunday in Ordinary Time

The second block of Ordinary Time Sundays concludes with a dramatic manifestation of Jesus' authority. The One who provided healing and teaching (Fifteenth and Sixteenth Sundays) and the bread of life (Seventeenth through the Twenty-first Sunday) now provides hearing and speech before turning toward Jerusalem where he will provide the world with salvation. Some of the gestures used in this healing were once ritual gestures in the ceremonies of the catechumenate. The first reading from Isaiah uses the same imagery as the gospel healing and also incorporates baptismal imagery: waters, streams, a pool, springs of water. Note that the *Revised Common Lectionary,* the Protestant adaptation of the Roman Catholic lectionary, prefixes this healing with the story of the Syro-Phoenician woman (verses 24–30), a dramatic profession of faith and a breaching of the boundaries between Jews and Gentiles. Today's passage from the semicontinuous reading of James challenges Christian communities to consider our hospitality toward those least welcome in worldly assemblies.

■ BLESSING OF PARISH OUTREACH AND SOCIAL JUSTICE MINISTRIES: The passages from James this Sunday and next are a powerful call to social justice. Next Sunday is usually designated as "Catechetical Sunday" and features a blessing of religious education workers in many parishes. This Sunday might be a good day to recognize and commission for ministry those who lead and serve in the community's outreach programs. See the blessing of those who exercise pastoral service in *Book of Blessings,* #1808ff, but consider replacing the rather vague collect there with the more to-the-point prayer from the Episcopal *Book of Occasional Services* (1994) "for parish visitors," 191.

MON 11 #437 (LMC, #193–227)   green
Weekday

Paul addresses a delicate issue forthrightly, calls the community to task for its complicity, and concludes with a magnificent Easter canticle: Christ our passover is sacrificed for us. The gospel charts a different course: Jesus heals on the Sabbath, the day designated by God for the remembrance and renewal of the covenant relationship. But this healing touch cannot penetrate hardened hearts, and instead of inspiring the religious authorities to praise, they are filled with fury.

TUE 12 #438 (LMC, #193–227)   green
Weekday

Yesterday's pattern continues in the first reading. Paul deals with serious issues, and concludes with some of the most beautiful words ever written: "You were washed, you were sanctified, you were justified in the name of the Lord Jesus Christ and in the Spirit of our God." After an all-night vigil on a mountain, Jesus chooses his apostles and comes down with them to a level place. Luke loves to picture Jesus at prayer, and these locations give us a sense of Jesus moving between his prayer and his ministry — a pattern for us to keep in mind.

SEPTEMBER

WED 13 #439 (LMC, #193–227) white
John Chrysostom, bishop and doctor of the church
MEMORIAL

To set context, the Canadian lectionary wisely adds two verses to the first reading, 7:1 and 7:17. Paul's exhortation to "keep one's place" has nothing to do with arbitrary self-limitation but reflects this community's preparation for what they believed to be the imminent end of all things. But no matter how much longer we have, for the Christian "the present form of the world is passing away." Best to make sure that we are on the right side of the great divide that Jesus describes in Luke's version of the beatitudes, four blessings and four woes. Unlike Matthew's third-person version, "Blessed are they," Luke's version has an immediacy, "Blessed are you . . . Woe are you."

In honor of today's saint, consult the Eastern-rite liturgy that bears his name (Liturgy of Saint John Chrysostom), and adapt its opening litany of intercession for the general intercessions today. The *Liturgy of the Hours* (all volumes) features excerpts from the homilies of John (+ 407), whose nickname means "the Golden Mouth." See his words on making donations to the church while ignoring service to the poor (volume IV, page 182).

THU 14 #638 (LMC, #370) red
Exaltation of the Holy Cross
FEAST

ORIENTATION

The official Latin title of this feast is "exaltation" of the cross. The title in the current sacramentary, "triumph of the cross," gets part of the day's focus but misses part. Exaltation may be taken first in a literal sense. The feast originated as a celebration of the dedication of the Basilica of the Holy Sepulchre, built by Constantine over the site of Christ's crucifixion (September 13, 335). The next day, the relic of the cross that was kept there was lifted up for the veneration of the faithful.

The title also has a scriptural connotation deriving from today's gospel: "Just as Moses lifted up the serpent in the desert, so must the Son of Man be lifted up." In John's gospel, "lifting up" means both the act of physically raising Jesus up on the cross, and his glorification by the Father in the splendor of the resurrection and his enthronement at God's right hand. Glorious exaltation and grace-assured salvation should echo through the liturgy today, making it a celebration in which Christ is exalted and Christ's people exult.

LECTIONARY

This suite of readings is well organized. The exodus story to which Jesus refers provides the first reading (Numbers). This juxtaposition of motifs in the first reading and the gospel, hurting and healing, serpent and staff, finds an echo in Venantius Fortunatus' classic hymn to the cross, "Pange, lingua" (*Worship* #437; *Hymnal 1982*, #166; and a creative translation in *Hymnal for the Hours*, #94A and B). The second reading is Paul's canticle to the "self-emptying" *(kenosis)* of Christ from Philippians.

SACRAMENTARY

The occurrence of this feast on a weekday may mean that the resources available may depend on the hour chosen for the liturgy. Since the "lifting up" of Jesus in John's gospel means not only the crucifixion but also the glorification of Jesus, let the celebration feature links to the Good Friday liturgy with a special emphasis on the glory of that day.

■ VESTURE: Do not use the red of Pentecost, but the red of Good Friday and of martyrs' celebrations. The feast is a further celebration of Jesus as "faithful witness, firstborn from the dead" (Revelation).

■ CROSS: If possible, let the processional cross be the cross that the community venerates at the Good Friday liturgy, now festively decorated. Some Eastern rites conclude Evening Prayer on this feast with a veneration similar to that of Good Friday. The difference is that on this feast the cross rests in an arrangement of fragrant September herbs, so

SEPTEMBER

that people bending or kneeling to kiss the cross are reminded of the sweetness of its blossoming in the resurrection of Jesus. The people are given a flower from this "cross garden" to take home as a fragrant reminder of the salvation won for us upon that wood.

■ MUSIC: Depending on available resources, sing the Eastertime Gloria, gospel and eucharistic acclamations, and use hymns like Fortunatus' mentioned above and "Lift high the cross."

■ PREFACE AND EUCHARISTIC PRAYER: The proper preface is the former Passiontide text, which contrasts the tree of our defeat in Eden with the tree of our salvation on Calvary. This is a venerable text. The preface Passion of the Lord I is powerful as well. The Eucharistic Prayer for Reconciliation I has the line, "Before he stretched out his arms between heaven and earth. . . ."

#441 or 639 (LMC, #193–227) white

FRI 15 Our Lady of Sorrows
MEMORIAL

ORIENTATION

The counterpart of yesterday's feast, this memorial is placed here to illustrate Mary's participation in the work and fruit of her Son's redemptive mission.

LECTIONARY

As on most memorials for which the sanctoral lectionary offers proper readings, the calendar suggests maintaining the weekday lectionary for the first reading and using the proper gospel. 1 Corinthians speaks of service and strength, both of which are seen in Mary's response to God's intervention in her life. Both gospel options, John's version of the crucifixion and Luke's account of Simeon's prophecy, emphasize Mary's role within the community of believers as one who must face the same choice and test required of all who would be faithful disciples of Jesus.

SACRAMENTARY

The sacramentary provides a proper Mass for this memorial, but also look at the wonderful formularies in the lenten section of the *Collection of Masses of the Blessed Virgin Mary,* Mary at the Foot of the Cross I, and II, the Commending of Mary. Since the sacramentary provides no proper preface, choose one from the *Collection* that corresponds to the gospel chosen. For the Lukan gospel, use the preface Mary and the Presentation of the Lord, *Collection of Masses of the Blessed Virgin Mary,* P-7; for the Johannine gospel, the preface Commending of the Virgin Mary, P-13.

MUSIC

Proper to today's liturgy, but more often associated with the Stations of the Cross, is the hymn "Stabat Mater Dolorosa" ("At the cross her station keeping"). As an optional sequence hymn today, it might fit into the liturgy of the word as a preparation for the gospel. A more suitable place, however, might be as a meditation after communion.

#442 (LMC, #193–227) red

SAT 16 Cornelius, pope and martyr, Cyprian, bishop and martyr
MEMORIAL

The scriptural equations are simple when Paul and Luke make them: one bread, one body; good tree, good fruit. But within those simple words lies any community's spiritual challenge of a lifetime. Jesus speaks about digging deeply and laying firm foundations. Translated into a practical program for the community of disciples, that means hearing the word and then acting on it.

The two bishops, Cornelius of Rome (+ 253) and Cyprian of Carthage (+ 258), exemplify how division in matters of theology was overcome by unity in the essentials: one Lord, one faith, one baptism. The two saints are named together in Eucharistic Prayer I, and their memorial suggests a self-examination: Do we work as a community at moving beyond our surface divisions to the one Lord who unites us?

#131 (LMC, #126) green

17 Twenty-fourth Sunday in Ordinary Time

AUTUMN: SUNDAYS 24–30

Autumn always seems to signal a return to seriousness of purpose. Could it be those memories of back-to-school days? The path of discipleship takes a serious turn during this block of Sundays, as the Gospel of Mark sets us on the road to Jerusalem and the liturgical calendar points us toward the return of

SEPTEMBER

Christ and the culmination of all things.

LECTIONARY

The autumn Sundays begin with what many commentators consider to be the hinge of Mark's gospel: Peter's confession of faith, followed immediately by his misunderstanding of the nature of Jesus' Messiahship. The selection ends with Jesus' proclamation of the conditions of discipleship (Twenty-fourth Sunday). On the next Sunday (Twenty-fifth Sunday) Jesus again predicts his suffering and calls his disciples to humble service. Subsequent Sundays explore the nature of discipleship in specific detail: gentleness in judging others, strictness towards oneself (Twenty-sixth Sunday); integrity of commitment and humility (Twenty-seventh Sunday); complete commitment and the danger of riches (Twenty-eighth Sunday); the key to greatness and the nature of authority in the kingdom (Twenty-ninth Sunday). As did the previous section of Ordinary Time, this block of Sundays concludes with a healing that teaches a message (Thirtieth Sunday).

The last lines of both this Sunday's gospel and the Thirtieth Sunday's gospel (October 29) announce a principal theme of this block of Sundays in Ordinary Time. Today Jesus says: "If any want to become my followers, let them deny themselves, take up their cross and follow me." The gospel of the Thirtieth Sunday ends by saying of the blind Bartimaeus, "Immediately the man regained his sight and followed Jesus on the way." The way is not only the road to Jerusalem but the path of discipleship. Today Jesus has to remind Peter that it is not for the disciple to give the Master directions. The Isaiah reading is a repeat from Passion (Palm) Sunday, the third of the Suffering Servant songs, and reinforces the gospel message: The Master knows where he is going. Those who are truly disciples will follow him along the path that leads to suffering but culminates in glory. The passage from James continues last week's challenge to live the gospel's message of social justice within the community and beyond it.

SACRAMENTARY

The penitential rite throughout these Sundays might focus on the nature of Jesus' messiahship and our discipleship:

> Lord Jesus, you are the Messiah who walked the path of suffering for our salvation: Lord, have mercy.
>
> Christ Jesus, you are the Master who came not to be served but to serve: Christ, have mercy.
>
> Lord Jesus, you are the Teacher who bids us take up our cross and follow in the way of discipleship: Lord, have mercy.

The standard set of general intercessions throughout this block could focus on the challenges of discipleship, perhaps singling out various vocations and ways of life within the community (married couples, ordained ministry, single people, senior citizens, the widowed and the young). One variable intercession each week could relate the day's scriptures to some current need. The Preface for Sundays in Ordinary Time *i* or *ii* might provide a link binding this block of Sundays together.

MUSIC

Two refrains given in the lectionary at #175 would be appropriate to this block of Sundays if the proper psalm for each week is not used. They are available in settings of every style: For Psalm 95: "If today you hear his voice, harden not your hearts"; for Psalm 100: "We are his people, the sheep of his flock."

Change the eucharistic prayer acclamations for this block of Sundays, perhaps returning to those used during Winter Ordinary Time or the first part of this summer's Ordinary Time.

For a communion processional try using the first verse of the "Bangor antiphonary" hymn as a refrain. Found in many hymnals, it is at #732 in *Worship*. The assembly simply sings the first verse after each verse by cantor or choir: "Draw near and take the body of your Lord, and drink with faith the blood for you outpoured."

Hymnody should emphasize discipleship and community.

■ DECORATIONS: Over the weeks of this block of Ordinary Time, late summer will be giving way to golden autumn in many places. Peter Mazar's *To Crown the Year* (pages 176 – 191) has ideas for incorporating images of autumn and harvest time, along with a few helpful warnings.

■ ANOINTING OF THE SICK: Some communities schedule a communal anointing during the autumn part of Ordinary Time. The gospel of the last Sunday of this block (Thirtieth Sunday) features a healing story.

■ BLESSING FOR CATECHETICAL SUNDAY: This weekend's scriptures provide a perfect setting for the parish's blessing of its

SEPTEMBER

catechists. The very word *education* is derived from the Latin verb *to lead forth,* an easy starting point for reflections on following, i.e., discipleship. The *Book of Blessings* (chapter 4) has a fine order for blessing.

MON 18 — #443 (LMC, #193–227) green
Weekday

Divisions, distinctions, discrimination: These elements were fatal to community life in the Corinth of Paul's day and in our own parishes today. The Lord's Supper, says Paul, must be everyone's supper or it is no one's supper, least of all the Lord's. From this first reading comes one of the memorial acclamations of the eucharistic prayer, "When we eat this bread and drink this cup . . . " Today's gospel features a character who shows up in Luke's works more than once. In fact, some commentators theorize that this particular man belonged to the community for whom Luke wrote the Gospel and Acts. The centurion is a God-loving Gentile, a man of power and means who uses these on behalf of the people whose country his government is occupying. In this outsider, faith shines brightly—more brightly, says Jesus, than in Israel. Luke always challenges the common presumptions regarding who is in and who is out in the eyes of God.

TUE 19 — #444 (LMC, #193–227) green
Weekday

Januarius, bishop and martyr, optional memorial/red. ▪ Paul's letter celebrates the diversity of the body of Christ but points out that we are, nevertheless, members of one body. The little-used Preface of Christian Unity (P-76) is inspired by this text. Luke's predilection for the outsider shines through today's gospel whose focus is as much on the widowed mother as on her dead son. Jesus again crosses the boundaries of ritual impurity: He touches the bier.

Bishop Januarius was martyred near Naples in the persecution under the Emperor Diocletian at the beginning of the fourth century.

WED 20 — #445 (LMC, #193–227) red
Andrew Kim Taegon, priest and martyr and Paul Chong Hasang, and their companions, martyrs
MEMORIAL

Paul's canticle on love is today's first reading. Jesus points out that to those who do not want to hear, no messenger from God will be acceptable. In light of this week's Pauline readings and today's gospel, two practical questions might be: Do we work as a community to move beyond our superficial divisions toward the one Lord who unites us? How often do we dismiss the message by finding something to criticize in the messenger?

The sacramentary's listing of proper readings is for communities that keep this memorial as a feast or solemnity, Korean communities, for instance. These nineteenth-century martyrs numbered over 100 and came from all walks of life. Prayers for Korea are in order as its people continue to expand their personal and political freedoms. New memorials, like today's, of saints from nations outside Europe or the Americas should remind us of the universality of the church.

THU 21 — #643 (LMC, #376) red
Matthew, apostle
FEAST

Matthew presents his vocation story to point out Jesus' ability to see not what we are but what we can be. Jesus' table-fellowship with sinners is a scandal to the religiously observant who always see participation at the Lord's table as a reward for righteousness rather than as healing therapy.

FRI 22 — #447 (LMC, #193–227) green
Weekday

Paul presents a simple question, the answer to which determines whether we Christians are on the edge of a new reality or simply deluded dreamers: If the new life of resurrection is for Jesus only, where is our salvation in that? In Luke's gospel, the parable of the sower (tomorrow's reading) is framed with the passage on the women who accompanied Jesus (today's reading) and the description of Jesus' true family (next Tuesday's reading). If there is no Saturday morning assembly, planners may wish to join Saturday's gospel to today's or to next Monday's.

SAT 23 — #448 (LMC, #193–227) green
Weekday

Blessed Virgin Mary, optional memorial/white. ▪ By coincidence both readings use the image of sowing seed. Paul uses the image of a seed to teach the Corinthians the truth of the resurrection. What we shall become in the risen life is the fulfillment of what we are now and yet a wondrous reality far beyond it. For Luke, those who bear fruit do so not only by their endurance but with the qualities prized by Luke's pagan world: "good and generous hearts."

SEPTEMBER

For the Saturday memorial of Mary, see #38, Mother of Unity, especially appropriate to our week of readings from 1 Corinthians; or #46, Gate of Heaven, in light of Paul's teaching on resurrection and Luke's teaching on fruitfulness.

24 — Twenty-fifth Sunday in Ordinary Time
#134 (LMC, #128)   green

On the way: these three words are important. They mean not only on the way to Jerusalem but also on the way of discipleship. So last week, Jesus asks the question about his identity while they are on the way. This week the argument about greatness takes place while they are on the way. Despite Peter's insight near Caesarea Philippi, the disciples clearly see very little. Mark is always realistic about the disciples' obtuseness: "They did not understand, and they were afraid to ask." He is also honest about the ambition that blinds them in this week's episode. This block of Sundays is perfect for examining issues of contemporary discipleship.

The passage from James fits in well: The contrast between envy and ambition on one hand and wisdom from above on the other is important at all times.

■ BLESSING LITURGICAL MINISTRIES: Because they celebrate discipleship as service, this Sunday's second reading and gospel provide an appropriate setting for blessing liturgical ministers or introducing new members of the pastoral staff. See *the Book of Blessings* for appropriate texts and the Episcopal church's *Book of Occasional Services* for collects specific to various ministries.

MON 25 — Weekday
#449 (LMC, #193–227)   green

Today the weekday lectionary begins a tour of the Hebrew Bible's wisdom literature. Proverbs, Ecclesiastes and Job will provide the first reading for the next two weeks. For an introduction to each of these books that is scholarly and accessible, see Dianne Bergant's commentary in the Reading Guide section of *The Catholic Study Bible* (Oxford University Press, 1990). The opening passage focuses on the dynamics of relationships. The gospel is Jesus' counsel to "wise listening." It makes little sense if we have not heard last Saturday's parable, which might, therefore, be joined to today's passage.

TUE 26 — Weekday
#450 (LMC, #193–227)   green

Cosmas and Damian, martyrs, optional memorials/red. ▪ "To do righteousness and justice is more acceptable to the Lord than sacrifice." This wisdom from Proverbs goes well with today's gospel, in which Jesus redefines the criteria for membership in his family circle. For Jesus, blood relationship yields to a broader "family resemblance": Those who hear and do God's word are "brother and sister and mother to me."

The Eastern church has a designation for a category of saints of whom today's saints are representatives: the "unmercenary ones." Cosmas and Damian (third century) were physicians who upon their conversion to Christ refused to accept fees for their practice of medicine. Pray today for all in the medical and health care fields who freely give in service to those unable to repay them.

WED 27 — Vincent de Paul, presbyter, religious founder
#451 (LMC, #193–227)   white
MEMORIAL

Proverbs calls for joy in sufficiency, trust in need, and generosity in any case. Jesus sends the twelve on mission with few possessions for themselves but with awesome power for others.

Vincent de Paul (+ 1660) welcomed and served the Christ in our midst in the poorest of the poor. "Do not become upset or feel guilty," he wrote his followers, "because you interrupted your prayer to serve the poor. God is not neglected if you leave him for such service" (Office of Readings). To this day, the parish organization dedicated to service bears his name.

THU 28 — Weekday
#452 (LMC, #193–227)   green

Wenceslaus, martyr; Lawrence Ruiz and his companions, martyrs; optional memorials/red. ▪ In prescribing Ecclesiastes at this time of year, the compilers of the lectionary were continuing the Jewish tradition that schedules this book for proclamation during the harvest celebration of Sukkoth. "It is not clear how this practice began or why Ecclesiastes was chosen. Perhaps the somber tone of the book, the seasoned reflections of an aging sage, fit the maturity of harvest and the dreariness of autumn." Note the appropriateness of Ecclesiastes for today: "Qoheleth never disparaged ingenuity or

SEPTEMBER

hard work. Rather he criticized those who judged the worth of human endeavor by the amount of output rather than the quality of input" (Bergant, 264–270). The gospel is a commentary on the futility of simply trying to see something that is new. Herod's curiosity about Jesus, unlike that of the tax-collectors and sinners, did not lead to newness of life.

The proper readings of tomorrow's feast supersede the most famous passage from Ecclesiastes. Although it would make for a long first reading, some presiders may wish the assembly to hear it. Its bleak evaluation of life as an endless cycle of alternating opposites, whose ceaseless repetition changes nothing and leads nowhere, may strike a chord with some.

"Good King Wenceslaus" (+ c. 929), tireless in charity and boundless in generosity toward his subjects, was murdered by his brother's followers for opposing their military atrocities. Lawrence Ruiz (+ 1633), a husband and father, was martyred in Nagasaki, together with other Dominican Third Order members, lay, religious and clerical, Asian and European.

FRI 29 — Michael, Gabriel and Raphael, archangels
#647 (LMC, #381) red
FEAST

If anyone doubts the contemporary interest in angels, simply look at the displays in any bookstore. Angels have always had a special place in Catholic life, both in our reflection on scripture and in popular devotion. Our two autumn angel days, today and October 2, provide an opportunity to rekindle and refocus this element of our heritage.

Check LTP's *Preparing Liturgy for Children and Children for Liturgy* (pages 58–62) for liturgical suggestions applicable to the whole assembly. See Gregory the Great's homily in the Office of Readings. The petitions in the Office's intercessions may provide inspiration for today's general intercessions. There is a special preface, and Eucharistic Prayer I mentions the ministry of angels in the community's eucharist. Two fine hymns for the feast are in the Episcopal *Hymnal 1982:* a translation from Latin, "Christ the fair glory of the holy angels" (#283 has an ancient and beautiful chant) and "O ye immortal throng" (#284), which synthesizes the scriptural references to angelic ministry.

SAT 30 — Jerome, presbyter and doctor of the church
#454 (LMC, #193–227) white
MEMORIAL

Our survey of Ecclesiastes concludes with some of the most beautiful but pessimistic poetry in scripture. The gospel seems to echo that pessimism, as Jesus predicts his passion to unperceiving disciples who are afraid to ask for clarification. Ecclesiastes knows death to be inevitable. Yet Jesus embraces death of his own free will on behalf of others, of us! This makes death not the end that Ecclesiastes is resigned to, but a passage to eternal life.

Jerome (+ 420) had a fierce temper, acerbic tongue and lethal pen. He also had the most exquisite sensitivity to God's presence in scripture and an undaunted commitment to put those scriptures into the language of God's people. Testifying to his love of scripture, this quote of his appears in Vatican II's *Constitution on Divine Revelation:* "Ignorance of the scriptures is ignorance of Christ!"

October

1 — Twenty-sixth Sunday in Ordinary Time
#137 (LMC, #132) green

If the unifying motif of this block of Sundays is discipleship, then the theme of today's gospel must be the continued misunderstanding of the disciples. The gospel offers several challenges to the disciples' following of Jesus — and our own:

- Disciples must broaden their vision of the community. Jesus' boundaries are inclusive: "Whoever is not against us is for us!"
- Disciples appreciate the least gesture of hospitality as worthy of gratitude and reward.
- Disciples must never be a stumbling block to those who come seeking Jesus.
- Discipleship demands uncompromising commitment.

Although each admonition is important, the point of the first reading is clearly intended to match the first point of the gospel. Christ has called his disciples to serve others, not to judge their motives. Meanwhile James has some sharp words for any community to ponder.

OCTOBER

MON 2
#650 (LMC, #193–227) white
Guardian Angels
MEMORIAL

The lectionary's survey of Job cannot do justice to this rich, deep book, universally appealing as its protagonist struggles with God, neighbor and his own soul over the problem of suffering. The preacher's few and carefully prepared words will have to fill in the blanks in the weekday lectionary's presentation. See Dianne Bergant's commentary in *The Catholic Study Bible*, Reader's Guide, 232–241. The gospel for the memorial focuses on the little ones the Guardian Angels watch over and on the disciples' need to become like children. Devotion to the Guardian Angels is traditionally a wonderful way to teach children about God's abiding love for each of us.

TUE 3
#456 (LMC, #193–227) green
Weekday

Suffering Job curses the day of his birth. Perhaps we've been there ourselves. Luke's gospel pictures Jesus "firmly resolved to proceed toward Jerusalem," the city of his own confrontation with suffering and death. For Jesus, as for Job, life is far from painless. But for Luke's Jesus suffering is freely borne for the redemption of others.

WED 4
#457 (LMC, #193–227) white
Francis of Assisi, religious founder
MEMORIAL

The "otherness" of the omnipotent and eternal God fills Job's thoughts as he reflects on his innocent suffering. The answers and explanations of his friends are not helpful to Job, for whom God is a God of mystery and silence. In the gospel, those who would follow Jesus must leave all else behind — perhaps even the desire to have all the answers now.

Neighbor to the planet and all its creatures was today's saint, Francis of Assisi (+ 1226). Honor him today by singing all the verses of his "Canticle of creation" ("All creatures of our God and King") and one of the many settings of his famous prayer, "Lord, make me an instrument of your peace."

THU 5
#458 (LMC, #193–227) green
Weekday

Faced with the silence of the mysterious God who permitted his suffering, Job professes his belief in the final vindication that God "my Redeemer" will bring. Like lambs in the midst of wolves, the disciples go forth with good news for those who will listen and a blessing of peace for those who will not.

FRI 6
#459 (LMC, #193–227) green
Weekday

Bruno, presbyter, hermit, religious founder; Blessed Marie-Rose Durocher, virgin, religious founder; optional memorials/ white. ▪ The first reading is the beginning of Job's interview with God. If there is no Saturday gathering, it might be helpful to conclude this week's cycle of Job readings by adding tomorrow's passage to today's. For Luke, seeing is not believing; changing one's life and doing the word is the only proof of having accepted Christ.

Today's saints bore witness in different ways. Bruno (+ 1101) founded the Carthusian order of hermits and Marie-Rose (+ 1849) was a Canadian educator who worked to provide young women with a quality education and a vibrant spiritual life.

SAT 7
#460 (LMC, #193–227) white
Our Lady of the Rosary
MEMORIAL

While some dispute the authenticity of the ending, the canonical text of the Book of Job provides today's happy ending. To the disciples' happy ending of their first mission, Jesus adds a gentle caution. Not what we accomplish but how God sees us: This ought to be the source of our true delight, and for this we need to become like the little children for whom Jesus praises his Father.

This memorial originally commemorated a Christian victory over the Muslims (October 7, 1570). Today, thankfully, the rosary is offered as a prayer for peace. If October is dedicated to praying the rosary, consider the scriptural form, which helps to focus the mind and heart on the succession of mysteries. See the CDs that feature the pope praying the rosary. He arranges the traditional prayer in a beautiful context of scriptural proclamation and communal song.

8
#140 (LMC, #135) green
Twenty-seventh Sunday in Ordinary Time

Authentic discipleship demands renewal in relationships. The Pharisees focus on the concession of divorce, but Jesus spotlights the ideal of marriage, appealing to the text of today's first reading. The story analyzes not the *what* of creation but the *why*, and teaches several truths. Woman is not created from dirt and is not to be treated like dirt. In God's plan, and in the kingdom proclaimed by Jesus,

OCTOBER

there is mutuality of dignity and rights between man and woman. Human sexuality is God's good gift, and the individual's fulfillment is found in community. On the other hand, Jesus' private answer to the disciples shows even this earliest gospel struggling to uphold Jesus' ideal of marriage in the face of contrary realities. For instance, the situation addressed by verse 12, a woman divorcing her husband, was impossible in the Judaism of Jesus' time, though not in the Greco-Roman world of Mark's community. The gospel concludes with Jesus embracing another disenfranchised segment of society. The disciples are busy chasing away children. But in the previous chapter of the gospel Jesus had told them to be like children!

From now until Advent, the second reading each Sunday is from the Letter to the Hebrews. Today's passage fits nicely with the other readings since it, too, focuses on relationships. Jesus becomes lowly so that he might be one with his brothers and sisters in the human condition and help us to see that together he and we have one Father.

MON 9 #461 (LMC, #193–227) green
Weekday

Denis, bishop and martyr, and his companions, martyrs/red; John Leonardi, presbyter, religious founder/white; optional memorials. ▪ From now through the beginning of next week, we read from the Letter of Paul to the "foolish Galatians," as he called them. The burning issue of the day was whether the prescriptions of the Jewish covenant bound Christians, or was faith in Christ all-sufficient? Contemporary-sounding questions flow from that ancient dilemma. *Leadership:* Who decides what and for whom? *Divisions:* Are some of us right and some of us wrong about this non-negotiable question? Is the question non-negotiable? How does the rest of the church cope when leadership is divided? Is this a scandal or a healthy sign? In the gospel, a student of the law asks, "Who is my neighbor?" The parable of the Good Samaritan teaches him, and us, that the proper question is "To whom can I be a neighbor?" The answer: "To anyone in need." The moral: "Go and do likewise!"

Denis (+ third century) is venerated as founder of the church in Paris. John Leonardi (+ 1609) gave his life tending the sick during an epidemic in Rome.

▪ COLUMBUS DAY: Mass prayers could be taken from a number of places in the sacramentary. The texts for civic observances might be appropriate (July 4 and Appendix X, #6). Today is also a day when immigrants celebrate citizenship: the formularies "For the Progress of Peoples" or "For Refugees and Exiles" might be suitable. Given our history with respect to Native Americans, the Masses "For Peace and Justice" might provide good texts. Use the new Eucharistic Prayer for Various Needs and Occasions, Form C, Jesus, Way to the Father, or Form D, Jesus, the Compassion of God.

TUE 10 #462 (LMC, #193–227) green
Weekday

Paul offers his vocation story to establish the legitimacy of his call and his authority in what he is about to say to the Galatians. In yesterday's gospel, Jesus said, "Go and do." In today's gospel, Jesus says, "Sit and listen." These are two sides of the same discipleship.

WED 11 #463 (LMC, #193–227) green
Weekday

Paul's confrontation with Peter in today's passage sets the stage for his private confrontation with the Galatians in tomorrow's reading. The church's growth in truth comes as the fruit of real honesty and patient sifting of insights to discern what the Spirit is saying. In the gospel, Jesus teaches his disciples a prayer whose simplicity can bring all sides together.

THU 12 #464 (LMC, #193–227) green
Weekday

Faith comes through hearing, and from looking upon Christ crucified as the image of the good news we have heard. That news always seems too good to be true! We don't have to *do* anything to be beloved by God; we just *are* loved! Once that sinks in, we will do wonderful things for all kinds of people; our salvation in Christ compels us to live out our faith in love for others. The gospel confirms Paul's message: ask, seek, knock. Everything good is a gift. Grace is everywhere.

▪ OPENING OF VATICAN II, 1962: Pope John XXIII's opening address an inspiration and challenge: "Our duty is not just to guard this treasure, as though it were some museum piece and we the curators, but . . . what is needed at the present time is a new enthusiasm, a new joy and serenity of mind."

FRI 13 #465 (LMC, #193–227) green
Weekday

Today, tomorrow and Monday, Paul presents faith apart from works as the source of salvation for Jews and Gentiles alike. He

OCTOBER

begins with the example of Abraham. The Canadian lectionary adds verse 6: "Just as Abraham 'believed God, and it was reckoned to him as righteousness,'" to make the transition to "all who believe are children of Abraham." The point Jesus makes in the gospel, interpreted in light of Paul's remarks, could be very timely. Any return to a legalistic vision of the spiritual life (a recurring temptation) can leave us worse than we were before.

SAT 14 — #466 (LMC, #193–227) green
Weekday

Callistus I, pope and martyr/red; Blessed Virgin Mary/white; optional memorials. ▪ Faith is the great equalizer, proclaims Paul: "There is no longer Jew or Greek, slave or free, male or female; all of you are one in Christ." Do we yet believe this? Hearing the word of God in such faith, says Jesus in the gospel, really hearing it (obey comes from *ob-audire,* to listen intently) leads to true blessedness. Thus Mary's blessedness is not the result of her motherhood but of her fidelity in hearing and obeying the word.

Callistus (+c. 222) was a born a slave and even served time as a convict. After his release, he served as deacon and was eventually elected Pope. Rigorists criticized him sharply for alleged laxity in church discipline. Callistus favored leniency toward those who had denied the faith under persecution and offered them reconciliation and a second chance. For the Saturday commemoration of Mary see *Collection of Masses of the Blessed Virgin Mary,* #10, Disciple of the Lord; or #25–27, Image and Mother of the Church, which is in keeping with the readings from both Galatians and Luke.

15 — #143 (LMC, #138) green
Twenty-eighth Sunday in Ordinary Time

On the way: The NRSV and the RNAB opt for the word "journey," to translate the Greek expression that punctuates this block of Sundays about discipleship. A more literal choice would be "on the way." On the way a would-be follower (Matthew says he was young) appears with a question: "What must I do to inherit eternal life?" It is an odd question, in that the verbs don't match: *do* and *inherit.* One does not inherit by doing, one inherits by receiving what someone else has already done something to achieve. So when Jesus tells him to go, sell and give, come and follow, he is not so much asking the man to *do* something as to *become* someone: a disciple whose trust is in God. Mark's version contains a poignant detail: "Jesus, looking at him, loved him." There is a personal dimension to this and every invitation to discipleship. But there is, likewise, what Bonhoeffer called "the cost of discipleship." Responding to Christ's invitation always involves some renunciation.

The first reading suggests some elements that can hinder communities and individuals from answering Christ's call: scepters and thrones (power); wealth and gems (money and material possessions); health and beauty (two of the "idols" of our age). The Book of Wisdom does not imply that any of these are evil, only that the gift of discernment will help us order our priorities aright. The self-examination, individual and communal, that this Sunday's scriptures presents does confirm Hebrews' picture of God's word as a double-edged sword.

MON 16 — #467 (LMC, #193–227) green
Weekday

Hedwig, married woman, religious; Margaret Mary Alacoque, virgin, religious; optional memorials/white. ▪ Paul returns to the story of Abraham to illustrate his assertion that believers in Christ are true descendants of this "father in faith" and at the same time free from the requirements of the Law. Preachers must avoid any disparaging remarks about the Sinai covenant or Judaism. "No longer Jew nor Greek," is the line we must remember. The continuity of our faith with the faith of Abraham's descendants could be brought out with the reminder that all of us, Jews and Christians, look at the promises through eschatological lenses. "Next year in Jerusalem," is the exclamation with which our Jewish friends end their Passover seder; "Christ will come again," we proclaim at our paschal feast as we look forward to its fulfillment in the new and eternal Jerusalem. At any rate, the gospel should keep us humble: We, too, have someone greater than Solomon or Jonah. Do we heed his wisdom? Have we repented at his word?

Hedwig (+ 1243) founded hospitals, served the poor and worked to secure peace among warring princes. Margaret Mary (+ 1690) bore with patient love the rejection and contempt of her religious superiors and others, and is largely responsible for the devotion to the Sacred Heart that provides many with a rich appreciation of the compassion of Christ.

OCTOBER

On this day in 1978, Cardinal Karol Wojtyla of Cracow, Poland, was elected the youngest pope in longer than a century and the first non-Italian bishop of Rome in 450 years.

TUE 17 — #468 (LMC, #193–227) red
Ignatius of Antioch, bishop and martyr
MEMORIAL

Paul states the core of Christian life: "The only thing that counts is faith working through love." In the face of rigid observances and unbending traditions, Jesus proclaims the cleansing power of practical charity toward those in need.

To today's great saint, Ignatius of Antioch (+ c. 107), we owe seven letters to the churches he passed through on his way to martyrdom in Rome. These letters provide insights into the life and structure of the early church.

WED 18 — #661 (LMC, #396) red
Luke, evangelist
FEAST

"Luke, the holy evangelist, is worthy of the church's praise, for he is the scribe of the gentleness of Christ." The poetry of Dante is an antiphon in today's Liturgy of the Hours, and many who read Luke's gospel agree. His gospel and Acts make up over a quarter of the New Testament, taking Jesus from Bethlehem to Jerusalem and then taking the church from Jerusalem to Rome, the heart of the Empire and the ends of the earth. In its pages we can all find ourselves: women, men, rich, poor, sinners and saints. Legend remembers Luke as an artist who painted a portrait of Mary. An American novelist, drawing on Colossians, called her fictionalized Luke "dear and glorious physician." Luke indeed paints a portrait of a compassionate God whose healing touch extends to everyone.

Worship and *RitualSong* have hymns based on Luke's Emmaus gospel (*Worship* #448; *Ritual Song* #597 and 816). Consider using the Eucharistic Prayer for Masses for Various Needs and Occasions, Form D, Jesus, the Compassion of God.

THU 19 — #470 (LMC, #193–227) red
Isaac Jogues and John de Brébeuf, presbyters, religious, missionaries and martyrs, and their companions, martyrs
MEMORIAL

For two weeks the lectionary takes us through the Letter to the Ephesians, thought to be the work of a "Paulinist" writer immediately after Paul's death. The style is not the personal approach Paul used to help local churches with problems. Ephesians has quite an advanced theology of the church and seems meant for a wider audience. Today's passage is a hymn of praise for what God has accomplished for believers in Christ. Rather than the eschatological note of Paul's personal letters, in which the blessings in Christ are yet to come for those who persevere, Ephesians celebrates a redemption and forgiveness already ours by our adoption in Christ. Jesus' criticism of the Pharisees and religious legal experts is something our own age needs to take to heart.

The eight North American martyrs (+ c. 1647), six Jesuit priests and two lay assistants, shared the gospel in the languages and idioms of the peoples they met. But their work was caught up in turmoil: a smallpox epidemic, battles between French and English trading interests and conflict among the Huron, Mohawk and Iroquois peoples. The church honors them for their zeal for the gospel, their love of the peoples to whom they ministered, and their steadfast courage in the face of torture. Today the Eucharistic Prayer for Special Needs, Form D, Jesus, the Compassion of God, would be appropriate.

FRI 20 — #471 (LMC, #193–227) green
Weekday

Paul of the Cross, presbyter, religious founder, optional memorial/white. • Who are we and what are we all about? The church in every age must always ask this question anew and embrace the answer again. Ephesians replies that we are "destined to live for the praise of Christ's glory . . . marked with the seal of the promised Holy Spirit . . . God's own people." Jesus warns his disciples against hypocrisy and bids them remember, in the midst of persecution, how precious they are to God, whose providential care will not fail them.

To combat the indifferentism of his time, Paul of the Cross (+ 1775) founded the Passionist congregation and combined a contemplative life with the preaching of parish missions that calls participants to conversion and commitment.

SAT 21 — #472 (LMC, #193–227) green
Weekday

Blessed Virgin Mary, optional memorial/white. • Echoing Romans, Ephesians calls the church "the body of Christ." As members of his body we are to know the hope to which we are called and to experience God's immeasurable power at work

OCTOBER

in us. This sense of "vocation in the world" is what Vatican II extolled as "the universal call to holiness." It is a sense that will transform all our relationships and give a touch of eternal purpose even to our ordinary daily work. In Luke's gospel, the "Gospel of the Holy Spirit," Jesus promises his followers the words they will need in the hour they will need them — all the gift of the Spirit.

For the Saturday memorial of Mary, choose from the *Collection of Masses of the Blessed Virgin Mary* #23, Temple of the Lord, or any of the formularies entitled Image and Mother of the Church, #25, 26, 27.

22 Twenty-ninth Sunday in Ordinary Time
#146 (LMC, #141) green

The first reading is an abbreviated version of Isaiah's Fourth Servant Song, which is proclaimed in its entirety on Good Friday. For the sake of context, the Canadian lectionary adds verse 4: "The servant of the Lord has borne our infirmities and carried our diseases; yet we accounted him stricken, struck down by God, and afflicted." In the gospel, the disciples' misunderstanding of what it means to follow Jesus is reaching the point of no return. Consider the progression of their inability to see what Jesus is all about. After Jesus' first prediction of his passion, Peter objects (Twenty-fourth Sunday). After the second prediction comes a discussion of greatness that embarrasses even the Twelve (Twenty-fifth Sunday). Today's passage comes after Jesus' third prediction of his own death. Jesus warns them all that becoming disciples means becoming suffering servants themselves.

In light of this message, it is hard to imagine choosing the short form of today's gospel. The two parts of this passage go hand in hand: The cost of discipleship is everything; the sacrifice required of those in leadership is everything. Even the Hebrews reading fits in with today's gospel: we may approach the throne boldly, not for power, but for grace.

■ MISSION SUNDAY: The proper way to work this concern of the universal church into the liturgy is through the general intercessions, a special collection and a fitting hymn whose theme is mission, service or discipleship. Some presidential prayers could be drawn from the Mass for the Spread of the Gospel. The Eucharistic Prayer for Various Needs, form C (Jesus, the Way to the Father) might be appropriate.

■ PAPAL ANNIVERSARY: Pray today for one whose ministry within the family of faith is a focus of unity and sometimes a source of division: Today is the twenty-second anniversary of the installation of John Paul II as bishop of Rome.

23 Weekday
#473 (LMC, #193–227) green

John of Capistrano, presbyter, religious, missionary, optional memorial/white. ■ Ephesians repeats a major Pauline doctrine: We are saved by grace through faith. The next point: This is not our own doing; therefore, no boasting. And, the gospel seems to add, no judging of others and no hoarding of God's bounty, given to us in trust as stewards who must share.

The Franciscan John of Capistrano (+ 1456) is remembered as a preacher and reformer who worked in what is now Austria, northern Italy and Serbia.

24 Weekday
#474 (LMC, #193–227) green

Anthony Mary Claret, bishop, religious founder, optional memorial/white. ■ Gentiles and Jews reconciled in one body; strangers no longer; peace to all, near and far. Ephesians' picture of the church comforts us by speaking of this wonder having been accomplished already, and challenges us, for we know that we have yet to live this reality. The gospel's warning of the master's certain return at an uncertain hour ought to be our inspiration act on the vision of Ephesians and keep the lamp of faith lit. For Luke, vigilance for the Lord's return and diligence in the kingdom's service are complementary aspects of discipleship.

Today's saint, Anthony Claret (+ 1870), founded the Claretians to spread the gospel by spoken and printed word. He served as archbishop in Cuba, laboring for spiritual and social reforms and championing especially the rights of indigenous peoples.

25 Weekday
#475 (LMC, #193–227) green

People in Paul's time were shocked. The Gentiles are fellow heirs with the Jews and members of one body. Had this been truly lived just a little over fifty years ago, would humanity have been spared the Holocaust? "Through the church," says the letter, "the wisdom of God in its rich variety" is to be made known. Do we see God's wisdom reflected in rich variety? Much has been given us, and much will be required; we have the Lord's own word for this.

THU 26 #476 (LMC, #193–227) green
Weekday

A family in whose heart Christ dwells by faith, rooted in love: Day after day, as we read through Ephesians, image after beautiful image of the church is held up before us. Mirror or mirage? The reality is beyond our power to accomplish, yet it surely demands and deserves our complete gift of self. Having spelled out the demands of discipleship, Jesus today talks to the disciples about the inevitable division which the choice for discipleship will cause.

FRI 27 #477 (LMC, #193–227) green
Weekday

Writing in Paul's name, the author pictures the apostle in prison, begging the church to live the litany of virtues required to maintain the unity which is the Spirit's gift. What is asked of us? Humility and gentleness, patience and loving forbearance of one another. What makes such a life possible? One Lord, one faith, one baptism.

SAT 28 #666 (LMC, #401) red
Simon and Jude, apostles
FEAST

Simon's nickname was "the Zealot," suggesting an affiliation with one of the radical Jewish resistance movements current at the time of Christ. Jude in Luke's gospel may be the same person as Thaddeus in Matthew and Mark. Because his name sounds like that of the traitor, the story goes, Jude was neglected as an intercessor, and this has led some Christians to consider him the patron of "hopeless causes." As we approach All Saints and All Souls, today's feast invites us to reflect on our communion with those gone before us, even those we know little about. We, too, have a place as living stones, forming with Simon and Jude and all those gone before us, the temple of God and the household of faith.

29 #149 (LMC, #144) green
Thirtieth Sunday in Ordinary Time

After weeks of misunderstanding on the part of the disciples, the autumn block of Sundays in Ordinary Time concludes with a miracle and a new disciple on the way. The Jeremiah reading is not from his "fountain of tears" oracles but from his "book of consolation." Hebrews, too, gives us comfort with its picture of Jesus as the compassionate high priest. The gospel message is good news to seekers in every age. Its description of Bartimaeus' response to Jesus' call is almost ritual and, in fact, has been interpreted as the response of a catechumen coming to faith: Bartimaeus threw off his cloak (cast off the old way), sprang up (an image of resurrection) and came to Jesus (embracing of the gospel). The immediate wonder in the story may be that Bartimaeus has received his sight, but given Matthew's stories of misunderstanding which we have heard in this block of Sundays, the real miracle is that he receives *insight*.

■ REFORMATION SUNDAY: Today has become a day for pulpit exchange and mutual intercession, even joy at the progress toward that unity for which Christ prayed. There is no interfaith dialogue that does not now admit that both sides were at fault in the Reformation, and both sides have much to learn from one another. "Wherever I see a wall dividing Christians," Pope John XXIII remarked, "I try to pull out a brick." Pope John Paul II's encyclical *Ut Unum Sint* would provide a good basis for reflection within or among the churches this weekend.

■ DEDICATION ANNIVERSARY: This Sunday can be a local solemnity observing the anniversary of dedication, especially in parishes whose dedication date is unknown, though even if the date is known, this Sunday may be chosen (footnote, paragraph 52c, General Norms for the Liturgical Year and Calendar, #3818 in *Documents on the Liturgy* [Collegeville: The Liturgical Press, 1983]).

NOVEMBER

- ANOINTING OF THE SICK: This Sunday's gospel of healing may suggest today as an appropriate occasion for communal anointing. The readings of Sunday would be used; perhaps some of the collects, the preface and the interpolations in the eucharistic prayer could be borrowed from the Mass of Anointing.

MON 30 #479 (LMC, #193–227) green
Weekday

Because Wednesday and Thursday have their own readings, today's reading and tomorrow's conclude our Ephesians' passages. They draw out the consequences of the image of the church presented thus far. The mutual forgiveness and love we are to offer one another have been modeled for us already by God in Christ. In the gospel, Jesus expands the obligations of the Sabbath law to embrace the care of anyone in need.

TUE 31 #480 (LMC, #193–227) green
Weekday

The society in which Ephesians was written was one in which authority lines were clearly drawn and beyond challenge. But Christian marriage, mutuality is to prevail. The first line is crucial: "be subject to one another out of reverence for Christ." This should color the interpretation of all that follows. Wives are to be subject to their husbands as to the Lord: that is, hardly as slave to master, for the church is the body of Christ. The image continues: "Husbands, love your wives, just as Christ loved the church and gave himself up for her." The image of the perfect Christian husband, then, is the crucifix. Marriages like that would be seeds that make a difference when grown to maturity, yeast kneaded into the dough of society and raising it up in a holy and wholesome way. The gospel continues the theme of promise and hope.

- HALLOWEEN: One of the few vigils to survive in the popular mind, Halloween has some trappings that derive from Druid festivals and other ancient pagan customs. Without negative preaching that presumes the worst (and accomplishes little), we need to emphasize the Jewish and Christian tradition that links harvest time with God's harvest, gathering in the faithful. Even ghosts and goblins, skeletons and cemeteries point toward the heavenly Jerusalem! See *Take Me Home* for fine pages for All Hallows' Eve and All Saints' Day. *Preparing Liturgy for Children and Children for Liturgy* provides recommendations suitable for adult and mixed assemblies as well as children's liturgies.

> Trick-or-treat is door-to-door hospitality. The jack-o-lantern is a welcoming light to guide us home. Masks and merriment and the edibles (it's harvest time) are all signs of God's reign, a place where rag-tag children remove their masks and we see who they truly are, the saints of God. (page 65)

November

ORIENTATION

November is a month when contrasting moods work together to create a diverse atmosphere:

- *Seasonally*, the world of nature has already begun its decline into winter. Flowers have faded, plants have died or gone into their winter hibernation, fruits and vegetables have been harvested and stored. As the weeks of November unfold, the days get noticeably shorter. The crisp cold air of early morning and evening clears the sinuses and focuses the mind.

- *Socially* and *commercially*, the holiday season is about to begin. Throughout November, as the world outside grows bleak and bare, the malls grow festive and bright. At home, moods collide. Increasing cold and lengthening darkness conspire to keep us inside. But we are lured out by the November sales that, like a secular Advent, herald the season of gift-giving. Fulfilling the obligations of love warms the heart and uplifts the spirit after a gray November day.

- *Liturgically*, Vatican II's calendar and lectionary have refined a long-standing Catholic tradition: November is a month-long celebration of the communion of saints, of remembrance and prayer for those gone before us, and of heightened anticipation of Christ's Second Coming. Within each of these themes are complementary liturgical moods.

The example of the saints, which is meant to challenge us, may also dishearten us as we reflect on how far we are from being the disciples that baptism calls us to be. Yet their intercession on our behalf makes them "a cloud of witnesses," an eternal cheering section of sisters and brothers urging us onward, convincing us that, by God's grace and not our own effort, the crown can be won. The memory of our departed loved ones is bound to be bittersweet. Yet the scriptures and prayers are filled with "the sure and certain hope" of resurrection and reunion. And, if there are some with whom we were not at peace, there is the promise of ultimate reconciliation in the kingdom where "every tear shall be wiped away." As we contemplate our own

NOVEMBER

death and judgment, we are filled with a surpassing hope that the God whose judgments are just is a God who is merciful and compassionate.

MASS IN NOVEMBER

Let all these thoughts and emotions find place in the choices that surround the liturgy of November:

Introductory Rites

One November custom is to use the litany of the saints, with local patrons included, as a processional before the principal Mass each Sunday. Melody and pace are important to avoid tedium. Most communities prefer a strong gathering song. Some use an All Saints hymn; other communities prefer a Jerusalem hymn or harvest anthem as a gathering song and an All Saints hymn at the preparation of the gifts or as a recessional. See the suggestions at "November Hymnody" below.

For the greeting, adapt a scriptural text that emphasizes the communion of saints:

> Citizens with the saints and members of the household of God: grace and peace be with you all. (see Ephesians 2:19)

For the penitential rite, use the invocations at C*ii* in the sacramentary, or let the rite of blessing and sprinkling set a paschal tone for these November Sundays.

Liturgy of the Word

Psalm 122 (lectionary, #175) is the month's common responsorial psalm. Among numerous settings:

- Christopher Willcock, "Let us go rejoicing," *Psalms for Feasts and Seasons* (Liturgical Press)
- Robert Kreutz, "I rejoiced when I heard them say," *Psalms* (OCP)
- A. Gregory Murray antiphon, Gelineau tone, *Worship* (#67)
- Joseph Smith, "I rejoiced when I heard them say" (GIA, G-2775)
- Michael Joncas, "Let us go rejoicing," *Gather*
- David Haas, "I was glad," *Gather*

The gospel acclamation for these last Sundays and weekdays of Ordinary Time should come from the verses at the end of each list in the lectionary (#164, 509).

See LTP's *Prayers for Sundays and Seasons, Year B* for intercessions based on the Sunday scriptures; or use a common set of intercessions throughout the month, including extra petitions for the dead (see the *Order of Christian Funerals* and the sacramentary, appendix I, #11).

Liturgy of the Eucharist

There are proper prefaces for All Saints, the Dedication of the Lateran Basilica and Christ the King. On All Souls, one of the prefaces for Christian Death is used. This could be repeated on the Thirty-second and Thirty-third Sundays and on weekdays, especially during the last two weeks. The same set of acclamations could be used or the Eastertime set, at least on All Saints, All Souls and Christ the King. A good eucharistic prayer might be Reconciliation II.

Concluding Rite

Solemn blessings are suggested for All Saints (#18), All Souls (#20) and the Dedication (#19). See the revision of the All Souls' text in the *Book of Blessings* (#1438). Use it also on the Thirty-third Sunday and perhaps on Christ the King.

NOVEMBER HYMNODY

Survey the topical and liturgical indices of your community's hymnal for headings that suggest this season: kingdom of God, reign of Christ, the church triumphant, pilgrimage, thanksgiving, second coming of Christ. Several genres are particularly appropriate to November:

- *Communion of saints:* "For all the saints" is a perennial favorite. Use the eschatological verse each time: "From earth's wide bounds, from ocean's farthest coast." See new texts set to familiar tunes in *The New Century Hymnal:* "For the faithful who have answered" (#384) and "Thank our God for sisters, brothers" (#397).

- *Thanksgiving:* Some of these carry associations with the heavenly harvest: "Come, ye thankful people, come," "For the beauty of the earth," "Sing to the Lord of the harvest," "For the fruit of your creation."

- *Christ the King:* These may be suitable throughout the month: "To Jesus Christ, our sovereign king," "Jesus shall reign," "Crown him with many crowns," "The king shall come when morning dawns," Paul Manz's anthem, "E'en so, Lord Jesus, quickly come," and Dan Damon's contemporary, "Eternal Christ, you rule" (*New Century,* #302).

- *Jerusalem hymns:* These weave together all the November themes, saints, dedication, judgment, ingathering, reign of God. Their melodies are as important as their texts for setting the mood of the season: "Jerusalem, my happy home," (LAND OF REST); John Mason Neale's translation of Peter Abelard's "O what their joy and their glory must be," (SLANE); "Light's abode, celestial Salem," and "Christ is made the sure foundation" (Sarum plainsong); "O holy city, seen of John" (MORNING SONG).

NOVEMBER

WORSHIP ENVIRONMENT

Overall Decorations

If they are to be used, begin the harvest-motif decorations November 1. As Peter Mazar notes in *To Crown the Year* (pages 192–197): "It's a mistake not to recognize how November 1 and 2 are clothed in the harvest — an intensely paschal image that the scriptures use over and over as a sign of the kingdom to come, as an emblem of resurrection."

Book of the Names of the Dead

A beautifully bound blank book in which members of the assembly may inscribe the names of the deceased could be placed near the baptismal font. This book can be honored with incense at least on All Saints and All Souls, if not on all the Sundays of the month, and the Easter candle lighted. Liturgy Training Publications publishes such a book for this purpose.

Cemeteries

The care taken of cemeteries is a sign of respect not only to the dead but also to the bereaved and to the descendants who visit. Parishes with cemeteries should think about decorating the entranceway, posting signs describing the significance of November and its feasts, and placing special prayers in weatherproof containers along walkways. A procession and blessing could be held on All Souls' Day.

- DOMESTIC PRAYER IN NOVEMBER: See *Catholic Household Blessings and Prayers* (pages 178–183) for prayers for this month and a family's visit to a cemetery. Liturgy Training Publication's *Sourcebook about Death* (1989) might be made available for parishioners to purchase throughout the month. See, too, the entries in *Take Me Home* and *Take Me Home, Too*.

W #667 (LMC, #402)   white
E **All Saints**
D SOLEMNITY

ORIENTATION

This feast, which honors all holy men and women in glory with Christ, began in the East as a commemoration of all martyrs, and by the eighth century was celebrated in Rome on this day. Honored are all, known or unknown, whose lives were modeled on the great commandment of love for God and neighbor.

As with all solemnities, this celebration begins with first vespers. There are several All Hallows' Eve possibilities. Communities should plan something that could involve all age groups.

HALLOWEEN MASS

An evening Mass with children, early enough to allow youngsters to go on their rounds, might be appreciated by their parents as well. Participation in costume can be fun, an eschatological sign; pushing for "saints only" costumes is not necessary. The sung litany of the saints is a good accompaniment to a great procession, perhaps including the children. The gathering rite may include a procession that passes all the statues, windows and icons that honor the saints. Perhaps after the procession has passed by these images, the deacon could return to honor them and then the whole assembly with incense while the entrance song or litany continues.

VIGIL SERVICES

There are three possibilities:

- VIGIL FOR THE EVE OF ALL SAINTS' DAY: (*Book of Occasional Services,* Episcopal). This calls for a service of light, three or more readings and psalms before the gospel, then sacraments of initiation or renewal of baptismal vows. Catholic tradition, of course, reserves initiation of adults to the Easter Vigil.

- SERVICE FOR ALL HALLOWS' EVE: (*Book of Occasional Services,* Episcopal). Combined with "suitable festivities and entertainment" or a communal visit to a cemetery, this rite begins with a service of light and continues with appropriate readings. The collects include Mary and the saints. The service concludes with a homily and the Te Deum.

- LITURGY OF THE HOURS: Use the proper texts for Evening Prayer I, the Office of Readings, and an extended vigil proper to this night.

MASSES ON THE SOLEMNITY

An entrance procession past the images of the saints might be appropriate today as well. The Beatitudes are the time-honored

SUMMER AND FALL ORDINARY TIME: NOVEMBER   217

gospel for this solemnity, and there are several versions of that text, set to various meters and melodies, which may be sung during the liturgy. There is a proper preface to use. Eucharistic Prayer I has two lists of saints, though some of these are obscure people associated with the early Roman church. Eucharistic Prayer III speaks of God as "the source of all holiness" and the object of praise "from east to west," and permits the naming of other saints. The most inclusive vision of sanctity is found in Reconciliation II. Solemn Blessing #18 is proper to this day and should be chanted.

#1011 – 1016 (668) (LMC, #403)
white/violet/black

THU 2 The Commemoration of All the Faithful Departed (All Souls)

ORIENTATION

Originating early in the Middle Ages in monastic communities as an annual day of prayer for the dead, All Souls' Day came to be celebrated throughout the church after the tenth century. The texts and traditions express faith in the communion of saints and our need to pray especially for those who have died in their human imperfection and await final entrance into the joy of heaven.

Imbued with a paschal character that befits our "sure and certain hope in the resurrection," today should be different from yesterday. Variations could include the transformation of yesterday's All Saints' procession into a procession to the parish cemetery if nearby. The incensation should be directed today to the parish's Book of Names of the Dead. The litany of the saints could be replaced today by a prayerful recitation or chanting of the names of all who have died since last year, with the refrain, "Grant them rest and peace, O Lord."

On All Souls' Day, white, violet or black vestments may be worn. Throughout the United States, white is now the standard color for funerals, even Eastertime's white to link Christian burial with the paschal mystery. All Souls' Day, however, seems to have a more emphatic note of our own preparation for death and judgment. Perhaps for that reason, a color associated with reflection and repentance might be appropriate: violet. This might also be the day to bring out any black sets from storage, if they are in good condition.

MUSIC

Hymns from the parish funeral repertoire would make an effective beginning for today's liturgy. The Taizé ostinato "Beati in domo domini" ("Happy they who dwell in God's house") would be appropriate, as would Jeremy Young's "We shall rise again" (GIA, G-2983; *Gather*). Its text is pastorally suited to those who grieve. "I heard the voice of Jesus say" is set, in *Worship,* to the tune KINGSFOLD. The Episcopal *Hymnal 1982* has several beautiful and useful pieces (#354 – 358): the "Adoro te" melody with the prayer "Jesus, Son of Mary"; an English version of the chant "In Paradisum"; and both a Russian chant and metrical version of the Eastern rite *kontakion,* "Give rest, O Christ, to your servants."

LECTIONARY

The liturgical calendar for the United States recommends: Daniel 12:1 – 3; Romans 6:3 – 9 or 6:3 – 4, 8 – 9; and the gospel John 6:37 – 40. The Canadian lectionary has a different set, offering a choice between the two evangelists of Year B, Mark and John: Isaiah 25:6 – 9; 1 Corinthians 15:12 – 26; and Mark 8:27 – 35 or John 1:1 – 5, 9 – 14.

CONCLUDING RITE AND CEMETERY VISIT

Solemn Blessing #20, rarely used because of the rite of commendation and farewell, is the proper blessing for today. See the *Book of Blessings* (chapter 57) for an Order for Visiting a Cemetery on All Souls' Day.

OTHER ALL SOULS LITURGIES

All Souls could conclude with Evening Prayer from the Office of the Dead. The Book of the Names of the Dead could be incensed along with the altar and assembly during the Magnificat. Solemn Blessing #20 should conclude the celebration with the singing of "In Paradisum," the *kontakion* noted above, or the parish's usual song of farewell, sung in the plural, of course.

NOVEMBER

FRI 3 — Weekday
#483 (LMC, #193–231) green

Martin de Porres, religious, optional memorial/white. ▪ Philippians begins with keynotes that recur throughout the letter: Despite persecution and imprisonment, Paul knows joy: joy in Christ and in the community gathered in Christ's name. Love, knowledge and insight are gifts already given, and Paul prays for their increase as the community works toward the final harvest. Jesus again tries to expand the Pharisees' vision of the Sabbath by healing someone in need — someone with "dropsy," a disease which Greek authors at the time of Luke used to symbolize avarice and greed. The miracle is thus connected with the rest of chapter 14. If there is no morning liturgy tomorrow, consider combining Saturday's gospel with today's to set up the block of teaching.

Martin de Porres (+ 1639) was an illegitimate child of mixed race who, as a Dominican brother, ministered especially to African slaves. One story claims that Martin rescued from extermination all the field mice who had taken up residence in the sacristy vesting cases. No word on where he took them, but the legend confirms his renown for gentleness and love toward outcasts.

SAT 4 — Charles Borromeo, bishop
#484 (LMC, #193–231) white
MEMORIAL

Paul proclaims the creed we should be praying in November: "To me, living is Christ and dying is gain." Paul's peace in the face of danger and even death stems from the fact that he has let go. He no longer judges or cares about the motives of others, so long as Christ is preached. The disciple, says Jesus, must be unconcerned about power, privilege and prestige. It is enough to be at the banquet; let the host decide where each of us should sit!

Charles Borromeo (+ 1584) had all the qualifications to turn out as be one of the living problems that had caused the Reformation: A papal uncle and an early appointment to a large benefice surely must have seemed like nepotism to his contemporaries. Yet with "Humility" as his motto, Charles set about translating the documents of Trent into a way of personal and ecclesial life. For us in the generation following Vatican II, Charles' love for the council of his day, its liturgical and ecclesial reforms and its call to personal holiness, is a fine example.

SUN 5 — Thirty-first Sunday in Ordinary Time
#152 (LMC, #193–231) green

The final block of Sundays in Ordinary Time places Jesus in Jerusalem, where his teaching takes place in and around the Temple. The first reading is from Deuteronomy, the great summary of Israel's covenant, the *Shema, Israel:* "Hear, O Israel, the Lord is our God, the Lord alone." Today's passage portrays him in perfect continuity with that covenant, for he responds to the scribe's question with the Shema they have both recited since childhood. To Deuteronomy, Jesus adds a quote from Leviticus regarding love of neighbor.

The scribe is delighted with Jesus' answer, and Jesus seems to like this scribe. "You are not far from the kingdom of God," says Jesus. Is that good? Not far is not bad, but neither is it far enough. For the scribe, as for the rich young man, indeed as for all of us, it is one thing to know what ought to be done and another to do it. How do we live out the covenant whose words we know so well but whose deeds we always find a challenge?

▪ FOOD COLLECTION: In many parishes, the month is dedicated to the "harvesting" of gifts that will be transformed into food baskets for Thanksgiving and Christmas. One parish gathers these gifts at the baptismal font: We are all members of one body. To make this a month-long project, this Sunday's announcements ought to include a request to bring canned goods on the next three Sundays.

MON 6 — Weekday
#485 (LMC, #193–231) green

Unity in love, humility in service: these are the keys to building Christian community. The arrogance and rivalry Paul feared ought to be laid aside. Let the community direct its energies toward those Jesus suggests for the kingdom's guest list: the poor, the lame and the blind, remembering that afflictions can be spiritual and emotional as well as physical.

TUE 7 — Weekday
#486 (LMC, #193–231) green

Paul's magnificent hymn of Christ's self-emptying love is a wonderful theme for this month of all saints: "Let that mind be in you which was in Christ Jesus" and in all our sisters and brothers gone before us into heaven's exaltation. How

NOVEMBER

blessed, even now, we who are invited to the kingdom's feast. As long as we remember the Lukan twist to the story: We are here by default, as it were, invited because those on the first list refused to come.

WED 8 — Weekday
#487 (LMC, #193–231) green

The November motif is easy to discern in today's readings. Paul sounds a call for perseverance that keeps the end of all things in view. Jesus calls would-be disciples to consider carefully the cost of discipleship (everything) and to calculate their resources (nothing but grace) before undertaking the project.

THU 9 — The Dedication of the Lateran Basilica in Rome
#671 (LMC, #406) white
FEAST

ORIENTATION

This dedication feast fits well with the eschatological thrust of the November liturgy. For the Christian, each worship space on earth is something of a reflection of the heavenly city. As the cathedral of the bishop of Rome, "the Lateran" once carried the same connotations as "the Vatican" does now. The inscription over the east entrance is accurate: Mother and Head of All Churches in the City and throughout the World. The observance of this feast is a token of our local church's communion with the church in Rome and with all the other churches that hold fast to similar bonds of communion.

LECTIONARY

Most lectionaries refer to the Common of Dedication, but choices abound. The liturgical calendar for the United States and the new Canadian lectionary specify texts that fit the style of November's liturgies: Ezekiel 47:1–2, 8–9, 12; 1 Corinthians 3:9c–11, 16–17; John 2:13–22.

November's common psalm, Psalm 122, is the premier dedication psalm. Keep whatever setting of the psalm's refrain the community is using for the month: "I rejoiced when I heard them say, 'Let us go up to the house of the Lord,'" the pilgrim song of the community across the centuries. ICEL's translation captures the sense of the Hebrew and the eschatological dimension of the feast: "Jerusalem the city so built, that city and temple are one."

SACRAMENTARY

In selecting sacramentary texts, remember to use those designated "Outside the Dedicated Church." There is a special preface, Dedication II, P-53, and solemn blessing (the first element of which will require some minor adaptation).

Otherwise there is no need to depart markedly from the November pattern. The dedication of any church recalls the heavenly Jerusalem that all church buildings symbolize and toward which November's liturgical spirit directs us. Hymns of Jerusalem and the communion of saints are appropriate, as are "Christ is made the sure foundation" and "The church's one foundation."

FRI 10 — Leo the Great, pope and doctor of the church
#489 (LMC, #193–231) white
MEMORIAL

For the enemies of Christ's cross, says Paul, destruction lies in store. But for us sinners, redeemed by that cross, the end will be citizenship in heaven, transformation of our mortal bodies, glory forever with our Savior. Jesus praises not the steward's dishonesty but his prudence and creativity in the face of his crisis. Are we anywhere near as industrious and generous in advancing the kingdom?

Leo the Great's (+ 461) gifts included political acumen, theological sophistication, the ability to preach clear and pastorally practical sermons, and the classical knowledge necessary to frame exquisite Latin phrases for liturgical texts of the Roman rite. These mercies of the Lord are not spent even in our own day. Vatican II has taught us to look beyond the hierarchy to find a wide variety of gifts among all the priestly people of God.

SAT 11 — Martin of Tours, bishop
#490 (LMC, #193–231) white
MEMORIAL

Paul proclaims that the all-sufficiency of Christ's strength is the source of his, and every disciple's, ability to bear witness. Fidelity with the gifts entrusted to us, and placing love of God before love of money: Jesus presents these as essential qualities for disciples.

NOVEMBER

This is the ancient memorial of Martin (+ 397), the gallant soldier who as a catechumen felt conscience-bound to leave his military career behind. He carried his love of peace into the church's service, rejecting the use of force and persecution in dealing with heretics and devoting his energy instead to evangelization and service of the poor. Together with Saints Justin and Cyprian, Martin is remembered for his nonviolent witness in the U.S. bishops' pastoral letter on peace.

■ VETERANS DAY: Martin's memorial coincides with this civil holiday that commemorates the end of World War I. Intercessions for peace and for the dead, especially for those who died in war, would be appropriate.

SUN 12 — Thirty-second Sunday in Ordinary Time
#155 (LMC, #150) green

Jesus continues to teach discipleship. The widow of Zarephath and the widow in the temple are set before the community as examples of those who give what they cannot afford for the glory of God and in service of others. The long form of the gospel (seven verses) ought to be proclaimed. The contrast between the characters is too striking, and the lesson for the church too pointed, to use the shorter form. Although the scribe of last week's gospel praised Jesus for getting the Law right, the scribes in this week' gospel get the Law all wrong. Perhaps among the widows whose savings these scribes have devoured is the poor woman whom Jesus points out to his disciples as an example of true wealth.

MON 13 — Frances Xavier Cabrini, virgin, religious, missionary
#491 (LMC, #193–231) white
MEMORIAL

This week begins with the Letter to Titus, probably written by a disciple of Paul toward the end of the first century. Today's passage shows the emerging structure of at least part of the early church in the work of the presbyters. The gospel deals with several matters. Scandals: we need no more. Forgiveness: we always need more. When the disciples ask Jesus for more faith, he responds that what is needed is not more, but deeper faith. A little faith, firmly rooted and daringly enacted, is the key to the kingdom.

To frightened immigrants in the New World, fellow immigrant Mother Cabrini (+ 1917), with the sisters she gathered to share her ministry, was a beacon of hope and benefactor filled with compassion and salty good humor.

TUE 14 — Weekday
#492 (LMC, #193–231) green

Today's passage from the Letter to Titus outlines the behavior expected of the rest of the community. The conclusion of the passage is the beautiful text read at the Christmas Midnight Mass: "The grace of God has appeared." This selection is also the source of the prayer that concludes the Lord's Prayer during the liturgy, "as we wait in joyful hope for the coming of our Savior Jesus Christ." November's theme is there: the culmination of all things. The mutual service envisioned by the Letter to Titus echoes in Luke's gospel which pictures all of us as servants doing our duty.

WED 15 — Weekday
#493 (LMC, #193–231) green

Albert the Great, bishop and doctor of the church, optional memorial/white. ▪ "Be subject to the government and take on honest employment." A late date is suggested for the composition of Titus in part because of today's selection. Conflict with the authorities seems to be past, at least for now, as does the expectation of the Lord's imminent return. In the gospel, a foreigner, a Samaritan, returns to give thanks. Eucharist means thanksgiving: Do we balance our prayers of petition with joyful thanks and praise, especially in the eucharistic prayer?

Albert (+ 1280) was a university professor, remembered not only for his own extraordinary learning, but for his most famous student, Thomas Aquinas. As Muslim influence and the importance of the Near East advanced throughout the world, Albert expanded his knowledge of natural sciences to include Jewish and Arabic studies, placing these, together with his expertise in Greek philosophy, at the service of theology.

THU 16 — Weekday
#494 (LMC, #193–231) green

Margaret of Scotland, married woman, queen; Gertrude the Great, virgin, religious; optional memorials/white. ▪ Philemon's dilemma touches each of us in one way or another. Nothing less was demanded of this early Christian than a total change of perspective. The eschatological note of Luke's gospel begins to come through as Jesus speaks

NOVEMBER

of his suffering and coming of "the Son of Man in his day."

Margaret (+ 1093) of Scotland presided energetically over a household of a devoted husband and eight growing children. She reformed the royal court and the church in her husband's kingdom while serving the poor and promoting education. Gertrude (+ c. 1302) is renowned for her devotion to the humanity of Jesus and for the mystical writings which still lead many by prayer into the heart of God.

FRI 17 — Elizabeth of Hungary, married woman, religious
MEMORIAL
#495 (LMC, #193–231) green

Another late composition, the Second Letter of John exhorts the community to mutual love and warns about deceit afoot in the world. For Christians waiting and watching, working and praying in these "last days" (gospel) the task is to bear witness to the immanent presence of the God who is surely coming.

Elizabeth (+ 1231) is another of several medieval widows who consecrated a time of life that could have been lonely into a time of loving service to others.

SAT 18 — Weekday
#496 or 679 (LMC, #193–231) green

Dedication of SS. Peter and Paul; Rose Philippine Duchesne, religious; Blessed Virgin Mary; optional memorials/white. • On our pilgrimage through life, the Third Letter of John reminds us how graciously we ought to offer the gift of hospitality to all whose paths cross ours. The gospel asserts that God's justice is certain, and that our faith needs to be bolstered by the conviction that permeates Luke's gospel: the Son of Man will come — and more quickly perhaps than we imagine. But Jesus wonders "will he find faith on earth?"

Rose Philippine Duchesne (+ 1852) was a religious of the Sacred Heart of Jesus who served as a teacher in her native France and in the cities of the United States. Her desire to teach Native Americans was frustrated by her inability to learn their languages, but she served among them and earned the name "Woman Who Prays Much." Her proper prayer (in the sacramentary supplement) is joined to the weekday readings.

For the Saturday memorial of Mary, consider *Collection of Masses of the Blessed Virgin Mary*, #40, Mother of Divine Providence.

SUN 19 — Thirty-third Sunday in Ordinary Time
#158 (LMC, #153) green

The end is near! But so is the beginning. The lectionary omits the details of "that suffering" (v. 24 refers to vv. 14–23) and chooses to focus instead on the great harvest that will follow the cosmic cataclysm. The harvest of the elect is vast: "From the four winds, from the ends of the earth to the ends of heaven." "Know the signs," counsels Jesus, adding paradoxically, though "no one knows that day or hour." Jesus' constant message about the end: the best way to *get* ready is to *be* ready. Daniel's vision of resurrection and judgment begins on a note of anguish. The Letter to the Hebrews offers blessed assurance: Forgiveness is ours in the all-sufficient sacrifice of Christ.

Ember days

In the United States, the three days before Thanksgiving are proposed as ember days, a kind of preparatory fast with a focus on practical care for those in need. See *Catholic Household Blessings and Prayers,* page 188 for suggestions.

MON 20 — Weekday
#497 (LMC, #193–231) green

Nothing could make the eschatological nature of the month more obvious than its final two weeks of scripture being drawn from Revelation. This frequently misinterpreted book requires careful preparation by the preacher. The assembly will most likely have heard some preacher somewhere misuse the book as a manual for the interpretation of current events. Conscientious homilists should offer some insight into the nature of apocalyptic and prophetic literature. In the midst of horrific persecution, this book told our ancestors in faith: "Don't give up, and don't give in!" Today, its point is simple and direct: How easy to fall away from the fervor of first love! If we can see that in ourselves, the remedy is in today's gospel. For Bartimaeus, faith leads to sight, and beyond sight to insight, and beyond that to "following Jesus, glorifying God."

TUE 21 — Presentation of the Blessed Virgin Mary
MEMORIAL
#498 (LMC, #193–231) white

No need to look to years past to find today's revelation fulfilled. Each community should be able recognize itself in the churches the author addresses. How often reality does not match reputation, how quickly fervor cools,

222 SUMMER AND FALL ORDINARY TIME: NOVEMBER

NOVEMBER

how easily we can fall prey to self-delusion. The prescription for these common ecclesial ailments: repentance and listening. In the gospel the harvest of the kingdom continues, as Jesus welcomes and is welcomed by the tax collector Zacchaeus.

Today's memorial is based on a story from the apocryphal Gospel of James. It may suggest the picture of Mary as "temple of the Lord" over whom the Spirit hovers, in whom the word becomes flesh. The sacramentary offers only a collect for this memorial. See the *Collection of Masses of the Blessed Virgin Mary,* Mass #23, Mary, Temple of the Lord, for evocative texts that relate the temple image to baptism.

WED 22 — Cecilia, virgin and martyr
#499 (LMC, #193–231) red
MEMORIAL

Today's revelation fills the hearts of worshipers with joyful expectation. The throne of the one reverently left unnamed, the rainbow that reminds God of the covenant with all creation, the priestly people, the scattered churches, all living creatures: The cosmic liturgy of praise has begun. This is the liturgy in which our worship even now participates! The gospel takes us from vision to reality: With a stern parable about trust and betrayal, rejection and slaughter, Luke concludes Jesus' long journey to Jerusalem.

Apart from legend, nothing is known of today's saint. Cecilia, presumably martyred during the early Roman persecutions, was popular enough to have her name given to a fourth-century church in Rome and inserted into the Roman Canon (Eucharistic Prayer I). In the sixteenth century she was named patron of musicians.

THU 23 — Weekday
#500 or 881–885 (LMC, #193–231) green or white

Clement I, pope and martyr/red; Columban, abbot/white; Blessed Miguel Augustín Pro, presbyter, religious, martyr/red; optional memorials. U.S.A.: Thanksgiving Day, civil observance/white.

ORIENTATION

This civil observance, like all national "feasts," must be celebrated with sensitivity to gospel values. On this day our praise for God's bounty must be joined to penitence for misuse of those blessings, and a commitment to share the Lord's gifts to us with others. Thoughtful selection of texts and music can balance these considerations.

LECTIONARY

An appendix to the 1970 lectionary has a selection of texts for Thanksgiving Day. Of these, Joel and Zephaniah correspond to the eschatological nature of these last weeks of Ordinary Time. Deuteronomy has a warning: "Be careful not to forget." The 1 Corinthians passage speaks of being "strengthened to the end." The selection from Luke 12 might be fitting in communities where the "good life" struggles with the "gospel life" for equal time, and the Luke 17 passage is the classic text on God's goodness and human ingratitude.

SACRAMENTARY

Some suggested texts for this observance:

- *Greeting:* May the Lord, who fills you with his bounty, be with you always (*Book of Blessings,* #1764).
- *Presidential prayers:* Votive Mass for Thanksgiving in sacramentary after November 30.
- *General intercessions:* For ideas see BB #1760; *Book of Common Prayer* (Episcopal), Litany of Thanksgiving, #837; *Book of Common Worship* (Presbyterian), Litany of Thanksgiving, #792.
- *Blessing of food:* If food is to be blessed for Thanksgiving Dinner or for distribution to those in need, use BB #1759–1761.
- *Eucharistic prayer:* The official preface in the current sacramentary, with its triumphalistic and nationalistic tone, strikes many as inappropriate. Use any of these eucharistic prayers with their own prefaces: Reconciliation II (the great feast for all peoples) or Eucharistic Prayer for Masses for Various Needs and Occasions, form B (God Guides the Church on the Way of Salvation) or form D (Jesus, the Compassion of God).

MUSIC

"Come, ye thankful people, come," the classic American Thanksgiving text, has an eschatological verse about God's great harvest. "We plow the fields," "We gather together" and "For the beauty of the earth" have long associations with this day. "Father, we thank thee" is an adaptation of the *Didache* prayer that can unite our civic Thanksgiving to the great thanksgiving of the eucharist. See "Thanksgiving" suggestions in the ideas for general hymnody during November, page 216.

DOMESTIC PRAYER

Make available one of the Litanies of Thanksgiving from the resources listed above and the prayer from *Catholic Household Blessings and Prayers,* page 200.

NOVEMBER

To one of today's saints, Clement I, pope at the end of the first century, we are indebted for eloquent writing on life in the early church. To another, the Irish monk-missionary Columba (+ 615), we owe the development of individual confession. The recently established optional memorial of Miguel Agustín Pro (+ 1927) is a powerful reminder that disciples can still face persecution. Executed as a conspirator against Mexico's revolutionary government, he was immediately hailed as a martyr. The widely circulated photograph of Miguel kneeling before his executioners became a twentieth-century icon of courage. His last words were a proclamation of Christ's lordship over all civil authorities: *"Viva el Cristo Rey!"* The prayer for his memorial is in the sacramentary supplement (Catholic Book, 1994).

FRI 24
#501 (LMC, #193–231) green

Andrew Dung-Lac, presbyter and martyr, and his companions, martyrs
MEMORIAL

What is the sweet and sour scroll John is given to eat? The scroll is sweet, say the commentators, because it announces the final victory of God's people. Sour, they add, because it also predicts the sufferings that will precede that victory (RNAB). The cleansing of the Temple is a symbolic act that portends the final days of the Temple and a religious-political statement that almost guarantees the end of Jesus.

Today's memorial celebrates the fidelity under persecution of Vietnam's martyrs, Andrew Dung-Lac and the 116 others (+ 1820 through 1862) who were canonized with him as representatives of thousands tortured and martyred in Vietnam between the seventeenth and nineteenth centuries. Their descendants in faith, displaced by war in decades past, are now a blessing in many communities worldwide. Parishes with Vietnamese parishioners should honor them today.

SAT 25
#502 (LMC, #193–231) green

Weekday

Blessed Virgin Mary, optional memorial/white. ▪ Jesus preaches about the new life we will enjoy in the resurrection, proclaiming God to be "God not of the dead but of the living." As the month of All Saints and All Souls draws to a close, we find new comfort in his promise that "to God, all of them are alive."

For the Saturday memorial of Mary see *Collection of Masses of the Blessed Virgin Mary,* #37, Mother of Divine Hope.

26
#161 (LMC, #156) white

Christ the King

ORIENTATION

When Pius XI established this feast in 1925, the rise of totalitarianism must have made it seem that apocalyptic forces had been unleashed on the world. Bolshevism reigned in Russia, Fascism in Italy, the bloodshed of civil war flowed in many places, and from every quarter came forebodings of new dictatorships. So the pope proclaimed: *Pax Christi in regno Christi:* "The peace of Christ in the reign of Christ!" At century's end, is the world very different? Some totalitarian walls have crumbled, but in many places new forces of oppression have rushed in, in some places enslaving bodies, in others hearts and minds in the bondage of consumerism. The feast is appropriate here, at the turning point of the church's year of worship and witness. All Western Christian churches share it now, sometimes under different titles, but with the same scriptures, proclaiming in every cycle of the lectionary the unique kingship of Jesus the Lord.

NOVEMBER

LECTIONARY

In each cycle of the lectionary, the scriptures for this solemnity portray a different aspect of the kingship of Christ. The framers of the lectionary were aware that the notion of "kingship" does not conjure up positive thoughts in the contemporary mind. Thus the selections proclaim that when Christians call Jesus "king" they mean something altogether different from any political connotations the word may have. In Year A, the shepherd-king of Matthew's gospel rewards those who have done good to the least of the brothers and sisters. In Year C, Luke's King Jesus, as he dies, welcomes into his kingdom its first citizen, a fellow criminal, the "good thief" hanging beside him.

In Year B, the gospel is taken not from Mark but from John. The passion account of the Gospel of John is different from that of the synoptics. John's is the "glorious passion," with Jesus in control and confident from beginning to end: "No one takes my life from me. I lay it down and I take it up again." From the liturgy's perspective, Jesus' royal portrait becomes clear over a period of time. He is prefigured in Daniel's night visions as the one "whose dominion is an everlasting dominion, and whose kingship will never be destroyed." He is the one known in Revelation as "the one who loves us and freed us from our sins by his blood and made us a kingdom." In the clear light of the gospel, he is the king who only seems to be bound before the powers of this world, but who is supremely free.

SACRAMENTARY

The gathering song should echo the glory given to the Lamb in Revelation (the original entrance antiphon): "Crown him with many crowns," "All hail the power of Jesus' name" and "To Jesus Christ our sovereign king" are but a few of such hymns. You might consider a hymn that could continue into Advent, such as "The king shall come when morning dawns." Let the greeting, too, draw on the second reading.

The preface of Christ the King sings a litany of qualities that should mark the life of Christ's community: truth and life; holiness and grace; justice, love and peace. Given Luke's portrait of Christ in today's gospel, the Eucharistic Prayer for Reconciliation I would be an appropriate choice. As a communion processional, consider a Beatitudes refrain the community may already know or "Jesus, remember me" (Taizé). Use the solemn blessing that has been in place throughout November. Then let the final hymn be strong and festive, sung by all together, ministers and assembly remaining in place for the whole piece.

EVENING PRAYER

A fitting way to end the liturgical year and prepare for the Advent season ahead is to celebrate Sunday vespers. Before the Office begins, there might be a reprise of Christ the King hymns from the morning liturgy. Parishes with bells should have these peal out the community's joy during the singing of the Magnificat or at the conclusion of the celebration.

MON 27 — #503 (LMC, #193–231) green
Weekday

With the exception of tomorrow's bleak passage, each Revelation reading for this last week of the liturgical year contains a positive element of victory and vindication. The mystical number of the redeemed, one hundred and forty-four thousand, represents a countless number: the twelve tribes of Israel and the twelve apostles of the Lamb multiplied together to infinity. Once we realize this, the vision is glorious, and the song they sing, we trust, will one day be our own. The gospel is brief and beautiful. Jesus speaks with reverent appreciation of a poor widow whose gift, "all she had to live on," is a foreshadowing of his own gift.

TUE 28 — #504 (LMC, #193–231) green
Weekday

Earth's harvest of violence is answered in today's reading from Revelation by a harvest initiated by the Son of Man. Jesus foretells destruction by natural disasters and human hands. Signs of the end? Luke doesn't think so, and speculation is vain. For every age, Jesus' warning is valid, "Don't follow those who claim 'I am he!' or 'The time is here!'" and his assurance comforting: "Do not be terrified."

WED 29 — #505 (LMC, #193–231) green
Weekday

God's wrath yields to a glorious vision of the victors playing harps and singing canticles. In the gospel, Jesus promises that persecution will yield to a glorious salvation.

NOVEMBER

THU 30 — Andrew, apostle
#684 (LMC, #423) red
FEAST

ORIENTATION

Saint John Chrysostom notes in today's Office of Readings: "Andrew's words reveal a soul waiting with the utmost longing for the coming of the Messiah, looking forward to his appearing from heaven, rejoicing when he does appear, and hastening to announce so great an event to others."

LECTIONARY

Paul's Letter to the Romans and Matthew's gospel of Andrew's call emphasize the responsibility of disciples to share the good news they have received. How beautiful are our feet upon the mountains of the workplace or the classroom? In John's account, Andrew brings his brother Peter to Jesus. In Matthew, both Peter and Andrew are sent fishing for people. To whom could we be apostles this coming Advent?

SACRAMENTARY

The second preface of the apostles emphasizes the call of the church to be "the living gospel for all to hear." Most hymnals have a generic saints' hymn, "By all your saints still striving," which has individual verses specific to particular saints, including one for Andrew. The words will fit the melody of "All glory, laud and honor."

December

FRI 1 — Weekday
#507 (LMC, #193–231) green

The harvest of God leads to a new heaven and a new earth, and the vision of the holy city, the new Jerusalem, descending as a bride for the wedding feast of the Lamb. Jesus calls us to attend to the signs that the kingdom is near, and the words come back to us: "He has put the signs of his coming in every generation, that every generation may expect his coming in their time" (Augustine).

SAT 2 — Weekday
#508 (LMC, #193–231) green

Blessed Virgin Mary, optional memorial/white. ▪ The Bible that began with a tree whose fruit was death ends with a vision of a new tree, ever yielding fruit, ever verdant, with leaves that are medicine for the healing of the nations. The journey has taken us from the Garden to the City, and this city is filled with such beauty and praise that our exile from the Garden appears a "happy fault." "Maranatha! Come, Lord Jesus!" sings the church in today's responsorial psalm. The gospel reminds us that disciples are to avoid both extremes: a life that is carefree and a life burdened with cares. The last word belongs to Jesus, the First and the Last, Alpha and Omega of this and every liturgical year: "Be on guard! Stay alert! Pray constantly! See, I am coming soon!"

For the Saturday memorial of Mary, see *Collection of Masses of the Blessed Virgin Mary*, #46, Mary, Gate of Heaven.